EARLY CHILDHOOD EDUCATION SERIES

Leslie R. Williams, Editor   Millie Almy, Senior Advisor

ADVISORY BOARD: Barbara T. Bowman, Harriet K. Cuffaro, Stephanie Feeney, Doris Pronin Fromberg, Celia Genishi, Stacie G. Goffin, Dominic F. Gullo, Alice Sterling Honig, Elizabeth Jones, Gwen Morgan, David Weikert

USING THE SUPPORTIVE PLAY MODEL

....

INDIVIDUALIZED INTERVENTION IN
EARLY CHILDHOOD PRACTICE

Margaret K. Sheridan
Gilbert M. Foley
Sara H. Radlinski

Foreword by G. Gordon Williamson

TEACHERS
COLLEGE
PRESS

Teachers College, Columbia University
New York and London

#31013366

If you would like separate copies of the Supportive Play Model chart found on pp. 17–38, they may be purchased for $6.00 each (price subject to change), plus minimum $2.50 shipping and handling. Send orders to:

Teachers College Press
1234 Amsterdam Avenue
New York, NY 10027
Fax (212) 678-4149
Attention: Marketing Manager

Published by Teachers College Press, 1234 Amsterdam Avenue, New York, N.Y. 10027

Cataloging-in-Publication Data

Sheridan, Margaret K., 1945–
     Using the supportive play model: individualized intervention in
     early childhood practice/Margaret Sheridan, Gilbert M. Foley,
     Sara H. Radlinski.
          p.   cm.—(Early childhood education series)
     Includes bibliographical references and index.
     ISBN 0-8077-3422-5 (paper)
     1. Play. 2. Early childhood education—United States. 3. Child
development—United States. 4. Individualized instruction—United
States. 5. Handicapped children—Education (Early childhood)—
United States. I. Foley, Gilbert M., 1947–   . II. Radlinski,
Sara Hunting. III. Title. IV. Series.
LB1139.35.P55S54   1994   94-32949
371.9′0472—dc20

ISBN 0-8077-3422-5 (paper)

Printed on acid-free paper
Manufactured in the United States of America
02 01 00 99 98 97 96 95   8 7 6 5 4 3 2 1

CONTENTS

FOREWORD

It is a rare occasion when one discovers an intervention approach that incorporates best practices of the therapeutic, educational, and mental health fields. The Supportive Play Model is such a find. It provides an interdisciplinary professional audience with (1) a systematic process for observing and understanding the play and development of young children with special needs, and (2) a decision-making structure for planning personalized intervention.

A prominent feature is the firm belief that "play is the child's genetically determined and inherent means of learning." Play provides an opportunity for the child to organize thoughts, feelings, and skills within the context of exploring the new and making sense of the familiar. Through this self-initiated, intrinsically rewarding activity, the child integrates the internal and external worlds. From an intervention perspective, play is both a means and an end—the primary vehicle for enhancing all areas of development and a reflection of the child's adaptive, functional well-being.

This book is an essential resource for practitioners who work with children from birth to 5 years of age. The Supportive Play Model has been field tested by parents and professionals involved in diverse settings such as early intervention, preschool, Head Start, and child care programs. Although the model focuses on children with special needs, it offers rich insights for creating play and learning experiences appropriate for all children.

Indeed, the book emphasizes ways to include children with disabilities in natural community environments. This frame of reference provides a process through which professionals from different disciplines can collaborate with parents to design intervention that is family centered, relationship based, and respectful of the inner life of the child.

The text provides a well written, informative description of the theoretical foundation for this approach. Topics include theories and stages of play, the interdependent relationship of play and development, and play skills and themes. A particularly interesting and relevant discussion is the differentiation between pretend and symbolic play.

The Supportive Play Model is presented in detail, including a helpful chart for guiding assessment, intervention, and outcome measurement. This comprehensive, ecological frame of reference addresses the child, family, and program. The child section offers age-referenced guidelines for observing the child in six developmental domains and determining characteristic patterns that foster and limit play behavior. Excellent intervention strategies are delineated for each developmental area as well as considerations for adapting play experiences. The family section covers such pertinent issues as family goals, parent–child interaction, and the home environment. Numerous techniques are suggested for supporting all family members. The program section has a similar format and concerns the availability of staff, peers, space, time, and materials and equipment. Attention to these program components is an innovative aspect of the model. Characteristics of the physical and social environments are evaluated as they relate to the child's play, and recommendations are offered for necessary modification.

Four case studies are provided to demonstrate application of the Supportive Play Model in practice. These representative examples present children who have challenges related to hearing impairment, spina bifida, pervasive developmental disorder, and compromised development due to multiple risk factors. In each case there is a thoughtful review of the literature concerning associated developmental issues, a summary of trends in intervention relevant to the condition, and a discussion of the use of the model to support inclusion of the child in a regular nursery school or Head Start program. These case examples are highly instructive. They serve to illustrate the practicality and effectiveness of this play-oriented, psychodevelopmental approach to intervention.

An underlying theme is an appreciation of the emotional life of the young child. Through play with self and others the child develops a personal identity and capacity for intimacy. Intervention that capitalizes on this enormous force is likely to be most successful. Such is the wisdom of this book.

G. Gordon Williamson, Ph.D., OTR
Director, COPING Project
John F. Kennedy Medical Center
Edison, New Jersey

Associate Clinical Professor
Rehabilitation Medicine Department
Columbia University
New York, New York

PREFACE

A configuration of shared convictions and experiences brought us together to write this book. We hold a common commitment to the value of attending to the inner lives of children, including children with disabilities. We believe the psychological development of a child stands at the center of all relating and learning. Attuning to the emotional life of children is not always easy, comfortable, or convenient for adults working with them. Children's feelings can be powerful beyond their stature, and complex beyond the simplistic and concrete qualities attributed to be characteristic of childhood. Likewise, there may be far more complexity to children's emotional development than that which is ascribed by virtue of their diagnosed disability. The inner world of children is a tapestry of representations and feelings that includes themselves, significant others, and the world as they know it. We believe that when the interventionist is as committed to the inner reality of the child as the more easily observable and measurable externalized behavior of the child, then authentic intervention can begin.

Play is a vehicle through which we can come to know the content of the inner life as well as the child's capacities to interact with the physical world. In a play-oriented milieu, children's spontaneous actions can be guided toward learning without the need for an imposed task. This notion transforms the concept of curriculum from activities applied to the child to experiences derived from the child. This shift in perspective should guide the learning and the teaching toward a dynamic and interpersonal process wrapped in a relationship.

Believing that play serves to wed the inner and outer life of the child, we developed the Supportive Play Model (SPM) to bring early intervention and infant mental health into a closer harmony. Traditionally, these approaches have had different emphases with early intervention focusing more on procedures, skill acquisition, content, and tasks; and infant mental health focusing more on relationships, processes, feelings, and styles. With the blending of concepts suggested in our model, we hope to encourage intervention that brings the technology and art of intervention into a new partnership and uses knowledge of normal development as a reference, but not as an invariant guide. Normal development provides us with orienting principles within which individual differences can be accommodated. When working with children with developmental problems, we must be free to follow and use their idiosyncratic patterns of development. Knowing the "rules" frees us to break them when necessary.

Our model also encourages an attention to the interrelatedness of the developmental zones, so that a strength or weakness in one developmental area is always recognized as a potential source of support or challenge to other developmental zones. It is our experience that for children with special needs the early emotional stages can cast a particularly powerful influence on areas of development that on the surface may appear free of emotional content. Additionally, the subtleties of learning styles that reflect neurological organization can contribute equally to the developmental complexity that is often presented as simplicity.

The current trend of including children with special needs in typical settings posed another motivation for the book. Mainstreaming and inclusion are currently popular directions in education because of legislation and as a result of a changing social and economic climate. The federal laws have mandated that all handicapped children from birth to age 21 are to be served in a free and appropriate educational program. The laws also discuss "least restrictive environment," which has been interpreted as providing opportunities for the child with disabilities to have a program provided as much as possible with typical peers. We see merits to inclusion, but in no way advocate it as a solution for every child. Rather, we view it as a useful option that needs to be exercised judiciously.

The current economic pressures on communities are great because a large portion of local school budgets involve special education costs. In spite of the original motivations that generated the concepts of mainstreaming and inclusion, some communities may see an economical advantage to including the children with special needs in regular education classes, thus alleviating the additional personnel required for special education services. It is our experience that intensive and highly individualized early intervention plans are economically cost effective in the long run. It may be appealing to place a child who has special needs in a program in which the teacher is willing but the services are minimal, in the hope that the child will rise to the challenge of the setting. It is our experience, however, that these less-than-ideal arrangements may look all right on the surface, but are ultimately at great cost to the child's development. The system may allow the child temporary harbor, but as more sophisticated skills are needed, both academically and socially, the situation is often doomed to fail. This failure model takes a toll on the child's self-esteem and may preclude a good readjustment in a more specialized setting.

When inclusion takes place, we advocate that it be designed with great care, which will most likely be at considerable initial cost. For instance, it is crucial that staff coverage and staff consultation are adequate to both the child's needs and the setting's needs. Successful plans often include a staff member who is initially available to focus on the child with special needs, but who can gradually disengage as the child becomes involved with peers and the program. There needs to be adequate time for the conferencing, coordination, and delivery of services, including speech and language, occupational therapy, and physical therapy, in collaboration with and in support of the parents. It is our experience that when the inclusion plan is carefully designed and clearly supportive of the child, family, staff, and peers, a successful placement results in real satisfaction to all involved.

The philosophy and its application of the intervention approach that has grown into the Supportive Play Model has unfolded out of the authors' cumulative experience in the field. The framework has evolved from work with over 1,000 children and their families in direct service and outreach projects, particularly the Connecticut College Child Development Department's Program for Children with Special Needs in New London, Connecticut, and the Family Centered Resource Project (FCRP) in Reading, Pennsylvania. The Connecticut College program is a state-approved, private school for children with special needs, which functions as a laboratory for undergraduate students, and the FCRP project was a model demonstration and outreach project funded by the United States Department of Education and sponsored by the Pennsylvania Department of Education. In our settings it has become clear that our emphasis on play, emotional and self-development, family-focused and relationship-centered early intervention has made our approach somewhat unique. The ongoing clinical and follow-up data of the effectiveness of this approach has strongly supported our commitment to intervention that is developmental in its design and play-driven in its day-to-day execution.

The authors all subscribe to the important assumption of the central role of the family in designing and implementing developmentally appropriate programs for their child. Parents are not only the "ground" in which children develop, they are also invaluable members of the team who work collaboratively in the process of the Supportive Play Model. Through our own work we have seen the impact of an effective early intervention program on families (acquiring advocacy skills, promoting marriage stability, enhancing effective parenting and sibling adjustment, increasing involvement of extended family members). Children with special needs, who otherwise may have been institutionalized, have been able to grow up in their homes. In many cases, families have chosen to have other children, who have benefited from the knowledge and resources the parents have acquired from their experiences with the special child. Family systems, *per se,* are not the focal point of this book. Instead, we have chosen to focus more directly on the issues raised when a child with special needs is mainstreamed into various early childhood settings. It is our belief, nevertheless, that parents are central to the Supportive Play Model and should be active partners in all stages of the process.

This book aims to serve as a bridge unifying the disciplines working with young children with handicaps. We envision that it will be used in preservice training (undergraduate), and in graduate training for the disciplines of child development, early childhood education, early childhood special education, clinical psychology, special education, school psychology, social work,

child life, and in the related disciplines of occupational therapy, physical therapy, and speech and language pathology. It also can be used for inservice training programs for nursery school, day care, early childhood special education, Head Start program staff, and state and private social service personnel. Additionally, this book can be used as a resource for a case approach to personnel preparation or as a catalyst for group learning and discussion (seminar format, staff meetings, case reviews). To aid the reader or student, a glossary of technical terminology follows the case studies section of the book.

This process has been field tested with approximately 500 undergraduate and graduate students in child development and school and developmental psychology over the past 5 years. Throughout the field testing phase, the process has been refined and modified. There have also been numerous conference presentations since 1987 at which the authors have presented the Supportive Play Model process to approximately 2,000 early childhood professionals, specialists in related fields, and parents. In addition to parents, participating professionals have included early childhood teachers, early childhood special education teachers, special education teachers, school administrators, Head Start staff, day care staff, physicians, nurses, psychiatrists, social workers, and psychologists. Audience members have been asked to participate in the process as cases were presented. Their feedback was used to revise and clarify this process over time. The national and International conferences at which the SPM process has been presented have included Council for Exceptional Child (CEC); Division of Early Childhood—Council for Exceptional Children (DEC); National Association for the Education of Young Children (NAEYC); Organization Mondiale pour l'Education Prescolaire (OMEP); American Speech-Language Hearing Association, and National Center for Clinical Infant Programs Training Institutes.

This book is divided into two parts. Part I begins with a chapter explaining the philosophical and historical underpinnings of the Supportive Play Model. Chapter 2 contains a descriptive and instructional overview of the SPM process and use of the chart, and Chapter 3 discusses issues related to placement of children with special needs.

Part II of the book contains four case studies that illustrate the developmental challenges often presented by young children with special needs and application of the SPM to ameliorate these problems. These cases are illustrative in that they are compilations from our actual clinical experience. The areas of disability that are discussed in these cases include a child who has moderate hearing impairment, a child with spina bifida, a child with moderate pervasive developmental disorder (PDD), and a child whose development is compromised by multiple risk factors. All of the children are mainstreamed in early childhood settings. The SPM is used as a method to help the staff and parents understand the children more completely and design developmentally appropriate programs within their nursery school, day care, or Head Start class setting.

ACKNOWLEDGMENTS

The Supportive Play Model has evolved through our collaborative effort over the past six years. During the prior 15 years, central concepts of the model were in formulation as we worked in early intervention and in college and graduate teaching. But throughout all of this time, ideas evolved with the support and stimulation of many children, families, friends, and colleagues. The list is a lengthy one, but we would like to name a few of the individuals who have made this book possible.

First, we would also like to thank the over 1,000 children and their families who participated in the our programs over the past 20 years. We have been fortunate to see these young children grow while benefiting from interventions that have brought together play, learning, and mental health. These children and their families were the catalyst for our ideas, and offered continuous feedback over these years to facilitate the development of this process.

Next, we must express our special gratitude and love to our families: Ron Radlinski and Tony, Keenan, and Tosh Sheridan for their patience, good humor, and unfailing encouragement, and for the numerous times that they have put aside their own needs so that we could work on "the book" over holidays, vacations, weekends, and evenings. Also we want to give our special appreciation to our parents: Lena D. and William G. Foley, Marvin and Grace Hunting, and Mary and Albert J. Keenan who provided us with loving and secure environments during our own formative years of development.

There have been numerous gifted and generous colleagues who influenced us academically and clinically, and who have assisted us as we formed the ideas that are central to the model. A. J. Pappanikou served as a major advisor for both Margaret and Sara, and John Mierzwa for Gilbert, during our doctoral programs. They were role models who encouraged us to express our positions clearly, and share them with our colleagues with conviction. They taught us to question, probe, and find the underpinnings of policies and practice. They taught us to believe that the educational process can and should be responsive to the individual. Additionally, thanks goes to Rachelle Dattner, Andrew Edminston, Robert Mellon, William Robbins, Joseph Rudolph, and Peter Sax who introduced and nurtured Gilbert in the art and science of the psychoanalytic investigation of the "inner life".

Also our thanks to our colleagues at the Connecticut College Child Development Department: Clara Allison, Camille Hanlon, Karen McLaughlin, and June Patterson; and to other key colleagues: Majorie Beeghly, Joanna Erikson, Margaret Holmberg, and Amy Powell. Their ongoing faith in our ideas and our work has been encouraging and revitalizing.

A special thanks goes to Terry Lawrence, who has served as a colleague to each of us, has encouraged us to conceptualize intervention and program design in a way that it can be shared, and has been an advocate and champion of the role of play in the early childhood education movement. She reminds us that good practice does not happen by chance, but takes careful planning and execution. Her convictions and energy have been sustaining.

The staff at the Connecticut College Program for Children with Special Needs have been integral to the development of this model. Our thanks to each of you for helping us face and solve the continual challenges in our careers; for making it a pleasure to come to work each day; for helping us look forward to each new year with its unknown challenges; and for sticking by us as we tried new approaches or added new programs. Your confidence and support has added to the growth of the SPM process. Many skilled, developmentally oriented professionals have worked in the program over the past 20 years and have offered invaluable insights and contributions to the stages of the development of this process. They helped field test the SPM and gave us ideas and feedback that have shaped the current process. Some of the recent long term staff who have made significant contributions are Fran Jeffreys, Mary Kuhn, Sharon Rowland, and Nancy Slimak. An additional special thanks to Marianne Kennedy for her unending support. Her ideas and insights were central in shaping this model and her masterful editing provided ongoing assistance for each phase of this book. We would like to offer our special gratitude to Marianne's input in the speech and language portions of the SPM.

We would also like to express our appreciation to Connecticut College and to the many funding agencies that have kept the Program for Children with Special Needs operating so that this model could evolve and develop. Without this financial support and commitment to the philosophy of the program, we would have been unable to proceed. The funding agencies and foundations include: The State of Connecticut Department of Children and Families, the Connecticut Department of Education, the Connecticut Department of Health, the Connecticut Department of Social Services, the Curtis Blake Foundation, and the F. L. Weyenberg Charitable Trust. All of these funding sources have had staff members who were supportive of our efforts to provide the crucial elements necessary to offer quality programs for young children and their families during times when our approach was not "in vogue".

Also deserving thanks are the clinical staff of the Family Centered Resource Project: Louise Bridges, Lynn Brown, Dee Creevey, Barbara Keene, Donna Malloy, Bonnie Marsden, Marcia McCrae, Joyce Perella, Luz Parco, and two colleages named Wendy Davis, all of whom significantly contributed to helping Gilbert form a more holistic and integrated view and approach to the child and family. Other significant colleagues for Gilbert include Drs. Haru Hirama and Anne Mosey who dramatically shaped Gilbert's developmental perspective. Additional thanks are extended to Marilyn Appell, Eula Boelke, Miriam Cherkes-Julkowski, Lois Davis, Jane DeWeerd, Joanna Erikson, Nancy Heyman, Margaret Hobin, Bill Isler, Martha Woodward Isler, Barbara Kelleher, Jack Kiss, Toni Linder, Mary Lovell, Brian McNulty, David Smith, Kathy Sims, Arlene Uss, and the U.S. Department of Education for providing opportunities for the development, demonstration, and dissemination of the Family Centered Resource Project.

When it came time to put our ideas into print several people stand out as having been helpful. Thanks to Donna Addison and Lisa Atkinson for the secretarial support throughout the process. They spent many extra hours helping us get over the hurdles we faced. Ashley P. Hanson was an invaluable resource to us in the Shain Library as she tackled unending bibliographic requests. Thanks also to Sam Gipstein, age 5, for being willing to share his art work for our cover. Numerous current and past college students were also involved in field testing, library research, case study research, and manuscript preparation. Key in these are Laurie Clark, Mary Fischer, Jennifer Fox, Elizabeth Holdridge, Deborah Leffingwell, Cecile Lewis, Kim Marcantonio, Sally Ravanelle, and Liza Wallace.

Another major contributor to the development process of the SPM has been Sue Wagner. Sue, a former Child Development major and past teacher in the program, has been our key technical assistant throughout all of the steps of preparing our manuscript for publication. Typing, library research, and editing all were parts of her job, which she attacked with vigor. She was tireless and an overall morale booster; she kept the process moving during those times when the task seemed too large to conquer. We are indebted to Sue's unfailing perseverance and hours of work and dedication.

Thanks also to Nancy Berliner for her thoughtful work in preparing our manuscript. Lastly a big thank you goes to Susan Liddicoat, our editor from Teachers College Press, who has been our guardian and advocate throughout the entire publishing process. She has been persistent and calm no matter the circumstances. We each thank her wholeheartedly.

To Eveline B. Omwake and Sally Provence, M.D.

*two women who through their work demonstrated that this practice is more than a technology—
it is an opportunity for the transformation of the self*

*who committed themselves to the guidance and formation of the forthcoming generation of
professionals in child development*

*and who illuminated the central role of relationships in human development and expressed utmost faith
in the potential of parents and children*

PART I

Foundations and Description of the Supportive Play Model

The first part of this book is divided into three chapters. It offers essential information related to the philosophical foundations, practical applications, and mechanics for using the Supportive Play Model. This background information serves as a prelude to the four case studies presented in Part II.

Chapter 1 examines the role of play in early intervention and describes the centrality of play in early development. Chapter 2 walks the reader through the steps of using the Supportive Play Model chart, which is the procedural framework of the model. Chapter 3 is a discussion of family adaptations to the birth a of child with special needs and the issues relevant to successful school placement.

CHAPTER 1

Play as the Mainstay of Early Development and Early Intervention

Since the passage of the Education for All Handicapped Children Act of 1975 (PL 94-142), the Education of the Handicapped Amendments of 1986—Part H (PL 99-457), the Americans with Disabilities Act of 1990 (PL 101-336), and the Education of the Handicapped Act Amendments of 1990 (PL 101-476) in 1990, early childhood teachers have faced increasingly the challenge of working with special needs children integrated into their typical classrooms. Although most preschool professionals are sympathetic with the underlying principle of "least restrictive environment" (LRE), the current move towards inclusion and the assumption that children with special needs may benefit from a normalized setting, many have found themselves frustrated by the unexpected demands placed on the staff and the class by the child with special needs. The developmental limitations of the child with special needs become particularly poignant when the child attempts to sustain social experience, master the demands of routine and environment, and participate fully in the play experiences that form the spine of the normal preschool curriculum. Children with special needs are often unable to engage spontaneously in play or derive the same richness from their play as typical children because of motor, symbolic, or social limitations. The inherently unfolding development of play themes may be compromised or confounded by their disability. The inability to participate fully in play may even impose a secondary deprivation on children whose development is already imperiled.

We developed the Supportive Play Model (SPM) to help teachers adapt their existing play strategies to meet the unique needs of the child with disabilities and optimize the benefit such children may derive from participating in a range of settings. This model offers the professional a systematic process for observing children with special needs, analyzing their play, and preparing developmentally appropriate play and learning environments, inclusive or special.

In the SPM, play is defined as the child's spontaneous, pleasurable, and naturally unfolding repertoire of actions on objects, others, and self, which leads to the discovery, expression, and mastery of physical reality, ideas, and feelings. Play is the child's genetically determined and inherent means of learning. It is our assumption that by supporting the child's inherent play patterns, development, learning, and adaptation will evolve in a naturalistic and organic way.

Within the traditional nursery school setting, the teacher is responsible for orchestrating an environment that is conducive to the child's innate motivation to play. This role, although typically seen as being distinctly unobtrusive, can be highly effective in supporting the emerging play skills of the normally developing child (Biber, 1984; Isaacs, 1930, 1940, 1960; Read & Patterson, 1980; Sigel, 1965; Stallibrass, 1989). However, when planning for children with special needs, we can not assume that a play-conducive environment and a supportive adult alone automatically produce the desired intellectual and social motivation needed to transform these children into active players and learners. With the help of the SPM, such children can be assisted in compensating, if not overcoming, some of the constraints that limit their play. If children are liberated to play, then surely they will learn.

This chapter describes developmental theories of play and approaches to practice which have contributed to the SPM. It also presents a paradigm of the stages of play from sensorimotor to symbolic as it relates to development.

THEORIES OF PLAY AND THEIR IMPLICATIONS FOR THE SUPPORTIVE PLAY MODEL

The concept of play weaves a central theme throughout the early childhood movement from its origin in 18th-century idealism to the present. In Froebel's (1897) kindergarten, the play of childhood was seen as the germinal stage of all later life development. In the contemporary preschool, three major lines of thought shape our understanding of play: the psychodynamic–affective model, the normative–maturational model, and the cognitive–interactional model. Each model has emphasized some specific attribute of play and its contribution to the total fabric of human development. In addition, the SPM utilizes the contribution of two major contemporary educational approaches, compensatory education and special education, to highlight teaching methods and the value of play in intervention.

Psychodynamic–Affective Model

In the psychodynamic–affective model, play is understood as children's action and expression through which they derive pleasurable mastery in a naturalistic and organic way, without the need for imposed intellectual tasks (Peller, 1954). Winnicott (1966) describes the child's capacity for play as deriving from the child's experience with a dependable object, which leads to trust, symbol use, and, ultimately, cultural experience. In play, children sense, experiment, and extract information from the environment as well as reduce tension, vent forbidden impulses, and master traumatic events in ways that allow them to transcend the limitations of their bodies and environment (Solnit, 1987). Most centrally, play serves as a window to the inner life and a medium through which the internalized conflicts and distortions of the world of objects, drives, and feelings can be adjusted.

Play has had direct application in both therapy and in nursery education. When using play as a mode of treatment, Anna Freud (1964, 1966b) believed that the adult should assume a broadly educational role, assisting the child to transform adaptively impulses through play, thereby strengthening ego development. Klein (1937) encouraged direct interpretation of the child's play content, focusing on understanding the dynamics of preoedipal and unconscious fantasy. Axline (1947) fostered a permissive, nondirective environment in which the child plays out problems with the participation of the therapist in a reflective and clarifying role. Erikson (1940, 1963) sees the therapist as a sympathetic adult who allows the child to play out natural ambivalence and insecurity (caused by hate and fear). This act of playing, with appropriate adult support, serves as a vehicle for natural teaching and healing, resulting in a sense of peace that leads to increased coping and mastery.

In nursery school settings, psychodynamic concepts have been translated into practice by many, including Selma Fraiberg (1965, 1980), Anna Freud (1964, 1966b), Susan Isaacs (1930, 1940, 1960), Eveline Omwake (1963, 1974), Lili Peller (1954), and Sally Provence (1967, 1983). In these settings, emotional expression is encouraged and sustained through the use of plastic materials, teacher dialogue, and reflection. The aim of these nursery schools is to redirect and transform the innate sexual and aggressive drives of the child toward mastery, learning, and adaptation. Similarly, in the SPM, the teacher encourages awareness and acceptance of the children's inner life as reflected through the psychodynamic themes in their play, which are used as a vehicle for promoting learning, adjustment, and self-realization.

Normative–Maturational Model

The influence of genetic inheritance and the innate unfolding of developmental life are emphasized in the normative–maturational model. Age norms are a mainstay of programs that adhere to this model, and readiness is an assumed prerequisite for the acquisition of any new skill. Play provides a dress rehearsal for roles and relationships that are part of the grown-up world and serves as a vehicle for the unfolding of the innate maturational plan.

John Dewey (1916), a major contributor to this model, laid the groundwork for the progressive education movement that was established on the precept that children, when stimulated by an appropriate environment on which they can act, and supported by meaningful adults, will grow, form interests, and learn when they are ready. Gesell (1940) and Gesell and colleagues (1974) formulated a sequential and stage-specific schedule of child development, derived from careful scientific observation, which is the basis of the contemporary normative–maturational approach.

This approach has had an impact on the SPM in that the normative data in the model provides a referent to assess and interpret a child's behavior. However, the curriculum and teaching techniques that are general outgrowths of the normative–maturational model are predominantly observational and too passive for many children with special needs. Although appropriate materials and environments may stimulate well-organized children to become active learners, the SPM advocates that the teacher be a more active participant in the learning process when working with children with special needs. "Readiness" and self-initiated learning may not unfold naturally in the special needs child without the support of more direct intervention.

Cognitive–Interactional Model

The cognitive–interactional view of development purports that knowledge is acquired by the child who is an active learner. Play is the means of learning through guided discovery in a prepared environment. Montessori (1912, 1965) emphasized the prepared environment and developed a wide array of teaching devices and materials that systematized children's discovery and learning experiences. Piaget (1952, 1962), in his theory of cognitive development, emphasized an interactive environment that is planned and monitored by a developmentally sensitive adult. The adult's use of Socratic dialogue and judicious use of disequilibrium guides the child's discovery process (Biber, Shapiro, & Wickens, 1977; Bredekamp, 1986; Read & Patterson, 1980). The SPM derives the principle of strategic design of the play environment from the cognitive–interactional approach in order to facilitate sequential discovery and promote curiosity through novelty and challenge. But, because of the learning and behavioral issues that are often the result of developmental differences, it is suggested in the SPM that a teacher may have to be a more active participant in the child's play and learning experience than is advocated in traditional cognitive–interactional approaches.

Compensatory and Special Education Intervention Models

As part of the compensatory models that flourished in the 1960s, the role of the sensitive and responsive cognitive–interactional teacher was expanded. At that time, educators realized that the natural unfolding of development was not equally experienced across all socioeconomic groups. Theorists, such as Shefatya (1990), Smilansky (1968), and Smilansky and colleague (1990), suggested that an active teaching orientation was preferable for children with normal intellectual potential but who lacked spontaneous motivation and expected progress. Specifically, in reference to the development of **sociodramatic play,** Smilansky rejects the concept of the observing and supportive teacher in favor of a more active and sensitive role as fellow player, modeler, and expander. Freyberg (1973) demonstrated that active facilitation of dramatic play with children from low socioeconomic backgrounds improved imagination, concentration, and affect. Wolfgang (1977) also demonstrated that the active role of the teacher promoted improved play and overall growth in aggressive or passive children.

From the special education literature we draw several contemporary lines of thought regarding play and the young child with special needs. Notable among these is the concept of the interrelatedness of development (Brazelton & Als, 1979; Greenspan, 1990a, 1990b, 1992; Prizant, 1990; Prizant & Wetherby, 1990) and the notion that assessment of play can provide important information about development as a whole (Fewell & Kaminski, 1988; Fewell & Vadasy, 1983; Foley & Appel, 1987; Kennedy, Sheridan, Radlinski, & Beeghly, 1991; Linder, 1990; Lowe & Costello, 1988; McCune, 1986a, 1986b; McCune-Nicolich & Fenson, 1984; Newson & Newson, 1979; Provence, Erikson, Vater, & Palmeri, 1994; Takata, 1974; Westby, 1980). These concepts have directly influenced intervention models and have led to developmentally oriented curricula that underscore the value of play in early development (Bromwich, 1978; Fewell & Vadasy, 1983; Gottfried & Brown, 1985; Knox, 1974; MacDonald, Gillette, Bickley, & Rodriguez, 1984; Mahoney & Powell, 1986; Michelmann, 1974; Newson & Newson, 1979; Schwartz & Miller, 1988; Wood, Combs, Gunn, & Weller, 1986). Occupational therapy and physical therapy literatures have contributed awareness of the value of play materials that are specifically adapted to compensate for the child's particular physical and motor disabilities (Florey, 1971; Musselwhite, 1986; Riddick, 1982). A concurrent and contrasting movement in early intervention emphasizes behavioral teaching of play skills through task analysis and a programmed training approach to specific skill acquisition (Coe, Matson, Fee, Manikam, & Linarello, 1990; Haring, 1985; Lefebvre & Strain, 1989; Sherburne, Utley, McConnell, & Gannon, 1988; Uline, 1982).

The SPM has selectively assimilated key components of these compensatory and special education approaches for application to children with special needs in typical settings. This model reflects the tenets that

- Early remediation can maximize development.
- Play is an effective means of assessing the child's development.
- Play is a mode of expression.

- Play acquisition positively affects interrelated areas of development.
- Play can be improved through the use of modified materials and toys.
- The judicious application of behavioral techniques can enhance the child's learning.

THE STAGES OF PLAY

In this section we propose a broad description of the developmental progression of play from concrete and sensory to symbolic and expressive. Although we characterize the child's spontaneous pleasurable activity on objects, self, and others across the age span as play, it changes dramatically in complexity, function, and form.

Our proposed stages, derived from existing literature and clinical experience, make an effort to define the salient changes in play over the course of development. We caution against the temptation to think of the stages as lock step and the zones discrete and suggest an image of them as evolving and interrelated with more formed stages synthesized out of the components of simpler stages. Rather than visualizing stage-wise development as blocks stacked tower-like, envision it as scoops of sand layered upon each other to create an expanding, plastic, and interrelated configuration.

In attempting to identify the essential features of play, Bergen's analysis (1987) proved helpful. She identifies three overlapping themes in the play literature that seem to summarize the central features:

- Play as it relates to action for its own sake and action on objects
- Play as it relates to pretense and symbolization
- Play as it relates to interaction with others

In our proposed stages, the pretense and symbolic features differ most notably from existing models, which we will explore in greater depth in the Play Skills and Themes section.

Sensorimotor Play

The **sensorimotor** stage of play dominates the early months of life. Much early behavior is reflex-mediated and undifferentiated from feeding and responses to physical care. This "protoplay" begins as pleasure experienced through sensory activation of the whole body and then, more specifically, the mouth. In this play, the baby makes little distinction between self and other. This undifferentiated play is gradually refined and organized around simple visual–sensory–motor manipulations, such as reaching, tasting, touching, swiping, grasping, inspecting, banging, and dropping. Through these seemingly accidental and haphazard object plays, the child gets acquainted with the qualities of objects, assimilates sensory information, regulates tension, and discovers the topography and action properties of the body.

Functional–Combinatory Play

This form of play assumes ascendance in the later months of the first year of life. This play is initially accidental, then repetitive in nature, leading to a limited anticipation of the effects of actions on objects. As babies "apply" information learned about the properties of objects, they discover purposeful actions and outcomes and then intentionally apply known means to new situations. That is, children begin to purposefully use objects in the ways intended. They make objects work, put objects together and discover action properties. Random explorations with a ball are transformed into purposeful nothing. The toy car, initially banged and mouthed, is purposefully pushed. Cup and cube, initially explored as two unrelated objects, are combined first in banging and then containment. Cups demand a saucer; spoons are contained in cups, and hats placed on heads.

Constructive Play

During this stage of play, in the second year of life, the child purposefully uses objects in the ways intended but also discovers novel compositions, elaborations, and new possibilities through active trial-and-error experimentation, often with a somber and serious demeanor. Out of this play, children discover, discriminate, and begin to categorize the shared and unique attributes between and among objects. They expand not only their knowledge of the sensory/physical properties of objects, but also their knowledge of functional relations, spatial relations, causal relations, and categorical relations (perceptual qualities) among objects (Fenson & Schell, 1986).

Out of this play children construct and revise their inner cognitive maps and working models of the world. Constructive play unfolds as a line across the subsequent stages of play, expanding rapidly in the preschool years. Towers are built to various heights and with a variety of foundations to test the limits of soaring. Cities sprawl expansively, and tea-time is fabricated from myriad materials. Constructive play can be representational, as in replica building, or symbolic and expressive, as in materializing an elaborate imaginary landscape. At its heart, constructive play can be categorized as action-oriented discovery, problem solving, and elaboration.

Autorepresentational Play

This stage of play also emerges in the child's second year. It includes the playful pretend use of objects on the self, thus the prefix *auto*. Objects are used in a conventional manner, through **deferred imitation** or mimicry, as seen in a child's pretend use of a toy phone (Fein & Apfel, 1979; Inhelder, Lezine, Sinclair, & Stambak, 1972; Lowe, 1975; Watson & Fischer, 1977). While we suspect the child possesses a mental "image" of the object–action, what is "in mind" is still tied in a one-to-one correspondence with the physical object. This type of play is similar to simple naming or labeling.

Allorepresentational Play

In this stage of play, children continue to use deferred imitation to reconstruct short play scenes, but do so in novel settings directed toward new persons or objects, thus the prefix *allo*, meaning "other." In this make believe, the child may feed the parent and then the teddy bear with a toy cup and spoon. This shift of focus from self to other in early pretend play begins around 18 months and becomes well incorporated into play after 2 years (Fein & Apfel, 1979; Lowe, 1975). Following age 2, play is increasingly decentered or directed to others (Piaget, 1962), decontextualized or recreated in novel settings (Werner & Kaplan, 1963), and integrated so that individual actions are connected in a behavior sequence forming the beginnings of scenes, themes, and scripts (Fenson & Schell, 1986).

Symbolic Play

In our scheme, play becomes symbolic when it reflects deferred imitation and liberation from the concrete referent. This tends to follow a developmental progress or form a hierarchy of abstraction. This progression begins at the level of object substitution, pretending that a block is a car, and proceeds to sociodramatic play in which children combine and expand on actions and ideas at the level of personal experience, and finally at the imaginative level where children create ideas beyond personal experience and break with convention in object use, scene or role. When children are able to move beyond the literal one-to-one correspondence between the material object and inner representation to effect a meaning, then they have moved from the level of sign or icon to true abstraction or symbol. Once this freedom of thought has been realized, children are at the threshold of expressive imagination and creativity. Thus, symbolic play is an ongoing opportunity for creative transformation and problem solving through an evolving capacity for divergent thinking. (Figure 1.1.)

Figure 1.1

Stages of Play	The Continuum of Social Complexity
Sensorimotor	Solitary
Functional–Combinatory	Interactive (synchronous
Constructive	and reflective)
Autorepresentational	Onlooker
Allorepresentational	Parallel
Symbolic	Associative
Object-centered	Cooperative
Sociodramatic	
Imaginative	

PLAY AND DEVELOPMENT: AN INTERDEPENDENT RELATIONSHIP

Play is a window through which we come to understand the child from both the outside and the inside. It gives us clues about children's repertoire of skills and abilities to negotiate with the world around them. Play gives us a glimpse of children's memories, feelings, wishes, fantasies, and theories about how the world works. Play is a condensed and intensified version of the larger spectrum of development, like poetry is an intensified language version of some larger human experience—"much in little." Through the aperture of play, outer physical/descriptive reality becomes part of the child's mental apparatus and the content of the inner life is externalized.

Because play is spontaneous and usually pleasurable, it is innocently revealing. Once the child has formed a demarcation between outer and inner reality, play serves yet another important function as transitional space, a safe stage on which experiences, feelings, and ideas can be rehearsed and revised before being internalized or externalized (Winnicott, 1966). Thus, by looking at children's play, we simultaneously partake in the evolving constructions of their inner and outer realities and can assess the status of the many skills that must converge to make a competent player.

As process, play and development support each other. Play offers the child a naturalistic opportunity without the need of an imposed task to master new skills, which in turn advance, expand, or change the play itself. The capacity for narration, for example, prunes the play of excessive action. Yet the very narrative that eventually liberates the play from overreliance on action might have had its origins in solitary constructive play during which the child rehearsed linking actions and words together to form a schematic play script. That outline might have been "fleshed out" later in sociodramatic play, resulting in a rich narration with word and gesture substituting for demonstration.

In the SPM we assume a psychodevelopmental position and hope the organization and content of the book speaks to our view. This bias is to encourage caregivers of typical and atypical children alike to be as attuned and attentive to the inner life of their "charges" as they are to their physical care and developmental competence. When we speak of the inner life of children, we refer to their sensorium (alert, responsive, attentive), internal disposition (comfortable, hungry, irritable), mood (elated, subdued), motivations, memories and subjective interpretations of experience. We include their feeling states; theories about how they and the world work; their wishes, worries, and conflicts; their fantasies and their fears. Although their inner world may be less tangible than walking and talking, it is no less real. Even from infancy, the inner state, though rudimentary, vastly influences behavior. As children grow in physical stature and skill, so grows the structure and content of their inner life of memories, theories, and feelings. Effecting harmony between inner and outer experience becomes an important focus of our work, because when they are in relative congruence the unfolding of development is both optimal and authentic.

Within the SPM, play behavior can be understood both as a reflection of a child's progress in the four developmental-centered zones (self/social/emotional, motor/self-help, communicative/language, and cognitive) and in terms of play skills and play themes. The Observational Impressions that are used in completing the SPM charts (see Chapter 2) are consequently divided into these six subdivisions. The developmentally centered zones are not intended, however, to stand alone as comprehensive "scales" of development *per se*. Rather, they are designed to afford the observer a systematically descriptive and qualitative appreciation of the child's relative level of capability in each area. The aim is to expand the observer's understanding of how these zones relate to each other thematically and, more pointedly, promote or confound the child's ability to play competently. The play-centered zones focus more specifically on play development itself, namely the means (skills) and the content (themes) of play.

The narrative that follows focuses first on the developmental-centered zones and then on play skills and play themes. Since there is considerable overlap between the developmental zones and the age-related play skills and play themes, we often fold the complementary material into one discussion area. Thus, the following sketches of each zone are not intended to be a direct narrative description of the content of *Section II: Observational Impressions* of the SPM charts. Rather, they aim to orient the reader to the spirit of the charts and to frame development in play.

Self/Social/Emotional Development

This area focuses primarily on the formation of self, relations to others, and feelings as they unfold in play. Throughout infancy, play serves survival by promoting attachment. Newborns come into the world with a complex repertoire of inborn patterns of action and reaction. Although initially reflex-mediated, parents are apt to personalize these behaviors as playful interactions. Thus, babies "woo" their parents into proximity, engagement, and empathy.

Play also serves as a source of comfort, tension reduction, and stimulus nurturance—what Wilbarger (1993) calls a sensory diet. These benefits accrue from the exchanges between parent and infant in physical care often framed as play, such as feeding, diapering, activating, engaging, and quieting. As these successful patterns of arousal, balanced by calming, comfort, and organizing, become internalized, the child learns to maintain a relative homeostasis independently and regulate his or her own sensory diet. Over the course of development, play continues to function as a discharge mode for uncomfortable tension and as a social activator by bringing parents and caregivers into pleasurable and assistive interaction.

Play initially focuses on the bodies of the child and caregiver. In junior toddlerhood, play serves as a bridge over which the child passes from the caregiver–infant envelope to a wider world of objects, people, and experiences. A transitional object (blanket or cuddly toy) sometimes emerges to assist children in negotiating this passage by giving them a kind of "mobile mother" to carry with them in their exciting and sometimes frightening adventures into new territory. These successive separations define for the child a demarcated self and promote the development of new and differentiated affects.

Consistent playful experience with stable human and nonhuman objects promotes a concept of constancy. The internalized memories of these pleasurable experiences form the nuclei around which inner representations are organized, including those of parents and self. The beginnings of object- and self-constancy hallmark a rudimentary psychological birth during toddlerhood (Mahler, Pine, & Bergman, 1975). This fledgling self is fragile and ambivalence characterizes the period. Children are beginning to wrestle with the problem of autonomy and independence. This launches them headlong into a fundamental conflict between the rather passive–receptive orientation of infancy and the more active instrumental possibilities of toddlerhood. The tension contributes to a period peppered by mood swings and the defense of autonomy counterpointed against infantile helplessness. "No" becomes a rallying cry and negativism serves as a means through which children make adult demands of being civilized their own. To accept reality *carte blanche* from caregiver would be far too threatening to the toddler's fragile autonomy. By indulging in the extremes and playing out the confusion, it is hoped the child will discover a graded middle ground that will neutralize the extremes and result in what we call "normal limits." The salient themes of this period center around matters of fusion and separateness, holding on and letting go, self-sufficiency and dependency. This serves as a transition to the expansive growth that will transpire in the preschool years.

Children's play during the early part of the preschool years centers on affirming, exploring, and expanding their newly formed selves. Children can be observed resolving matters of what is "me" and "mine" and what is not "me" or "mine." Play affords children a safe venue to experiment with these matters and serves as a prelude to what will become social skills. Children must also learn how to manage strong and sometimes conflicting impulses and feelings. Struggling to make a puzzle piece fit, children may wrestle with the impulse to jam in or break the obstinate piece. With guided rehearsal in play, children learn to cope with the frustrating and aggressive impulse by anticipating a pleasurable outcome, in accomplishment.

Being small in physical stature means that children may often feel at the mercy of the larger world. In play, they can be giants or parents and assert themselves in ways not possible in reality. Play affords the child a way to explore acceptably those mysteries that are a part of the hidden and forbidden realities of daily life: social roles, family composition, sex, gender, and bodily functions. Play allows children to make intangible social–emotional reality knowable and their own.

With a more consolidated sense of self, and an amplified repertoire of emotional skills to manage anxiety (e.g., increased frustration tolerance, displacement to activation on a toy, turning passive to active), children's play turns more to the social sphere during the later portion of the preschool period, the benefits of which are many. Skilled sociodramatic players are able not only to attract peers and adults but maintain their interaction in a mutually satisfying way, thereby expanding their own social development (Rubin, Fein, & Vandenberg, 1983). Pretend social play reinforces and amplifies children's capacity for reciprocity, explaining, negotiating, and accommodating—the foundations of prosocial behavior (Connolly, Doyle, & Reznick, 1988). Children who play competently and cooperatively are less likely to argue and are more likely to receive peer acceptance and positive teacher assessment (Ladd & Price, 1987; Ladd, Price, & Hart, 1988; Pellegrini, 1988; Rubin, 1986).

As children's understanding of social rules and interactions becomes more abstract and their cognitive and verbal skills expand, the psychological and social aspects of play become more elaborate. As children grow less dependent on the concrete reality of the environment and defined roles to organize themselves, they are able to submerge in the "as if" (Fein, 1986; Isaacs, 1940) an important inventive means to elaborating self-identity and promoting individuation.

Motor Development and Self-Help Skills

Almost all play involves action, so motor skill is a fundamental part of becoming a competent player. This zone focuses on the development and contribution of posture, movement, dexterity, and self-sufficiency to the unfolding of play.

As was described previously, postural reflexes and early intentional motor activity are key in promoting a baby's connection to the world. As the baby's movements progress from random to intentional actions, the lifelong process of exploration and discovery begins. As repeated actions cause repeated reactions, infants not only learn the rudiments of causality, but gain trust in the predictability of their surroundings and their bodies (Kaplan-Sanoff, Brewster, Stillwell, & Bergen, 1987).

The attainment of postural control and locomotion expands the babies' sphere of experience, and reinforces the self as locus of control. Of particular importance, however, is not just the attainment of motor milestones, but mastery of the components of movement (**stability, disassociation, equilibrium, rotation, mobility, and motor planning**) that serve as the underpinnings of motor competence. The infant practices these adroitly and inherently in the course of playing.

Tracking, localizing, and inspecting people and things in **interactive play** all contribute quite naturalistically to the stabilization and control of the infant's head. Pivoting while prone to swipe at a dangling toy, with the reinforcement of parental delight, allows the baby to practice visually directed reaching, stabilization of the spine, and antigravitational control. Bearing weight on extended arms and reaching to grasp a ring contributes to stabilizing the **proximal joints** and provides practice in weight shifting, an antecedent of balance. Sitting perched on mom's lap, face to the world, and reaching back to touch her, not only reassures the baby of her physical presence and affords emotional refueling, but also serves as an opportunity to engage in disassociation of movement and trunk rotation. Creeping to retrieve a ball playfully rolled out of reach affords the child an opportunity to practice weight shifting, balance, and rotation in motion—a dynamic prelude to walking. Mobility allows for a shift from a mother-centered world to an environment-centered world that includes mother. Through developing motor skills, particularly upright locomotion, toddlers learn to control their own bodies, become instrumental, and influence other people (Kaplan-Sanoff, Brewster, Stillwell, & Bergen, 1987).

In toddlerhood and beyond, children spend a good deal of energy in motor planning and refining and combining fundamental gross motor skills to perfect complex activities such as jumping, running, throwing, and catching. Innate developmental potential interacts with environmental and cultural factors in determining the progression and extent to which these skills are refined (Gallahue, 1982; Kaplan-Sanoff, Brewster, Stillwell, & Bergen, 1987).

The ability to execute complex motor actions enables children to master tasks of self-sufficiency (feeding, dressing, toileting) and use objects in accord with their prescribed purposes (spoons for feeding, pots for cooking, tables for setting and eating). These skills are refined in play and in turn press the play itself toward increasing social and expressive complexity.

Communicative/Language Development

This zone focuses on the communicative structure of play, including the receptive and expressive, verbal and gestural modalities. While there is a relationship between language and play, the exact interaction of these skills is not fully understood. In infancy, interactive play seems critical in promoting and shaping the formation of "protopragmatic skills," such as eye contact, shared attention, social–emotional attunement, and turn-taking (Bloom, Johnson, Bitler, & Christman, 1986). It is hypothesized that these skills are antecedents to the more elaborate pragmatic language skills that include conversational reciprocity, topic maintenance and expansion, and felicity.

At 2 months, mother–baby interactive play promotes babbling, and approximately one third of all infant language production can be explained by mother–infant interaction (Tamis-LeMonda, 1993). At later ages, research points out that certain phases of symbolic language and symbolic play occur together (Hill & McCune-Nicolich, 1981; Ingram, 1977; McCune-Nicolich & Fenson, 1984; Nicolich & Raph, 1978). However, research does not clearly establish a casual relationship between pretend play and the achievement of language and cognitive abilities (Watson & Fischer, 1977).

In the child's earliest expressions of symbolic play there appears to be an association between the ability to combine words and combine play acts. This may suggest that these different modes of behavior share some underlying symbolic competencies (McCune-Nicolich, 1981; Shore, O'Connell, &

Bates, 1984). Play has been described as integral to the "evolution of communication and metacommunication" (Bateson, 1976). This is supported by longitudinal research that indicates that competent players who were late talkers but good comprehenders were, in the long run, more competent communicators than those with earlier speech but poorer play skills and receptive language (Tamis-LeMonda, 1993). Children have been found to have different communication skills, depending on whether they intend their behavior to be perceived as play or not. Garvey (1979) describes how the child is also able to use verbal rituals within play to establish and change relationships and roles. There is also evidence to suggest that gesture, a component of play, may be the missing link between language comprehension and production (Bates, Bretherton, Snyder, Shore, & Volterra, 1980; Bates, Thal, Whitesell, Fenson, & Oakes, 1989).

As pretend play develops toward decontextualization and symbolism, new relationships are observed between language use and play behavior. Children use language with gestures to animate dolls and other objects, but find it easier to express internal states (wants, needs, feelings) with words rather than action (Fenson, 1984). In the earliest stages of pretend play, however, pretense is conveyed by action only for the vast majority of children, with only a small percentage of play action being narrated. But once the child is over 2 years old, language-supported action or independent narrative outstrips action–pretense alone. Thus, the child relies increasingly on the more precise and efficient modality of words to convey the symbolic intent and content of the play action (Fenson, 1984; Fenson & Schell, 1986).

As social pretend play develops to more advanced levels in the preschooler, the language used to support action becomes more complex. Sociodramatic play involves the development of verbal play scripts that evolve collaboratively. This interplayer negotiation can be compared to the interactive process between an author and editor, in which one participant's suggestion leads to another's adaptation and redesign of an idea. Some theorists suggest that children's language skills and play skills are thus the foundations upon which writing skills are built, and whereby children learn how to communicate their ideas to an audience and begin to understand "voice" (Fromberg, 1992).

Cognitive Development

This zone focuses on the conceptual underpinnings of play and, simultaneously, on how play contributes to the content of cognitive structure. The role of play in cognitive development has attracted many theorists and much research. Piaget (1962) and Montessori (1912) favored constructive play as the important contributor to cognitive formation. They, like other cognitive–interactionists, saw both sensorimotor and pretend play as formats for assimilation but not activities that lead to new learning. On the other hand, they believed that constructive play allowed for instrumental and creative learning by serving as a vehicle for problem solving, hypothesis testing, and the formation of new mental constructs, not just imitating or cataloging information (Bretherton, 1985; Bruner, Jolly, & Sylva, 1976; Fenson & Schell, 1986; Freyberg, 1973; Leslie, 1987; Seidman, Nelson, & Gruendel, 1986; Singer, 1973; Smilansky, 1968; Smith, 1986; Vygotsky, 1976).

The metacommunication needed to play also contributes to the consolidation of cognitive constructs. To communicate role, scene, and action to playmates requires concept formation and mental mapping (Garvey, 1979). In turn, opportunities to play with older children challenge a child's thinking and may encourage

more mature social cognition in play (Fromberg, 1992; Pellegrini, 1984). Pretend-play opportunities that involve challenging and complex schemata can support, strengthen, or integrate existing knowledge or effect new learning by triggering dissonance and revision of existing cognitive maps (Rubin, 1986). Some theorists believe that the ability to be playful contributes to a capacity for divergent thinking and later creativity (Cowie, 1984; Hutt & Bhavnani, 1976; Johnson, 1976; Lieberman, 1977; Schaefer, 1969).

The interplay of the social, linguistic, communicative, and cognitive components of play are described in transformational dynamics, or "script model" research (Auwärter, 1986; Bretherton, O'Connell, Shore, & Bates, 1984; Eckler & Weininger, 1989; Eiser, 1989; Garvey & Kramer, 1989; Kreye, 1984; Mandler, 1983; Nelson & Gruendel, 1986; Roskos, 1990). These data suggest that children design their **play scenarios** out of their cultural reality and daily living experiences. They weave the predictable routines and roles into a "stock" story line out of which they improvise novel variations of the expected processes and outcomes. In sociodramatic experience, the "script" reflects the shared cognitive themes related to cultural understanding and skills, but is modified in production (Fromberg, 1992). This improvisational dimension contributes to a capacity for cognitive flexibility, decentering, and creativity.

PLAY SKILLS AND THEMES

Not unlike art, play can be understood, albeit somewhat simply, in terms of means (materials, techniques, processes) and content (themes, forms, feelings), hence our delineation of play skills and play themes within the SPM. These sections focus on the developmental progression of play itself, and they synthesize material from across zones into an integrated scheme. The Play Skills section addresses play action and action on objects, pretense and symbolization, and the social progression of play, whereas the Play Themes section focuses more on the content of play as an expression of the organization and dynamics of the inner life. In reality, play skills and play themes are surely not so separate as we may have portrayed them, but intertwine and interweave in the unfolding of development. Therefore, the observer needs to engage in an ongoing reflective process of examining the child's play skills and play themes in relation to each other, within the larger configuration of development, and, finally, within the broad frame of family and environment.

Play Skills

The seemingly random and undifferentiated sensorimotor activities of infancy become increasingly discrete, repetitive, and playful. As knowledge of the material world expands, so the focus of the play shifts from "descriptive" to purposeful and combinatory to constructive and experimental. The banging of the toy car becomes purposeful pushing. Stacking blocks becomes replica building in which the child discovers how high the tower can be built before toppling or how far a platform can be cantilevered off a building before falling.

Action experiences on objects, people, and self and the multisensory information assimilated from these experiences are encoded in the mental apparatus. Out of visual, **tactile**, proprioceptive, and **vestibular** data, inner representational **schemes** are formed. These images correspond to the concrete object and serve a mutually activating sign function, thus effecting a one-to-one correspondence between inner and outer reality, pushing play toward symbolization and pretense (Langer, 1962).

In reviewing the literature in this area we encountered considerable semantic confusion, specifically related to the distinction between play as sign or icon and play as symbol or expression. In an effort to clarify and, hopefully, not confound this matter, we propose a slightly modified taxonomy derived from clinical experience, theoretical formulations, and the aesthetic literature. Our particular interest in this area of symbolic formation stems from a belief that it stands at the threshold of what makes us consummately human. Symbol making liberates us from enslavement to the concrete and heralds the age of concept and creativity.

Children's first representations are egocentric in nature. Although some authors refer to this autorepresentational level of play as symbolic, as explained earlier, we believe this designation is premature because the play is still intimately tied to the concrete referent and thus more aligned with **imitation** or mimicry. Although it is true that the play cup, for example, does not contain a liquid, to pretend to drink is so consonant with the prescribed and conventional use of a cup that it does not constitute a sufficient leap from the concrete to qualify as a symbolic act. At best, this pretend is more akin to displacement than imaginative projection.

In toddlerhood, the deferred imitation begun on self begins to generalize to others, and experiences can be reconstructed outside their typical contexts. At this level we may see a child feeding a doll or puppet from an empty cup or recreating scenes from daily life in new environments. We suggest that this is still representational and not yet truly symbolic.

The Greek root of the English word "symbol" translates to "throw," and Read (1960) suggests the implication is "to throw together," as in "to combine," to create a new idea or meaning. We suggest another association: to "throw" could be to "hurdle or leap" from the literal, suggesting the passage from sign to symbol. That juncture is traversed when play and language become sufficiently liberated from a one-to-one correspondence with physical reality to allow "a throw" to greater abstraction through thought and imagination.

The social evolution of play begins with early onlooker and **parallel play** (Parten, 1932). These forms persist throughout childhood into adulthood because they afford the opportunity to learn passively through observation without the risk of scrutiny, criticism, or failure. **Solitary play** is a haven most children return to repeatedly for retreat, refueling, and the pleasure of unbridled reverie. It affords an opportunity to master the tenuous without the fear of embarrassment or reproach.

In the preschool years, the social line of play forges forward rapidly. The early interactive skills, incorporating interpersonal sychrony and reciprocity, spawned over the first 18 months expand into a capacity for association. The child can now not only greet and initiate a social exchange, but begins to sustain an engagement. This is typically centered around a concrete play theme, such as building or recreating some simple scene from daily life. Although often prompted by necessity, children begin to use toys from a common stock pile, experiment with turn taking, contribute to the play of another, allow another to amplify their play, and, eventually, maintain mutuality around a play theme and work toward a common goal. The latter is characterized as cooperative play.

In the preschool years, children become truly constructive and symbolic, both in play and in language. They can substitute one object for another, invest it with meaning, combine symbols (words) to make new ideas, create scenes free of slavish dependence on direct experience, and elaborate creatively and imaginatively as well as construct replicas. Throughout this time, the social line progresses from **associative play** to true **cooperative play**. Symbolization may well be contributory. The ability to hold an idea or symbol may quell the urgency to have and to hold the material world; thus, the child develops an increasing capacity to tolerate delay and work with others toward the realization of a common goal. A growing repertoire of internal abstractions affords children a "symbol currency" with which to trade and negotiate as well as a rapidly expanding mental life that they "express and fabricate." This translates operationally into a rapidly expanding capacity on the part of the child to wait a turn, negotiate, bargain, share, and create within the framework of play.

Play Themes

In infancy, play themes are directly tied to bodily experience and the drive to survival through nurturance. What is called play is pleasure bound, and pleasure is an important organizer of development. The pleasure garnered from feeding and bodily care serves as "raw sensory material" around which ego development will coalesce. The aim that pleasure or comfort should dominate over pain or discomfort in this early period stems not only from the notion that it colors the child's first emotional perception of the world, but also from the fact that pleasure renders the baby more available and motivated to tackle subsequent developmental tasks. It is important to realize that, from the beginning, aggression is a powerful developmental force expressed in biting, scratching, throwing, and poking. Play serves as a medium for balancing pleasure and aggression into socialized ways of tolerating frustration and acting on the world.

The play of the baby at this early age is related to discovery of what is internal and what is external. As children "get and take in" experience from the outside, they begin to make rudimentary distinctions between that which emanates from within, as from the viscera, and that which comes from the outside, as the breast. This crucial demarcation helps them to develop body boundaries and a primitive differentiation between what is "me" and what is "not me."

Throughout the stormy interlude of toddlerhood, squeezing, smearing, pressing, pounding, building, pulling, pouring, and splashing dominate children's play. Such behaviors may represent efforts to integrate ambivalent feelings of love and hate, dependence and autonomy, cleanliness and messiness, and holding on and letting go. This restlessness gradually gives way to an increasing conformity with adult rules and gaining entry to the civilized world.

By age 3, the child has not only become a novice in the civilized world, but also has a rudimentary inner life that includes relatively stable representations of self and parents formed out of memories, feelings, words, and wishes. As the symbolic and expressive capacities expand, play is increasingly driven from the inside out. The child becomes less focused on the body and more centered on the role of the body in human relationships, particularly as it relates to sexuality and the organization of the family. The child's play begins to center on matters of sex differences, the functioning of the genitals, the architecture and mechanics of the family, and the intense affects evoked by intimate relationships: love, loss, jealousy, envy, and hate. Because the adult at this time is so envied, competitiveness and rivalry emerge, and children try to test their own desirability and potential to the limits. These themes saturate the play. They imagine what they could be by taking dramatic leaps into the future, pretending to be firefighters and doctors, Indian chiefs and heroes, even figures bigger than life itself—supermen and superwomen. This expressive play is vitally important because it gives form to feelings and fantasies that could loom gargantuan if left to unfold unbridled in the boundless world of the inner life. Expressive play affords children the opportunity to shape roles that may influence them across the life span and master emotionally charged themes related to authority, control, and identification (Schwartzman, 1978). Play provides the child both a stage and dress rehearsal for life, through which to find a balance between the fantasized and the real, the grandiose and the accomplishable, the wish and the fear.

A great deal of learning occurs through showing and watching. The expected sexually driven exhibitionism and voyeurism of this period can be sublimated in play toward constructive ends. The wish to peek and show is a source of excitation and pleasure. These motivations can be transformed into a capacity for observation and demonstration charged with feeling—important aspects of learning. Through play, which permits exciting flirtations with the "forbidden," passion and curiosity can be wedded, bearing fruit in a love of learning.

SUMMARY

In keeping with Anna Freud's (1966a) concept of the lines of development, play is the spawning ground for the capacity to recreate and work. Constructive play with objects enables children to delay gratification, to imagine possibilities, to complete a task, and then to displace what is learned to the larger reality arena of human endeavors and possibilities. In play, children can take experience apart and reconstruct it according to their own schemes and ideas. This becomes the prototype for creative work, in which adults deconstruct external reality and recreate it in novel ways and in new contexts. Play is the antecedent to creative problem solving and the well spring for future products. The adult capacity to recreate also contains the same play skills germinated in childhood, but remains more closely wedded to pleasure and aggression than does work.

Play serves the child in so many ways: a form of discharge, a way of learning, a dress rehearsal for life, a source of refueling and a respite in adaptive regression—a way to dream and a means to correct emotional injury. Play allows children to come face-to-face with the forbidden, the magical, and the miraculous, so that these elusive aspects of inner experience can be externalized and made knowable and manageable. Play serves as a concrete prototype for adult mental play in the form of reverie. The richness of early play may return at a later time in "aha" insights and solutions. It may reappear, transformed in art, to the degree that painting speaks to the playful infantile wish to smear, and the "play" serves the forbidden desire to peek. Play holds a noble and nodal place in human development.

Because play is so powerful and so central in early development, we see it as the mainstay to the SPM. Because of changing beliefs and practices, many early childhood settings are now enrolling many young children who have special needs; staff in these centers may be frustrated by their inability to understand and adequately serve these children. The SPM has been developed to provide professionals and parents with a philosophical perspective and a system that enables the design of a developmental intervention plan. In this first chapter we have reviewed key aspects of the role of play in development and in early intervention. Historical, legal, and theoretical foundations of play and intervention theory have been outlined to clarify their contributions to the SPM. Play stages and their interrelationships with other developmental zones have been described, and play skills and play themes have been discussed. With this overview, the reader is prepared to proceed with the specifics of the Supportive Play Process delineated in Chapter 2.

REFERENCES

Americans with Disabilities Act of 1990, 42 U.S.C. § 12101. (1990)

Auwärter, M. (1986). Development of communicative skills: The construction of fictional reality in children's play. In J. Cook-Gumperz, W. A. Corsaro, & J. Streeck (Eds.), *Children's worlds and children's language* (pp. 205–230). New York: Mouton deGruyter.

Axline, V. M. (1947). *Play therapy*. New York: Ballantine Books.

Bates, E., Bretherton, I., Snyder, L., Shore, C., & Volterra, V. (1980). Vocal and gestural symbols at 13 months. *Merrill-Palmer Quarterly, 26*(4), 407–423.

Bates, E., Thal, D., Whitesell, K., Fenson, L., & Oakes, L. (1989). Integrating language and gesture in infancy. *Developmental Psychology, 25*(6), 1004–1019.

Bateson, G. (1976). A theory of play and fantasy. In J. S. Bruner, A. Jolly, & K. Sylva (Eds.), *Play—Its role in development and evolution* (pp. 119–129). New York: Basic Books.

Bergen, D. (1987). Stages of play development. In D. Bergen (Ed.), *Play as a medium for learning and development* (pp. 49–66). Portsmouth, NH: Heinemann.

Biber, B. (1984). *Early education and psychological development*. New Haven: Yale University Press.

Biber, B., Shapiro, E., & Wickens, D. (1977). *Promoting cognitive growth* (2nd ed.). Washington, DC: National Association for the Education of Young Children.

Bloom, L. A., Johnson, C. E., Bitler, C. A., & Christman, K. L. (1986). *Facilitating communication change: An interpersonal approach to therapy and counseling*. Rockville, MD: Aspen.

Brazelton, T. B., & Als, H. (1979). Four early stages in the development of mother–infant interaction. *Psychoanalytic Study of the Child, 34*, 349–369.

Bredekamp, S. (Ed.). (1986). *Developmentally appropriate practice*. Washington, DC: National Association for the Education of Young Children.

Bretherton, I. (1985). Pretense: Practicing and playing with social understanding. In C. C. Brown & A. W. Gottfried (Eds.), *Play interactions: The role of toys and parental involvement in children's development* (pp. 69–79). Skillman, NJ: Johnson & Johnson.

Bretherton, I., O'Connell, B., Shore, C., & Bates, E. (1984). The effect of contextual variation on symbolic play development from 20 to 28 months. In I. Bretherton (Ed.), *Symbolic play* (pp. 271–298). Orlando, FL: Academic Press.

Bromwich, R. (1978). *Working with parents and infants*. Austin, TX: PRO-ED.

Bruner, J. S., Jolly, A., & Sylva, K. (Eds.). (1976). *Play: Its role in development and evolution*. New York: Basic Books.

Coe, D., Matson, J., Fee, V., Manikam, R., & Linarello, C. (1990). Training nonverbal and verbal play skills to mentally retarded and autistic children. *Journal of Autism and Developmental Disorders, 20*(2), 177–187.

Connolly, J. A., Doyle, A. B., & Reznick, E. (1988). Social pretend play and social interaction in preschoolers. *Journal of Applied Developmental Psychology, 9*, 301–313.

Cowie, H. (Ed.). (1984). The value of imaginative writing. In H. Cowie, (Ed.), *The development of children's imaginative writing*. New York: St. Martin's Press.

Dewey, J. (1916). *Democracy and education*. New York: MacMillan.

Eckler, J. A., & Weininger, O. (1989). Structural parallels between pretend play and narratives. *Developmental Psychology, 25*(5), 736–743.

Education for All Handicapped Children Act of 1975, 20 U.S.C. § 1401. (1975)

Education of the Handicapped Act Amendments of 1986, Part H—Handicapped Infants and Toddlers, § 101, 20 U.S.C. § 1400. (1986)

Education of the Handicapped Act Amendments of 1990, 20 U.S.C. § 1400. (1990)

Eiser, C. (1989). "Let's play doctors and nurses": A script analysis of children's play. *Early Child Development and Care, 49,* 17–25.

Erikson, E. H. (1940). Studies in the interpretation of play: I. Clinical observation of play disruption in young children. *Genetic Psychology Monographs, 22,* 557–671.

Fein, G. G. (1986). The affective psychology of play. In A. W. Gottfried & C. C. Brown (Eds.), *Play interactions* (pp. 31–39). Lexington, MA: Lexington Books.

Fein, G. G., & Apfel, N. (1979). Some preliminary observations on knowing and pretending. In N. R. Smith & M. B. Franklin (Eds.), *Symbolic functioning in childhood.* Hillsdale, NJ: Erlbaum.

Fenson, L. (1984). Developmental trends for action and speech in pretend play. In I. Bretherton (Ed.), *Symbolic Play: The development of social understanding.* New York: Academic Press.

Fenson, L., & Schell, R. E. (1986). The origins of exploratory play. In P. K. Smith (Ed.), *Children's play: Research and developments and practical applications: Vol 6. Special aspects of education* (pp. 17–38). New York: Gordon & Breach.

Fewell, R. R., & Kaminski, R. (1988). Play skills development and instruction for young children with handicaps. In S. L. Odom & M. B. Karnes (Eds.), *Early intervention for infants and children with handicaps* (pp. 145–158). Baltimore: Paul H. Brookes.

Fewell, R. R., & Vadasy, P. F. (1983). *Learning through play.* Allen, TX: Developmental Learning Materials.

Florey, L. (1971). An approach to play and play development. *American Journal of Occupational Therapy, 25*(6), 275–280.

Foley, G. M., & Appel, M. H. (1987). *The cognitive observation guide.* Tucson, AZ: Communication Skill Builders.

Fraiberg, S. H. (1965). *The magic years.* New York: Scribner.

Fraiberg, S. (Ed.). (1980). *Clinical studies in infant mental health.* New York: Basic Books.

Freud, A. (1964). *The psychoanalytical treatment of children.* New York: Schocken Books.

Freud, A. (1966a). The concept of developmental lines. In A. Freud, *Normality and pathology in childhood: Assessment of development* (pp. 11–30). New York: International Universities Press.

Freud, A. (1966b). *Psychoanalysis for teachers and parents.* New York: Emerson Books.

Freyberg, J. T. (1973). Increasing the imaginative play of urban disadvantaged kindergarten children through systematic training. In J. L. Singer (Ed.), *The child's world of make believe* (pp. 129–154). New York: Academic Press.

Froebel, F. (1897). *The education of man.* (W. N. Hailmann, Trans.). New York: Appleton.

Fromberg, D. P. (1992). A review of research on play. In C. Seefeldt (Ed.), *The early childhood curriculum: A review of current research* (2nd ed.). New York: Teachers College Press.

Gallahue, D. L. (1982). *Understanding motor development in children.* New York: Wiley.

Garvey, C. (1979). Communicational controls in social play. In B. Sutton-Smith (Ed.), *Play and learning* (pp. 109–125). New York: Gardner.

Garvey, C., & Kramer, T. L. (1989). The language of social pretend play. *Developmental Review, 9*(4), 364–382.

Gesell, A. (1940). *The first five years of life.* New York: Harper & Brothers.

Gesell, A., Ilg, F. L., Ames, L. B., & Rodell, J. L. (1974). *Infant and child in the culture of today* (revised ed.). New York: Harper & Row.

Gottfried, A. W., & Brown, C. C. (Eds.). (1985). *Play interactions.* Lexington, MA: Lexington Books.

Greenspan, S. I. (1990a). An intensive approach to a toddler with emotional, motor, and language delays: A case report. *Zero to Three, 9*(1), 20–22.

Greenspan, S. I. (1990b). Comprehensive clinical approaches to infants and their families: Psychodynamic and developmental perspectives. In C. J. Meisel & J. P. Shonkoff (Eds.), *Handbook of early childhood intervention.* New York: Cambridge University Press.

Greenspan, S. I. (1992). *Infancy and early childhood: The practice of clinical assessment and intervention with emotional and developmental challenges.* Madison, CT: International Universities Press.

Haring, T. G., (1985). Teaching between-class generalization of toy play behavior to handicapped children. *Journal of Applied Behavior Analysis, 18*(2), 127–139.

Hill, P. M., & McCune-Nicolich, L. (1981). Pretend play and patterns of cognition in Down's syndrome children. *Child Development, 52,* 611–617.

Hutt, C., & Bhavnani, R. (1976). Predictions from play. In J. S. Bruner, A. Jolly, & K. Sylva (Eds.), *Play—its role in development and evolution.* New York: Basic Books.

Ingram, D. (1977). Sensori-motor intelligence and language development. In A. L. Lock (Ed.), *Action, gesture and symbol: The emergence of language.* New York: Academic Press.

Inhelder, B., Lezine, I., Sinclair, H., & Stambak, M. (1972). Les debuts de la fonction symbolique. *Archives de Psychologie, 41,* 187–243.

Isaacs, S. (1930). *Intellectual growth in young children.* New York: Harcourt, Brace.

Isaacs, S. (1940). *Social development in young children.* London: Routledge.

Isaacs, S. (1960). *The nursery years.* London: Routledge.

Johnson, J. E. (1976). Relations of divergent thinking and intelligence test scores with social and nonsocial make-believe play of preschool children. *Child Development, 47,* 1200–1203.

Kaplan-Sanoff, M., Brewster, A., Stillwell, J., & Bergen, D. (1987). The relationship of play to physical/motor development and to children with special needs. In D. Bergen (Ed.), *Play as a medium for learning and development* (pp.137–162). Portsmouth, NH: Heinemann.

Kennedy, M. D., Sheridan, M. K., Radlinski, S. H., & Beeghly, M. (1991). Play-language relationships in young children with developmental delays: Implications for assessment. *Journal of Speech and Hearing Research, 34,* 112–122.

Klein, M. (1937). *The psycho-analysis of children (2nd ed.).* (A. Strachey, Trans.). London: Holgarth Press.

Knox, S. H. (1974). A play scale. In M. Reilly (Ed.), *Play as exploratory learning* (pp. 247–266). London: SAGE.

Kreye, M. (1984). Conceptual organization in the play of preschool children: Effects of meaning, context, and mother–child interaction. In I. Bretherton (Ed.), *Symbolic play* (pp. 299–336). Orlando, FL: Academic Press.

Ladd, G. W., & Price, J. M. (1987). Predicting children's social and school adjustment following the transition from preschool to kindergarten. *Child Development, 58,* 1168–1189.

Ladd, G. W., Price, J. M., & Hart, C. H. (1988). Predicting preschoolers' peer status from their playground behaviors. *Child Development, 59,* 986–992.

Langer, S. K. (1962). *Philosophy in a new key.* New York: Mentor Books.

Lefebvre, D., & Strain, P. S. (1989). Effects of a group contingency on the frequency of social interactions among autistic and nonhandicapped preschool children: Making LRE efficacious. *Journal of Early Intervention, 13*(4), 329–341.

Leslie, A. J. (1987). Pretense and representation: The origins of "theory of mind". *Psychological Review, 94*(4), 412–426.

Lieberman, J. N. (1977). *Playfulness: Its relationship to imagination and creativity.* New York: Academic Press.

Linder, T. W. (1990). *Transdisciplinary play-based assessment.* Baltimore, MD: Paul H. Brookes.

Lowe, M. (1975). Trends in the development of representational play in infants from one to three years—An observational study. *Journal of Child Psychology and Psychiatry, 16,* 33–47.

Lowe, M., & Costello, A. J. (1988). *Symbolic play test* (2nd ed.). Windsor, England: NFER-NELSON.

MacDonald, J. D., Gillette, Y., Bickley, M., & Rodriguez, C. (1984). *Conversation routines.* Columbus, OH: Ohio State University.

Mahler, M. S., Pine, F., & Bergman, A. (1975). *The psychological birth of the human infant.* New York: Basic Books.

Mahoney, G., & Powell, A. (1986). *Transactional intervention program.*

Farmington, CT: Pediatric Research and Training Center.

Mandler, J. M. (1983). Representation. In P. H. Mussen (Ed.), *Handbook of child psychology* (Vol. 3, pp. 420–494). New York: Wiley.

McCune, L. (1986a). Play–language relationships: Implications for a theory of symbolic development. In A. W. Gottfried & C. C. Brown (Eds.), *Play interactions* (pp. 67–79). Lexington, MA: Heath.

McCune, L. (1986b). Symbolic development in normal and atypical infants. In G. Fein & M. Rivkin (Eds.), *The young child at play: Reviews of research: Vol. 4* (pp. 45–61). Washington, DC: National Association for the Education of Young Children.

McCune-Nicolich, L. (1981). Toward symbolic functioning: Structure of early pretend games and potential parallels with language. *Child Development, 52,* 785–797.

McCune-Nicolich, L., & Fenson, L. (1984). Methodological issues in studying early pretend play. In T. D. Yawkey & A. D. Pellegrini (Eds.), *Child's play: Developmental and applied* (pp. 81–104). Hillsdale, NJ: Erlbaum.

Michelmann, S. S. (1974). Play and the deficit child. In M. Reilly (Ed.), *Play as exploratory learning* (pp.157–207). Beverly Hills, CA: SAGE.

Montessori, M. (1912). *The Montessori method* (2nd ed.). (A. E. George, Trans.). New York: Stokes.

Montessori, M. (1965). *Spontaneous activity in education.* (F. Simmons, Trans.). Cambridge, MA: Schocken Books.

Musselwhite, C. R. (1986). *Adaptive play for special needs children.* San Diego: College Hill Press.

Nelson, K., & Gruendel, J. (1986). Children's scripts. In K. Nelson, *Event knowledge: Structure and function in development.* Hillsdale, NJ: Erlbaum.

Newson, J., & Newson, E. (1979). *Toys and playthings.* New York: Pantheon Books.

Nicolich, L. M., & Raph, J. B. (1978). Imitative language and symbolic maturity in the single-word period. *Journal of Psycholinguistic Research, 7,* 401–417.

Omwake, E. B. (1963). The child's estate. In A. J. Solnit & S. A. Provence (Eds.), *Modern perspectives in child development.* New York: International Universities Press.

Omwake, E. B. (1974). *Connecticut College Program for Children with Special Needs: A modified nursery school model.* Unpublished manuscript, Connecticut College, New London, CT.

Parten, M. B. (1932). Social participation among pre-school children. *Journal of Abnormal and Social Psychology, 27,* 243–269.

Pellegrini, A. D. (1984). The social cognitive ecology of preschool classrooms: Contextual relations revisited. *International Journal of Behavioral Development, 7,* 321–332.

Pellegrini, A. D. (1988). Elementary-school children's rough-and-tumble play and social competence. *Developmental Psychology, 24*(6), 802–806.

Peller, L. E. (1954). Libidinal phases, ego development, and play. *The Psychoanalytic Study of the Child, 9,* 178–198.

Piaget, J. (1952). *The origins of intelligence in children.* (M. Cook, Trans.). New York: International Universities Press.

Piaget, J. (1962). *Play, dreams and imitation in childhood.* (C. Gattegno & M. F. Hodgson, Trans.). New York: Norton.

Prizant, B. (1990). Assessing the communication of infants and toddlers: Integrating a socioemotional perspective. *Zero to Three, 9*(1), 1–12.

Prizant, B. M., & Wetherby, A. M. (1990). Toward an integrated view of early language and communication development and socioemotional development. *Topics in Language Disorders, 10*(4), 1–16.

Provence, S. (1967). *Guide for the care of infants in groups.* New York: Child Welfare League of America.

Provence, S. (Ed.). (1983). *Infants and parents.* New York: International Universities Press.

Provence, S., Erikson, J., Vater, S., & Palmeri, S. (1994). *IDA: Connecticut Infant–Toddler Developmental Assessment.* Chicago: Riverside.

Read, H. E. (1960). *The forms of things unknown.* London: Faber & Faber.

Read, K., & Patterson, J. (1980). *The nursery school and kindergarten.* New York: Holt, Rinehart & Winston.

Riddick, B. (1982). *Toys and play for the handicapped child.* London: Croom Helm.

Roskos, K. (1990). A taxonomic view of pretend play activity among 4- and 5-year-old children. *Early Childhood Research Quarterly, 5*(4), 495–512.

Rubin, K. H. (1986). Play, peer interaction, and social development. In A. W. Gottfried & C. C. Brown (Eds.), *Play Interactions* (pp. 163–174). Lexington, MA: Lexington Books.

Rubin, K. H., Fein, G. G., & Vandenberg, B. (1983). Play. In P. H. Mussen (Ed.), *Handbook of Child Psychology: Vol. 4* (4th ed., pp. 693–774). New York: Wiley.

Schaefer, C. E. (1969). Imaginary companions and creative adolscents. *Developmental Psychology, 1,* 747–749.

Schwartz, S., & Miller, J. E. H. (1988). *The language of toys.* Kensington, MD: Woodbine House.

Schwartzman, H. B. (1978). *Transformations.* New York: Plenum.

Seidman, S., Nelson, K., & Gruendel, J. (1986). Make believe scripts: The transformation of ERs in fantasy. In K. Nelson, *Event knowledge: Structure and function in development.* Hillsdale, NJ: Erlbaum.

Shefatya, L. (1990). Socioeconomic status and ethnic differences in sociodramatic play: Theoretical and practical implications. In E. Klugman & S. Smilansky (Eds.), *Children's play and learning* (pp. 137–155). New York: Teachers College Press.

Sherburne, S., Utley, B., McConnell, S., & Gannon, J. (1988). Decreasing violent or aggressive theme play among preschool children with behavior disorders. *Exceptional Children, 55*(2), 166–172.

Shore, C., O'Connell, B., & Bates, E. (1984). First sentences in language and symbolic play. *Developmental Psychology, 20,* 872–880.

Sigel, I. (1965). Development considerations of the nursery school experience. In P. B. Neubauer (Ed.), *Concepts of development in early childhood education* (pp. 84–111). Springfield, IL: Thomas.

Singer, J. L. (Ed.). (1973). *The child's world of make-believe* (pp. 231–259). New York: Academic Press.

Smilansky, S. (1968). *The effects of sociodramatic play on disadvantaged preschool children.* New York: Wiley.

Smilansky, S., & Shefatya, L. (1990). *Facilitating play: A medium for promoting cognitive, socio-emotional and academic development in young children.* Gaithersburg, MD: Psychosocial & Educational Publications.

Smith, P. K. (1986). Play research and its applications: A current perspective. In P. K. Smith (Ed.), *Children's play: Research and developments and practical applications: Vol. 6. Special aspects of education* (pp. 1–15). New York: Gordon & Breach.

Solnit, A. J. (1987). A psychoanalytic view of play. *The Psychoanalytic Study of the Child, 42,* 205–219.

Stallibrass, A. (1989). *The self-respecting child.* Reading, MA: Addison-Wesley.

Takata, N. (1974). Play as prescription. In M. Reilly (Ed.), *Play as exploratory learning* (pp. 209–246). Beverly Hills, CA: SAGE.

Tamis-LeMonda, C. (1993, January). *Longitudinal perspectives on language development in infancy and childhood.* Paper presented at Bellevue Hospital, New York.

Uline, C. (1982). Teaching autistic children to play: A major teacher intervention. In P. Knoblock (Ed.), *Teaching and mainstreaming autistic children.* London: Love.

Vygotsky, L. S. (1976). Play and its role in the mental development of the child. In J. S. Bruner, A. Jolly, & K. Sylva (Eds.), *Play—Its role in development and evolution* (pp. 537–554). New York: Basic Books.

Watson, M. W., & Fischer, K. W. (1977). A developmental sequence of agent use in late infancy. *Child Development, 48,* 828–836.

Werner, H., & Kaplan, B. (1963). *Symbol formation.* New York: Wiley.

Westby, C. E. (1980). Assessment of cognitive and language abilities through play. *Language, Speech and Hearing Services in the School, 11,* 154–168.

Wilbarger, P. (1993, April). *Sensory intervention for infants and young children.* Paper presented at the meeting of the New York Chapter of Zero to Three Study Group on Sensory Functions in Infancy, New York.

Winnicott, D. W. (1966). The location of cultural experience. *International Journal of Psycho-Analysis, 48,* 368–372.

Wolfgang, C. H. (1977). *Helping aggressive and passive preschoolers through play.* Columbus, OH: Merrill.

Wood, M. M., Combs, C., Gunn, A., & Weller, D. (1986). *Developmental therapy in the classroom.* Austin, TX: PRO-ED.

CHAPTER 2

Understanding the Supportive Play Model

The SPM offers an operational process that takes as its first order the assumption that play is the child's genetically determined and inherent method of learning. However, when children's development is compromised by a disabling condition, so may be their play and learning. As a result of the impact of these limitations, we have found that the educator must assume a more active and instrumental role in intervention, moving beyond the function of guide or facilitator of play by directly compensating for the developmental components that may be lacking. The SPM provides the educator with a framework to rethink and redesign relevant aspects of the teaching role and early childhood setting to allow for more successful programming for the child with special needs. The model can be used in a self-contained special education setting or in a mainstreamed setting to help the intervention team and the parents make placement adjustments, monitor a child's progress, and evaluate the effectiveness of facilitative techniques.

The SPM is not a curriculum in the standard sense, but rather a systematic process that assists the adult in observing a child, assessing developmental play status, identifying limiting factors, and formulating play adaptations developmentally suited to the individual child. This is not a "cookbook" of specific activities, but a method to help professionals apply their own knowledge and create an individualized intervention rather than merely implement a curriculum. The process is not intended to be implemented in programmatic isolation, but in team collaboration involving observation, reflection, dialogue, and planning, with application of the facilitating techniques across the child's program. The chart that follows at the end of this chapter serves as a guide for the organization of observational impressions, data formulation, summation, and ongoing monitoring of progress. Although this chart examines an array of developmental areas, it does not a provide a comprehensive evaluation of function, but is intended to focus on the relationship among these developmental competencies as they contribute to the ability to play successfully. The outcome of this process is descriptive and qualitative, rather than quantitative, in its nature. The structure of the model supports an interactive process between parents and staff members that allows a thoughtful review of a child's strengths and concerns and an analysis of the child's behavior in a particular setting.

OVERVIEW OF THE SUPPORTIVE PLAY MODEL CHART

Located at the end of this chapter is the chart that serves as a guide for the SPM process. In this section, we acquaint you with the structure of the chart before describing its step-by-step use in the next section of the chapter. For ease of reference as you read the descriptions in the text, you may want to keep a marker at the beginning of the chart.

The first page of the chart, *Section I: Cover Sheet*, provides space to identify and describe the program and the child, including the purpose for initiating the SPM.

The rest of the chart is divided into three main parts: Child, Family, and Program. Looking through the Child part, you will notice six developmental areas:

Self/Social/Emotional
Motor/Self-Help
Communicative/Language
Cognitive
Play Skills
Play Themes

For each of these six areas, *Section II: Observational Impressions* provides compilations of established age-referenced information (Ainsworth, 1979; Ainsworth & Bell, 1970; Beaty, 1990; Curry & Johnson, 1990; Erikson, 1940, 1963; Fowler, 1980; Furuno et al, 1984; Gould, 1972; Healy, McAreavey, Saaz von Hippel, & Jones, 1978; Henry, 1965; Knox, 1974; Lally, Provence, Szanton, & Weissbourd, 1986; McCormick & Schiefelbusch, 1990; Michelmann, 1974; Musselwhite, 1986; Newson & Newson, 1979; Patterson, 1977; Peller, 1954; Schwartz & Miller, 1988; Smith, 1986; Takata, 1974; Westby, 1980). Section II is subdivided into three levels corresponding to the following age ranges: Level 1, birth to 18 months; Level 2, 19 to 36 months; and Level 3, 37 to 60 months. These developmental guides are intended to assist in reviewing a child's developmental status and do not constitute either a standardized assessment or a standardized sequential developmental progression.

Turning to the Family and Program parts of the chart, you will see that Section II is termed *Observational Guide* because it highlights items to focus on in data collections (Beaty, 1990; Cohen, Stern, & Balaban, 1983; Foley, 1982; Harmes & Clifford, 1980; Irwin & Bushnell, 1980; Patterson, 1977; Trad, 1990). The Program part is further subdivided into:

Staff
Peers
Space
Time
Materials and Equipment

Progressing through the chart, you will find that Section III provides space for you to record observations of the target child within the group setting and facts germane to family and program that should be considered in light of the child's immediate developmental needs. In the Child part, Section III is headed *Skills and Outstanding Characteristics Observed*, and in the Family and the Program parts it is *General Description*.

In all three parts of the chart (Child, Family, and Program), Section IV is termed *Characteristic Patterns Limiting Play*. This is a list of factors that may arise from problems or delays in any of the six developmental areas or from issues related to family or program. The characteristic patterns listed are not all-inclusive, but catalog significant recurrent problems found across a large number of children with special needs in typical settings, in families who have a child with special needs, and in programs that are working with a child who has special needs.

Section V is the *Discrepancy Analysis* located at the back of the chart. It provides a format to compare and contrast a child's developmental progress intrapersonally (personal strengths and weaknesses across the six developmental areas, skill scatter, and skill inconsistency) and interpersonally (in comparison to broadly age-referenced standards). It also offers space for the adult to summarize significant discrepancy issues that may be inhibiting play as they relate to child, family, and program.

Returning to the main body of the chart, you will find that *Section VI: Intervention Goals/Facilitating Techniques* lists suggestions compiled from early childhood and early intervention literature for each of the six specified developmental areas of the Child part as well as for Family and Program parts (Curry & Johnson, 1990; Forman & Kuschner, 1983; Fowler, 1980; Freyberg, 1973; Greenspan, 1992; Knox, 1974; Lally, Provence, Szanton, & Weissbourd, 1986; Lanser & McDonnell, 1991; Lawrence & Brown, 1987; MacDonald, Gillette, Bickley, & Rodriguez, 1984; Musselwhite, 1986; Provence, Naylor, & Patterson, 1977; Rogers & Sawyers, 1988; Smilansky, 1968; Smilansky & Shefatya, 1990; Wolfgang, 1977). The techniques are not all-inclusive, but strive to offer a wide range of ideas to help a teacher work toward the specified goals stated under every area of facilitating techniques.

The last column of the chart includes two sections: *Section VII: Individualized Supportive Play Adaptations and Experiences* is used to record the adaptations that are planned by staff and parents to assist the child's adjustment and progress and *Section VIII: Results and Outcomes* is used to record results and outcomes once changes have been implemented in the setting.

USING THE SUPPORTIVE PLAY MODEL

Having reviewed the structure of the SPM chart, let us now explain how to proceed through each step of the process, using the chart at the end of this chapter. Figure 2.1 provides a summary of the process.

For this process to be effective it is essential to carry out several aspects of preparation. No matter who initiates this process, communication and coordination are two areas that require time, but, when attended to, greatly increase the success of intervention plans.

Concerns expressed by either parents or staff about a child's functioning and experience in a group may be the initiating reason to use the SPM. The individual who is going to be responsible for conducting the observation and directing the process should review any personal feelings about the child before beginning the observation. This individual must be aware of what emotions a particular child arouses and how personal reactions can color objectivity and inferences. What expectations are developmentally appropriate behavior for this child's age? What knowledge does this individual have about the child's disabili-

ty and how this disability places limitations on the child's development? Discussion of these issues among team members can be very helpful in lowering anxiety level and in increasing personal understanding. Once aware of their personal reactions, it may be easier to support fellow team members, determine appropriate roles, and seek outside consultation and support.

When the program staff are initiating the process, it is essential to discuss the staff concerns with the parents, obtain permission from parents to undertake the process, and include parents in all steps of the SPM. Parents and staff need to have the opportunity to discuss their concerns and to see if they perceive the child's issues and needs similarly. This discussion helps staff understand the parental perception of the child's progress in the setting and to incorporate any concerns and goals that they consider important. Since this discussion is not the same as a clinical intake interview, in-depth background information does not need to be discussed, but it is very informative to review a family's perspective on their child. Some areas you can explore are suggested by the following questions: What is daily life like at home with the child? What are the child's habits of sleeping, eating, toileting, and recreation? What are the child's favorite toys and activities? Who is involved in daily care, and what is a daily schedule like? How do the parents envision their child in 6 months or a year from now? What do they expect to happen next in their child's development? Do they have a single most pressing concern about their child? Have any major things happened in their life or in the child's life since joining in this preschool setting? In some cases, it may also be appropriate and helpful to arrange for a home visit.

If the child has come into this setting through a public school placement, it may be necessary to have a case planning meeting before starting the process. If the child has an identified special need, it is also crucial to include the special education personnel who are involved in case management. In some situations, the SPM may be used by the special education case management staff, the family, and the preschool staff in designing the appropriate adaptations needed in a preschool setting even before a placement is made.

Section I: Cover Sheet

Having gained parental permission to carry out the process, you, as the staff member in charge of coordinating the SPM, begin by completing *Section I: Cover Sheet*. Summarize key aspects of the early childhood program, such as location, philosophy, curriculum focus, and schedule. Next, review the child's history and any existing classroom observation records, then summarize any patterns that are relevant and indicate the reasons for initiating the model, including parental and staff concerns regarding the child's success in the placement.

Child: Sections II, III, and IV

Next, conduct several observations with attention to collecting a representative sample of the child's behavior in a variety of activities, in and out of play. Throughout the observation process and in the summary of these findings, use *Section II: Observational Impressions, Section III: Skills and Outstanding Characteristics Observed*, and *Section IV: Characteristic Patterns Limiting Play*. While completing *Section II: Observational Impressions*, work through levels 1, 2, and 3 for each of the six developmental areas. Underline the skill or behavior item being observed and then code it, using the code key at the top of the chart. If the under-

Figure 2.1

SUPPORTIVE PLAY MODEL PROCESS

PREPARE

- Obtain permission from parents to undertake process
- Inquire
- Discuss review

OBSERVE

- Review history and records; conduct several observations to collect representative sample of behavior

FORMULATE

I.   **Cover Sheet:** Complete form

CHILD

II. **Observation Impressions:** Underline[a] and code observed skills and behavior; star (*) and underline working themes
III. **Skills and Outstanding Characteristics Observed:** Summarize key skills and outstanding characteristics
IV. **Characteristic Patterns Limiting Play:** Underline[a] and/or note significant characteristics

FAMILY

II. **Observational Guide:** Review
III. **General Description:** Summarize key family information
IV. **Characteristic Patterns Limiting Play:** Underline[a] and/or note significant characteristics

PROGRAM (staff, peers, space, time, and materials and equipment)

II. **Observational Guide:** Review items for program
III. **General Description:** Summarize key program information
IV. **Characteristic Patterns Limiting Play:** Underline and/or note significant characteristics

V.   **Discrepancy Analysis:** (at back of charts)
     Complete discrepancy analysis for Child, Family, and Program
VI. **Intervention Goal/Facilitating Techniques:** Review goal, underline[a] and/or note techniques for Child, Family, and Program
VII. **Individualized Supportive Play Adaptations and Experiences:** Design and summarize, with parental input, for Child, Family, and Program

IMPLEMENTATION

- Initiate appropriate adaptations and experiences

FOLLOW-UP

VIII. **Results and Outcome**
      Record progress

---

[a]Items that you would underline are shown in *italics* for ease of readability.

---

lined behavior or skill is fully acquired or mastered (generally performed spontaneously and with good quality), mark an A in the column to the left of the item. Mark a P, for practicing, if the behavior or skill is reoccuring, but has not yet been fully mastered or acquired. Mark an E, for emerging, if the child attempts the skill or behavior and it is not well established at this time. Mark an N if the behavior is not observed or is not part of the child's behavioral repertoire.

Now you should selectively underline and star, using an asterisk (*), the working theme in each of the six developmen-

tal areas that appears to be the focal point in the child's development at this time. The themes offer a summary of the major developmental goals and processes that are intrinsic to the area of development being observed and that typically lie within the time line of the particular level. The starred working theme is the area in which the child appears to be spending most of his or her developmental energy at this time or where lags in development are preventing the child from moving freely ahead to the next level. There is usually a sense that the working theme contains unresolved developmental issues, and that the child is displaying significant tension with several of the specified behaviors or skills outlined. There is no absolute rule in determining the working theme, but usually it will be the lowest level in which there are a number of items coded E, P, and N. It is possible, and actually somewhat common, for children with special needs to have significant scatter in their skill acquisition. This means that the observer may be able to code several items in a level as achieved or mastered (A), but still return to a lower level when designating the working theme. For instance, as we will demonstrate in Chapter 4, a motorically competent 5-year-old boy who is hearing impaired has several skills in place at Level 3, but because he has little sense of personal safety and impulse control, he is designated as having a working theme at Level 2. This toddler-like impulse control dramatically affects how this 5-year-old functions and needs to be supervised in a nursery school group. At first glance this child's Level 3, age-appropriate skills may lead the adults working with him to plan motor activities that are far beyond what this child can safely handle. Once the SPM highlights the significant deficit at Level 2, relative to judgment of personal safety and impulse control, it is easier for the staff to be confident in designing appropriate activities. Establishing the working theme requires some clinical judgment and this decision may be greatly facilitated by discussion with teammates (Provence, personal communication, October 5, 1989). By working through the SPM, staff and parents obtain the observational data and the mechanism to highlight these interrelated aspects of development and to make more appropriate developmental decisions.

Once the working theme has been established in each area, write in *Section III: Skills and Outstanding Characteristics Observed* any particular strengths and characteristics that are helpful in gaining a full picture of the child's development. You may want to comment on specific qualities about the child that are not mentioned in *Section II: Observational Impressions*, such as personality characteristics, unique behavior patterns, and specific physical qualities. Then, for each developmental area that you completed in Sections II and III, you are now prepared to underline and note related and relevant items in *Section IV: Characteristic Patterns Limiting Play*.

Family and Program: Sections II, III, and IV

These two parts of the SPM charts focus on the family and the program. The Program part is subdivided into Staff, Peers, Space, Time, and Materials and Equipment. The procedure used in the Family and Program parts differs from that followed in the Child part. Rather than underlining items in *Section II: Observational Guide*, use this column to guide your observations and to assist with data collection. Note and summarize your observations in *Section III: General Description*. Next, underline and note any additional information related to family and program in *Section IV: Characteristic Patterns Limiting Play*.

Section V: Discrepancy Analysis

At this point you should have an enriched sense of some of the issues that are interfering with the identified child's adjustment or progress in the particular setting. With this data in mind, turn to the last page of the SPM chart and undertake *Section V: Discrepancy Analysis* of the six areas of development. In the boxes provided, note the level in which the child's chronological age falls (the same age level is recorded in all six developmental areas). Next, write the level numbers of the working themes of each developmental areas in their boxes

and, finally, note on the line to the right of the boxes whether the child is within age level, above age level, or below age level in each of the six developmental areas. Star any working theme where the child displayed scatter with numerous skills above the working theme level and outstanding gaps in development. Working themes are often interrelated across developmental areas, but many children show a range in the level of the themes that they are currently working on. It is this range in skill mastery and theme focus, which causes some of the tension often observed in the child with special needs, that will be highlighted by *Section V: Discrepancy Analysis*. This page also provides space for a brief narrative statement highlighting significant discrepancy issues within the Child, Family, and Program. Completing the *Discrepancy Analysis* is often very helpful in beginning to understand some of the unique qualities and patterns in the child's development.

- Consider the discrepancy between chronological age of the child and the level of each working theme. Is the child delayed across all areas to a similar magnitude? What are the child's most developed and most underdeveloped areas?
- Consider the relative discrepancies among the working theme levels. Are this child's play skills or play themes out of synchrony with other aspects of development? If there is an uneven pattern of development, how does this affect the child's functioning with peers? Does an outstanding skill area camouflage areas of delay? Does the child have a pattern of scattered skills and developmental gaps that deceives adults into believing the child is more developmentally advanced than is, in fact, true?
- Consider what intrinsic factors (discrepancy in skills, handicapping condition) and extrinsic factors (adults, peers, environment, or family variables) may be inhibiting this child.
- Comment on qualitative aspects of the child's behavior. Is the child easily distracted? Is the child enthusiastic? Does the child have high or low energy?
- Make brief comments relative to family and program where there is a discrepancy. Is the parent's attachment to the child of concern? Is the family's daily schedule compatible with the developmental needs of the child? Is the ratio of adult to child adequate? Is the group an appropriate size to enable a target child's needs to be met?

Section VI: Intervention Goals/Facilitation Techniques

Turn to Section VI in the main body of the chart and review the goal for each of the areas. Then underline or note specific facilitating techniques that may remediate, modify, or compensate for developmental issues that have been identified thus far in the SPM. Keep in mind working themes and limiting patterns that were specified in *Section IV: Characteristic Patterns Limiting Play* and the issues highlighted in *Section V: Discrepancy Analysis*.

Section VII: Individualized Supportive Play Adaptations and Experiences

Use the insights and ideas gained in Section VI, along with other information gained thus far in the SPM, to design a customized strategy for intervention. Record this information in the space provided in *Section VII: Individualized Supportive Play Adaptations and Experiences*. Once a plan has been agreed on, initiate appropriate adaptations and experiences in a timely fashion.

Section VIII: Results and Outcomes

At the conclusion of the initial use of the SPM process the team should decide when a review of the plan that is being implemented should occur. This could be in 1 month, but usually this review should occur from 3 to 6 months after the initial summary meeting.

At the follow-up meeting the team should record progress relative to each supportive play adaptation and experience in *Section VIII: Results and Outcome*. When new team members join the process, reincorporate the preparation step in the follow-up process. Some interventions may have a dramatic and quick effect, while others may take much longer to show a positive result. Some of the techniques attempted may prove to be ineffective. The team, including the parents, must monitor and communicate regularly to assess how the child and the group are reacting to the designed changes. It is important to conduct reviews of the total process on an ongoing basis, being sure to include the parents, and then make appropriate readjustments as necessary.

SUMMARY

This review of the mechanics of the SPM chart, both form and process, provides the interventionist and the parent a structure to organize observational material within a developmental system. Facts then can be gathered and analyzed in a systematic way that leads to the planning of intervention that is developmentally appropriate. Before showing in Part II how the SPM is used with selected examples of children with special needs, Chapter 3 addresses two topic areas that are central to the successful implementation of the SPM, the impact of the child with special needs on the family and the planning and placement of the child in an educational setting.

REFERENCES

Ainsworth, M. D. S. (1979). Infant–mother attachment. *American Psychologist, 34*(10), 932–937.

Ainsworth, M. D. S., & Bell, S. M. (1970). Attachment, exploration, and separation: Illustrated by the behavior of one-year-olds in a strange situation. *Child Development, 41,* 49–67.

Beaty, J. J. (1990). *Observing development of the young child* (2nd ed.). Columbus, OH: Merrill.

Cohen, D. J., Stern, V., & Balaban, N. (1983). *Observing and recording the behavior of young children* (3rd ed.). New York: Teachers College Press.

Curry, N. E., & Johnson, C. N. (1990). *Beyond self-esteem: Developing a genuine sense of human value.* Research monograph of the National Association for the Education of Young Children, Volume 4. Washington, DC: National Association for the Education of Young Children.

Erikson, E. H. (1940). Studies in the interpretation of play: I. Clinical observation of play disruption in young children. *Genetic Psychology Monographs, 22,* 557–671.

Erikson, E. H. (1963). *Childhood and society* (2nd ed.). New York: Norton.

Foley, G. (1982). The principles of observation. In M. Frank (Ed.), *The puzzling child: From recognition to treatment* (pp. 13–17). New York: Haworth Press.

Forman, G. E., & Kuschner, D. S. (1983). *The child's construction of knowledge: Piaget for teaching children.* Washington, DC: National Association for the Education of Young Children.

Fowler, W. (1980). *Infant and child care: A guide to education in group settings.* Boston: Allyn & Bacon.

Freyberg, J. T. (1973). Increasing the imaginative play of urban disadvantaged kindergarten children through systematic training. In J. L. Singer (Ed.), *The child's world of make believe* (pp. 129–154). New York: Academic Press.

Furuno, S., Inatsuka, T., O'Reilly, K., Hosaka, C., Zeisloft, B., & Allman, T. (1984). *Help Checklist (Hawaii Early Learning Profile).* Palo Alto, CA: VORT Corporation.

Gould, R. (1972). *Child studies through fantasy.* New York: Quadrangle Books.

Greenspan, S. I. (1992). *Infancy and early childhood: The practice of clinical assessment and intervention with emotional and developmental challenges.* Madison, CT: International Universities Press.

Harmes, T., & Clifford, R. M. (1980). *Early childhood environment rating scale.* New York: Teachers College Press.

Healy, A., McAreavey, P., Saaz von Hippel, C., & Jones, S. H. (1978). *Mainstreaming preschoolers* (pp. 126–131). Washington, DC: US Government Printing Office.

Henry, J. (1965). Death fear and climax in nursery school play. In P. B. Neubauer (Ed.), *Concepts of development in early childhood education* (pp. 112–143). Springfield, IL: Thomas.

Irwin, D. M., & Bushnell, M. M. (1980). *Observational strategies for child study.* New York: Holt, Rinehart & Winston.

Knox, S. H. (1974). A play scale. In M. Reilly (Ed.), *Play as exploratory learning* (pp. 247–266). London: SAGE.

Lally, J. R., Provence, S., Szanton, E., & Weissbourd, B. (1986). Developmentally appropriate care for children from birth to age 3. In S. Bredekamp (Ed.), *Developmentally appropriate practice.* Washington, DC: National Association for the Education of Young Children.

Lanser, S. & McDonnell, L. (1991). Creating quality curriculum yet not buying out the store. *Young Children, 47*(1), 4–9.

Lawrence, T. M., & Brown, M. L. (1987). *Guided play.* Unpublished workshop materials.

MacDonald, J. D., Gillette, Y., Bickley, M, & Rodriguez, C. (1984). *Conversation routines.* Columbus, OH: Ohio State University.

McCormick, L., & Schiefelbusch, R. L. (1990). *Early language intervention* (2nd. ed.). New York: Merrill.

Michelmann, S. S. (1974). Play and the deficit child. In M. Reilly (Ed.), *Play as exploratory learning* (pp.157–207). Beverly Hills, CA: SAGE.

Musselwhite, C. R. (1986). *Adaptive play for special needs children.* San Diego: College-Hill Press.

Newson, J., & Newson, E. (1979). *Toys and playthings.* New York: Pantheon Books.

Patterson, J. (1977). The criterion model for preschool curriculum. In S. Provence, A. Naylor, & J. Patterson, *The challenge of daycare* (pp. 251–270). New Haven: Yale University Press.

Peller, L. E. (1954). Libidinal phases, ego development, and play. *The Psychoanalytic Study of the Child, 9,* 178–198.

Provence, S., Naylor, A., & Patterson, J. (1977). *The challenge of daycare.* New Haven: Yale University Press.

Rogers, C. S., & Sawyers, J. K. (1988). *Play in the lives of children.* Washington, DC: National Association for the Education of Young Children.

Schwartz, S., & Miller, J. E. H. (1988). *The language of toys.* Kensington, MD: Woodbine House.

Smilansky, S. (1968). *The effects of sociodramatic play on disadvantaged preschool children.* New York: Wiley.

Smilansky, S., & Shefatya, L. (1990). *Facilitating play: A medium for promoting cognitive, socio-emotional and academic development in young children.* Gaithersburg, MD: Psychosocial & Educational Publications.

Smith, P. K. (1986). Play research and its applications: A current perspective. In P. K. Smith (Ed.), *Children's play: Research and developments and practical applications: Vol. 6. Special aspects of education* (pp. 1–15). New York: Gordon & Breach.

Takata, N. (1974). Play as prescription. In M. Reilly (Ed.), *Play as exploratory learning* (pp. 209–246). Beverly Hills, CA: SAGE.

Trad, P. V. (1990). *Infant previewing.* New York: Springer-Verlag.

Westby, C. E. (1980). Assessment of cognitive and language abilities through play. *Language, Speech and Hearing Services in the School, 11,* 154–168.

Wolfgang, C. H. (1977). *Helping aggressive and passive preschoolers through play.* Columbus, OH: Merrill.

Supportive Play Model

Section I. Cover Sheet

Name: _____   **Observers:** _____

Age: _____

Date of birth: _____   **Date:** _____

BRIEFLY DESCRIBE:

Program (location, philosophy, curriculum focus, schedule):

Child (reason for conducting observation; any outstanding developmental issues; parental concerns and staff concerns)

Date of next review _____

II: Observational Impressions

A = attained or mastered   E = emerging   * = working theme
P = practicing   N = not observed

LEVEL 1 (BIRTH–18 MONTHS)

WORKING THEME   Develops attachment to and trust of caregiver(s), with feelings of affection and pleasure predominating over aggression and pain, leading to the emergence of awareness of self (separation and individuation), leading to autonomy

WHAT YOU OBSERVE
Signals needs, pleasure, and discomfort
Explores in an oral and sensorimotor manner
Shows progressive awareness of and interest in others
Increases gradually in self-regulation: waits, anticipates, soothes self for short time
Reciprocates affect and activity with caregivers
Displays caution with strangers (neither paralyzed by fear nor indiscriminately friendly)
Practices separating from caregiver (leave taking and reunion)
Seeks comfort from caregiver when hurt or distressed
Uses comfort objects during transitions
Increases in range of emotions (joy, anger, pleasure in mastery, humor)
Increases in aggression and assertiveness

LEVEL 2 (19–36 MONTHS)

WORKING THEME   Establishes the beginnings of constancy (sustained emotional investment in and feelings about self, others, things, and concepts)

WHAT YOU OBSERVE
Experiments with negotiation in interpersonal relationships
Experiences marked variations of mood; behavioral change may be abrupt with pinching, hitting, tantrums, etc.
Attunes progressively to feelings and goals of others
Increases in shared experiences (interaction and imitation of others, goal-directed partnership)
Grows in self-identity, resulting in formation of constancy (identifies self in picture, tolerates separation from parent)
Shows robust and differentiated expression of emotion (glee, aggression, fear, anger, humor)
Increases in impulse control and self-regulation with intermittent regression and expression of resentment

LEVEL 3 (37–60 MONTHS)

WORKING THEME   Develops initiative, gender identity, fusion of learning and feeling, and definition of role within family and with peers

WHAT YOU OBSERVE
Increases in curiosity about sex differences, roles, and relationships
Experiments with adult roles and relationships (Oedipal themes), which affirm sexual identification and gender role, leading to internalized sense of right and wrong
Plans ahead and briefly delays gratification
Experiences mood stabilization with growth in awareness of own internal states; communicates feelings; experiments with transition from actions to words to express strong feelings such as anger and envy
Grows in understanding of differences between dreams, fantasies, and reality
Grows in formulation of self-image and self-esteem
Develops capacity for empathy, rule attunement, and social sensitivity
Develops peer relationships
Launches and sustains interest in play projects with enthusiasm and zest

III: Skills and Outstanding Characteristics Observed

IV: Characteristic Patterns Limiting Play

Excessive need to control or extreme passivity and apathy
Prolonged regressive behavior or delayed behavior
Unusual demand for caregiver's time; adult preferred over peers
Poor self-regulation, resulting in extremes in emotional responses (inappropriate intensity and range of affect; inability to settle)
Identity and self-esteem conflicts resulting from past failures and frustrations
Poor reading of social cues, situations, expectations of others
Poor relatedness and engagement, poor eye contact, inadequate shared attention and turn-taking
Excessive and indiscriminate familiarity with strangers or inability to tolerate separation
Inflexible, unable to anticipate or handle transitions, overanxious, fearful, difficult to comfort

Other:

V: Discrepancy Analysis (GO TO LAST PAGE OF CHARTS)

VI: Intervention Goal/Facilitating Techniques

GOAL Provide evolving adult relationship to promote psychosocial development: attachment, separation, and individuation; affect range and self-regulation; initiative and social affiliation (beginnings of group membership)

WHAT YOU CAN DO

Make adult available for emotional refueling, reinvolvement, and as an outside regulator

Increase adult availability in the group

Establish primary adult caregiver in group for consistency

Determine and accept current level of behavior (strengths and weaknesses); move incrementally toward realistic goals

Reinforce successful approximations of appropriate behavior

Focus curriculum on social–emotional development, not exclusively on intellectual achievement

Recognize and verbalize needs and emotions (when child can not)

Wean gradually from primary adult to interact with several adults; gradually introduce appropriate peers

Stay calm; be shockproof; do not reinforce extremes

Experiment with strategies to engage, activate, and calm the child

Help child gain pleasure in process rather than focusing exclusively on product/performance

Overstate social signals (facial expression, gesture, voice tone)

Engage child by establishing eye-contact and physical proximity before sending cues

Model socially appropriate behavior

Avoid battle of wills, but clearly communicate to child that the adult will provide protection and that the child will not be able to decide or choose some things

Advise child of impending transitions, new experiences, changes in routines

Avoid undue haste

Sustain basic routine to bolster child's security, make all changes gradually, but adapt routine to match child's needs

Provide appropriate opportunities within child's daily life to make choices and exercise control (Use "You may do blocks or puzzles now," rather than "Do you want to play with blocks?")

Allow alternative modes of expression for child's fears and anxieties (through play, art, motor activities)

Accept periods of regression as typical and appropriate in development

Other:

VII: Individualized Supportive Play Adaptations and Experiences

VIII: Results and Outcomes

II: Observational Impressions

A = attained or mastered E = emerging * = working theme
P = practicing N = not observed

LEVEL 1 (BIRTH–18 MONTHS)

WORKING THEME Practices stability, disassociation, equilibrium, and rotation in preparation for postural security, locomotion, and prehension; establishes rhythmic patterns in eating, sleeping, elimination, and activity level

WHAT YOU OBSERVE

Lifts head in pull to sit; rolls segmentally; sits unsupported; sits well in chair; creeps

Pulls to stand, stands unsupported, cruises, walks with hand held, walks

Climbs onto and off of furniture

Creeps up/down stairs; walks up/down stairs, two feet each step, hand held

Squats and recovers to retrieve object; runs stiffly with some falling

Puts hands, feet, objects to mouth; eyes follow objects; develops eye–hand coordination—reaches, grasps, stores, transfers

Picks up small objects with raking and then pincer grasp, puts objects in container, pokes and examines objects with index finger

Uses marker on paper

Turns page of book; towers two blocks; shows initial hand preference

Begins to finger feed, use cup and spoon independently

Removes shoes, socks; indicates wet pants

Begins to comply to adult restrictions regarding safety issues

LEVEL 2 (19–36 MONTHS)

WORKING THEME Refines patterns of locomotion and prehension; gains independence in self-help; shows growing capacity to wait and briefly inhibit action

WHAT YOU OBSERVE

Stands and walks three steps on tiptoes; walks backward; stands on one foot

Walks up/down stairs holding rail; walks up, alternating feet, when hand held; jumps off one step; kicks and throws large ball

Stands up and pushes riding toys; uses push-and-pull toys

Assists in dressing, can undress

Eats independently with spoon and fork; indicates toilet needs

Scribbles with marker or crayon with fisted hand or fingers; towers six cubes; strings beads; turns knobs; unscrews and screws lids; uses scissors to snip (immature grasp); imitates horizontal crayon stroke; draws a circle; completes simple inset puzzle

Increasingly able to self-regulate motor activity level

Shows inconsistent judgment concerning personal safety; initially resistive and progressively more compliant to adult guidelines

LEVEL 3 (37–60 MONTHS)

WORKING THEME Masters motor planning of complex gross and fine movements and self-help skills; progressively self-monitors appropriate motor activity level

WHAT YOU OBSERVE

Matches objects using tactile (texture) cues; rolls clay into ball; draws a primitive person, progresses to body and limb features on person

Builds tower of nine blocks; cuts paper on straight and curved lines

Balances on one foot; catches ball; rides tricycle; swings

Walks downstairs, alternating feet; hops on one foot; somersaults

Skips to music; throws/catches ball, first using arms and body, then just hands

Buttons and unbuttons; dresses and undresses; brushes teeth, hair; bathes with supervision; toilets independently

Pours from pitcher; spreads with knife and then cuts with knife

Internalizes awareness of safety for self and others

Can wait, redirect, slow down, and exercise some judgment before action

III: Skills and Outstanding Characteristics Observed

IV: Characteristic Patterns Limiting Play

Delayed motor milestones, locomotion; avoidance of movement

Orthopedic or neurological impairments, hypertonicity (high motor tone) or hypotonicity (low motor tone), which compromises stability, balance, control, posture, and movement

Hyposensitivity or hypersensitivity to touch, texture, light, sound; sensory integration problems

Postural insecurity: timid to move, fearful of sudden movements, varying environmental heights, and exaggerated protective reactions

Poor motor planning of complex movements, leading to clumsiness

Visual–motor delays affecting eye–hand coordination, immature patterns of grasp

Perceptual problems related to visual field reduction; deficits in figure–ground discrimination, directionality, spatial relationships; or reduced visual acuity

Poor oral motor skills, including problems with chewing, mouth closure, drooling and swallowing, oral hyposensitivity or hypersensitivity to sensation

Self-pacing problems: not an active explorer or overactive and unaware of safety issues

Lack of striving for independent mobility, self-feeding, self-dressing, toileting

Other:

V: Discrepancy Analysis (GO TO LAST PAGE OF CHARTS)

VI: Intervention Goal/Facilitating Techniques

GOAL Provide child with sensory and movement opportunities to gain maximum competence with components of movement (stability, disassociation, equilibrium, rotation, locomotion) in order to gain competence with his or her body (fine and gross motor skills and self-help skills, body image and self regulation)

WHAT YOU CAN DO (The following are suggestions that are more generic in nature; consult with occupational therapist and physical therapist to plan specific adaptations for motor problems)

Attend to postural needs: use appropriate furniture for stability and body alignment (table and chair size, etc.); make sure child's feet are on a supporting surface when seated

Provide stability at center of body and proximal joints for low tone child

Provide opportunities to play in a flexed position (side sitting, cross-legged sitting) for high tone child

Apply occupational therapist and speech and language pathologist prescription for classroom adaptations necessary for oral–motor needs

Use consultation to provide opportunities that match child's visual needs and skills (choice of materials, adaptive equipment, material placement, lighting, predicable physical environment, adult verbal cueing to support visual perception)

Provide activities that promote visually directed movement: reaching, grasping, threading, pegboard, puzzle; use mirror to provide added feedback

Provide high-contrast materials to aid in figure–ground discrimination

Provide daily structured opportunities for large motor activities; verbally interpret and physically model motor activities to increase successful experiences; help peers to understand and tolerate child's compromising motoric conditions

Provide structured opportunities for child to experiment with and practice mastery of self-care skills, expression of personal needs when tired, sick, hungry

Reinforce child's care of personal and group belongings

Instruct child concerning personal safety

For the overactive child, structure activity, refocus on task, limit complexity and number of materials and stimuli, complement child's style, encourage group involvement without requiring total conformity; provide well supervised, calming sensory and tactile experiences (kneading clay, pouring water, bean and rice bins, bubble balls)

For the underactive child, encourage movement and engagement in activities, provide sensory and tactile experiences, encourage group involvement without requiring total conformity

Accept and mirror child's spontaneous movement; gradually shape approximations to next developmental level for underactive child

Other:

VII: Individualized Supportive Play Adaptations and Experiences

VIII: Results and Outcomes

II: Observational Impressions

A = attained or mastered   E = emerging   * = working theme
P = practicing   N = not observed

LEVEL 1 (BIRTH–18 MONTHS)

WORKING THEME   Explores sounds leading to awareness of social and prelinguistic communication and early word use

WHAT YOU OBSERVE
Turns to source of sound
Progresses from vocal play to babbling, jargoning, and first words
Smiles socially with mutual gaze, leading to joint attention and action rituals focused on environmental objects and activities
Looks for family members or pets when named
Follows simple commands
Imitates sounds, gestures, and words
Points to regulate adult activity
Uses intentional communication; reciprocal exchanges
Uses words to attract attention, comment, request, protest, greet, socialize

LEVEL 2 (19–36 MONTHS)

WORKING THEME   Uses sociocommunicative skills egocentrically in conjunction with rapidly developing linguistic skills, including vocabulary, grammar, and pragmatic skills

WHAT YOU OBSERVE
Uses word combinations, then phrases and simple sentences
Begins to develop grammatical structure
Refers to objects and persons not present, past experiences
Calls self by name, uses pronouns
Identifies pictures, listens to story
Uses rapidly increasing vocabulary
Follows three-part command
Asks and answers simple questions
Begins to use language to pretend during play
Uses private speech
Uses language to: request, greet, protest, assert, ask for comment and information; give comments, orders, and information; make rules

LEVEL 3 (37–60 MONTHS)

WORKING THEME   Uses rapidly developing linguistic skills for private speech and to communicate with peers and family

WHAT YOU OBSERVE
Uses sentences to converse
Develops and stabilizes grammar, uses complex forms
Speaks more intelligibly
Responds to abstract information: events in past and future, feelings
Understands and uses conversational rules
Expresses subtle differences in attitudes and affect
Communicates for entertainment and creative value
Develops metalinguistic awareness of language (understands how language works)
Comprehends complex directions
Participates effectively in two-way conversations

III: Skills and Outstanding Characteristics Observed

IV: Characteristic Patterns Limiting Play

Lack of or delay in language and communication competency: comprehension of speech; development of functional, understandable speech or augmentative communication system (signing, language boards, computers)
Lack of or delay in interpersonal skills that are precursors to language: eye-contact, shared attention, turn taking
Difficulties with social aspects (pragmatics) of language and communication: turn taking, topic maintenance, topic expansion, felicity (greeting, asking, giving, initiating, taking, closing, and the niceties of verbal and nonverbal communication)
Perceptual and attentional disabilities that interfere with development of language and communication
Difficulty comprehending verbal and nonverbal communication unless message is simplified
Nonsequential, fragmented, or unusual communication and language production and comprehension (immediate and delayed echolalia, chatter)
Need for augmentative and multiple communication options
Hearing problems, chronic or intermittent (middle-ear infections)

Other:

V: Discrepancy Analysis (GO TO LAST PAGE OF CHARTS)

VI: Intervention Goal/Facilitating Techniques

GOAL   Provide relationship and setting that elicits and sustains the social, nonverbal, and verbal aspects of communication: eye-contact, shared attention, turn taking, pleasure with sound making, gestures, receptive and expressive language, augmentative communication modes (signing, language boards, computers)

WHAT YOU CAN DO

Determine developmental level; coordinate classroom expectations with speech and language specialist's and hearing specialist's goals and guidelines

Establish preverbal communication and interpersonal exchange skills (eye-gaze, turn taking, shared meaning as keys to communication)

Explore ways of augmenting and facilitating communication when necessary (signing, language boards, pictures, computer programs, language master, wireless auditory trainer)

Use concrete objects and actions; reinforce with real-life photo cards and photo books of child, family, peers at home, school, or neighborhood

Provide multimodel and multisensory activities

Adapt and simplify all communication: clear, short statements, reinforced by body language and props

Determine most effective communication approach with child: open-ended discussion, yes/no choices, direct questioning, reflection, and indirect questioning

Use parallel talk, imitation, and exaggerated (sing-song) intonation to promote vocalization

Imitate and reflect vocal production

Model with gesture and heightened verbal and nonverbal expression

Other:

VII: Individualized Supportive Play Adaptations and Experiences

VIII: Results and Outcomes

II: Observational Impressions

A = attained or mastered   E = emerging   * = working theme
P = practicing   N = not observed

LEVEL 1 (BIRTH–18 MONTHS)

WORKING THEME Increases in attention, perception, and sensorimotor exploration, leading to rudimentary understanding of intentionality, object permanence, cause and effect

WHAT YOU OBSERVE
Discovers hands, puts hands in mouth, puts hands together
Swipes, reaches, grasps objects
Explores objects with motor schemes: shaking, banging, dropping, clapping
Combines objects by putting in, taking out, and banging together
Seeks and finds hidden object
Removes and replaces large peg into board; completes simple non-interlocking puzzle
Uses pull toy intentionally
Identifies self in mirror
Enjoys books; looks at named picture; pats named picture
Identifies one body part
Enjoys simple seek and discover games with familiar adult

LEVEL 2 (19–36 MONTHS)

WORKING THEME Develops representational thought, object permanence, and deferred imitation

WHAT YOU OBSERVE
Solves simple problems (retrieves toy with stick, looks for missing object or person)
Enjoys process of using creative materials
Follows simple rules in interactive exchanges with adults and peers
Enjoys and reenacts nursery rhymes, nonsense rhymes, finger plays, poetry, favorite stories, picture books, and songs
Matches objects to picture, sound to source, and shapes and colors
Identifies six body parts
Understands concept of one anything
Knows own sex and sex of others
Completes 3–4-piece interlocking puzzle
Increases attention, memory, and awareness of viewpoint of others

LEVEL 3 (37–60 MONTHS)

WORKING THEME Expands rapidly in concept formation: space, time, quantity, possession, causality, category; begins to problem solve with a marked increase in symbolic thought

WHAT YOU OBSERVE
Recognizes similarities and differences in size, shape, color, quantity, movement, direction, sequence, and time components of objects and events
Becomes aware of own thought process (metacognition)
Identifies colors
Counts to 10 with one-to-one correspondence
Classifies by one characteristic
Becomes aware of significance of letters, words
Pretends to read favorite story
Identifies own name in print
Becomes aware of concept of money
Knows words and actions to several songs
Enjoys learning activities shared with peers
Expands in awareness of viewpoint of others

III: Skills and Outstanding Characteristics Observed

IV: Characteristic Patterns Limiting Play

Fragmented or scattered cognitive skills
Cognition compromised by neurological, developmental, social–emotional issues; lack of experience
Difficulty reaching potential without concrete, multisensory, and multimodal materials and approaches
Delays and inconsistencies in attention, curiosity, self-motivation, problem-solving skills, and ability to generalize and expand
Perseveration (rigid and restrictive persistence) and preoccupation interferes with full exploration and experiences with objects
Delays and confusion in understanding concepts: cause and effect, object permanence, imitation, sequencing, categorization
Extended focus on process and lack of investment or understanding of product
Lack of motivation and interest

Other:

V: Discrepancy Analysis (GO TO LAST PAGE OF CHARTS)

VI: Intervention Goal/Facilitating Techniques

GOAL Create learning environment that attracts and sustains child's attention, provides motivating activities, shapes and reinforces motivation, and promotes exploration and discovery, all leading to progressive stages of cognition and mastery

WHAT YOU CAN DO

Determine level of cognitive functioning; consult with psychologist for diagnostic differentiation, if more in depth information or interpretation is necessary

Create an irresistible invitation to a higher level of functioning by offering challenges that are not too far above current level of performance, but have a quality of novelty; create play situations that help child experience, assimilate, and utilize concepts, such as causality, object permanence, intentionality, imitation, sequencing, and representation

Avoid premature conceptionalization, but, as ready, encourage simple concepts, such as texture, color, like/different, big/small

Provide a variety of meaningful concrete materials and experiences, beginning with large-scale, representational, three-dimensional toys with attention to objects' weight, color, texture, and action properties that respond to child's spontaneous object–choice and play–action interests

Reinforce child's discovery and learning process by techniques like "say, show, do, and review"

Employ a "touch-demonstrate-say" teaching style for visual–spatial learners

Support child's current level of development: if primarily process-focused, supply activities that allow for variation and exploration; if primarily product-focused, supply activities that encourage child to notice and enjoy process

Provide opportunity to share knowledge and enjoy learning activities with peers

Other:

VII: Individualized Supportive Play Adaptations and Experiences

VIII: Results and Outcomes

II: Observational Impressions

A = attained or mastered   E = emerging   * = working theme
P = practicing   N = not observed

LEVEL 1 (BIRTH–18 MONTHS)

WORKING THEME Engages in sensorimotor, functional-combinatory, early constructive, and autorepresentational play in solitary, onlooker, parallel, and interactive situations

WHAT YOU OBSERVE
Discovers and enjoys body parts and movement
Experiments with action on self, objects, and others; mouthing, banging, dropping, swiping, poking, and fitting in
Engages in mobility oriented play; pushes, pulls, throws, runs
Enjoys solitary play balanced by interactive play with caregiver: peek-a-boo, mirroring, and imitating
Engages in onlooker and parallel play with peers and adults
Engages in functional play: briefly uses object in purposeful ways (squeaks toy, pushes car)
Engages in functional–combinatory play by using two objects in way intended with sober and serious demeanor (stirs spoon in cup)
Engages in simple constructive play: builds tower of three cubes
Engages in autorepresentational play: playful conventional use of object on self or mimicry of routine experiences (drinks from empty cup, puts head down and pretends to sleep)

LEVEL 2 (19–36 MONTHS)

WORKING THEME Engages in constructive, autorepresentational, and allorepresentational play in solitary and associative situations

WHAT YOU OBSERVE
Continues to enjoy solitary play
Initiates chasing and hiding games
Expands functional–combinatory actions on objects: pouring, filling, carrying, loading, and unloading
Enjoys constructive materials and activities for building up and breaking down and creating simple replicas
Responds to realistic props; imitates daily experiences in play
Briefly takes on persona of another person or animal
Uses deferred auto- and allorepresentational play through imitation to recreate short scenes outside of their typical setting in which pretend action is extended to self, others, and objects (feeds self, teacher and doll from empty cup)
Beginning to use toys from common stock pile

LEVEL 3 (37–60 MONTHS)

WORKING THEME Engages in allorepresentational and symbolic play in solitary and cooperative situations

WHAT YOU OBSERVE
Uses symbolic play through object substitution (uses block as car, big spoon as telephone)
Works together with peers toward common goals, following rules, taking turns with limited resources, negotiating and accommodating (cooperative)
Uses symbolic play with planned sequence, longer episodes, props, players, roles, scripts, and scenarios based on realistic experience, increasingly substituting language for action and solving problems (sociodramatic)
Builds complex dramatic scenes which expand on actions and ideas beyond personal experience with imaginary roles, companions, and fantasy plots

III: Skills and Outstanding Characteristics Observed

IV: Characteristic Patterns Limiting Play

Fixated at sensorimotor or functional level; perseverative in auto- or allorepresentational use of objects or in play scenarios, themes, and routines
Preference for solitary and noninteractional activities
Delay in communicative, cognitive, sensory, motoric, and interactive skills inhibits development of symbolic and sociodramatic play
Rigidity to own purpose in play style and activity choice
Precipitation of sensory overstimulation and or emotional excitation through play, leading to regression in play skills, cessation of play, or disorganization and frenzy
Extended need for realistic props
Limited play skills may require active teacher support or involvement
Fearful of imaginative play
Lack of conceptual, attentional, sequencing skills and understanding of cause and effect, which inhibits linking of play acts and leads to fragmented play
Lack of life experiences that support play skill development
Lack of comprehension of social dynamics of turn taking, rule use
Overspecific preference for adult as play associate, little desire for peer interaction in play
Lack of pleasure in play, general apathy

Other:

V: Discrepancy Analysis (GO TO LAST PAGE OF CHARTS)

VI: Intervention Goal/Facilitating Techniques

GOAL   Provide relationship, environment, and materials that support pleasurable learning of progressively more complex object use and social interactions through play

WHAT YOU CAN DO

Create an environment in which play is fun and valued as the natural behavior of every child

Create an environment in which developmentally appropriate play is the focal emphasis in the planned curriculum

Design play environment through choice of specific toys and scenes that teach targeted concepts, interactions, or social relations (e.g., cars on block roadway with stop signs may teach turn taking, inhibition, and social rules)

Engage the child by being responsive to his or her preferred actions and activities; tune into the child's gestural and verbal interactive (two-way) communications; facilitate these messages by reciprocating through imitation and expansion, adjusting pace and affect to match or complement child's emotional energy

Provide numerous opportunities for sensorimotor and functional play, if child is still primarily involved with these levels; be an active partner in play, help peers accept this child's play level

Create situations so that child can first observe peers, then be near peers, sharing space and materials, even if play levels are dissimilar

Simplify play expectations to better match child's play-skill level

Provide direct support to compensate and adapt for compromised skills

Model subskills of play behavior to help child learn and practice more advanced play behavior

Allow for child's extended need for realistic props; incrementally remove pieces or parts of the play scene, evoking memory and imagination for the missing object

Substitute more adaptive or functional play experience for preoccupation with rigid, repetitive, and restrictive activity, but, if perseveration interferes with all learning experiences, modify pattern in small increments of change, model more adaptive behavior, redirect behavior or bargain (first this, then that); when all else fails, remove the object that leads to perseveration

Support progressive involvement in sociodramatic play by adult's modeling roles and use of props, adult partnership with peer and friend to assist in roles and purpose, adult monitoring of peers in roles and prop use

Other:

VII: Individualized Supportive Play Adaptations and Experiences

VIII: Results and Outcomes

II: Observational Impressions

A = attained or mastered   E = emerging   * = working theme
P = practicing   N = not observed

LEVEL 1 (BIRTH–18 MONTHS)

WORKING THEME Seeks pleasure from bodily sensation and movement to get and take in experience, leading to a balance of pleasure from nurturance (trust) with growing urge for self-sufficiency

WHAT YOU OBSERVE
Expresses personal and shared pleasure (feeding, sucking, mouthing, cuddling, physical care), as well as oral and motor aggression (biting, scratching, throwing, poking)
Enjoys early imitative play as a way to maintain an emotional connection with the caregiver (attachment)
Seeks and derives pleasure and comfort from activities involving own body (mouth, other body openings, skin) and caretaker's body, leading to the enjoyment of soft transitional objects
Derives pleasure and feelings of elation from mobility, robust–action schemes, and from movable toy

LEVEL 2 (19–36 MONTHS)

WORKING THEME Integrates ambivalent feelings of love and hate, dependence and autonomy, holding on and letting go, leading to cooperating with adult rules of social interaction, safety, and self-care

WHAT YOU OBSERVE
Experiments in play with vacillation between intake/elimination, hoarding/sharing, filling/dumping, hurting/being hurt, messiness/cleanliness, construction/destruction, elation/soberness, nurturing/destroying, impulsivity/regulation to strike a balance between extremes
Expresses daily living and family caregiving themes through repetitive and ritualized actions with unchanging plot
Displays negativeness and combativeness as a way to defend autonomy and accept adult rules on their own terms
Experiments with use of rules, rituals, routines, and fastidiousness to control unruly impulses
Uses emerging locomotion and play themes to assert independence and act out ambivalence about fusion and separateness, devouring/being devoured, (shadowing and darting, chasing and catching, hide-and-seek)

LEVEL 3 (37–60 MONTHS)

WORKING THEME Seeks mastery of sexual and social roles and place in family, leading to internalization of sexual identity, social rules regarding eating and bodily hygiene, and social conventions of interaction

WHAT YOU OBSERVE
Shows high-spirited, repeated sociodramatic plots that recreate family drama and romance, feeling states and emotions, hero and aggressor fantasies with exhibitionism and voyeurism counterpointed against privacy and modesty
Plays repetitive games that reflect fascination with expression of affection, sexual intimacy vs. aggression; use, function and differences of genital organs; birth, death and vulnerability; wish for affiliation with adults and jealousy of their skill, power, and relationships; wishes to be grown up; shows frustration at personal limitations; preoccupied with love, rage, fear of retaliation, and the loss of the love of the love object
Displays competitiveness (envy, jealousy, rivalry, possessiveness, bids for attention, winning exclusive relationship with preferred adult), leading to an increase in protectiveness, generosity, curiosity, and nurturance
Exhibits body mastery through challenging and vigorous activity
Uses symbolic, dramatic insignia, emblems, costumes and props (police badge, fire hat, nurse hat, etc.) to experiment with character roles and imaginary roles
Displays emerging passion for learning with pleasure in finished product

III: Skills and Outstanding Characteristics Observed

IV: Characteristic Patterns Limiting Play

Egocentricity or disturbed attachment (overdependent, insecure, ambivalent, unattached), interfering with resolution of themes related to body competencies, needs, and controls; separation/individuation, dependency/independence; sexual identification
Fixation on sensory and functional dimensions
Impoverishment of themes or content
Perseveration on themes
Excessive or insufficient inhibition around fear and aggression themes
Resistance to expansion of themes
Inability to adapt to adult or peer suggestions or involvement
Advancement of play skills elicits extremes of emotional experience, loss of control, and fear for safety
Emotionally charged play themes lead to overexcitement and overstimulation
Mismatch existing between play skill level and the level of themes being processed
Mismatch existing between cognitive level and the level of themes being processed
Play themes being inhibited by passivity, withdrawal, lack of motivation, overaggression, and overactivity
Play being inhibited by grief and sadness related to issues of real or imagined loss (death, hospitalization, divorce), confusion around finding a place in family and in adjusting to roles in the family, feelings of anger, entrapment, helplessness, and hopelessness imposed by limitations related to disability
Play themes inhibited by problems with oral intake, elimination, gross and fine motor skills, sensory functioning, state regulation, confused gender identity
Play themes inhibited by lack of appropriate role models, inability to organize and synthesize roles and play schemes (too loosened), inability to differentiate between reality and fantasy, limited or no motivation to play, hoarding and inability to share
Excessive passivity or competitiveness interferes with play

Other:

V: Discrepancy Analysis (GO TO LAST PAGE OF CHARTS)

VI: Intervention Goal/Facilitating Techniques

GOAL Provide relationship, environment, and materials that support expression and resolution of developmental crises: body, love, relationship, and membership

WHAT YOU CAN DO

Consult with play therapist and, when appropriate, refer child and family for therapy

Accept the need for persistent themes; gradually challenge the repeated play scene by introducing minor variations in the sequence, content, and object use

Accept and woo the passive and withdrawn child

Assist child to identify and label feelings

Offer child words and explanations that foster understanding of worries or confused play themes

Provide toys and props that allow child to play out and experiment with bodily themes of feeding and being fed, elimination, and hygiene

Provide toys and props that allow child to play out and experiment with separation and reunion, hide-and-seek, run-and-catch

Provide toys and props that allow child to play out and experiment with themes of gender role and identity

Provide reassurance about fears of bodily injury and support bodily integrity with materials and activities such as mirrors, doctor kits, grooming materials, fantasy and realist heroic figures

Allow child to take control and show power in play; avoid battle of wills; tolerate child's normal ambivalence without overreaction

Accept expression of anxious feelings; developmental progress in play may induce regression and increased anxiety

Support exploration of unresolved themes that may be aided by return to presymbolic play; provide more adaptive outcomes in play scenarios; suggest/evoke alternative solutions to problems/conflicts that arise in play scenarios

Strive to strike a balance between opportunities for messiness and conformity to social rules of cleanliness and tidiness

Provide through play opportunities to practice rule attunement: slowing down, stopping, changing directions, cleaning up, eating, toileting, waiting, redirection of aggression, finishing, social order

Provide appropriate sensory and motor adaptive toys and props to facilitate the development of play themes

Other:

VII: Individualized Supportive Play Adaptations and Experiences

VIII: Results and Outcomes

II: Observational Guide

Type and frequency of contact between family and staff (attend parent's meetings; exchange daily log with staff; participate in regular conferences with parent coordinator or other staff member; participate in planning and placement team meetings; make regular classroom observations)

Family goals and motivation for child's placement in preschool (family's concerns about child's development and projection for future developmental outcome and programming)

Child's attachment patterns within the nuclear and extended family (preferred adult for varied activities and routines; separation and reunion issues at different setting)

Role and relationship of siblings with observed child and within family (nurturing, rejecting, baiting, etc.)

Extended family constellation, roles and functioning

Child's routine within the family's daily/weekly schedule

Details of child's home environment (sleeping arrangements, available toys, available play space indoors and outdoors, amount of television viewing, playmates in neighborhood, pets)

Availability of professional resources and family utilization of available resources

III: General Description

IV: Characteristic Patterns Limiting Play

Expectations mismatched to child's development

Temperament or style mismatch between child and parents

Overinvestment in child's dependency

Overprotectiveness or defensiveness concerning peer reaction and lack of social interaction

Detachment and distancing

Lack of understanding of development and its implications

Provision of limited opportunities for child to experience outside the household

Overexposure of child to stimulation, activities, and experiences beyond his or her development and understanding

Driven search for innovative treatments

Inability to advocate for child

Use of education, health, and related service system in an adversarial and self-defeating way

Sibling relationships counterproductive for child or siblings

Limitations or lack of family resources and support systems

Home environment not supportive to child's individual developmental needs

Family environment not providing consistency and predictability of caregiving

Patterns of blaming and emotional unavailability between key family members, making coping difficult

Verbal commentary focusing on child's negative behavior and characteristics setting the stage for a self-fulfilling prophecy

Discussion of provocative and anxiety-ridden topics in child's presence

Other:

V: Discrepancy Analysis (GO TO LAST PAGE OF CHARTS)

VI: Intervention Goal/Facilitating Techniques

GOAL   Help family gain appreciation and understanding for child's unique qualities and developmental needs; help family maintain a system that supports mental health of all members; help family develop advocacy role in planning and management of child

THINGS YOU CAN DO

Accept parents' current level of functioning and understand that parenting is developmental process that needs nurturing

Assist family in establishing developmentally appropriate routine, environment, and expectations for child's temperament and style

Assist parents in the selection and organization of appropriate toys, materials, and play-time experiences that match child's current development needs

Encourage and guide parent–child play for its own sake and for pleasure

Support parental awareness of differences in temperament and style in their child and help them to accommodate these differences

Support family in understanding that sensorimotor exploration and play are precursors and subskills of preacademic and academic goals

Support parents as individuals in their own right

Support parents to reinforce self-identity and couple identity and total family focus so as not to become absorbed and overfocused on special child

Assist the family in helping to find a special place for the child in the family, rather than the child being at the center of the family

Assist parents in finding resources related to issues of disability and other issues

Reinforce parents' need to build support network (babysitters, respite care, therapy, support groups, etc.)

Support parents in maintaining a personal life, rather than being entrapped into "professional parent of the handicapped child" role

Work on reinforcing positive experiences shared between parent and child

Give positive feedback to parent about child's performance and positive characteristics

Understand that overprotection may be reflection of separation fears and issues of ambivalence

Allow parent appropriate access to program

Integrate parents of child with special needs into regular parent group

Assist parents in assessing strengths and limits of available services

Assist parents in selection of reasonable program of support therapies for themselves, siblings, and the child

Support family's effective advocacy for their child

Support parents in coping with what may be chronic nature of child's disability and its impact on the family

Heighten parents' awareness of the potential risk of the child's misunderstanding of anxiety-ridden and provocative commentary; worrisome material can be discussed, but at appropriate times and places, out of earshot of the child

Other:

VII: Individualized Supportive Play Adaptations and Experiences

VIII: Results and Outcomes

II: Observational Guide

Number of adults available in group

Adult-to-child ratio

Adequate time available for training, staff meetings, team meeting with parents, consultation

Roles and responsibility of staff members

Affective tone of staff members with group and with observed child

Staff's ability and commitment to play

General description of adults' interactions with group and with observed child

Adults' style (directive/nondirective), tolerance of children's behavior and range of development

Adults' use of language, general relationship with child and children

Adults' teaming style and the overall school climate

III: General Description

IV: Characteristic Patterns Limiting Play

Unresponsive or unempathetic to child's immediate needs, behaviors, or feelings

Inconsistent interest or acceptance toward child

Style and pace poorly matched to child's

Poorly defined roles and responsibilities

Communication and language poorly matched to affect and developmental level of child

Inadequate training to meet observed child's needs

Uninvolved with child's play

Too involved or controlling

Not reinforcing child's attempts for object mastery or peer affiliation

Confused about accepting the protective and guiding role (over permissive or authoritarian; inconsistent and ambivalent)

Anxious about child's disability

Poor team work

Inadequate adult-to-child ratio

Other:

V: Discrepancy Analysis (GO TO LAST PAGE OF CHARTS)

VI: Intervention Goal/Facilitating Techniques

GOAL Provide individualized relationship to support all areas of child's development and to accommodate a family-focused approach; incrementally release child to relate with other adults and peers

WHAT YOU CAN DO

Provide adult-to-child ratio of one-to-one, progressing to one-to-five; consider special child to be equivalent to two or three normally developing children when establishing adult-to-child ratio

Seek and use network support system to increase skills for working with child (consult specialists, attend workshops, read about condition)

Prepare personally for working with child: empathy exercises, exploration of personal reaction to child (sadness, hopelessness, helplessness, fear, vulnerability, anger, and disappointment)

Accept and reach out to family for collaboration, to develop mutual support and respect

Adapt teaching style and interactive style to child's needs (activity level and passivity, loudness, verbal intensity and rate of speech, use of physical contact)

Know and believe that task is to assist in the child's growth and development, not to "cure" the child (progress, not perfection); accept some misbehavior and regression

Be alert to nonintrusive ways that child's developmental skills can be supported

Build team collaboration and consistency for communication and management

Be available as play partner by being actively involved in child's play; gradually disengage and allow child to play with other adults and peers

Prepare environment and give child emotional and physical space that allows him or her to experience, explore, experiment, and discover through trial and error; let child's product be his or her own—do not use art models

Reinforce discovery and learning by using techniques like "say, show, do, and review"

Accept that child sometimes needs to experience failures, bumps, and falls

Actively facilitate child-to-child interaction: verbally model, prompt, cue, and coach; physically and verbally support greetings, partings, negotiations, material and space sharing, and turn taking

Allow child to retreat, when necessary, from group activities or engage in solitary play; "tuning out" for interludes may allow child to reorganize and then reenter group activities

Support by sitting near child at group time, praising child's attempt at task, reinforcing child's approach to peers

Resist temptation to comment critically or sarcastically (to discuss any child while children present); all classroom conversation should be appropriate for children to hear and be centered on child's experiences and activities

Prepare family and staff for the reality that regression is a normal part of development; sometimes you have to go back to regroup in order to go forward

Other:

VII: Individualized Supportive Play Adaptations and Experiences

VIII: Results and Outcomes

PEERS

II: Observational Guide

Total number of peers in group
Age range of peers
Male–female ratio of group
Ratio of normally developing children to children with disabilities
Interaction and style of peers with observed child during various
    activities
Pace of group
Child's awareness and involvement with peers
Peers' level of awareness, involvement, and interest in the
    observed child
Relative difference in developmental age of peers and observed
    child

III: General Description

IV: Characteristic Patterns Limiting Play

Inappropriate group size or composition
Peer-driven climate and activity preferences incompatible with
    child
Group social behavior and play level unable to accommodate
    observed child
Peers intolerant of, uninterested in, or display lack of understand-
    ing of child with special needs
Pace too fast or too slow

Other:

SPACE

II: Observational Guide

Size of room and playground
Scale, division, and organization of play spaces
Defined areas for activities of daily living spaces: feeding,
    sleeping, toileting, hand washing, tooth brushing, group and personal
    storage
Defined play spaces: fine motor, constructive and dramatic play,
    expressive arts, gross motor
Traffic flow, circulation space
Variety of flooring and ground surfaces (hard and soft; varying
    textures)
Acoustics (separation of quiet and noisy areas, sound-absorbing
    surfaces, general noise level)
Attention to appropriate stimulation level: decor, use of color,
    lighting level, window treatment, visual clutter
Open and closed storage facilities
Areas for relaxation, retreat, and comfort
Display areas
Handicapped accessible

III: General Description

IV: Characteristic Patterns Limiting Play

Disorganized, cluttered, or unsafe space
Sterile and uninviting or overplanned space
Too large, overstimulating, and unstructured space
Indoor and outdoor space not planned to respond to child's needs
Unclear division between activity areas
Inadequate opened and closed storage areas
Acoustics and lighting inadequate or inappropriate
Inconvenient or inappropriate toileting area
No space allocation for quiet, solitary, messy uses, clean-up
Inadequate large motor areas, indoors and outdoors
Traffic flow interferes with effective use of play spaces
Inadequate or inappropriate hard and soft play surfaces
No discrete display areas
Inadequate accessibility

Other:

V: Discrepancy Analysis (GO TO LAST PAGE OF CHARTS)

VI: Intervention Goal/Facilitating Techniques

GOAL   Help normal peers to relate in a positive fashion to their peers with special needs, to gain understanding and tolerance of individual differences

WHAT YOU CAN DO

Form small, compatible, and complementary subgroups that contain children who show a balance in activity level, play and social level and in the range of verbal, cognitive, and motor skills

Educate normal peers for presence of child with special needs in group (peers may be unable to understand child's problem or intention, fear child's condition, and fantasize something similar is going to happen to them, and show disinterest, which may represent a form of avoidance or denial)

Emphasize strengths and interests of child with special needs; empower the child with interesting activities and materials to draw other peers to him

Support peers to include child with special needs, even if play is at lower level

Support peers to allow child with special needs not to participate in all group activities or to participate in a different way

Other:

VII: Individualized Supportive Play Adaptations and Experiences

VIII: Results and Outcomes

V: Discrepancy Analysis (GO TO LAST PAGE OF CHARTS)

VI: Intervention Goal/Facilitating Techniques

GOAL   Design an environment that responds adaptively to the child's unique needs for flexible space

WHAT YOU CAN DO

Design flexible and accessible space: open and closed, movable and fixed elements and partitions, appropriately stimulating, clear divisions for activities and materials, logical and adequate storage, accessible sink and bathroom areas, messy activity area, large motor area outdoors/indoors, varied room textures

Give special consideration to acoustics (soft background music, white noise, rugs as sound absorption, ceiling height) and lighting (nonfluorescent lights, window shades, task spot lighting, mirror use)

Consult appropriate specialists concerning lighting and acoustics when child's needs are visual, auditory, motoric, or attention related

Other:

VII: Individualized Supportive Play Adaptations and Experiences

VIII: Results and Outcomes

TIME

II: Observational Guide

Daily schedule and length of activities
Sequences of activities
Balance of active and quiet activities
Schedule responsive to children's needs, interests, moods, and
  daily tempo
Coordination and synchronization of arrival and departure with
  school schedule, transportation schedule and family needs

III: General Description

IV: Characteristic Patterns Limiting Play

Inflexible routine or no clear routine
Activities, all group-focused, long, and required
Imbalance of active or quiet activities
Routine pace too rushed, too slow, nonresponsive
Disruption in routine because of unscheduled arrival and depar-
  ture

Other:

MATERIALS AND EQUIPMENT

II: Observational Guide

Scale, size, weight, texture, color, and composition of furniture,
  materials, and equipment
Quantity, categories, and appropriateness of toys, materials and
  equipment available
Large and small motor material and equipment
Suspended equipment for vestibular and sensorimotor stimulation
Sensory materials (sand and water, paint, clay and play dough,
  etc.)
Constructive and dramatic materials and equipment
Adaptive and augmentative materials and equipment
Conceptual and creative materials
Availability of furniture and equipment for activities of daily liv-
  ing (feeding, hygiene, napping)
Maintenance of materials and equipment
General accessibility to materials and equipment

III: General Description

IV: Characteristic Patterns Limiting Play

Choices and supplies inappropriately constrict child's selection of
  and experimentation with objects
Restrictive range of available materials
Poorly matched to child's needs (developmental level, size, etc.)
Not reflective of child's experiences
Not multisensory or creative in nature
Disorganized and poorly presented
Insufficient number of duplicate materials requiring premature
  sharing
Not adapted and accessible to child's specific limitations (chair and
  table height, grip handles on puzzles, etc.)
Broken, dirty, torn, and incomplete items
Inappropriate scale, size, weight, texture, color, and composition
Unavailable or insufficient toys that promote expanded play deal-
  ing with play themes

Other:

V: Discrepancy Analysis (GO TO LAST PAGE OF CHARTS)

VI: Intervention Goal/Facilitating Techniques

GOAL   Design an environment that responds adaptively to the child's unique needs for responsive routine.

WHAT YOU CAN DO
Provide predictable and responsive routine with adjustments for fatigue, illness, overstimulation, or regression
Experiment with schedule and activity variations relative to child's biological rhythms (slow starter, highly active, morning napper, etc.)
Allow ample time for solitary play, but encourage group participation
Allow sufficient periods in schedule to accommodate varying levels of play (solitary, interactive, onlooker, parallel, associative, cooperative)
Collaborate to identify and resolve scheduling problems

Other:

VII: Individualized Supportive Play Adaptations and Experiences

VIII: Results and Outcomes

V: Discrepancy Analysis (GO TO LAST PAGE OF CHARTS)

VI: Intervention Goal/Facilitating Techniques

GOAL   Design an environment that responds adaptively to the child's unique needs for adaptive materials and equipment.

WHAT YOU CAN DO
Consult, if necessary, with physical therapist, occupational therapist, speech and language specialist, audiologist, vision specialist, or other specialists for appropriately adaptive materials and equipment
Use toys, materials and equipment that promote a full range of learning, feeling, and playing experiences matched to children's developmental needs
Use materials that promote multisensory experiences (tactile: water, sand, clay, shaving cream; vestibular: swings, hammock, bolsters; auditory: earphones, tape player, instruments, background music, language master; visual: computer, light box, pictures, books, language master cards)
Choose materials with attention to tactile defensiveness, vestibular instability, and sensory problems; be attentive to material qualities that relate to size, weight, and volume
Repair or replace broken materials and equipment

Other:

VII: Individualized Supportive Play Adaptations and Experiences

VIII: Results and Outcomes

Supportive Play Model

Section I. Discrepancy Analysis

Name: _____

Date of birth: _____

Date: _____

Developmental Area	CA Level	Working Theme Level	Differences (below age level, age level, above age level)
Self/Social/Emotional	☐	☐	_____
Motor/Self-Help	☐	☐	_____
Communicative/Language	☐	☐	_____
Cognitive	☐	☐	_____
Play Skills	☐	☐	_____
Play Themes	☐	☐	_____

Highlight significant discrepancy issues:

CHILD:

FAMILY:

PROGRAM:

CHAPTER 3

The Supportive Play Model in the Context of Family and School

The SPM provides a framework for dialogue between parents and the involved professionals. In this process we aim to bring the unique characteristics of the child and the individual needs of the family into harmony. In the parent–professional dialogue we become more aware of the family's goals for their child with special needs, for themselves, as parents, and for the family as a whole. To be effective in this interchange, the interventionist needs to be knowledgable about family systems theory, the developmental stages of parenthood, and the stages of the family life cycle, along with the more specific issues that relate to raising a child with special needs. In addition, the interventionist needs to be familiar with current philosophy and practice regarding the continuum of services and placements for children with special needs. Thus, to prepare the reader more fully to participate in the use of the SPM, this chapter gives an overview of key issues that relate to the family and the school placement choice.

Interventionists need to be both empathetic and responsive in this work because a child with special needs may be demanding economically, emotionally, and physically on the family system. All intervention plans should account for parental wishes for their child, as well as the realities of the specific programs and services that are available to the child in the community. Program planning needs to reflect cultural and community beliefs and practices about rearing young children, as well as being developmentally appropriate for the child, in order to maximize the child's membership in a broad social community.

This chapter first reviews several issues regarding the family and the professional's role in regard to the family. Second, this chapter contains a review of issues that focus on placement philosophy and priorities as they have evolved since mainstreaming and least restrictive environment (LRE) were introduced by the Education for All Handicapped Children Act of 1975 (PL 94-142).

ISSUES RELATED TO FAMILY

Families are clearly challenged by the birth of a child with special needs. Some of their responses are emotional and psychological in nature, others need to be pragmatic in nature. This section discusses some of the issues of grief and stress that may be part of the familial response to their baby's birth. Family reactions, as understood in family-systems theory, are briefly described. The potential of a family adjusting to the needs of this new child while also tending to all the other members of the family is a viable goal. Many families do cope well, and some of the variables that make this possible are described. Professionals

working with families need to be aware of these family dynamics and should be conscious of how they can assist the family in a way that best matches the family's strengths and needs.

Emotional Reactions to the Birth

All parents experience a range of emotions with the birth of a new baby. When the baby has special needs, the range and intensity of the emotions may be magnified and may include grief and mourning (Solnit & Stark, 1961). Emotions, including feelings of mourning, are normal and should not be judged as psychopathological, but rather as a natural and responsive adaptation to feelings such as loss and powerlessness. For instance, guilt related to the baby's problems may be an unconscious way to counteract feelings of powerlessness (Gardner, 1969; Oster, 1984; Trout & Foley, 1989). Parents may also show denial as a healthy reaction to an overload of information regarding their child's condition and the suggested interventions (Oster, 1984; Trout & Foley, 1989).

An early emotional task for parents is to adjust to the loss of their "wished-for" baby. Even as they adjust to the reality of their baby's developmental issues, they may find that their relationship with their child is missing the expected positive quality and feelings. Foley (1986) identified the following stages of grief from following 20 families longitudinally who had a child with a handicap: shock/panic, searching, acknowledgment–depression, recovery, and maintenance. He also identified two psychological accomplishments that seemed to promote a remission from grief. The first is the formulation of a "personal mythology" that helped families make sense of their disorienting experience. The second is a reformation of the mental representation of the "wished for" child to bring it into greater congruence with the real child. Even as emotional adjustments are made by the parents and the family, raising a child with special needs may produce stress within the family.

Stress

One of the known possible causes of stress for parents who are raising children with special needs is the difference in interactive quality that may be integral to the child's condition. Specifically, many children with disabilities are likely to be less responsive, which may strain parent–child interactions (Gunn & Berry, 1985). Before 1980, these interaction issues were likely to be perceived as the result of a deficit in the parents, particularly the mother's ability to relate to her child (Shonkoff, Hauser-Cram, Krauss, & Upshur, 1992). Research now shows that children with disabilities are less interactive and responsive, demonstrate less affect, have social cues that are difficult to read, and demonstrate social behavior that is less spontaneous than with the normal child (Brooks-Gunn & Lewis, 1982; Buckhalt, Rutherford, & Goldberg, 1978; Cicchetti & Sroufe, 1976; Eheart, 1982; Goldman & Johnson-Martin, 1987; MacTurk, Hunter, McCarthy, Vietze, & McQuiston, 1985; Maurer & Sherrod, 1987; Stoneman, Brody, & Abbott, 1983).

It is important for the professional to realize that uncontrolled stress is not an inevitable outcome in families who have young children with special needs (Frey, Fewell, & Vadasy, 1989; Gowen, Johnson-Martin, Goldman, & Appelbaum, 1989). Some of the variables that may lead to the presence of stress include the severity and type of handicap and the expected outcome and prognosis for the child. The more pervasive handicaps generally cause the most stress in families (Beckman, 1983; Donovan,1988; Holroyd & McArthur, 1976; Kashani, 1986). Depending on a family's coping abilities, stress within the family can lead to depression, social isolation, role restriction, and marital discord, which may interfere with family functioning (Shonkoff et al., 1992). Family system theory helps clarify how stress can affect various aspects of a family's functioning and life experience.

Family Systems Theory and Coping

It is now understood that the birth of the child with special needs often has an impact not just on the parents, but on the entire family. Family systems theory implies that each member of the family is connected to another in an interdependent way. This theory suggests that change in one part of the family affects the whole family system. For instance, each phase of the child's development causes reaction within the family, and the family's reactions, in turn, affect the child's development. Families may function differently at different times in their child's life, but those differences do not necessarily mean that the family is deviant. Some studies have found that having a child with a disability can have a negative effect on a marriage and family systems, while others have shown that marriages and families have grown closer and stronger (Barber, Turnbull, Behr, & Kerns, 1988; Gath, 1977; Hare, Laurence, Paynes, & Rawnsley, 1966). Another formulation for family dysfunction is that the child with a disability amplifies stress that may have already existed in the family system.

In the past, much of the research and intervention focused on family distress rather than on the understanding and supporting family coping skills. Coping may include family members' accepting that the child is handicapped, acknowledging what that means to the family, and searching for ways to improve the outcome of the handicap. Shapiro (1983) outlines styles of coping that are related to control and can include such maneuvers as protective denial, positive mental imagery, insight and acceptance, support seeking, expression of feelings, rationalization, humor, prayer, stress reduction, negative techniques such as obsessional hypervigilance, dysfunctional denial and avoidance, intellectualization and denial of affect, capitalizing, focusing on helplessness and hopelessness, pervasive dependency, low self-esteem, and giving-up.

A family's ability to cope positively with their child with a disability depends greatly on family-system variables such as family size and form, cultural background, socioeconomic status, and geographic location. Barber, Turnbull, Behr, and Kerns (1988) describe and discuss the significant components of a family system that directly affect family coping, including family resources, family interactions, family functions, and family life cycle.

Family Resources

Important family resources are the characteristics and strengths of both the individual family members and the family as a whole. Characteristics of the child's handicapping condition, such as timing of the diagnosis of the exceptionality, financial costs that are not covered by insurance, the amount of care giving that is required, the needs of the individual and extended family members, and the family's perception of the stigma attached to the handicapping condition, are all variables that affect the family resources (Barber, et al., 1988; Fewell, 1986; Gallagher, Beckman, & Cross, 1983; Goffman, 1963; Lipsky, 1985). In general, it has been found that there is a positive relationship between available social support and parents' well-being (Beckman, 1991; Dunst & Trivette, 1990; Levitt, Weber, & Clark, 1986). Adequate support may act as a buffer to stress because in families in which there are support systems there is less maternal depression and an increased sense of competence (Gowen et al., 1989; Koeske & Koeske, 1990).

Family Interactions

Important to the understanding of a family system is a review of its interaction patterns. These include the varying dimensions of communication both within the family system and with outside systems. These interactions can include sharing affection, planning for the future, resolving problems, accomplishing daily tasks, or teaching new skills. The ability of families to share the emotional, psychological, and physical stress they experience appears to be a key factor in their ability to cope.

Marital roles and parental roles are often affected by the needs of the child with a disability. Working through the changes in the relationship as a couple, sharing the responsibilities of care, and differing styles or paces in grieving and coping all can cause a need for major reorganization in the marital relationship. Mothers and fathers show different concerns in relation to their child with handicaps. Mothers tend to focus more on matters related to the nuclear family, such as child care and other daily tasks, emotional strain, and family harmony, while fathers express concern about societal acceptance, stigmatization of the family, the child's future, and cost of care (Gumz & Gubrium, 1972). These differences in focus can interfere with the sharing of the experience of parenting the child with special needs until the couple develops a sense of collaboration in reacting to the child's and their own needs.

Siblings must also make adjustments to the birth of the child with special needs. A disproportionate amount of time, energy, and family resources are absorbed by the child with special needs. Factors that may affect normally developing siblings' adjustments to their disabled sibling relate to their age and position in the family, how much responsibility they feel in the care of their sibling now and over the life span, family norms relative to mutual care expectations, and heightened family expectations for the normally developing children to excel and be highly responsible. Some siblings report greater understanding, compassion, and tolerance as well as a greater appreciation for their own abilities, while other siblings express anger, frustration, and distress about their personal experiences (Vadasy, Fewell, Meyer, & Schell, 1984).

Interaction patterns extend beyond the immediate family. Family members must all interact with the extended family and community members, including friends and professionals. Some families rely heavily on extended family members and friends for emotional support and direct assistance in child care. Other families may retreat from all outsiders because they believe that people outside the nuclear family do not understand the child's needs and place blame on the parents for the child's problems. Families that are able to foster positive interaction both within the family unit, in the broader circle of extended family, and in the community have many more resources available to help them to fulfill family functions.

Family Functions

Family functions relate to the tasks of daily survival that must be carried out by family members. Economic survival, socialization, managing domestic and health care needs, self-definition as individuals and as a family unit, fulfilling educational and vocational needs, recreational needs, and the need for affection are all key family functions that may be affected by the birth of a child with special needs (Barber et al., 1988; Turnbull & Turnbull, 1986). The necessity for extra caregiving for the child with special needs may tax all family resources, including time and finances. Formal and informal support networks may need to be tapped to assist the family in dealing with the complex needs of their child with disabilities. Often, the first family functions to be set aside are recreation and outside socialization. This can increase the family's fragmentation and feeling of isolation and desperation. Families that can care for the child with special needs while still fulfilling these important functions for all family members are more successful in coping. The ability to cope, though, may fluctuate at different points in time because of the cyclical demands on the family system and its resources.

Family Life Cycle

A family has a life cycle that evolves with the changing needs of individual members. Each stage of the family life cycle has several issues that may affect the parents and other issues that may affect the siblings (Barber et al., 1988). During the preschool years of the child with special needs, parents may be very focused on obtaining a diagnosis for their child and searching for the causes of the developmental disability. Family and extended family members need to be informed about the disability. Issues related to the stigma of disability must be faced. On the philosophical side, parents need to find some meaning in the exceptionality and to formulate a personal ideology to help them in making all the decisions they face. On the pragmatic side, a great deal of time may have to be spent in finding and coordinating appropriate services for their child with special needs. During these same early years, siblings may feel the loss of both parental time and energy, which can lead them to feelings of jealousy. They may also be confused about the nature of their sibling's disability, which can cause fear and misunderstanding in their thinking. Older siblings may find themselves bearing more than typical responsibility in both child care and domestic responsibilities.

Family–Professional Relationship

It is the assumption that the relationship that is shared between professionals and families will be one that strives to support and facilitate the natural strengths present in all families. Families of handicapped children, although they may be experiencing stress, are not different from families of nonhandicapped children in their basic needs and functions (Moroz, 1989). Professionals working with families need to respect the competence of the family in knowing their own child and in deciding the course and limits of the intervention plan. The professional must appreciate the boundaries of the family and the cultural and personal belief systems that are intrinsic to the family. These cultural beliefs and parental styles naturally influence the intervention goals that families set. Professionals must also be prepared to help parents accept the limits of the emotional support and services available within an educational setting. The high need level and intensity of emotions experienced throughout the grieving process may lead to unrealistic expectations and "magical" thinking that is focused on program staff's curing the child rather than assisting the parents to learn to accept the child's unique development. On the other hand, professionals also need to respect the fact that parents must think about the needs of the entire family, not just the child with special needs (Moroz, 1989).

The range of family desire regarding intervention may include developmental monitoring, crisis intervention, help with day-to-day needs (such as finding babysitters), educationally focused intervention, even to psychotherapy. Intervention at its most intensive includes a focus on the inner life of families, the conflicts that arise from rearing a handicapped child, and the relationships among the members of the family (Fraiberg, 1980; Foley, 1986). Even if families are not interested in directly dealing with family systems or psychodynamic material, the interventionist who is aware of the blatant or latent family issues will be far more effective in helping a child and the family.

As professionals work in a family-centered style they will find that responsive intervention and guided discovery are more fruitful than direct instruction (Trout & Foley, 1989). The responsive interventionist can expand behavior already in place between the parent and child by using a teaching style that employs "suggestion, demonstration, practice, and coaching" (Trout & Foley, 1989, p. 65). The primary goal is to increase the pleasure and reciprocity experienced by the parents with their child within play and activities of daily living. Intervention must always be interactive and relationship-based (Bromwich, 1981; Trout & Foley, 1989). The interventionist must build the relationship through being consistent, predictable, warm, and empathetic. The professionals must possess a high level of self-awareness because their own psychological history will affect their interpretation of the familial dynamics and will influence their responses (Trout, 1988). It is also a challenge for professionals to establish a balance between closeness and distance. Too much distance blocks empathy. Too much closeness threatens objectivity and loosens the boundaries necessary to set limits, test reality, and stimulate the optimal stress that may be needed to promote movement (Foley, Hochman, & Miller, 1994).

As the family works through the SPM process with the staff, benefits that are likely to be gained include a clear expression of parental wishes and concerns regarding their child, a heightening of observation skills, reinterpretation of their child's development in light of their child's unique strengths and style, and a greater appreciation for the value of play and the social–emotional aspects of development. As a family becomes more focused on their child's unique qualities, the family often becomes less frustrated by their child's behavior and finds the child more endearing.

ISSUES RELATED TO THE EARLY CHILDHOOD PLACEMENT

As explained in Chapter 1, over the last two decades we have moved away from the practice of isolating individuals with disabilities and have seen a growth in public awareness and acceptance of the personal rights of individuals who have special needs. As a result of these changes, early childhood placements have moved toward a continuum of options that stress least restrictive environments. There has been an evolution of terminology and placement design that has progressed from self-contained special education settings to settings that offer mainstreaming, integration, or inclusion.

With the multiplicity of choices regarding placement plans, parents and staff may be perplexed in knowing what will best serve a child's needs at a given time. Working through the SPM allows the professionals and parents to explore key aspects of the child's placement and to determine if the plan matches the child's developmental needs. Another major change that is a direct result of federal legislation and shifts in societal attitude is the need for interventionists to plan interactively with the family. Program planning should be responsive to children and their families, rather than expecting the children and families to mold themselves to the available services and settings. The SPM can help the interventionist plan with families in a collaborative fashion, and the process can help parents and professionals select or adapt available programs to better match children's needs.

Terminology

A number of terms have surfaced in the literature and in practice that are the result of legal and societal changes. Some of the most significant terms include normalization, least restrictive environment, mainstreaming, integration, and inclusion.

- *Normalization.* As defined by Nirje (1985), normalization refers to "making available to all persons with disabilities patterns of life and conditions of everyday living which are as close as possible to the regular circumstances and ways of life of society" (p. 67).
- *Least restrictive environment.* This speaks specifically to the type of school placement for the child with special needs— "to the maximum extent appropriate, handicapped children, including children in public or private institutions or other care facilities, are educated with children who are not handicapped (Education for All Handicapped Children, 1975). Defining the LRE for a particular child entails deciding the setting that is least restrictive, but still allows the child to experience social and academic success. Although the LRE can include a full range of possible placements, from institutional care to full-time participation in a regular education setting, most people have come to believe that LRE is synonymous with a mainstreamed placement.
- *Mainstreaming.* This concept incorporates the idea of children with special needs having part or all of their educational experience in a regular education setting, side-by-side with children who do not have identified special education needs. As reported by the R. W. Johnson Foundation (*Serving handicapped children*,1988), of the 10% of school children having special needs, 96% attend regular schools, and the vast majority of these are receiving partially or totally mainstreamed educational experiences. Most educators focus on the educational aspects of mainstreaming (Fewell & Oelwein, 1990; Taylor, Biklen, Lehr, & Searl, 1987), but, in practice, mainstreaming has included everything from a child with special needs going into the playground or into the lunch room with the regular education students to full academic participation in a regular education program. Mainstreaming has also evolved, particularly in the preschool years, to include the idea of reverse mainstreaming, in which normally developing peers are brought into a special education setting to act as models for the children who have special needs (McLean & Hanline, 1990; McLean & Odom, 1988; Odom, 1989; Odom & McEvoy, 1988). Gradually, the concept of mainstreaming has been replaced by a broader concept of "integration." Self-contained programs that serve only children who have special needs is referred to as "segregated."
- *Integration.* The concept of integration reflects a desire for the child with special needs to have access to the full school environment, not just the academic program (Fewell & Oelwien, 1990; McLean & Hanline, 1990; Taylor et al., 1987). This idea of integration is reflective of the societal goal of normalization, which includes physical, social, and academic accessibility (Taylor et al., 1987).
- *Inclusion.* The most current conceptual transition is a progression away from integration to the idea of "inclusion" (Salisbury, 1991; "CEC Policy", 1993). Integration is described as having the unstated message that one group is from the "mainstream" (the individuals without disability) and, consequently, that the other group, those who have disabilities, are not from the "mainstream." Therefore, the process of integration requires bringing the individuals who are different into the mainstream. Inclusion, on the other hand, suggests starting from a very different mind set. Specifically, that all children, no matter how diverse their needs, should expect to be served in the regular education setting that they would attend at any specific age. Thus, only after "supplementary aides and supports have been tried (within the regular setting) and found to be insufficient, then and only then, should alternative service delivery options be considered" (Salisbury, 1991, p. 147).

Within contemporary early education there are proponents of mainstreaming, reverse mainstreaming, integration, segregation, and inclusion. The challenge is in sifting through the philosophies and the research findings and then designing a plan that is appropriate and supportive to specific children and their families. Maintaining a developmental focus requires careful consideration of the potential outcomes and concerns regarding the placement choices. For simplicity, within the next sections we have chosen to use mainstreaming as the generic term to discuss the LREs that are being reported on from the literature.

Social Outcomes

Given a good intervention plan and strong support services, there is much indication in the literature that many children have benefited from the various opportunities to interact with normal peers that have been built into their intervention programs. For instance, for preschool children, especially those with mild to moderate special needs, researchers have found improvements in children's social behavior and play in typical settings (Bailey & McWilliam, 1990; Esposito & Koorland, 1989; Guralnick, 1986, 1990b; Guralnick & Groom, 1987, 1988; Jenkins, Odom, & Speltz, 1989; McLean & Hanline, 1990). Leonoff and Craig (1989, as quoted in Guralnick, 1990a) find that social acceptance is maximized if mainstreaming is full time. Friendship patterns at school have been found to have a broad positive effect on social inclusion in the community (Green & Stoneman, 1989). Many parents are committed to mainstreaming because they believe it is valuable in their children's preparation for the real world and that it leads to increased acceptance of their children into the community (Bailey & Winton, 1987; Green & Stoneman, 1989).

Not all research, however, is unanimous regarding the benefits of mainstreaming when specific groups of children and their families are studied. Parents whose child with a disability is enrolled in a typical setting may find themselves very isolated from the parents of normally developing children and without needed family support systems (Bailey & Winton, 1987). While it can be established that most educational systems have worked to prepare themselves to serve the academic needs of students with disabilities, it has been questioned if the social and emotional needs of these students have been adequately addressed and understood (Gliedman & Roth, 1980). The naiveté and optimism of the mainstreaming movement assumed that placement of children with handicaps in a regular education program would mitigate the psychological and interpersonal consequences of growing up with a disability (Gresham, 1984). Unfortunately, mainstreaming alone can not counteract the societal and personal issues intrinsic in the psychosocial life of the individual who has a disability. Throughout their educational experience these students may experience subtle or blatant prejudice, academic frustration, low self-esteem, low aspirations, superficial peer relationships, social isolation, and the conflicts associated with self-perceived differences (Bursack, 1989; Dubow, 1989; Gliedman & Roth, 1980; Lord, Varzos, Behrman, Wicks, & Wicks, 1990).

Complicating the social adjustment of children who are developmentally delayed is that fact that many of these children have social interaction deficits that are more delayed than expected on basis of their developmental levels (Guralnick & Weinhouse, 1984; Taylor, Asher, & Williams, 1987). Social interaction skills should be of major concern during the preschool years because such deficits during this period have been associated with subsequent and ongoing social problems, especially for children with disabilities (Anastasiow, 1986; Hartup, 1983; Hartup & Sancilio, 1986; Odom, Peterson, McConnell, & Ostrosky, 1990). Preschoolers with disabilities make fewer social initiations and social responses (Peterson & McConnell, 1993; Spicuzza, McConnell, & Odom, 1991; Strain, 1983), are less likely to engage in classroom activities that have a social context (Odom et al., 1990), and are generally less skilled in the strategies that are necessary for successful peer interactions (Guralnick, 1992). Adding to their lack of social skills is the fact that in typical settings some research finds that children without disabilities socialize and interact most frequently with other nondisabled children, leaving the children with disabilities as a separate social group with lower social status; this separation is extenuated by the degree of disability (Guralnick, 1990b; Guralnick & Groom, 1987). In addition to this tendency are findings that children with disabilities experience more isolation from their peers, need disproportionate amounts of adult availability, have attentional problems, and are the recipients of a disproportionate amount of negative behavior from their normally developing peers (Burstein, 1986; Honig & McCarron, 1988; Hundert & Houghton, 1992; Novak, Olley, & Kearney, 1980; White, 1980).

Preparing the Program

The adults in the integrated setting must have prepared the environment, the peers, and the specific intervention plan to enhance the opportunity for true integration to take place (D'Alonzo & Ledon, 1992; Gottlieb, 1990). "Integration is not easy because it represents fundamental change in the nature of who does what to whom, where and with what resources" (Strain, 1990, p. 293). Suc-

cessful mixing of children who are developing normally and children who have special needs does not happen of its own accord. It is well established that physical proximity of children with special needs and normally developing children does not, of its own accord, lead to social integration and socially positive interaction (Field, Roseman, DeStefano, & Koewler, 1982; Guralnick, 1981b; McLean & Hanline, 1990; Peterson, 1982; Strain, 1984).

Teaching Strategies

Some interventionists stress that the curriculum approach, the general quality of the program, and the quality of teaching style are of greater significance in establishing an effective intervention plan than the peers who share the setting with a child (Bailey & Winton, 1987; D'Alonzo & Ledon, 1992; Fewell & Oelwein, 1990; Green & Stoneman, 1989). For any intervention program to be highly effective, staff development must be a priority (Green & Stoneman, 1989; Klein & Sheehan, 1987). Staff must know how to create an environment that is conducive to developmentally appropriate learning and peer interaction. For instance, there is evidence that when working with young children, much more attention must be paid to the affective and emotional development of each child, not just to the intellectual and skill-specific learning that is often stressed in intervention plans. The social and emotional development of children must be nurtured and monitored as directly as motor skills and cognitive skills (Hundert & Houghton, 1992; Odom, Hoyson, Jamieson, & Strain, 1985; Sancilio, 1987). Teachers need to plan and structure experiences for social interactions (Guralnick, 1981a, 1990c; Jenkins, Odom, & Speltz, 1989).

For preschoolers, play is the natural setting for social interaction, but, unfortunately, many preschool teachers do not take advantage of play activities as a method of instruction (Mahoney, O'Sullivan, & Fors, 1989). This adds to the progressive decline in social skills for children with special needs. To support and expand social skills, teachers need to know how to use toys that encourage peer interaction, how to organize play activities in small spaces that encourage contact and how to directly mediate and facilitate play interactions (McConnell, McEvoy, & Odom, 1992). Effective teaching strategies for all young children include incidental teaching, peer and adult modeling, and allowing for spontaneity and for some error in learning (Bailey & McWilliam, 1990; Warren & Kaiser, 1986).

Concerns

The direct result of the mainstreaming, normalization, integration, and inclusion movements is that many young children with special needs are now attending a variety of day care and nursery school settings. When this works out well, it is gratifying and exciting for all involved—the child, family, staff, and peers. But if the child is not ready for the setting, or the setting is not ready for the child, the results may be negative if not destructive. These arrangements are attractive to parents because they may believe that a typical setting affords their children a more normal social experience. This type of placement plan can also be very attractive to public school systems because it fulfills the current direction of normalization and may relieve the public school from the challenge of organizing their own preschool programs. Also, if public funds are tight, it can look like a bargain to use community programs for early intervention. But Bailey and McWilliam (1990) caution us that the use of day care centers and nursery schools should be undertaken very carefully because some centers are understaffed and underprepared to deal with the intervention strategies required for young children with special needs. Some placement plans set up periodic consulting between specialists from the public schools and the staff in the day care and nursery school. This concept is popular because it seems a cost-effective method of serving a range of children in a range of settings, but here, too, efficiency alone can not be the motivating force.

Essential Components

High quality early intervention requires highly motivated and trained staff willing to work with parents and in teams to create an effective environment. Bruder (1993) reports on the specific characteristics that need to be in place for successful placement in community settings. Any proposed program adjustments must be consistent with the overriding program philosophy and must be open to family involvement and team planning. The staff must have the skills and motivation to collaborate with a broad range of outside agencies. They need the knowledge, materials, and equipment to carry out the instructional objectives that are designed by the planning and placement team. The program needs a strong commitment to staff training, and there must be an ongoing evaluation of program effectiveness.

Making the decision as to what constitutes the least restrictive environment for a particular child requires that parents and professionals objectively evaluate the child's developmental level and readiness for the challenges and benefits encountered in each available setting. Maintaining a continuum of available services, models, and programs is a prudent goal (CEC, 1993). The enthusiasm for mainstreaming, integration, and inclusion needs to be balanced by a careful analysis of what is best for a given child at a given point in his or her development. Agreeing to a premature plan for placement in a typical setting may serve to deny the severity and complexity of the developmental problem. It may be comforting to believe that by surrounding a child with normal peers, his or her developmental needs will be dissipated magically. Inappropriate placement raises the risk of children experiencing unnecessary failure or isolation. In the same way, inclusion should be initiated as soon as the child and system are deemed prepared, in order for the child to avoid unnecessary isolation. Placement of children who have special needs with their typical peers is an appropriate ultimate goal, but a carefully designed individualization plan that meets developmental needs should be the immediate goal. The philosophical pendulum is fast moving toward total inclusion, which worries some who have worked to focus on the child, not on the trend. Bailey and colleague (1990), Rimland (1993), and Strain (1990) all caution that oversimplification of the intervention planning and the blanket adoption of one model of placement for all children is imprudent.

Mainstreaming and the Supportive Play Model

Deciding on the best placement for a child is a difficult and time-consuming process. The SPM helps the staff and parents to highlight a child's current needs and to anticipate the types of service that must be in place for the child to be successful. The analysis of the observations may also help the staff realize that a particular setting is inappropriate for the child at this particular time. The decision that a child is currently in an inappropriate placement may be emotionally wrenching for most staff members to face, because we are trained to be helpful and accepting of all children. Sometimes, making the difficult decision that a child

can not function successfully in a setting and that the setting does not have the ways and means to adapt to the child is the most humane and ultimately helpful decision. When the setting can access the resources to be appropriately adaptive, then the SPM provides a wide range of suggestions for adaptations and facilitating techniques to increase the likelihood of a successful adjustment of the child.

Working through the SPM helps focus on the child's abilities and skills. At the same time, the process helps highlight some of the dynamics of the child's condition that may be impeding play, as well as circumstances of the setting that may be interfering in the child's success. The process dramatizes the interrelatedness of development in such a way that the staff and parents can understand how a disability in one area of development has ramifications across development that can complicate and compromise adjustment to a setting. Additionally, the SPM clarifies how deceptive **splinter skills** and scatter in skills can be. It is easy to set unrealistic expectations for children based on areas of apparent competency that camouflage areas where key components of development are undeveloped. Once developmental gaps have been clarified, it may be easier to understand difficulties in behavior and adjustment. The child's oppositional behavior may be the result of the lack of fit between the expectations of the setting and the child's immediate developmental needs. This insight reduces the adult's frustration with a child, making it easier to maintain motivation to work with the child.

The process of working through the SPM also encourages the staff to look carefully at their own anxieties and concerns about the child and the child's disability. Once these concerns have been discussed with team mates, the adult may find it easier to work with the child and be less apt to deny or be fixed on the manifestations of the disability. Successful mainstreaming of a child with special needs may take a great deal of energy and stir surprising emotions in the adults involved. The process can provide a wonderful stimulus for personal growth and learning on behalf of staff, but it is often not accomplished without some struggle at the personal and systems levels. Increasing staff knowledge about a disability is crucial, as is providing appropriate consultants to the staff to facilitate the process.

Increasing adult coverage in the group is also a consideration that should be explored. The presence of a child with a disability has the potential of being a very positive growth experience for the peers in the group, but not if the needs of the child with a disability leave the rest of the group deprived of appropriate adult supervision and attention. The ratio of children with special needs to normal peers also needs to be considered in order to maintain a balance in the population. In planning overall group size, it may be helpful to consider a child with special needs as being comparable to several normally developing children. Depending on the specific needs of the children with disabilities, two or three such children may be the maximum number that can easily be placed in a typical nursery class.

For the placement plan to work, it is also crucial that the normal peers be prepared and supported in this experience. Certain disabilities may be very provocative or anxiety producing to preschool children who are naturally struggling with their own feelings of mastery, physical competence, and bodily integrity and constancy. The natural competitiveness among children for attention can be exaggerated when one child requires so much individual attention and appears to live by different classroom rules.

The SPM will help staff to review these issues and be prepared for some of the realistic stresses and tensions that must be addressed to successfully support the development of the child with special needs, the normally developing peers, the family, and the staff. Mainstreaming is a developmentally appropriate goal for all children, but the extent and the timing of the plan need to be judiciously considered.

SUMMARY

The reality of the 1990s is that many children with special needs are being placed in regular nursery schools and day care settings. This change in attitude and practice is the outcome of our society's increasing awareness of the needs of children with disabilities to experience rich and full lives with their peers. It is also a recognition that children who are developing normally benefit from growing up as friends with people who are different from themselves in significant ways.

Unfortunately, even with the best intentions, if a child is placed into a setting that is not developmentally appropriate and responsive, the child can experience unnecessary distress and failure. Sometimes, a placement has been made prematurely or without adequate support systems built in for the child or the staff. In this situation, the SPM may help parents and the staff identify the areas of a program that must be fortified or redesigned. It may even happen that, after reviewing a child's program with the SPM, it becomes clear that the placement is developmentally inappropriate and that a different placement must be found.

Most typically, though, the SPM enables the early childhood team to analyze and adapt the typical nursery school environment to better meet the unique needs of these young children with special needs. This process is based on a normal developmental model and emphasizes play as a critical element in promoting normalcy across developmental areas. This model helps to keep play at the center of any intervention and facilitates compensation for the characteristic patterns that may limit typical play behavior in the special needs child.

REFERENCES

Anastasiow, N. J. (1986). *Development and disability: A psychobiological analysis for special educators.* Baltimore: Paul H. Brookes.

Bailey, D. B., Jr., & McWilliam, R. A. (1990). Normalizing early intervention. *Topics in Early Childhood Special Education, 10*(2), 33–47.

Bailey, D. B., Jr., & Winton, P. J. (1987). Stability and change in parents' expectations about mainstreaming. *Topics in Early Childhood Special Education, 7*(1), 73–88.

Barber, P. A., Turnbull, A. P., Behr, S. K., & Kerns, G. M. (1988). A family systems perspective on early childhood special education. In S. L. Odom & M. B. Karnes (Eds.), *Early intervention for infants and children with handicaps* (pp. 179–198). Baltimore: Paul H. Brookes.

Beckman, P. J. (1983). Influence of selected child characteristics on stress in families of handicapped infants. *American Journal of Mental Deficiency, 88*(2), 150–156.

Beckman, P. J. (1991). Comparison of mothers' and fathers' perceptions of the effect of young children with and without disabilities. *American Journal on Mental Retardation, 95*(5), 585–595.

Bromwich, R. M. (1981). *Working with parents and infants: An interactional approach.* Baltimore: University Park Press.

Brooks-Gunn, J., & Lewis, M. (1982). Development of play behavior in handicapped and normal infants. *Topics in Early Childhood Special Education, 2*(3), 14–27.

Bruder, M. B. (1993). The provision of early intervention and early childhood special education within community early childhood programs: Characteristics of effective service delivery. *Topics in Early Childhood Special Education, 13*(1), 19–37.

Buckhalt, J. A., Rutherford, R. B., & Goldberg, K. E. (1978). Verbal and nonverbal interaction of mothers with their Down's syndrome and nonretarded infants. *American Journal of Mental Deficiency, 82*(4), 337–343.

Bursack, W. (1989). A comparison of students with learning disabilities to low achieving and higher achieving students on three dimensions of social competence. *The Journal of Learning Disabilities, 22*(3), 188–194.

Burstein, N. D. (1986). The effects of classroom organization on mainstreamed preschool children. *Exceptional Children, 52*(5), 425–434.

CEC Policy on Inclusive Schools and Community Settings. (1993, May). *Teaching Exceptional Children, 25*(4) (Suppl.).

Cicchetti, D., & Sroufe, L. A. (1976). The relationship between affective and cognitive development in Down's syndrome infants. *Child Development, 47*, 920–929.

D'Alonzo, B. J., & Ledon, C. (1992). Successful inclusion of children with disabilities with nondisabled peers in early intervention and preschool settings. *The Transdisciplinary Journal, 2*(4), 227–283.

Donovan, A. M. (1988). Family stress and ways of coping with adolescents who have handicaps: Maternal perceptions. *American Journal on Mental Retardation, 92*(6), 502–509.

Dubow, S. (1989). "Into the turbulent mainstream"—A legal perspective on the weight to be given to the least restrictive environment in placement decisions for deaf children. *Journal of Law and Education, 18*(2), 215–228.

Dunst, C. J. & Trivette, C. M. (1990). Assessment of social support in early intervention programs. In S. J. Meisels & J. P. Shonkoff (Eds.), *Handbook of early childhood intervention.* Cambridge: Cambridge University Press.

Education for All Handicapped Children Act of 1975. 20 U.S.C. §1401. (1975)

Eheart, B. K. (1982). Mother–child interactions with nonretarded and mentally retarded preschoolers. *American Journal of Mental Deficiency, 87*(1), 20–25.

Esposito, B. G., & Koorland, M. A. (1989). Play behavior of hearing impaired children: Integrated and segregated settings. *Exceptional Children, 55*(5), 412–419.

Fewell, R. R. (1986). A handicapped child in the family. In R. R. Fewell & P. F. Vadasy (Eds.), *Families of handicapped children* (pp. 3–34). Austin, TX: PRO-ED.

Fewell, R. R., & Oelwein, P. L. (1990). The relationship between time in integrated environments and developmental gains in young children with special needs. *Topics in Early Childhood Special Education, 10*(2), 104–116.

Field, T., Roseman, S., DeStefano, L. J., & Koewler, J., III. (1982). The play of handicapped preschool children with handicapped and nonhandicapped peers in integrated and nonintegrated situations. *Topics in Early Childhood Special Education, 2*(3), 28–38.

Foley, G. M. (1982). The principles of observation. In M. Frank (Ed.) *The puzzling child: From recognition to treatment* (pp. 13–17). New York: Haworth Press.

Foley, G. M. (1983). The grief cycle. In N. J. Anastasiow, *Development and disability: A psychobiological analysis for special educators.* Baltimore: Paul H. Brookes.

Foley, G. M. (1986). Family development planning: An intervention model for working with parents of handicapped children. In J. Levy, P. Levy, & B. Niven (Eds.), *Model program and new technologies for people with disabilities.* New York: Young Adult Institute.

Foley, G. M., Hochman, J. D., & Miller, S. (1994). Parent–professional relationships: Finding an optimal distance. *Zero to Three, 14*(4), 19–22.

Fraiberg, S. (1980). *Clinical studies in infant mental health.* New York: Basic Books.

Frey, K. S., Fewell, R. R., & Vadasy, P. (1989). Parental adjustment and changes in child outcome among families of young handicapped children. *Topics in Early Childhood Special Education, 8*(4), 38–57.

Gallagher, J. J., Beckman, P. J., & Cross, A. H. (1983). Families of handicapped children: Sources of stress and its amelioration. *Exceptional Children, 50*(1), 10–19.

Gardner, R. A. (1969). The guilt reaction of parents of children with severe physical disease. *American Journal of Psychiatry, 126*(5), 636–644.

Gath, A. (1977). The impact of an abnormal child upon parents. *British Journal of Psychiatry, 130,* 405–410.

Gliedman, J., & Roth, W. (1980). *The unexpected minority: Handicapped children in America.* New York: Harcourt Brace Jovanovich.

Goffman, E. (1963). *Stigma.* Englewood Cliffs, NJ: Prentice-Hall.

Goldman, B., & Johnson-Martin, N. (1987, March). *Understanding babies' cues: A comparison of parents of normally developing and handicapped infants.* Paper presented at the biennial meeting of the Society for Research and Child Development, Baltimore.

Gottlieb, J. (1990). Mainstreaming and quality education. *American Journal on Mental Retardation, 95*(1), 16–17.

Gowen, J. W., Johnson-Martin, N., Goldman, B. D., & Appelbaum, M. (1989). Feelings of depression and parenting competence of mothers of handicapped and nonhandicapped infants: A longitudinal study. *American Journal on Mental Retardation, 94*(3), 259–271.

Green, A. L., & Stoneman, Z. (1989). Attitudes of mothers and fathers of nonhandicapped children. *Journal of Early Intervention, 13*(4), 292–304.

Gresham, F. M. (1984). Social skills and self-efficacy for exceptional children. *Exceptional Children, 51*(3), 253–261.

Gumz, E. J., & Gubrium, J. F. (1972). Comparative parental perceptions of a mentally retarded child. *American Journal of Mental Deficiency, 77*(2), 175–180.

Gunn, P., & Berry, P. (1985). The temperament of Down's Syndrome toddlers and their siblings. *Journal of Child Psychology and Psychiatry, 26*(6), 973–979.

Guralnick, M. J. (1981a). Programmatic factors affecting child–child social interactions in mainstreamed preschool programs. *Exceptional Education Quarterly, 1*(4), 71–91.

Guralnick, M. J. (1981b). The social behavior of preschool children at different developmental levels: Effects of group composition. *Journal of Experimental Child Psychology, 31*(1), 115–130.

Guralnick, M. J. (1986). The application of child development principles and research to preschool mainstreaming. In C. J. Meisel (Ed.), *Mainstreaming handicapped children: Outcomes, controversies, and new directions* (pp. 21–41). Hillsdale, NJ: Erlbaum.

Guralnick, M. J. (1990a). Major accomplishments and future directions in childhood mainstreaming. *Topics in Early Childhood Special Education, 10*(2), 1–17.

Guralnick, M. J. (1990b). Peer interactions and the development of handicapped children's social and communicative competence. In H. C. Foot, M. J. Morgan, & R. H. Shute (Eds.), *Children helping children* (pp. 275–305). Chichester, England: Wiley.

Guralnick, M. J. (1990c). Social competence and early intervention. *Journal of Early Intervention, 14*(1), 3–14.

Guralnick, M. J. (1992). A hierarchical model for understanding children's peer-related social competence. In S. L. Odom, S. R. McConnell, & M. A. McEvoy (Eds.), *Social competence of young children with disabilities: Issues and strategies for intervention* (pp. 37–64). Baltimore: Paul H. Brookes.

Guralnick, M. J., & Groom, J. M. (1987). The peer relations of mildly delayed and nonhandicapped preschool children in mainstreamed playgroups. *Child Development, 58,* 1556–1572.

Guralnick, M. J., & Groom, J. M. (1988). Peer interactions in mainstreamed and specialized classrooms: A comparative analysis. *Exceptional Children, 54*(5), 415–425.

Guralnick, M. J., & Weinhouse, E. (1984). Peer-related social interactions of developmentally delayed young children: Development and characteristics. *Developmental Psychology, 20*(5), 815–827.

Hare, E. H., Laurence, K. M., Paynes, H., & Rawnsley, K. (1966). Spina bifida cystica and family stress. *British Medical Journal, 2,* 757–760.

Hartup, W. W. (1983). Peer relations. In P. H. Mussen (Ed.), *Handbook of child psychology: Vol. IV* (4th ed., pp. 103–196). New York: Wiley.

Hartup, W. W., & Sancilio, M. F. (1986). Children's friendships. In E. Schopler & G. B. Mesibov (Eds.), *Social behavior in autism* (pp. 61–79). New York: Plenum.

Holroyd, J., & McArthur, D. (1976). Mental retardation and stress on the parents: A contrast between Down's syndrome and childhood autism. *American Journal of Mental Deficiency, 80,* 431–436.

Honig, A. S., & McCarron, P. A. (1988). Prosocial behaviors of handicapped and typical peers in an integrated preschool. *Early Child Development and Care, 33,* 113–125.

Hundert, J., & Houghton, A. (1992). Promoting social interaction of children with disabilities in integrated preschools: A failure to generalize. *Exceptional Children, 58*(4), 311–320.

Jenkins, J. R., Odom, S. L., & Speltz, M. C. (1989). Effects of social integration on preschool children with handicaps. *Exceptional Children, 55*(5), 420–428.

Kashani, J. H. (1986). Self-esteem of handicapped children and adolescents. *Developmental Medicine and Child Neurology, 28,* 77–83.

Klein, N., & Sheehan, R. (1987). Staff development: A key issue in meeting the needs of young handicapped children in day care settings. *Topics in Early Childhood Special Education, 7*(1), 13–27.

Koeske, G. F., & Koeske, R. D. (1990). The buffering effect of social support on parental stress. *American Journal of Orthopsychiatry, 60,* 440–451.

Levitt, M. J., Weber, R. A., & Clark, M. C. (1986). Social network relationships as sources of maternal support and well-being. *Developmental Psychology, 22,* 310–316.

Lipsky, D. K. (1985). A parental perspective on stress and coping. *American Journal of Orthopsychiatry, 55*(4), 614–617.

Lord, J., Varzos, N., Behrman, B., Wicks, J., & Wicks, D. (1990). Implications of mainstream classrooms for adolescents with spina bifida. *Developmental Medicine and Child Neurology, 32,* 20–29.

MacTurk, R. H., Hunter, F. T., McCarthy, M. E., Vietze, P. M., & McQuiston, S. (1985). Social mastery motivation in Down Syndrome and nondelayed infants. *Topics in Early Childhood Special Education, 4*(4), 93–109.

Mahoney, G., O'Sullivan, P., & Fors, S. (1989). Special education practices with young handicapped children. *Journal of Early Intervention, 13*(3), 261–268.

Maurer, H., & Sherrod, K. B. (1987). Context of directives given to young children with Down Syndrome and nonretarded children: Development over two years. *American Journal of Mental Deficiency, 91,* 579–590.

McConnell, S. R., McEvoy, M. A., & Odom, S. L. (1992). Implementation of social competence interventions in early childhood special education classes: Current practices and future directions. In S. L. Odom, S. R. McConnell, & M. A. McEvoy (Eds.), *Social competence of young children with disabilities: Issues and strategies for intervention* (pp. 277–306). Baltimore: Paul H. Brookes.

McLean, M., & Hanline, M. F. (1990). Providing early intervention services in integrated environments: Challenges and opportunities for the future. *Topics in Early Childhood Special Education, 10*(2), 62–77.

McLean, M., & Odom, S. (1988). *Least restrictive environment and social integration.* Division for Early Childhood White Paper. Reston, VA.

Moroz, K. (1989). Educating autistic children and youths: A school–family–community partnership. *Social Work in Education, 11*(2), 107–122.

Nirje, B. (1985). The basis and logic of the normalization principle. *Australia and New Zealand Journal of Developmental Disabilities, 11*(2), 65–68.

Novak, M. A., Olley, J. G., & Kearney, D. S. (1980). Social skills of children with special needs in integrated and separate preschools. In T. M. Field, S. Goldberg, D. Stern, & A. M. Sostek (Eds.), *High-risk infants and children* (pp. 327–346). New York: Academic Press.

Odom, S. L. (1989). *LRE, mainstreaming and integration for young children with disabilities: A decade of research.* Chapel Hill, NC: National Early Childhood Technical Assistance System (NECTAS).

Odom, S. L., Hoyson, M., Jamieson, B., & Strain, P. S. (1985). Increasing handicapped preschoolers' peer social interactions: Cross-setting and component analysis. *Journal of Applied Behavior Analysis, 18,* 3–16.

Odom, S. L., & McEvoy, M. A. (1988). Integration of young children with handicaps and normally developing children. In S. L. Odom & M. B. Karnes (Eds.), *Early intervention for infants and children with handicaps: An empirical base* (pp. 241–268). Baltimore: Paul H. Brookes.

Odom, S. L., Peterson, C., McConnell, S., & Ostrosky, M. (1990). Ecobehavioral analysis of early education/specialized classroom settings and peer social interaction. *Education and Treatment of Children, 13*(4), 316–330.

Oster, A. (1984). Keynote address of the conference "Comprehensive Approach to Disabled and At-Risk Infants, Toddlers and Their Families". December 1984, Washington, DC. Reprinted in *Equals in this partnership: Parents of disabled and at-risk infants and toddlers speak to professionals* (pp. 26–32). Washington, DC: National Center for Clinical Infant Programs.

Peterson, N. L. (1982). Social integration of handicapped and non-handicapped preschoolers: A study of playmate preferences. *Topics in Early Childhood Special Education, 2*(2), 56–59.

Peterson, C. A., & McConnell, S. R. (1993). Factors affecting the impact of social interaction skills interventions in early childhood special education. *Topics in Early Childhood Special Education, 13*(1), 38–56.

Rimland, B. (1993). Inclusive education: Right for some. *Autism Research Review: International, 7*(1), 3.

Salisbury, C. L. (1991). Mainstreaming during the early childhood years. *Exceptional Children, 58*(2), 146–155.

Sancilio, M. F. M. (1987). Peer interaction as a method of therapeutic intervention with children. *Clinical Psychology Review, 7*, 475–500.

Serving handicapped children: A special report. (1988). Boston: Robert Wood Johnson Foundation.

Shapiro, J. (1983). Family reactions and coping strategies in response to the physically ill or handicapped child: A review. *Social Science and Medicine, 17*(14), 913–931.

Shonkoff, J. P., Hauser-Cram, P., Krauss, M. W., & Upshur, C. C. (1992). Development of infants with disabilities and their families: Implications for theory and service delivery. *Monographs of the Society for Research in Child Development, 57*(6, Serial No. 230).

Solnit, A. J. & Stark, M. H. (1961). Mourning and the birth of a defective child. *The Psychoanalytic Study of the Child, 16*, 523–537.

Spicuzza, R. J., McConnell, S. R., & Odom, S. L. (1991, May). *Normative analysis of social interaction behavior for children with and without disabilities: Implications for intervention.* Paper presented at the 14th annual conference of the Association for Behavior Analysis, Atlanta, GA.

Stoneman, Z., Brody, G. H., & Abbott, D. (1983). In-home observations of young Down syndrome children with their mothers and fathers. *American Journal of Mental Deficiency, 87*, 591–600.

Strain, P. S. (1983). Identification of social skill curriculum targets for severely handicapped children in mainstream preschools. *Applied Research in Mental Retardation, 4*, 369–382.

Strain, P. S. (1984). Social behavior patterns of nonhandicapped and developmentally disabled friend pairs in mainstream preschools. *Analysis and Intervention in Developmental Disabilities, 4*(1), 15–28.

Strain, P. S. (1990). LRE for preschool children with handicaps: What we know, what we should be doing. *Journal of Early Intervention, 14*(4), 291–296.

Taylor, A. R., Asher, S. R., & Williams, G. A. (1987). The social adaptation of mainstreamed mildly retarded children. *Child Development, 58*, 1321–1334.

Taylor, S. J., Biklen, D., Lehr, S., & Searl, S. J. (1987). *Purposeful integration . . . inherently equal.* Syracuse, NY: Center on Human Policy, Syracuse University.

Trout, M. (1988). Infant mental health: Monitoring our movement into the twenty-first century. *Infant Mental Health Journal, 9*(3), 191–200.

Trout, M., & Foley, G. (1989). Working with families of handicapped infants and toddlers. *Topics in Language Disorders, 10*(1), 57–67.

Turnbull, A. P., & Turnbull, H. R., III (1986). Stepping back from early intervention: An ethical perspective. *Journal for the Division of Early Childhood, 10*(2), 106–117.

Vadasy, P. F., Fewell, R. R., Meyer, D. J., & Schell, G. (1984). Siblings of handicapped children: A developmental perspective on family interactions. *Family Relations, 33*, 155–167.

Warren, S. F., & Kaiser, A. P. (1986). Incidental language teaching: A critical review. *Journal of Speech and Hearing Disorders, 51*, 291–299.

White, B. N. (1980). Mainstreaming in grade school and preschool: How the child with special needs interacts with peers. In T. M. Field, S. Goldberg, D. Stern, & A. M. Sostek (Eds.), *High-risk infants and children* (pp. 347–371). New York: Academic Press.

Case Examples Using the Supportive Play Model

Each of the chapters in Part II focuses on a major area of developmental disability: hearing impairment, motor impairments with related chronic medical issues, autism and pervasive developmental disorders, and children affected by multiple risk factors. Each chapter includes a review of the literature concerning the developmental issues frequently found associated with the area of disability. Additionally, each chapter contains an illustrative case study that demonstrates the application of the SPM. These fictitious case studies are composites from our experience in the field and from real case material. In all case studies, we have disguised any specific identifying information that would breach confidentiality. We constructed each case example to demonstrate a range of applications related to the various aspects of the SPM. Included in the first case study of the child with hearing loss (Chapter 4) is a completed SPM chart. By reviewing this filled-out chart, the reader can see an example of how a team can use the SPM to design changes needed for this particular child. Chapters 5, 6, and 7 each contain an additional case study that is representative of many of the children with disabilities who are currently attending nursery school, Head Start, or special education programs, but these last three chapters do not include completed SPM charts. Instead it is recommended that you experiment with completing the chart found at the end of Chapter 2 for each case while reading through the chapter. Our narrative in these chapters explains our main observations about the child and describes in detail some of the interventions that we recommend. In these chapters, you can compare your decisions as recorded on the chart with our suggestions. There is no set answer or solution to the issues that are raised in using this process with a child, but by practicing with these three last case studies, you will gain confidence and experience using the SPM process and will be ready to use the process in the field.

CHAPTER 4

Application of the Supportive Play Model to a Child with a Moderate Hearing Impairment

It is currently recommended that the majority of children with hearing impairments be mainstreamed into regular classroom settings with appropriate support services (Paul & Quigley, 1990). Because these children often look normal, have average or above average intelligence, and are believed to have had their problem minimized by their hearing aids, it is often assumed that their needs can be quite easily met in a regular education setting. Although it is well known that hearing impairment results in speech and language problems, it may be surprising for teachers to discover that hearing impairment can have a dramatic and penetrating impact on a child's overall development. With reduced, altered, modified, or no auditory information, children may experience a great deal of difficulty structuring their sense of reality as well as perceiving and interpreting the experience of others, objects, and themselves (Sanders, 1980).

This chapter includes general background information on hearing impairment and its impact on self/social/emotional;

communicative/language; cognitive; and play development. There is a discussion of medical and educational interventions that are used with children who have hearing impairments. Many of the developmental and intervention issues discussed are then illustrated by a case study of a child with moderate hearing impairment who is mainstreamed in a nursery school. The use of the SPM is briefly described and the notations are recorded on a completed SPM chart at the end of the chapter.

GENERAL BACKGROUND ON HEARING IMPAIRMENT

Approximately 1% of all children are born with or grow up with a persistent hearing loss (Glorig & Roberts, 1977). One third of the children with hearing impairments also have either visual, learning, or mental disabilities (Karchmer, 1985). It can be assumed that the current incidence rate of hearing impairment is declining because some causes are under better control (for example, because of the availability of rubella vaccine), but other current medical changes, such as the increased success in saving very premature and low-birth-weight infants, have led to the incidence rate staying relatively unchanged (Robertson & Whyte, 1983).

There are several types of hearing loss that may affect a child's development. Sensorineural loss is the result of damage to the inner ear or to the auditory nerve. This damage can happen either prenatally or be acquired through illness or from insult by medication or injury. This type of loss is typically not treatable by medication or surgery (except in cases where a **cochlear implant** is feasible), but can be modified by sound amplification. Conductive losses are the result of malfunction of the Eustachian tube, resulting from middle-ear infections, or may be caused by a range of problems, such as structural anomalies in the outer or middle ear, genetic syndromes, or traumatic head injury. Some of these conductive losses can be helped medically, but amplification of sound may also be necessary. Hearing loss may also be due to a combination of sensorineural and conductive losses; this is referred to as mixed hearing loss. Only about 20% of hearing loss is unilateral (affecting one ear), with the vast majority of hearing impairment being bilateral (affecting both ears) (Bess & Tharpe, 1984).

Degree of hearing loss is an important factor in understanding its impact on development. Hearing impairment is generally defined by the decibel (dB) amount of hearing loss experienced by the individual in the better ear, without hearing aids. Across the life span, a mild loss (27–40 dB) is experienced by approximately 40% of individuals with hearing impairment. Northern and Downs (1991) believe that, in children, this category should be expanded downward to include those with a hearing loss of even 15 dB, because this degree of loss is considered significant enough to cause problems in language perception and acquisition in the young child. Individuals with mild hearing losses may be able to understand conversations when they are in a face-to-face situation, but they may miss auditory information when there is environmental noise, and they are also likely to experience a mild language delay. A moderate hearing loss (41–55 dB) is experienced by 20% of the hearing-impaired population. Children with a moderate loss miss 50 to 80% of normal conversation; they have problems with auditory learning and articulation and experience language and speech delays. Those with moderate to severe loss (56–70 dB) miss all unamplified speech information and may not be able to under-

stand amplified speech; they have delayed language and syntax, atonal voice, and reduced speech intelligibility. An additional 20% experience a severe loss (71–90 dB) and another 20% of this population have a profound loss (over 90 dB). Individuals with severe and profound losses may not hear a loud voice right near their ear, can not even hear amplified speech, may not develop oral speech, and have speech and language disorders (Anderson, 1991; Glorig & Roberts, 1977; Paul & Quigley, 1990; "Report of the Ad Hoc Committee," 1975). Gaining clear oral language is most difficult for the prelingually hearing impaired who have never clearly heard the human voice. Having hearing for part of infancy or into toddlerhood has a major impact on a child's success in developing oral communication (Northern & Lemme, 1982). In general, the more severe the hearing loss, the greater the impact on the rate of language learning (Ling, 1984a,1984b).

Half of the causes of hearing impairment are genetic, half are environmental (National Information Center on Deafness, 1989). One in 20,000 children suffers from 1 of 200 inherited disorders, such as Down syndrome, cleft palate, Waardenburg's syndrome, and Hunter's syndrome, that are associated with hearing impairments (Kirk, Gallagher, & Anastasiow, 1993; Konigsmark & Gorlin, 1976; National Information Center on Deafness, 1989). Maternal diabetes, Rh negative factor, toxoplasmosis, rubella, cytomegalovirus, and herpes simplex virus are the major environmental and prenatal causes of deafness in the United States (Kirk et al., 1993). Other acquired causes include noise pollution; infections, such as **meningitis,** mumps, measles, and chicken pox; asphyxia; complications from prematurity and low birth weight; and damage to the cochlea from certain antibiotics and head trauma (Harada, Iwamori, Nagai, & Nomura, 1986; Kirk et al., 1993; Miller, Cradock-Watson, & Pollock, 1982; Northern & Downs, 1991; Salamy, Eldredge, & Tooley, 1989).

Of acquired losses, the vast majority are conductive and caused by chronic otitis media (middle ear infections) (Northern & Downs, 1991). Many children are susceptible to middle ear infections because of the structure of the young child's ear, but children with cleft palate and Down syndrome are particularly susceptible. One in 900 children are born with cleft palate. Their susceptibility to persistent middle ear infections may result in conductive hearing loss (Grant, Quiney, Mercer, & Lodge, 1988). Children with Down syndrome also have a high incidence rate of middle ear infection and accompanying hearing loss (Batshaw & Perret, 1992). Chronic otitis media can be deceptive in its role in hearing loss: frequently, the level of hearing loss fluctuates, so that a child may pass a hearing screening, yet, within a few days, experience a period of appreciable hearing loss.

There is often an extended delay in diagnosing hearing impairment, and serious underestimation of the impact of hearing loss (McCrae, 1986). Despite great strides in the technology and techniques available for diagnosing hearing loss in infants and young children, many children are not diagnosed until they are between the ages of 2 and 5 (Batshaw & Perret, 1992; Coplan, 1987). The under-identification of children with hearing impairment may be due to the subtlety of the early symptoms. Even when severely hearing impaired, infants in the first 6 months all utter the same kind of sounds, making it difficult to notice behavioral differences. Children with mild and moderate losses can become very skilled at interpreting tone and gesture, even if they do not easily understand all words, so that it may take a clear delay in language development before parents or pediatricians seek out hearing testing.

THE IMPACT OF A HEARING IMPAIRMENT ON EARLY DEVELOPMENT

It is logical that a hearing impairment will affect speech development, but, as discussed earlier, it may not be as immediately clear that a hearing loss can have a far more global impact on a child's development. This section highlights some of the key areas of development that may be compromised by a hearing loss. We have organized the following sections to coincide with major developmental areas that are used in the SPM chart. The area of motor development is not included because this area has not received emphasis in the available research, and play skills and play themes are combined into the single area of play.

Self/Social–Emotional Development

Sound is very important in early development, not only for the ultimate development of language, but also because hearing is a sense that connects the prenatal and newborn infant to his or her immediate environment and offers a source of relationship building. Sensory deprivation experienced by children who are blind and visually impaired has been studied extensively as a source of challenge to early psychosocial development (Burlingham, 1965; Fraiberg, 1968; Omwake, 1968). Hearing impairment may have some of the same complications in the development of the young child, although these ideas are not as thoroughly defined in the literature. We do know that from the 7th month of the pregnancy, babies are able to hear and respond to sound and that, typically, newborns prefer female voices and, most specifically, their mother's voice (Brazelton, 1975; DeCasper & Fifer, 1980). In a child with normal hearing, the reception and processing of sound provides a continuity of sensory experience that bridges the prenatal and neonatal periods (DeCasper & Spence, 1986). The neonate responds specifically to sound in a fashion that shows attunement by matching its body movements to the patterns of human speech (Brazelton, Tronick, Adamson, Als, & Wise, 1975; Condon & Sander, 1974). This subtle response to the spoken word may be crucial in early relationship-building behavior between a baby and its parents. Terhune (1979) suggests that the ability to hear and respond to the human voice may be the first agent of early ego organization.

The auditory and vocal contribution to ego organization is complex. The mother's voice is a source of comfort and pleasure. Infants, knowing their mother's voice, are able to be calmed, to stop agitated physical action, to be helped in regulation of impulses, and to wait for a short period of time to have their needs met. This power of regulation indicates an awareness of a need-gratifying object. The memory of the mother's voice, being able to hear the mother's comings and goings, and the mother being able to call out and reach the baby, even over a distance, serves as a contribution to the construction of **object permanence** and object constancy. The human voice is saturated with feeling, so it is true deprivation when the baby is not able to hear the parent's voice. From the parent's perspective, the infant's early gestural responses to sound are part of the two-way communication pattern that is crucial to attachment. If the baby is not hearing sound well, and the parents do not realize it, their baby's signals can be subtly different from and out of synchrony with the parents' attempts to verbally comfort and communicate. The more handicapped the baby is in joining these communication exchanges, the more at risk is the infant–parent attachment (Kessler, 1988).

In preschoolers, communicative competence between children with hearing impairments and their parents has a strong positive relationship to levels of attachment (Greenberg & Marvin, 1979). Similarly, parents who were able to use both verbal and manual methods (sign language, finger spelling, pantomimes, and gestures) with their children who were profoundly hearing impaired, had a more successful interchange, with more touching, child compliance, eye contact, laughter, and play (Greenberg, 1980).

Much of the research supports that social–emotional development is imperiled in children with hearing impairment. Such children have demonstrated an increased risk of behavioral and psychological problems as well as social isolation because their skills inhibit friendship patterns (Cohen, 1980; Davis, 1977; Davis, Elfenbein, Schum, & Bentler, 1986; Freeman, Malkin, & Hastings, 1975; Gentile & McCarthy, 1973; Harris, 1978; Jensema & Trybus, 1975; Macklin & Matson, 1985; Meadow, 1980,1984; Schwartz, 1987). These difficulties may be the result of subtle neurological problems associated with some of the genetic or environmental causes of their hearing impairment, or they may be the result of a full range of family, school, and environmental issues that exaggerate the social–emotional consequences of the hearing impairment.

Repeated research has identified specific characteristics in many individuals with hearing impairments, such as rigidity, egocentricity, absence of inner controls, impulsivity, and suggestibility (Meadow, 1980). Chess and Fernandez (1980) and Meadow (1980) argue, however, that there is no "deaf personality type," but rather a true diversity in individuals who have hearing disabilities that reflects their individual experiences, their education, and their skill in communication. Interestingly, Meadow (1984) did not find social–emotional maladjustment in preschoolers who had hearing impairment and no other handicaps. She suggests that hearing impairment may have a cumulative impact on social adjustment and social interaction that may not be as discernible in this young population, but that can become more apparent as social interaction skills become more complex and communication expectations become more demanding.

Communitive/Language Development

Speech, language, and communication development is typically affected to some degree by the presence of hearing loss. The degree of impairment in these areas varies with several factors, including type and severity of hearing loss, age of onset, general developmental status, the presence of other developmental disorders or conditions, and environmental factors.

Because of rapid brain development in the first 2 years of life, the current emphasis in early intervention is to encourage alternative communication rather than oral speech in the young child who has a hearing impairment. The spurt in brain development, particularly between the 1st and 2nd birthday, provides the child with the internalized capacity for memory and symbolism (McCrae, 1986). It is now understood that a language (oral speech, sign language, or finger spelling) needs to be acquired during the critical early years or there may be long-term communicative, social, and academic consequences. Children with hearing impairments who have parents who are also hearing impaired have an advantage in that their parents are more attuned to the early gestural behaviors that are the precursors of a signed system of speech. These parents are also more able to develop effective responsive interactions that are based on visual signals (Spencer, Bodner-Johnson, & Gutfreund, 1992). Research has also shown that with early diagnosis and amplification, babies and toddlers who have hearing mothers are capable of producing a normal level of intentional preverbal or gestural communications, but that they develop delays in their production of **formal symbolic communication** by 18 months (Spencer, 1993). Other than delays in language production, children with hearing impairments may also have difficulty in generating the rules of grammar and in understanding the pragmatics of language use that are integral to effective communication (Paul & Quigley, 1991). Early intervention with a consistent exposure to oral and gestural language, both at home and at school, is essential for infants and toddlers to have the maximum opportunity to develop the internalized symbolic system that will allow for their most advanced social, communicative, and cognitive development (Kirk et al., 1993).

Cognitive Development

It is important to emphasize that the majority of children with hearing impairment have normal intelligence, but documenting this presents challenges because most IQ tests place an emphasis on verbal skills (Schlesinger, 1983). Research also repeatedly highlights the life-long difficulty many persons with deafness and hearing impairment have with language-based academic tasks (Gleason, 1985; Quigley, 1969; Trybus & Karchmer, 1977). Currently, there is some research indicating improved long-term academic performance in individuals who are deaf and hearing impaired, a trend that may reflect the current increase in early intervention and a more flexible philosophy regarding communication and language (Allen, 1986; Brown & Karchmer, 1987; Moores, 1989). But it is still true that, in general, individuals with hearing impairment do not fare as well academically as would be expected based on their innate intelligence, nor do they approach national norms. The factors that carry the most weight in academic success are similar to those associated with communication outcomes: the time of onset and degree of hearing loss suffered, the age at amplification and initiation of therapy, and the richness of language and experience available to the child (Jensema, 1975; Paul & Quigley, 1990). Early diagnosis, the provision of effective amplification and auditory training, speech and language therapy, and, if appropriate, the availability of sign and total communication, all affect the child's learning potential, along with his or her self/social/emotional adjustment with family and peers.

Play Skills and Themes

Because play is such a crucial aspect of the preschooler's learning and social experience, a hearing impairment may affect play development subtly and negatively. Although there is little research that looks directly at the play skills of young children with hearing impairments (Quinn & Rubin, 1984; Rubin, Fein, & Vandenberg, 1983), play at the sensorimotor level is generally assumed to be unaffected by hearing impairment (Rogers, 1983), and symbolic play skills are generally normal (Mayberry, Wodlinger-Cohen, & Goldin-Meadow, 1987). However, delays in object substitution and imaginative play have been documented in the learning of children with hearing impairment; these delays may vary by socioeconomic status, age of onset of hearing loss, age at amplification, and language experience (Darbyshire, 1977; Mogford, 1977).

Findings indicate that children with normal hearing spend more time in associative imaginative play than do equally competent children with hearing impairments. The latter tend to prefer solitary imaginative and noninteractive construction activities (Higginbotham & Baker, 1981; Mann, 1981, 1984; Schirmer, 1989a, 1989b). Even at the preschool age, hearing children initiate play more frequently with another hearing child than with a child who is hearing impaired (Arnold & Tremblay, 1979). Research has shown that it is communicative competence, not language skill *per se*, that has a facilitating affect on the interactive–imaginative play of children with hearing impairments with their parents (Greenberg, 1980; Pien, 1984) and peers (Lederberg, Ryan, & Robbins, 1986). Additionally, it is suggested by Kaplan and McHale (1979) that hearing peers need to be taught to repeat and modify communication efforts that may be initially ignored by the child with hearing impairment. Without such persistent efforts on the part of hearing peers, the child with a hearing impairment may be deprived of sufficient play interactions and suffer undue isolation. Mann (1981, 1984) suggests that the teacher must become an active play partner with the child with a hearing impairment to directly facilitate interactive play.

TRENDS IN INTERVENTION

There are two major aspects of intervention that must be investigated for any child who is discovered to have a hearing loss. Currently, interventions for children with hearing impairment can include medical and/or surgical management, amplification decisions, speech and language training, and educational interventions. This section will highlight issues relative to these topics and give background information that will be helpful to the reading of the case study.

Medical Intervention

As was previously explained, ear infections are one common cause of hearing loss. It is crucial that all ear infections in children be treated rapidly and consistently in order to reduce the risks of permanent hearing loss (Bluestone & Klein, 1988). Generally, the treatment is with antibiotics, but when infections are persistent, surgical incision of the eardrum (myringotomy), accompanied by placement of pressure equalizing tubes to drain the middle ear, may be warranted. Some children may have their adenoids removed at the same time, if they are so swollen as to interfere with hearing (Batshaw & Perret, 1992). Cochlear implants are now being performed on children who are older than 2 years, have a profound loss, and who have not experienced any improvement in sound reception from hearing aids. The implant is surgically attached to the cochlea, a receiver is buried in the temporal bone, and the individual wears a microphone and transmitter that receive incoming sound and convey it to the implant. The implant provides electrical current to stimulate the remaining auditory nerve fibers, allowing sound impulses to be transmitted to the brain where the individual can learn to interpret them. The degree of improved language recognition varies greatly among individuals, but as this surgery becomes more common, children with cochlear implants will be more common in the preschool-age and school-age population (House, Berliner, & Luxford, 1987; Kveton & Balkany, 1991).

Amplification and Education

The Education for All Handicapped Children Act of 1975 (PL 94-142), the Education of the Handicapped Act Amendments of 1986—Part H (PL 99-457), and the Education of the Handicapped Act Amendments of 1990 (PL 101-476) have all mandated services for hearing impairments, including hearing testing, hearing aid fittings, assistive technology, speech–language therapy, and special education services (Ferguson, Hicks, & Pfau, 1988). Early amplification and early intervention are crucial because even mild hearing losses, if not remediated, can lead to permanent loss in language development and academic success (Meadow, 1980; Northern & Lemme, 1982). Although proper amplification through hearing aids can raise the range of sound that a child hears by 10 to 60 decibels (Sandlin, 1988), it does not provide normal hearing. Specialized training is necessary for children to gain maximum benefit from their amplification. Most children who wear hearing aids can be helped further, especially while in group settings, by being fitted with a wireless auditory training system that allows a teacher, parent, or peer who wears a wireless microphone to send a direct auditory signal to the child. This device transmits the speaker's voice louder than surrounding environmental sounds and allows the speaker to move away from the child without loss of volume.

Historically, there have been strong philosophical differences among specialists teaching children who are hearing impaired and deaf. There was a time in the late 19th century and early in this century when educators believed that every child, no matter how severe his or her hearing loss, should be trained to use oral speech. More recently, many educators have come to accept that total dependency on oral communication is not realistic for some individuals with a hearing impairment. Currently, the strictly oral approach (where lip reading, amplification, and oral-only communication are used) is declining in favor, with most interventionists preferring a combination of teaching approaches that include speech, sign, natural gesture, finger spelling, lip reading, speech–language training, and amplification training (Kirk et al., 1993). Total communication approaches, which combine the simultaneous use of sign and speech, are preferred by most parents (Matkin & Matkin, 1985). American Sign Language, a distinct language with its own grammar, is sometimes referred to as the "native language" of the deaf community in the United States (Lane, 1984); however, fewer than 2% of hearing parents learn this language well enough to communicate effectively with their school-age children who have hearing impairments (Matkin & Matkin, 1985). Sign systems, such as signed English, that use English word order and grammar are easier for parents to learn (Meadow, 1980). Currently, 70% of students with hearing impairment use some type of signing, but only 35% of their families are able to use the same method to communicate at home (Paul & Quigley, 1990).

Early intervention places a great deal of emphasis on developing communication skills in the young child and on establishing reciprocal interactions between the child and parents. These interactive skills, such as reading each others' verbal and nonverbal cues, as well as understanding and enjoying each other in the context of daily activities, are crucial for emotional, social, communicative, and cognitive development in the children and for positive emotional attachment between the parents and children. Research suggests that the current emphasis on total communication may be fostering more gratifying and suc

cessful interaction between parents and their children (Greenberg, 1980), especially when compared to parent–child interaction with children who are receiving only oral training (Meadow, Greenberg, Erting, & Carmichael, 1981). No matter what communication approach is chosen by parents and professionals for the young child with hearing impairment, the intervention typically requires a high degree of dedication and involvement on behalf of the parents. The parents play a key role in the development of an intervention plan because they know best the strengths and needs of their family. Their role in direct therapy must be designed with sensitivity to their needs as well as to the child's. Since the consequences of their child's hearing impairment may make their relationship strained, it is important to be aware of the primacy of parents' enjoying their child and, within that context, to see language and communication as part of overall development.

INCLUSION OF A CHILD WITH A MODERATE HEARING IMPAIRMENT IN A NURSERY SCHOOL

The following case study illustrates some of the ways that a moderate hearing impairment can change the experience of a preschool child in nursery school. Descriptive material about the child and his current adjustment is followed by a narrative that reviews the steps of the SPM. The observational material and process steps are recorded on the charts at the end of the chapter. Finally, some of the outcomes that resulted from the intervention plan are specified.

Background Information and Initial Observation

Beginning with the fall semester, 5-year-old Peter, who has a hearing impairment, is placed in a nursery school class with 17 4-year-old classmates. Peter is the only child with identified special needs in this class. Peter wears bilateral behind-the-ear hearing aids and has a moderate hearing loss after correction. Although his speech is quite intelligible, he does have some articulation problems, and his language and communication skills are somewhat delayed. His lip-reading skills are good, but he sometimes intentionally turns away from the speaker when he suspects the message may interfere with his immediate plans. Peter has worn hearing aids since he was 3 1/2 years old and he has had speech therapy through his local public school for the past 18 months. This is his first group experience.

Peter's parents were both in their middle forties when he was born. Peter is their first and only child. They are very active advocates for Peter, but find his energy level challenging and exhausting. Peter and his parents live on a small farm where there are no neighbors who have children. His parents have registered Peter in this nursery school because they were concerned that, although Peter has above average intelligence, his lack of exposure to peers and his delayed social skills will leave him unprepared for kindergarten.

This group has a teacher, Carol, and a full-time aide, Anna. The classroom is large and open, appropriately divided by low shelving to form four major activity areas. The morning schedule includes 1 hour of free choice activities with four activities concurrently available to all the children (block corner, kitchen and dress-up, cooking today's snack, and mural painting), followed by an all-group story and singing circle time, snack, and then outside play time. Carol and Anna are available throughout the morning to observe and support the children's play and participation.

Peter's first month in this setting has been difficult from the viewpoint of the staff and peers. Peter's inability to share activities and his delay in many social skills are making his adjustment difficult. Several children are beginning to avoid him because they are afraid of his reactions. Some children are still eager to play with him because his creativity makes his play appealing. The staff is afraid that unless Peter learns how to interact more appropriately, all of the children will begin to avoid him. Peter's parents are also worried that, if this group experience can not become more successful, Peter will begin to feel negatively about school in general. It has been decided at a conference, including Peter's parents, nursery staff, and the speech and language **pathologist**, to use the SPM to gather specific information about Peter's behavior in the group. The speech and language pathologist offers to observe him for several mornings; her observations are recorded on the SPM chart at the end of this chapter. The following vignette, which takes place in the last week of September, is representative of Peter's behavior during free play, group activity, snack, and outdoor play.

For the first 20 minutes of the observation, Peter has been building a space station by himself in the block corner. Several times he has called out to Anna to show her some aspect of his project. Two children approach, admire his project, step into the block corner, and ask to help.

ANNA: Beth and Tommy like your building.
PETER: (yells) This mine. No!
ANNA: Can you show them how your rocket launches?
PETER: I fixin' the rocket. Can't fly.
ANNA: Beth or Tommy could help fix it.
PETER: No.
ANNA: There are more blocks and a rug area over there. (points to other half of the rug) Tommy and Beth can work over there.
PETER: Don't touch mine.
ANNA: Maybe in a few minutes you can let Tommy and Beth play.
PETER: No.

During the singing and story circle that follow, Peter refuses to join the group. He continues to work by himself in the block corner and makes enough noise with the blocks to cause an ongoing distraction to the group story time. When snack is prepared, he eagerly joins a table with seven other children and Anna. He seems disinterested in the conversation taking place with the children but is talkative with Anna, managing to sustain her attention and keeping her from conversing with the other children at the table.

During outdoor play, Peter is delighted to take a bike and demonstrates excellent motor control in riding it throughout the yard. When a small group of boys decide to set up a roadway using the traffic signs, Peter is unwilling to conform to the rules of the road and rides his bike recklessly through the paths, knocking down signs and narrowly missing the other children. After ignoring repeated requests for him to stop, Anna removes Peter from the playground and brings him inside. He quickly recovers from his anger and is content to sit on the couch looking through familiar story books until his mother arrives to pick him up. When he sees his mother, he bolts out the door, runs through the sandbox crushing several projects, and yells good-bye to the teachers.

Utilizing the Supportive Play Model

Now use the material in the vignette as the basis of working through the SPM for Peter. Refer to the completed SPM charts at the end of the chapter as we walk you through the steps of the process. Note that for ease of readability, items that you would underline if you were actually completing the chart are shown in *italics,* and comments that you would write in are shown in special type. The information presented in the charts is more detailed than you can glean from this single vignette because the

process is actually completed after several observations and when staff and parents concur that they have collected a representative sample. But the vignette will give you enough data to relate to the general trends reported in the charts.

Section I: Cover Sheet

On the *Cover Sheet* of the SPM chart, we note that both the staff and Peter's parents are concerned about him. Although Peter is a bright and creative child, he is not mixing well in the group and is showing signs of anxiety, aggression, and frustration in this nursery school setting.

Child: Sections II, III, and IV

In *Section II: Observational Impressions*, the underlining, which summarizes observational impressions, and codes reveal an uneven developmental pattern with a scatter of skills at the age-appropriate level, but with all working themes at the more toddler-like Level 2. His scatter is most evident in the motor, cognitive, and play skill areas, but in each case serious gaps in his development keep his working theme depressed at Level 2. Note that the most relevant working theme in each developmental area has been starred.

In completing *Section III: Skills and Outstanding Characteristics Observed*, note Peter's developmental skills as reported in the vignette and from information his teachers have gained from working with him since he joined the group. It is immediately clear that Peter has a wide variety of skills, and that, in spite of his sometimes difficult behavior, his lively and enthusiastic approach to learning make him appealing to adults. He appears to be a child who, if helped to adjust to this setting and supported in the process of recapitulating and amending the weak or missing developmental components, has a good chance of eventually taking full advantage of an integrated elementary school experience.

Next we proceed by underlining items in *Section IV: Characteristic Patterns Limiting Play*, which highlight issues that are impeding Peter's adjustment. Peter's poor impulse control, his need to control interactions with adults, and his delay in social skills with peers are all inhibitors of his play. Excellent motor skills are compromised by high activity level and lack of awareness for safety. Hearing problems directly affect communication skills and participation in all aspects of a group setting. Strong intellectual potential and an emerging capacity for symbolic content in play are compromised by fluctuating attention and limited preschool experiences. These factors limit his tolerance for peer inclusion in his play and opportunities for social learning. His play themes reflect a toddler-like egocentricity and anxiety.

Family and Program: Sections II, III, and IV

The SPM process continues with Family and Program. *Section II: Observational Guide* offers suggestions of areas to note under *Section III: General Description* regarding Family and Program. Peter's parents are highly invested in his development, but their small nuclear family and remote home environment have not provided Peter with opportunities to gain skills with peers. Peter's parents are somewhat overwhelmed by his energy level and are having a difficult time establishing consistent patterns of behavior management.

Turning to Program, note under Staff that they are pleased

about Peter's presence in their group, but stressed by his behavior. Peter's behavior requires a great deal of adult attention, and the teachers worry that the other children are losing out because Peter interrupts the activities and needs more direct supervision than most of the other children.

Peers are curious about Peter and interested in his play skills, but they are being repeatedly rebuffed by him. Peers are more socially oriented in their play and are still eager to include Peter, but do not succeed in establishing joint play experiences.

Space is generally adequate, but needs acoustic adaptations and an indoor gross motor area. Under Time, note that the schedule is basically suitable for Peter, and under Materials and Equipment it is recorded that technical and gross motor equipment need to be increased to improve Peter's experience.

The underlining in *Section IV: Characteristic Patterns Limiting Play* shows that Peter's family has inappropriately high social goals for him and Peter has a lack of neighborhood peers with whom to play. In his current school program, note that the number of adults working is inadequate to provide the individual attention he needs, and there are issues regarding the pace and interactional style of the staff. Other issues include the number of peers with whom Peter must interact, the group focus of most activities, and the mismatch between Peter's play needs and the group play interactions. The Space, Time, and Materials and Equipment concerns are underlined relative to acoustics, indoor gross motor space, the amount of time focused on group activities, and the range and type of materials available.

Section V: Discrepancy Analysis

Peter's Discrepancy Analysis (found at the end of the chart) assists staff to design adaptations that will better meet his developmental needs. First, the chronological age level was written beside the 6 developmental skill areas (Level 3); then the 6 working theme levels were filled in (all Level 2). Next, relative discrepancies between chronological age level and working theme levels were noted on the line to the right (all below age level). Then any areas of development that showed significant internal scatter were starred (Motor/Self-Help and Play skills). Lastly, significant discrepancy issues were summarized in brief narrative under Child, Family, and Program at the bottom of the page.

Peter has many Motor/Self-Help skills that are age-appropriate, but because of his lack of impulse control and poor **self-regulation**, his working theme was set at Level 2. Similarly, he is showing some age-appropriate play skills in material use and representational and symbolic play, but his serious delays in the social skills required for interactive and associative play retain his working theme at Level 2. The discrepancies among Peter's skills are very significant in assessing the appropriateness of Peter's current placement, understanding his current developmental needs, and designing appropriate adaptations for this setting. Because Peter gives the initial impression of being so capable, it would be easy for a teacher to assume that he will be able to adapt quickly to the group expectations of children who are, on the average, a full year younger. Unfortunately, this assumption has caused Peter to be placed in a setting that is only minimally adapted to his needs at this time.

Section VI: Intervention Goals/Facilitating Techniques

Now, with the information collected thus far (Sections I–V), the staff is ready to review Section VI, in which there are numerous suggestions for approaches and adaptations that may improve Peter's experience in this setting. The underlinings in Section VI under Child reflect the belief that it is imperative that Peter have the support of a strong relationship with a key adult to augment his developing ego skills and to assist him in mastering tasks related to attachment–separation–individuation, affective expression, and self-regulation. Peter's age-appropriate motor skills are a strength, but his poor impulse control and tendency to become overstimulated require clear limits and consequences for safety.

Considering Peter's degree of hearing impairment and his late acquisition of hearing aides, his language development is a relative strength, but it is still not fully age appropriate. His linguistic skills are stronger than his communication skills. This area of intervention requires technological support and the assistance of specialists who can work with speech and language development.

Because many of Peter's cognitive skills are approximately age appropriate, the teacher wants to sustain a learning environment that builds on Peter's strengths. But it is important not to allow Peter to rely on his intellectual skills to avoid more challenging interpersonal encounters with peers. Peter has a vivid imagination and can create extended play scenes in solitary play, but does not possess the interpersonal skills necessary for socially interactive play. The emotional content of Peter's play as reflected in the play themes is more like that of a 2- or 3-year-old. Control issues dominate his management of materials, regulation of his body, and the themes of his play scenarios. Latent conflict related to bodily integrity and loss and attachment and autonomy may contribute to his immature social skills. His growing awareness of his hearing loss and his fantasies about the cause of his disability may be contributing to these themes. An expression of these themes may emerge in his play and could be used by the adult to assist him to replace action with words and fantasy with understanding.

In Section VI under Family, the observation that Peter's parents need support in better understanding his current developmental needs and in expanding his day-to-day life experiences was highlighted. Problems that the parents are having with Peter are most often the result of their lack of understanding of how his hearing loss has compromised developmental areas. Staff need to include parents in the intervention process and support their parenting strengths.

In Section VI under Program, note that adults interacting with Peter in the group need to offer more individualized support, help him compensate for his delays, and serve as a bridge to the broader world of peers.

Peers, in turn, need to better understand Peter's unique needs and to interact with him in ways that do not threaten his need for control, but at the same time promote a desire for cooperation.

The Environment requires adaptations in order to be more appropriate.

Section VII: Individualized Supportive Play Adaptations and Experiences

Because it is not possible to implement all of the facilitating techniques at one time, the staff and parents must prioritize the changes that will become part of Peter's immediate school and home experience. Section VII summarizes the most pertinent individualized adaptations planned by the staff and parents to assist Peter in his adjustment to this mainstreamed setting. These adaptations focus on helping Peter gain a better balance with regard to control and peer interactions.

Crucial to the success of this process is the establishment of a strong supportive relationship between one staff member and Peter. In this case Anna was selected because she and Peter are comfortable together, and he seems responsive to her management approaches. At this time in his development, Peter needs an adult to acknowledge, accept, mirror, and help him to label his emotions and needs. This key adult also needs to be available to help him cope more effectively with the stresses posed by group life, thereby relieving some of his anxiety through serving as an **auxiliary ego**.

Because motor skills are a relative strength for Peter, the aim is to include daily opportunities for indoor gross motor play, which will help Peter not only expend energy, but also increase his status with peers. Outdoor motor opportunities need to be expanded and include activities away from the large group. These could be organized by Anna and shared by Peter and a peer, to provide sufficient adult supervision in order to support his development of impulse control and safety consciousness.

Placing a child with hearing impairments into a regular education setting means that staff must be receptive to expanding their knowledge and skills about learning differences, behavioral interventions, and technological innovations. The public school speech and language pathologist who has been working with Peter for the past 18 months needs to arrange for the purchase of a wireless auditory trainer, as designated at the Planning and Placement Team (PPT) meeting. The wireless auditory trainer would help Peter function in this busy noisy environment and may help in increasing his attention. (The wireless auditory trainer can also be directly connected to audio-visual equipment used in the classroom to aid in his auditory reception). The staff needs to become more empathetic to the issues related to the hearing-impaired child, by consultation and in-service from speech and language pathologists and **audiologists**. When relating to Peter, emphasis should be placed on the interactive features of language, such as communicative intent, shared attention, turn taking, and gesture reading.

Peter's strong cognitive potential needs to be fostered by increased exposure to novel experiences through a rich learning environment and field trips into the community. He needs to be supported in understanding and constructing increasingly more complex concepts and in relating his experiences to adults and peers.

Peter's play skills are relatively strong, except when cooperative interaction with peers is a part of the expectation. Anna will be available to gradually help Peter tolerate more proximate parallel play and then associative activity. While wearing the wireless auditory trainer, Anna will be able to narrate Peter's play and, acting in a transitional and regulatory role, introduce peers for short exchanges. Sensorimotor and **kinesthetic** play experiences may be the least threatening play context to introduce these social forays.

The development of play themes can also be promoted through the shared play relationship with Anna. By offering words, identifying emotions, clarifying confusions, and solving problems, Anna can use the play as a tool for emotional growth. As the trust alliance strengthens and Peter shows a tolerance for sharing Anna, the play partnership between them can be expanded to include peers for interludes of increasing duration.

The family can also be encouraged to invite nursery school companions home, so Peter can practice social play beyond the confines of the classroom. Instructing Peter's parents to promote and shape age-appropriate behavior, while helping them to tolerate and ignore some of Peter's toddler like qualities, is an important part of the family plan. The family's motivation to understand Peter better and their willingness to share personal experiences with the whole program are to be carefully encouraged.

Central to the staffing adaptations is the arrangement for a volunteer to join the group three mornings a week to afford Anna additional time with Peter. Peers need to be familiarized with Peter's handicapping condition and auditory equipment. Peter's speech and language pathologist or audiologist can be asked to explain and demonstrate the equipment to the class. Accentuating Peter's strengths will make him more desirable to peers as a playmate and friend.

Environmental adaptations include consultation regarding the acoustics of the classroom and design of an indoor gross motor space. With regard to the funding of these renovations, the public school is responsible for those that are deemed central to Peter's programming. Other adaptations and improvements could be funded by parent fund raisers or civic donations—these will be of benefit not just to Peter, but to all of the children in the program. Appropriate time and scheduling changes that would be helpful include variations in the format of the day to allow more sensory, vestibular, and gross motor activity in the early part of the morning. Greater availability of duplicate materials will also allow Peter to tolerate more parallel and associative peer involvement with less anxiety about loss and finding a position in the group.

Supportive Play Model Adaptation

Four months after staff initiated the *Individualized Supportive Play Adaptations and Experiences*, a second observation reflects some changes in Peter's behavior and adjustment to the classroom. After consultation with an audiologist, the classroom was modified by the installation of wall-to-wall carpeting, except in the arts area and other messy areas. The audiologist suggested that, when possible, the ceiling be resurfaced with acoustical tiling. Because Peter's hearing is diminished in a busy classroom, the public school system in charge of Peter's special services provided a wireless auditory trainer system, and the speech and language pathologist has instructed the teacher and Anna in its use. Anna is wearing the wireless auditory trainer microphone and Peter is wearing the receiver; this allows Anna's speech to be transmitted directly to Peter, thereby allowing her voice to be heard by Peter over the classroom noise. A volunteer has joined the group three mornings a week, freeing Anna to play individually with Peter when it is appropriate. Free choice time now includes a sensorimotor activity each day (sand, water, clay). Ceiling hooks have been installed in one area to allow for the inclusion of a small platform swing and hammock. An indoor slide, tunnel, and small climbing structure have been added for an indoor gross motor area. Circle time and snack now take place in three smaller groups with Peter always joining the group with the adult who is wearing the wireless auditory trainer microphone. Outdoor playtime has been reorganized to encourage more large motor, vestibular, and **sensorimotor activities**. Because Peter is most relaxed during gross motor activities, Anna takes him, with one friend, for a walk, to play ball, to run, or to fly paper kites in a nearby field. The goal is to gradually increase the outdoor play group to three or four children for these gross motor activities.

The following vignette begins during the indoor activity choice hour. Within the brackets in the vignette we have added reflective commentary on Peter's behavior and Anna's interaction with him.

Peter first chooses to spend 10 minutes in the gross motor corner. While Peter is being pushed by Anna in the hammock, he spontaneously begins to sing "row, row, row your boat." When Jack approaches the hammock, Anna helps him to climb in beside Peter and both children enjoy several minutes of shared swinging and singing. *[Peter's choice of a motor activity demonstrates how this type of activity is relaxing to him and assists him in making his entry into the school day. The repetitive vestibular activity is soothing and organizing as demonstrated by Peter's spontaneous singing. Anna is actively involved in pushing him on the hammock, and he is able to expand the activity to include another child for a brief period. The repeated pattern of going away and coming back that is experienced in this activity is helpful for all children as they deal with the themes of separation and reunion.]*

For the free-choice activity, Peter has been building a farm scene by himself in the sand table. This choice is an outcome of a recent field trip to a small local dairy farm. Anna has pulled up a small chair and is attentively watching him create his farm. Several times he has spoken to Anna to point out some aspect of his project. Two children approach, admire his project, step near the sand table, and ask to help.

ANNA: (to peers) Do you like Peter's farm. Maybe we can just watch while Peter feeds the animals.
PETER: (yells) This mine. No!
ANNA: Peter, do you want to play by yourself?
PETER: Yeah, my farm.
ANNA: You worked hard to build that farm. Maybe later Beth and Tommy can come back and see your farm.
PETER: (Nodding and turning to play.) OK.
ANNA: (touches Beth and Tommy's shoulders) You wanted to play with Peter's farm, but Peter wants to work alone today. Let's help him by letting him finish, and I can help you find something else to play with. Let's look around the room.
PETER: Teacher, look at this.
ANNA: Peter, I'm helping Beth and Tommy now. In a few minutes I'll be back to see your farmyard.

[In this dialogue, Anna shows how to reflect, clarify, and negotiate with Peter. She realizes that it is still too threatening for Peter to have peers enter into his play at this moment. She accepts this and provides a voice for Peter, directly supporting his ego functioning by mediating the situation and setting some boundaries for his peers.]

After helping Beth and Tommy select another activity, Anna returns to sit beside Peter as he works on the farm scene. Peter is bringing in the cows for milking. He is receptive to Anna helping to line up all the cows inside the play barn. As Anna helps, she speaks to Peter, naming the animals and talking about the fresh milk. They fill many small buckets with pretend milk. Anna says she is hot and thirsty, so they pretend to have a snack of the raw milk. When Beth and Tommy come back to see the developments in the farmyard, Anna suggests to Peter that he might like to share some of the milk with his friends. Peter shows Beth and Tommy the little buckets and asks them if they want some fresh milk. All three children drink the pretend milk from the buckets with exaggerated slurping and lip smacking. *[By giving Peter enough time, Anna has set the stage for a successful collaboration between Peter and his peers. If Anna had previously pushed him beyond his tolerance, he might not have been able to participate in and enjoy this shared **fantasy play**. Perhaps the nature of the play scenario with its focus on self-feeding and simple oral motor expression allowed Peter to participate with less anxiety.]*

Anna plans the snack sitting arrangement to include Beth and Tommy at her table with Peter. Anna mentions to Peter that the milk might have come from his pretend dairy farm. Peter is not able to extend the imaginative scenario into the snack situation. He whines and resists this line of conversation. Anna accepts Peter's comments and redirects the conversation to another topic that includes Beth and Tommy. *[When Anna tries to extend the play at the snack table, Peter is resistive and unable to participate. Superimposing the fantasy theme upon the reality of snack may be too confusing and threatening for Peter. Again, Anna accepts the signals of distress given by Peter and does not force the issue.]*

Anna and Peter decide that it is time for a short walk in the immediate neighborhood. Anna has established certain basic guidelines for Peter's behavior during these excursions, including the need for him to hold her hand whenever they cross a street and to obey her verbal requests and directions. For the past week Peter has been allowed to take one self-selected friend on these little trips. Today Peter selected Tommy to join him on his walk to the nearby field with Anna. Both boys enjoyed rolling down a small incline and playing with a playground ball. When Peter is told by Anna that it is nearly time for his father to pick him up and that they must return to school, Peter bolts and heads in the opposite direction. Using a firm voice she tells him to stop, reaches him, and says, "You like to play here, but it makes me worry when you run away." She tells him that now she must take his hand for the entire walk back to school because she wants him to be safe. As they walk she reminds Peter and Tommy that another day they can return with her to the field to play again. She returns to the building holding both Tommy and Peter's hands as they sing a skipping song. *[Throughout this vignette we see Anna finding a balance among empathy, structure, and limits. She is skilled at attending to Peter's motivation and his feeling tone. She also shows attention to what stands behind the rules—in this case, his safety. She understands that his opposition is likely to be an attempt to express his unhappiness with the end of a pleasant and exciting activity. She connects his behavior to his feelings and helps him prepare for separation and endings, an area of difficulty for Peter. She introduces a song that helps Peter organize for the transition back to the classroom, and then to home. She wants him to succeed, but she respects his pace and his coping skills. Because she is giving him appropriate time and space to grow, he is rising to the challenge.]*

Section VIII: Results and Outcomes

The changes that are in place by the end of January, as described in this vignette, are summarized in Section VIII. Clearly, the adaptations are already having a positive impact on Peter's overall experience in this nursery school setting. His developmental issues have not disappeared, but the more individualized approach and the more appropriate developmental goals have greatly reduced the stress on Peter, the staff, and his peers. By treating Peter as a capable and energetic 5-year-old child who still is working on emotional, social, and communicative issues in a way similar to a 2- or 3-year-old, the staff are able to more successfully match the group expectations and experiences to meet Peter's current needs. Within this newly sensitized setting, it now appears more possible for Peter to be successful.

At the end of the year, review of this case indicates that the original adaptations continued to be useful in facilitating Peter's development. Throughout the school year he maintained a strong bond with Anna and enjoyed some individual play time with her each day. Gradually, Anna was able to step back from many activities and provide only verbal support using the wireless auditory trainer. Peter established two strong friendships with classmates and learned to interact successfully with the majority of the children in the group. His two best friends were 4-year-old boys with high energy levels and well established imaginations. Together, these boys engaged in elaborate construction play and by spring were planning and carrying out sociodramatic sequences. Peter still struggled when his peers' ideas did not totally match his conceptualization of a play scenario, but ,with Anna's help he gained skill in talking through these disagreements and learned how to carry out verbal negotiation, without seemingly losing his sense of self. By the end of the school year it was clear that Peter was ready to proceed to a half-day kindergarten, with an afternoon placement in a resource room for speech and language therapy and the speech and language pathologist consulting with the kindergarten teacher.

SUMMARY

This case demonstrates the complexity of including a child with a hearing impairment in a nursery school setting. As is often the case, Peter's apparent competence led to a placement in which his needs were not initially recognized. Because this nursery school relies on self-initiated exploration and play as the major learning modality, a child like Peter, if left unsupported, would not benefit from the potential richness of the setting. In spite of areas of developmental strengths and Peter's clear potential, his current generalized delays and inconsistencies in his skills require a reorganization of both approach and expectations to reflect an understanding of his Self/Social/Emotional, Communicative/Language, and Play Theme development. Through the use of the SPM, his parents and the staff have joined in the examination of this child's developmental levels and the specific qualities of the setting, including the role of the family, program adults, peers, and environment. The significance of implementing individualized supportive play adaptations and experiences has been demonstrated. His parents have become more involved with Peter's immediate needs and have a fuller understanding of the broader long-range developmental needs of this little boy. With these more developmentally appropriate family expectations, modified staff strategies, compensatory play-focused milieu, and a more developmentally appropriate environment, Peter has been able to develop more closely in line with his innate potential. The secondary benefits that are the result of the use of the SPM are that the classroom is more stimulating and enriched for all the children and the normally developing children are beginning to appreciate and enjoy Peter as a playmate and peer.

REFERENCES

Allen, T. (1986). Patterns of academic achievement among hearing impaired students: 1974–1983. In A. Schildroth & M. Karchmer (Eds.), *Deaf Children in America* (pp. 161–206). San Diego: College Hill Press.

Anderson, K. L. (1991). Hearing conservation in the public schools revisited. *Seminars in Hearing, 12,* 340–364.

Arnold, D., & Tremblay, A. (1979). Interaction of deaf and hearing preschool children. *Journal of Communication Disorders, 12,* 245–251.

Batshaw, M. L. & Perret, Y. M. (1992). *Children with Disabilities: A Medical Primer* (3rd ed.). Baltimore: Paul H. Brookes.

Bess, F. H., & Tharpe, A. M. (1984). Unilateral hearing impairment in children. *Pediatrics, 74*(2), 206–216.

Bluestone, C. D., & Klein, J. O. (1988). *Otitis media in infants and children.* Philadelphia: Saunders.

Brazelton, T. B. (1975). Discussion of J. H. Kennel, M. A. Trause, & M. H. Klaus, Evidence for a sensitive period in the human mother. In, *Parent–Infant Interaction {Ciba Foundation Symposium 33}* (pp. 95–102). Amsterdam: Elsevier.

Brazelton, T. B., Tronick, E., Adamson, L, Als, H., & Wise, S. (1975). Early mother–infant reciprocity. In, *Parent–Infant Interaction {Ciba Foundation Symposium 33}* (pp. 137–154). Amsterdam: Elsevier.

Brown, S. C., & Karchmer, M. A. (1987). Who will be served? *Gallaudet Today, 18*(1), 4–7.

Burlingham, D. (1965). Some problems of ego development in blind children. *The Psychoanalytic Study of the Child, 20,* 194–208.

Chess, S., & Fernandez, P. (1980). Do deaf children have a typical personality? *Journal of the American Academy of Child Psychiatry, 19,* 654–664.

Cohen, B. K. (1980). Emotionally disturbed hearing-impaired children: A review of the literature. *American Annals of the Deaf, 125,* 1040–1048.

Condon, W. S. & Sander, L. W. (1974). Neonate movement is synchronized with adult speech: Interactional participation and language acquisition. *Science, 183,* 99–101.

Coplan, J. (1987). Deafness: Ever heard of it? Delayed recognition of permanent hearing loss. *Pediatrics, 79,* 206–213.

Darbyshire, J. O. (1977). Play patterns in young children with impaired hearing. *Volta Review, 79*(1), 19–26.

Davis, J. (Ed.). (1977). *Our forgotten children: Hard of hearing pupils in the schools.* Minneapolis: University of Minnesota.

Davis, J. M., Elfenbein, J., Schum, R., & Bentler, R. A. (1986). Effects of mild and moderate hearing impairments on language, educational, and psychological behavior of children. *Journal of Speech and Hearing Disorders, 51,* 53–62.

DeCasper, A. J., & Fifer, W. P. (1980). Of human bonding: Newborns prefer their mothers' voices. *Science, 208,* 1174–1176.

DeCasper, A. J., & Spence, M. J. (1986). Prenatal maternal speech influences newborns' perception of speech sounds. *Infant Behavior and Development, 9,* 133–150.

Education for All Handicapped Children Act of 1975. 20 U.S.C. § 1401. (1975)

Education of the Handicapped Act Amendments of 1986, Part H— Handicapped Infant and Toddlers. § 101, 20 U.S.C. §1400. (1986)

Education of the Handicapped Act Amendments of 1990. 20 U.S.C §1400. (1990)

Ferguson, D. G., Hicks, D. E., & Pfau, G. S. (1988). Education of the hearing impaired learners. In N. J. Lass, L. V. McReynolds, J. L. Northern, & D. E. Yoders (Eds.), *Speech, Language, and Hearing* (pp. 1265–1277). Toronto: Decker.

Fraiberg, S. (1968). Parallel and divergent patterns in blind and sighted infants. *The Psychoanalytic Study of the Child, 23,* 264–300.

Freeman, R. D., Malkin, S. F. & Hastings, J. O. (1975). Psychosocial problems of deaf children and their families: A comparative study. *American Annals of the Deaf, 120,* 391–405.

Gentile, A., & McCarthy, B. (1973). *Additional handicapping conditions among hearing impaired students, United States, 1971–1972* (Gallaudet College Office of Demographic Studies, Series D, No. 14). Washington, DC: Gallaudet College Press.

Gleason, J. B. (1985). Studying language development. In J. B. Gleason (Ed.), *The development of language* (pp. 1–34). Columbus, OH: Merrill.

Glorig, A., & Roberts, J. (1977). *Hearing levels of adults by age and sex.* (Series 11, No. 11. U.S. Vital Health Statistics). Bethesda, MD: National Center for Health Statistics.

Grant, H. R., Quiney, R. E., Mercer, D. M., & Lodge, S. (1988). Cleft palate and glue ear. *Archives of Disease in Childhood, 63,* 176–179.

Greenberg, M. T. (1980). Social interaction between deaf preschoolers and their mothers: The effects of communication method and communication competence. *Developmental Psychology, 16*(5), 465–474.

Greenberg, M. T., & Marvin, R. S. (1979). Attachment patterns in profoundly deaf preschool children. *Merrill-Palmer Quarterly, 25,* 265–279.

Harada, T., Iwamori, M., Nagai, Y., & Nomura, Y. (1986). Ototoxicity of neomycin and its penetration through the round window membrane into the perilymph. *Annals of Otology, Rhinology, & Laryngology, 95,* 404–408.

Harris, R. I. (1978). Impulse control in deaf children: Research and clinical issues. In L. S. Liben (Ed.), *Deaf children: Developmental perspectives* (pp. 137–156). New York: Academic Press.

Higginbotham, D. J., & Baker, B. M. (1981, April). Social participation and cognitive play differences in hearing-impaired and normally hearing preschoolers. *Volta Review, 83*(3), 135–149.

House, W. F., Berliner, K. I., & Luxford, W. M. (1987). Cochlear implants in deaf children. *Current Problems in Pediatrics, 17*, 345–388.

Jensema, C. (1975). *The relationship between academic achievement and the demographic characteristics of hearing impaired children and youth.* (Series R, No. 2) Washington, DC: Gallaudet College, Office of Demographic Studies.

Jensema, C., & Trybus, R. J. (1975). *Reported emotional/behavioral problems among hearing impaired children in special education programs: United States, 1972–73* (Series R, No. 1) Washington, DC: Gallaudet College, Office of Demographic Studies. (Abstract)

Kaplan, B. J., & McHale, F. J. (1979, March). *Communication and play behaviors of a deaf preschooler and his younger sibling.* Paper presented at the Biennial Meeting of the Society for Research in Child Development, San Francisco, CA. (ERIC Document Reproduction Service No. 182 003).

Karchmer, M. A. (1985). A demographic perspective. In E. Cherow, N. D. Matkin, & R. J. Trybus (Eds.), *Hearing-impaired children and youth with developmental disabilities* (pp. 36–58). Washington, DC: Gallaudet College Press.

Kessler, J. W. (1988). *Psychopathology of Childhood* (2nd ed.). Englewood Cliffs, NJ: Prentice Hall.

Kirk, S. A., Gallagher, J. J., & Anastasiow, N. J. (1993). *Educating exceptional children* (7th ed.). Boston: Houghton Mifflin.

Konigsmark, B. W., & Gorlin, R. J. (1976). *Genetic and metabolic deafness.* Philadelphia: Saunders.

Kveton, J., & Balkany, T. J. (1991). Status of cochlear implantation in children. *Journal of Pediatrics, 118,* 1–7.

Lane, H. (1984). *When the mind hears.* New York: Random House.

Lederberg, A. R., Ryan, H. B., & Robbins, B. L. (1986). Peer interaction in young deaf children: The effect of partner hearing status and familiarity. *Developmental Psychology, 22,* 691–700.

Ling, D. (1984a). Early oral intervention: An introduction. In D. Ling (Ed.), *Early intervention for hearing-impaired children: Oral options* (pp. 1–14). San Diego: College Hill Press.

Ling, D. (1984b). Early total communication intervention: An introduction. In D. Ling (Ed.), *Early intervention for hearing-impaired children: Total communication options* (pp. 1–14). San Diego: College Hill Press.

Macklin, G. F., & Matson, J. L. (1985). A comparison of social behaviors among nonhandicapped and hearing impaired children. *Behavioral Disorders, 11*(1), 60–65.

Mann, L. F. (1981, November). *Play and the non-verbal child.* Paper presented at the Annual Meeting of the National Association for the Education of Young Children, Detroit, MI. (ERIC Document Reproduction Service No. ED 212 381)

Mann, L. F. (1984, June). *Play behaviors of deaf and hearing children.* Paper presented at The International Symposium on Cognition, Education, and Deafness, Washington, DC. (ERIC Document Reproduction Service No. 247 722).

Matkin, A. M., & Matkin, N. D. (1985). Benefits of total communication as perceived by parents of hearing-impaired children. *Language, Speech and Hearing Services in Schools, 16,* 64–74.

Mayberry, R., Wodlinger-Cohen, R., & Goldin-Meadow, S. (1987). Symbolic development in deaf children. In D. Cicchetti & M. Beeghly (Eds.), *Symbolic development in atypical children.* San Francisco: Josey-Bass.

McCrae, M. Q. (1986). *Medical perspectives on brain damage and development.* Reading, PA: Family Centered Resource Project.

Meadow, K. P. (1980). *Deafness and child development.* Berkeley, CA: University of California Press.

Meadow, K. P. (1984). Social adjustment of preschool children. Deaf and hearing, with and without other handicaps. *Topics in Early Childhood Special Education, 3*(4), 27–40.

Meadow, K. P., Greenberg, M. T., Erting, C., & Carmichael, H. (1981). Interactions of deaf mothers and deaf preschool children: Comparisons with three other groups of deaf and hearing dyads. *American Annals for the Deaf, 126,* 454–468.

Miller, E., Cradock-Watson, J. E., & Pollock, T. M. (1982). Consequences of confirmed maternal rubella at successive stages of pregnancy. *Lancet, 2,* 781–784.

Mogford, K. (1977). The play of handicapped children. In B. Tizard & D. Harvey (Eds.), *Biology of play.* Philadelphia: Lippincott.

Moores, D. F. (1989). *Educating the deaf* (3rd ed.). Boston: Houghton Mifflin.

National Information Center on Deafness. (1989). *Deafness: A fact sheet.* National Information Center on Deafness, Gallaudet University, 800 Florida Ave., N.E., Washington, DC 20002–3695.

Northern, J. L., & Downs, M. P. (1991). *Hearing in Children* (4th ed.). Baltimore: Williams & Wilkins.

Northern, J. L., & Lemme, M. (1982). Hearing and auditory disorders. In G. H. Shames & E. H. Wiig (Eds.), *Human communication disorders: An introduction.* Columbus, OH: Merrill.

Omwake, E. (1968). The impact of blindness on the development of the child. *Connecticut Medicine, 32,* 598–605.

Paul, P. V., & Quigley, S. P. (1990). *Education and Deafness.* White Plains, NY: Longman.

Pien, D. (1984). *The development of language functions in deaf infants of hearing parents.* Paper presented at The International Symposium on Cognition, Education, and Deafness, Washington, DC. (ERIC Document Reproduction Service No. 247 723).

Quigley, S. (1969). *Some effects of hearing impairment upon school performance.* Springfield, IL: Office of the Superintendent of Public Instruction.

Quinn, J. M., & Rubin, K. H. (1984). The play of handicapped children. In T. D. Yawkey & A. D. Pelligrini (Eds.), *Child's play: Developmental and applied* (pp. 63–80). Hillsdale, NJ: Erlbaum.

Report of the Ad Hoc Committee to Define Deaf and Hard of Hearing. (1975). *American Annals of the Deaf, 120,* 509–512.

Robertson, C., & Whyte, L. (1983). Prospective identification of infants with hearing loss and multiple handicaps: The role of the neonatal follow-up clinic. In G. T. Mencher & S. E. Gerber (Eds.), *The multiply handicapped hearing impaired child* (pp. 27–54). New York: Grune & Stratton.

Rogers, S. J. (1983). Cognitive characteristics of handicapped children's play: A review. *Journal of the Division of Early Childhood, 12*(2), 161–168.

Rubin, K. H., Fein, G. G., & Vandenberg, B. (1983). *Play.* In P. H. Mussen (Ed.), *Handbook of child psychology: Vol. 4. Socialization, personality, and social development* (4th ed.). (pp. 693–774). New York: Wiley.

Salamy, A., Eldredge, L., & Tooley, W. H. (1989). Neonatal status and hearing loss in high-risk infants. *Journal of Pediatrics, 114,* 847–852.

Sanders, D. A. (1980). Psychological implications of hearing impairment. In W. M. Cruickshank (Ed.), *Psychology of exceptional children and youth* (4th ed.). (pp. 218–254). Englewood Cliffs, NJ: Prentice-Hall.

Sandlin, R. E. (1988). Clinical application of sound-field audiometry. In R. E. Sandlin (Ed.), *Handbook of hearing aid amplification Vol. II: Clinical considerations and fitting practices* (pp. 257–278). Boston: College Hill Press.

Schirmer, B. R. (1989a, July). *Language and cognitive development of deaf and hearing twin sisters.* Paper presented at The International Symposium on Cognition, Education, and Deafness, Washington, DC. (ERIC Document Reproduction Service No. 313 842).

Schirmer, B. R. (1989b). Relationship between imaginative play and language development in hearing-impaired children. *American Annals of the Deaf, 134*(3), 219–222.

Schlesinger, H. (1983). Early intervention: The prevention of multiple handicaps. In G. T. Mencher & S. E. Gerber (Eds.), *The multiply handicapped hearing-impaired child* (pp. 83–116). New York: Grune & Stratton.

Schwartz, S. (1987). *Choices in Deafness: A parent's guide.* Montgomery, MD: Woodbine House.

Spencer, P. E. (1993). Communication behaviors of infants with hearing loss and their hearing mothers. *Journal of Speech and Hearing Research, 36,* 311–321.

Spencer, P. E., Bodner-Johnson, B. A., & Gutfreund, M. K. (1992). Interacting with infants with a hearing loss: What can we learn from mothers who are deaf? *Journal of Early Intervention, 16*(1), 64–78.

Terhune, C. B. (1979). The role of hearing in early ego organization. *The Psychoanalytic Study of the Child, 34*, 371–383.

Trybus, R., & Karchmer, M. (1977). School achievement scores of hearing impaired children: National data on achievement status and growth patterns. *American Annals of the Deaf, 122*, 62–69.

Supportive Play Model

Section I. Cover Sheet

Name: _Peter_____   Observers: _____

Age: _5_____

Date of birth: _July 24, 1989____   Date: _September_____

BRIEFLY DESCRIBE:

Program (location, philosophy, curriculum focus, schedule):

The nursery school class consists of seventeen 4-year-olds, a teacher (Carol), and a full-time aide (Anna). The school is located in the wing of a community church that is located on the edge of a small town. The large open classroom is divided by shelving into four activity areas. The daily schedule includes free choice time, group story and singing, snack, and outside play time. The program philosophy is described as a developmental one, and the staff plan the program and schedule in 1-month blocks.

Child (reason for conducting observation; any outstanding developmental issues; parental concerns and staff concerns)

Staff are concerned that at school Peter is unable to share activities, and demonstrates delays in many social skills. A few of the children are afraid of his reactions and avoid him. However, some of the children are attracted to the creativity involved in his play.

   Peter's parents are concerned that if this experience is a negative one, this will affect how he feels about school in the future. They worry about his activity level and his readiness for kindergarten.

Date of next review _PPT to follow SPM Process_____

II: Observational Impressions

A = attained or mastered   E = emerging   * = working theme
P = practicing   N = not observed

LEVEL 1 (BIRTH–18 MONTHS)

WORKING THEME   Develops attachment to and trust of caregiver(s), with feelings of affection and pleasure predominating over aggression and pain, leading to the emergence of awareness of self (separation and individuation), leading to autonomy

WHAT YOU OBSERVE

A   *Signals needs, pleasure, and discomfort*
A   *Explores in an oral and sensorimotor manner*
P   *Shows progressive awareness of and interest in others*
P   *Increases gradually in self-regulation: waits, anticipates, soothes self for short time*
A   *Reciprocates affect and activity with caregivers*
A   *Displays caution with strangers (neither paralyzed by fear nor indiscriminately friendly)*
A   *Practices separating from caregiver (leave taking and reunion)*
P   *Seeks comfort from caregiver when hurt or distressed*
A   *Uses comfort objects during transitions*
A   *Increases in range of emotions (joy, anger, pleasure in mastery, humor)*
A   *Increases in aggression and assertiveness*

LEVEL 2 (19–36 MONTHS)

*   **WORKING THEME**   *Establishes the beginnings of constancy (sustained emotional investment in and feelings about self, others, things, and concepts)*

WHAT YOU OBSERVE

P   *Experiments with negotiation in interpersonal relationships*
P   *Experiences marked variations of mood; behavioral change may be abrupt with pinching, hitting, tantrums, etc.*
E   *Attunes progressively to feelings and goals of others*
E   *Increases in shared experiences (interaction and imitation of others, goal-directed partnership)*
P   *Grows in self-identity, resulting in formation of constancy (identifies self in picture, tolerates separation from parent)*
A   *Shows robust and differentiated expression of emotion (glee, aggression, fear, anger, humor)*
E   *Increases in impulse control and self-regulation with intermittent regression and expression of resentment*

LEVEL 3 (37–60 MONTHS)

WORKING THEME   Develops initiative, gender identity, fusion of learning and feeling, and definition of role within family and with peers

WHAT YOU OBSERVE

E   *Increases in curiosity about sex differences, roles, and relationships*
E   *Experiments with adult roles and relationships (Oedipal themes), which affirms sexual identification and gender role, leading to internalized sense of right and wrong*
E   *Plans ahead and briefly delays gratification*
E   *Experiences mood stabilization with growth in awareness of own internal states; communicates feelings; experiments with transition from actions to words to express strong feelings such as anger and envy*
P   *Grows in understanding of differences between dreams, fantasies, and reality*
E   *Grows in formulation of self-image and self-esteem*
N   Develops capacity for empathy, rule attunement, and social sensitivity
N   Develops peer relationships
E   *Launches and sustains interest in play projects with enthusiasm and zest*

III: Skills and Outstanding Characteristics Observed

Trusts and uses adults to support goals
High energy, enthusiastic
Appealing to adult, reinforcing to work with
More attuned to adults than to peers
Strong personality and presentation of self
Interesting child
Emotionally responsive and strong willed
Poor impulse control
Strong pretend and fantasy skills
Poor reading of social expectations
Anxiety level high, leading to strong need to control

IV: Characteristic Patterns Limiting Play

Excessive need to control or extreme passivity and apathy
Prolonged regressive behavior or *delayed behavior*
Unusual demand for caregiver's time; adult preferred over peers
Poor self-regulation, resulting in extremes in emotional responses (inappropriate intensity and range of affect; inability to settle)
Identity and self-esteem conflicts resulting from past failures and frustrations
Poor reading of social cues, situations, expectations of others
Poor relatedness and engagement, poor eye contact, *inadequate shared attention and turn-taking*
Excessive and indiscriminate familiarity with strangers or inability to tolerate separation
Inflexible, unable to anticipate or handle transitions, overanxious, fearful, difficult to comfort

Other:

V: Discrepancy Analysis (GO TO LAST PAGE OF CHARTS)

VI: Intervention Goal/Facilitating Techniques

GOAL Provide evolving adult relationship to promote psychosocial development: attachment, separation, and individuation; affect range and self-regulation; initiative and social affiliation (beginnings of group membership)

WHAT YOU CAN DO

Make adult available for emotional refueling, reinvolvement, and as an outside regulator

Increase adult availability in the group

Establish primary adult caregiver in group for consistency

Determine and accept current level of behavior (strengths and weaknesses); move incrementally toward realistic goals

Reinforce successful approximations of appropriate behavior

Focus curriculum on social–emotional development, not exclusively on intellectual achievement

Recognize and verbalize needs and emotions (when child can not)

Wean gradually from primary adult to interact with several adults; gradually introduce appropriate peers

Stay calm; be shockproof; do not reinforce extremes

Experiment with strategies to engage, activate, and calm the child

Help child gain pleasure in process rather than focusing exclusively on product/performance

Overstate social signals (facial expression, gesture, voice tone)

Engage child by establishing eye-contact and physical proximity before sending cues

Model socially appropriate behavior

Avoid battle of wills, but clearly communicate to child that the adult will provide protection and that the child will not be able to decide or choose some things

Advise child of impending transitions, new experiences, changes in routines

Avoid undue haste

Sustain basic routine to bolster child's security, make all changes gradually, but adapt routine to match child's needs

Provide appropriate opportunities within child's daily life to make choices and exercise control (Use "You may do blocks or puzzles now," rather than "Do you want to play with the blocks?")

Allow alternative modes of expression for child's fears and anxieties (through play, art, motor activities)

Accept periods of regression as typical and appropriate in development

Other:

VII: Individualized Supportive Play Adaptations and Experiences

Establish primary adult for child as case manager and primary facilitator

Support his delayed social–emotional needs and help bridge developmental discrepancy with peers as he interacts in group

Provide opportunity for solitary and parallel activities; not yet ready for total group involvement

Follow routine; verbally prepare for transitions to alleviate anxiety and tearfulness

Recognize and verbalize child's emotions and needs. Anticipate potential problems and conflicts; adult to move to child and support verbally

Plan for more activities that ensure child's interest and success (e.g., use transportation themes)

Acquire wireless auditory trainer for use in classroom

VIII: Results and Outcomes

Peter is responding well to aides increased attention and support

Wireless auditory trainer is assisting in relationship building with aide and in preparing Peter for transitions and is helping Peter to understand more of group process

Aide is serving as bridge to peers and as a playmate to Peter

Aide is helping children understand and allows Peter to play independently

Aide is verbalizing Peter's feelings to help him label his emotions and to help other children interpret his behavior

Aide plans motor focused activities for Peter and one peer to begin friendship experience

II: Observational Impressions

A = attained or mastered   E = emerging   * = working theme
P = practicing   N = not observed

LEVEL 1 (BIRTH–18 MONTHS)

WORKING THEME Practices stability, disassociation, equilibrium, and rotation in preparation for postural security, locomotion, and prehension; establishes rhythmic patterns in eating, sleeping, elimination, and activity level

WHAT YOU OBSERVE

A Lifts head in pull to sit; rolls segmentally; sits unsupported; sits well in chair; creeps

A Pulls to stand, stands unsupported, cruises, walks with hand held, walks

A Climbs onto and off of furniture

A Creeps up/down stairs; walks up/down stairs, two feet each step, hand held

A Squats and recovers to retrieve object; runs stiffly with some falling

A Puts hands, feet, objects to mouth; eyes follow objects; develops eye–hand coordination—reaches, grasps, stores, transfers

A Picks up small objects with raking and then pincer grasp, puts objects in container, pokes and examines objects with index finger

A Uses marker on paper

A Turns page of book; towers two blocks; shows initial hand preference

A Begins to finger feed, use cup and spoon independently

A Removes shoes, socks; indicates wet pants

P Begins to comply to adult restrictions regarding safety issues

LEVEL 2 (19–36 MONTHS)

* **WORKING THEME** Refines patterns of locomotion and prehension; gains independence in self-help; shows growing capacity to wait and briefly inhibit action

WHAT YOU OBSERVE

A Stands and walks three steps on tiptoes; walks backward; stands on one foot

A Walks up/down stairs holding rail; walks up, alternating feet, when hand held; jumps off one step; kicks and throws large ball

A Stands up and pushes riding toys; uses push-and-pull toys

A Assists in dressing, can undress

A Eats independently with spoon and fork; indicates toilet needs

A Scribbles with marker or crayon with fisted hand or fingers; towers six cubes; strings beads; turns knobs; unscrews and screws lids; uses scissors to snip (immature grasp); imitates horizontal crayon stroke; draws a circle; completes simple inset puzzle

A Increasingly able to self-regulate motor activity level

E Shows inconsistent judgment concerning personal safety; initially resistive and progressively more compliant to adult guidelines

LEVEL 3 (37–60 MONTHS)

WORKING THEME Masters motor planning of complex gross and fine movements and self-help skills; progressively self-monitors appropriate motor activity level

WHAT YOU OBSERVE

A Matches objects using tactile (texture) cues; rolls clay into ball; draws a primitive person, progresses to body and limb features on person

A Builds tower of nine blocks; cuts paper on straight and curved lines

A Balances on one foot; catches ball; rides tricycle; swings

A Walks downstairs, alternating feet; hops on one foot; somersaults

A Skips to music; throws/catches ball, first using arms and body, then just hands

A Buttons and unbuttons; dresses and undresses; brushes teeth, hair; bathes with supervision; toilets independently

A Pours from pitcher; spreads with knife and then cuts with knife

E Internalizes awareness of safety for self and others

N Can wait, redirect, slow down, and exercise some judgment before action

III: Skills and Outstanding Characteristics Observed

Age-appropriate skill mastery
Competent in all age appropriate visual/motor, fine and gross motor, and self-help skills
Becomes overactive in playground
Poor sense of safety
Poor impulse control
Poor compliance

IV: Characteristic Patterns Limiting Play

Delayed motor milestones, locomotion; avoidance of movement

Orthopedic or neurological impairments, hypertonicity (high motor tone) or hypotonicity (low motor tone), which compromises stability, balance, control, posture, and movement

Hyposensitivity or hypersensitivity to touch, texture, light, sound; sensory integration problems

Postural insecurity: timid to move, fearful of sudden movements, varying environmental heights, and exaggerated protective reactions

Poor motor planning of complex movements, leading to clumsiness

Visual–motor delays affecting eye–hand coordination, immature patterns of grasp

Perceptual problems related to visual field reduction; deficits in figure–ground discrimination, directionality, spatial relationships; or reduced visual acuity

Poor oral motor skills, including problems with chewing, mouth closure, drooling and swallowing, oral hyposensitivity or hypersensitivity to sensation

Self-pacing problems: not an active explorer or overactive and unaware of safety issues

Lack of striving for independent mobility, self-feeding, self-dressing, toileting

Other:

V: Discrepancy Analysis (GO TO LAST PAGE OF CHARTS)

VI: Intervention Goal/Facilitating Techniques

GOAL Provide child with sensory and movement opportunities to gain maximum competence with components of movement (stability, disassociation, equilibrium, rotation, locomotion) in order to gain competence with his or her body (fine and gross motor skills and self-help skills; body image and self-regulation)

WHAT YOU CAN DO (The following are suggestions that are more generic in nature; consult with occupational therapist and physical therapist to plan specific adaptations for motor problems)

Attend to postural needs: use appropriate furniture for stability and body alignment (table and chair size, etc.); make sure child's feet are on a supporting surface when seated

Provide stability at center of body and proximal joints for low tone child

Provide opportunities to play in a flexed position (side sitting, cross-legged sitting) for high tone child

Apply occupational therapist and speech and language pathologist prescription for classroom adaptations necessary for oral–motor needs

Use consultation to provide opportunities that match child's visual needs and skills (choice of materials, adaptive equipment, material placement, lighting, predicable physical environment, adult verbal cuing to support visual perception)

Provide activities that promote visually directed movement: reaching, grasping, threading, pegboard, puzzle; use mirror to provide added feedback

Provide high-contrast materials to aid in figure–ground discrimination

Provide daily structured opportunities for large motor activities; verbally interpret and physically model motor activities to increase successful experiences; help peers to understand and tolerate child's compromising motoric conditions

Provide structured opportunities for child to experiment with and practice mastery of self-care skills, expression of personal needs when tired, sick, hungry

Reinforce child's care of personal and group belongings

Instruct child concerning personal safety

For the overactive child, structure activity, refocus on task, limit complexity and number of materials and stimuli, complement child's style, encourage group involvement without requiring total conformity; provide well supervised, calming sensory and tactile experiences (kneading clay, pouring water, bean and rice bins, bubble balls)

For the underactive child, encourage movement and engagement in activities, provide sensory and tactile experiences, encourage group involvement without requiring total conformity

Accept and mirror child's spontaneous movement; gradually shape approximations to next developmental level for underactive child

Other:

VII: Individualized Supportive Play Adaptations and Experiences

Increase challenging motor and self-help activities to reinforce strong development

Provide adequate gross motor opportunity indoors and outdoors for energy release

Practice socially oriented motor behavior with one peer away from large group

Establish clear rules for motor activities and clear method of communicating acceptable behavior, stressing safety expectations

VIII: Results and Outcomes

Indoor motor options have been added for daily choice

Outdoor motor activity with one peer to support peer affiliation has been added

Safety rules have been established and are continually being reinforced

Motor activities are being used as an acceptable energy release

II: Observational Impressions

A = attained or mastered   E = emerging   * = working theme
P = practicing   N = not observed

LEVEL 1 (BIRTH–18 MONTHS)

WORKING THEME Explores sounds leading to awareness of social and prelinguistic communication and early word use

WHAT YOU OBSERVE

P   *Turns to source of sound*
A   *Progresses from vocal play to babbling, jargoning, and first words*
A   *Smiles socially with mutual gaze, leading to joint attention and action rituals focused on environmental objects and activities*
A   *Looks for family members or pets when named*
A   *Follows simple commands*
P   *Imitates sounds, gestures, and words*
A   *Points to regulate adult activity*
P   *Uses intentional communication; reciprocal exchanges*
A   *Uses words to attract attention, comment, request, protest, greet, socialize*

LEVEL 2 (19–36 MONTHS)

*   **WORKING THEME** *Uses sociocommunicative skills egocentrically in conjunction with rapidly developing linguistic skills, including vocabulary, grammar, and pragmatic skills*

WHAT YOU OBSERVE

P   *Uses word combinations, then phrases and simple sentences*
P   *Begins to develop grammatical structure*
A   *Refers to objects and persons not present, past experiences*
A   *Calls self by name, uses pronouns*
P   *Identifies pictures, listens to story*
P   *Uses rapidly increasing vocabulary*
E   *Follows three-part command*
P   *Asks and answers simple questions*
P   *Begins to use language to pretend during play*
P   *Uses private speech*
E   *Uses language to: request, greet, protest, assert, ask for comment and information; give comments, orders, and information; make rules*

LEVEL 3 (37–60 MONTHS)

WORKING THEME Uses rapidly developing linguistic skills for private speech and to communicate with peers and family

WHAT YOU OBSERVE

E   *Uses sentences to converse*
E   *Develops and stabilizes grammar, uses complex forms*
P   *Speaks more intelligibly*
E   *Responds to abstract information: events in past and future, feelings*
E   *Understands and uses conversational rules*
E   *Expresses subtle differences in attitudes and affect*
E   *Communicates for entertainment and creative value*
N   Develops metalinguistic awareness of language (understands how language works)
N   Comprehends complex directions
E   *Participates effectively in two-way conversations*

III: Skills and Outstanding Characteristics Observed

Simple grammar
Short sentences
Intelligible to familiar adults in familiar setting
Conversation aimed toward adults
Uses simple language in play
Uses private speech
Comprehends simple directions
Receptive speech compromised in busy classroom
Immature social skills interfere with use of language
Language not yet employed to express emotions
Little use of reciprocal conversation patterns—he controls conversational flow
Hearing aides essential for classroom participation

IV: Characteristic Patterns Limiting Play

Lack of or *delay in language and communication competency: comprehension of speech;* development of functional, understandable speech or augmentative communication system (signing, language boards, computers)
Lack of or delay in interpersonal skills that are precursors to language: eye-contact, shared attention, turn taking
*Difficulties with social aspects (pragmatics) of language and communication: turn taking, topic maintenance, topic expansion, felicity (greet*ing, asking, giving, initiating, taking, *closing, and the niceties of verbal and nonverbal communication)*
Perceptual and attentional disabilities that interfere with development of language and communication
Difficulty comprehending verbal and nonverbal communication unless message is simplified
Nonsequential, fragmented, or unusual communication and language production and comprehension (immediate and delayed echolalia, chatter)
Need for augmentative and multiple communication options
Hearing problems, chronic or intermittent (middle-ear infections)

Other:

V: Discrepancy Analysis (GO TO LAST PAGE OF CHARTS)

VI: Intervention Goal/Facilitating Techniques

GOAL Provide relationship and setting that elicits and sustains the social, nonverbal, and verbal aspects of communication: eye-contact, shared attention, turn taking, pleasure with sound making, gestures, receptive and expressive language, augmentative communication modes (signing, language boards, computers)

WHAT YOU CAN DO

Determine developmental level; coordinate classroom expectations with speech and language specialist's and hearing specialist's goals and guidelines

Establish preverbal communication and interpersonal exchange skills (eye-gaze, turn taking, shared meaning as keys to communication)

Explore ways of augmenting and facilitating communication when necessary (signing, language boards, pictures, computer programs, language master, wireless auditory trainer)

Use concrete objects and actions; reinforce with real-life photo cards and photo books of child, family, peers at home, school, or neighborhood

Provide multimodel and multisensory activities

Adapt and simplify all communication: clear, short statements, reinforced by body language and props

Determine most effective communication approach with child: open-ended discussion, yes/no choices, *direct questioning, reflection,* and indirect questioning

Use parallel talk, imitation, and exaggerated (sing-song) intonation to promote vocalization

Imitate and reflect vocal production

Model with gesture and heightened verbal and nonverbal expression

Other:

VII: Individualized Supportive Play Adaptations and Experiences

Coordinate with speech and language pathologist and audiologist about approaches and adaptations

Learn about hearing aids and wireless auditory trainer

Introduce technological equipment (computer, language master, etc.)

Be mindful of hearing impairment, face child before vocalizing, maximize child's auditory abilities by sitting near teacher, use wireless auditory trainer

Communicate in simplified and direct fashion—avoid open-ended questions and choices

Support interpersonal behaviors that relate to communication: waiting turns, turn taking, simple dialoguing

VIII: Results and Outcomes

Speech and language pathologist and audiologist have trained teacher, aide, and volunteer concerning hearing aids and wireless auditory trainer and appropriate communication techniques for working with the hearing impaired

Staff has explained hearing aids and wireless auditory trainer to children in group

Speech and language pathologist has shown short movies on hearing and has shown group model of ear

Consultants have helped in ordering language master for classroom

Public school will lend a computer for a trial period during the winter

II: Observational Impressions

A = attained or mastered   E = emerging   * = working theme
P = practicing   N = not observed

LEVEL 1 (BIRTH–18 MONTHS)

WORKING THEME Increases in attention, perception, and sensorimotor exploration, leading to rudimentary understanding of intentionality, object permanence, cause and effect

WHAT YOU OBSERVE

A *Discovers hands, puts hands in mouth, puts hands together*
A *Swipes, reaches, grasps objects*
A *Explores objects with motor schemes: shaking, banging, dropping, clapping*
A *Combines objects by putting in, taking out, and banging together*
A *Seeks and finds hidden object*
A *Removes and replaces large peg into board; completes simple non-interlocking puzzle*
A *Uses pull toy intentionally*
A *Identifies self in mirror*
A *Enjoys books; looks at named picture; pats named picture*
A *Identifies one body part*
A *Enjoys simple seek and discover games with familiar adult*

LEVEL 2 (19–36 MONTHS)

* **WORKING THEME** *Develops representational thought, object permanence, and deferred imitation*

WHAT YOU OBSERVE

A *Solves simple problems (retrieves toy with stick, looks for missing object or person)*
A *Enjoys process of using creative materials*
E *Follows simple rules in interactive exchanges with adults and peers*
P *Enjoys and reenacts nursery rhymes, nonsense rhymes, finger plays, poetry, favorite stories, picture books, and songs*
P *Matches objects to picture, sound to source, and shapes and colors*
A *Identifies six body parts*
A *Understands concept of one anything*
A *Knows own sex and sex of others*
A *Completes 3–4-piece interlocking puzzle*
E *Increases attention, memory, and awareness of viewpoint of others*

LEVEL 3 (37–60 MONTHS)

WORKING THEME Expands rapidly in concept formation: space, time, quantity, possession, causality, category; begins to problem solve with a marked increase in symbolic thought

WHAT YOU OBSERVE

E *Recognizes similarities and differences in size, shape, color, quantity, movement, direction, sequence, and time components of objects and events*
E *Becomes aware of own thought process (metacognition)*
E *Identifies colors*
P *Counts to 10 with one-to-one correspondence*
P *Classifies by one characteristic*
P *Becomes aware of significance of letters, words*
A *Pretends to read favorite story*
A *Identifies own name in print*
N Becomes aware of concept of money
A *Knows words and actions to several songs*
N Enjoys learning activities shared with peers
N Expands in awareness of viewpoint of others

III: Skills and Outstanding Characteristics Observed

Curious, energetic, and enthusiastic learning
Rapid assimilation of new concepts
Expands on themes with pleasure and exuberance
Enjoys showing off intellectual skills
Age-appropriate attention span in self-selected activities
Good problem solver
Prefers self-initiated and solitary learning experiences

IV: Characteristic Patterns Limiting Play

Fragmented or scattered cognitive skills
Cognition compromised by neurological, developmental, *social–emotional issues; lack of experience*
Difficulty reaching potential without concrete, *multisensory, and multimodal materials and approaches*
Delays and *inconsistencies in attention,* curiosity, self-motivation, problem-solving skills, and ability to generalize and expand
Perseveration (rigid and restrictive persistence) and preoccupation interferes with full exploration and experiences with objects
Delays and confusion in understanding concepts: cause and effect, object permanence, imitation, sequencing, categorization
Extended focus on process and lack of investment or understanding of product
Lack of motivation and interest

Other:

V: Discrepancy Analysis (GO TO LAST PAGE OF CHARTS)

VI: Intervention Goal/Facilitating Techniques

GOAL Create learning environment that attracts and sustains child's attention, provides motivating activities, shapes and reinforces motivation, and promotes exploration and discovery, all leading to progressive stages of cognition and mastery

WHAT YOU CAN DO

Determine level of cognitive functioning; consult with psychologist for diagnostic differentiation, if more in depth information or interpretation is necessary

Create an irresistible invitation to a higher level of functioning by offering challenges that are not too far above current level of performance, but have a quality of novelty; create play situations that help child experience, assimilate, and utilize concepts, such as causality, object permanence, intentionality, imitation, sequencing, and representation

Avoid premature conceptionalization, but, as ready, encourage simple concepts, such as texture, color, like/different, big/small

Provide a variety of meaningful concrete materials and experiences, beginning with large-scale, representational, three-dimensional toys with attention to objects' weight, color, texture, and action properties that respond to child's spontaneous object–choice and play–action interests

Reinforce child's discovery and learning process by techniques like "say, show, do, and review"

Employ a "touch-demonstrate-say" teaching style for visual–spatial learners

Support child's current level of development: if primarily process-focused, supply activities that allow for variation and exploration; if primarily product-focused, supply activities that encourage child to notice and enjoy process

Provide opportunity to share knowledge and enjoy learning activities with peers

Other:

VII: Individualized Supportive Play Adaptations and Experiences

Provide rich learning environment with interconnected multiexperiential theme development (shipbuilding and marine life, air and space, farming)

Provide conceptual framework for understanding progressively more abstract concepts (time, relationships, sequences)

Support more indepth and broadened conceptualization

Slow and enrich learning process allowing process to be valued (anxiety compels child to constantly strive for finished product)

Help child verbalize actions and goals, establish simple verbal plan to enable child to summarize and discuss activities and experiences with peers and adults

Use carefully planned and progressive field trips to broaden life experiences

Use computer and other technology to challenge intellect and allow for appropriate peer interaction

Provide ongoing learning opportunities that can be shared with another child, and then with a small group

VIII: Results and Outcomes

More multisensory experiences are being provided to help Peter gain more in depth comprehension of concepts

Aide is encouraging Peter to experience more relaxed exploration of materials and play themes

Peter is participating in group field trips and in small group motor activities away from school grounds

A record player with earphones is now available for story listening

A language master is in use

A computer will be on loan in a few months

Learning activities support involvement with peers

II: Observational Impressions

A = attained or mastered   E = emerging   * = working theme
P = practicing   N = not observed

LEVEL 1 (BIRTH–18 MONTHS)

WORKING THEME Engages in sensorimotor, functional-combinatory, early constructive, and autorepresentational play in solitary, onlooker, parallel, and interactive situations

WHAT YOU OBSERVE

A *Discovers and enjoys body parts and movement*
A *Experiments with action on self, objects, and others; mouthing, banging, dropping, swiping, poking, and fitting in*
A *Engages in mobility oriented play; pushes, pulls, throws, runs*
A *Enjoys solitary play balanced by interactive play with caregiver: peek-a-boo, mirroring, and imitating*
P *Engages in onlooker and parallel play with peers and adults*
A *Engages in functional play: briefly uses object in purposeful ways (squeaks toy, pushes car)*
A *Engages in functional–combinatory play by using two objects in way intended with sober and serious demeanor (stirs spoon in cup)*
A *Engages in simple constructive play: builds tower of three cubes*
A *Engages in autorepresentational play: playful conventional use of object on self or mimicry of routine experiences (drinks from empty cup, puts head down and pretends to sleep)*

LEVEL 2 (19–36 MONTHS)

* **WORKING THEME** *Engages in constructive, autorepresentational, and allorepresentational play in solitary and associative situations*

WHAT YOU OBSERVE

A *Continues to enjoy solitary play*
P *Initiates chasing and hiding games*
A *Expands functional–combinatory actions on objects: pouring, filling, carrying, loading, and unloading*
A *Enjoys constructive materials and activities for building up and breaking down and creating simple replicas*
A *Responds to realistic props; imitates daily experiences in play*
P *Briefly takes on persona of another person or animal*
P *Uses deferred auto- and allorepresentational play through imitation to recreate short scenes outside of their typical setting in which pretend action is extended to self, others, and objects (feeds self, teacher and doll from empty cup)*
N Beginning to use toys from common stock pile

LEVEL 3 (37–60 MONTHS)

WORKING THEME Engages in allorepresentational and symbolic play in solitary and cooperative situations

WHAT YOU OBSERVE

A *Uses symbolic play through object substitution (uses block as car, big spoon as telephone*
N Works together with peers toward common goals, following rules, taking turns with limited resources, negotiating and accommodating (cooperative)
E *Uses symbolic play with planned sequence, longer episodes, props, players, roles, scripts, and scenarios based on realistic experience,* increasingly substituting language for action and solving problems (sociodramatic)
E *Builds complex dramatic scenes which expand on actions and ideas beyond personal experience with imaginary roles,* companions, and fantasy plots

III: Skills and Outstanding Characteristics Observed

Prefers solitary play; tolerates some adult involvement but rejects all peers
Play skills strong but not being used at age-appropriate level for social interaction
Good imagination, strong imitation of adults, enthusiastic player
Enjoys object substitution
Plans sequence and excellent attention span in self-directed play
Builds structures
Uses people figures in play
Displays strong problem solving in play scenarios

IV: Characteristic Patterns Limiting Play

Fixated at sensorimotor or functional level; perseverative in auto- or allorepresentational use of objects or in play scenarios, themes, and routines
Preference for solitary and noninteractional activities
Delay in communicative, cognitive, sensory, motoric, and interactive skills inhibits development of symbolic and sociodramatic play
Rigidity to own purpose in play style and activity choice
Precipitation of sensory overstimulation and or emotional excitation through play, leading to regression in play skills, cessation of play, or disorganization and frenzy
Extended need for realistic props
Limited play skills may require active teacher support or involvement
Fearful of imaginative play
Lack of conceptual, attentional, sequencing skills and understanding of cause and effect, which inhibits linking of play acts and leads to fragmented play
Lack of life experiences that support play skill development
Lack of comprehension of social dynamics of turn taking, rule use
Overspecific preference for adult as play associate, little desire for peer interaction in play
Lack of pleasure in play, general apathy

Other:

V: Discrepancy Analysis (GO TO LAST PAGE OF CHARTS)

VI: Intervention Goal/Facilitating Techniques

GOAL Provide relationship, environment, and materials that support pleasurable learning of progressively more complex object use and social interactions through play

WHAT YOU CAN DO

Create an environment in which play is fun and valued as the natural behavior of every child

Create an environment in which developmentally appropriate play is the focal emphasis in the planned curriculum

Design play environment through choice of specific toys and scenes that teach targeted concepts, interactions, or social relations (e.g., cars on block roadway with stop signs may teach turn taking, inhibition, and social rules)

Engage the child by being responsive to his or her preferred actions and activities; tune into the child's gestural and verbal interactive (two-way) communications; facilitate these messages by reciprocating through imitation and expansion, adjusting pace and affect to match or complement child's emotional energy

Provide numerous opportunities for sensorimotor and functional play, if child is still primarily involved with these levels; be an active partner in play, help peers accept this child's play level

Create situations so that child can first observe peers, then be near peers, sharing space and materials, even if play levels are dissimilar

Simplify play expectations to better match child's play-skill level

Provide direct support to compensate and adapt for compromised skills

Model subskills of play behavior to help child learn and practice more advanced play behavior

Allow for child's extended need for realistic props; incrementally remove pieces or parts of the play scene, evoking memory and imagination for the missing object

Substitute more adaptive or functional play experience for preoccupation with rigid, repetitive, and restrictive activity, but, if perseveration interferes with all learning experiences, modify pattern in small increments of change, model more adaptive behavior, redirect behavior or bargain (first this, then that); when all else fails, remove the object that leads to perseveration

Support progressive involvement in sociodramatic play by adult's modeling roles and use of props, adult partnership with peer and friend to assist in roles and purpose, adult monitoring of peers in roles and prop use

Other:

VII: Individualized Supportive Play Adaptations and Experiences

Use wireless auditory trainer to directly communicate with child during group activities and play (support receptive auditory problems and social interpretive problems)

Direct teacher support to use well established symbolic play skills and to gradually increase tolerance of peers: assist in entrance of peers to play and ultimately have adult step out of play

Provide multiple play opportunities daily for enriched solitary and parallel play leading to cooperative/sociodramatic and symbolic play

Provide adult support and sharing in child selected dramatic play sequences with gradual introduction of expansion of form and conceptualization and expansion of role variability and inclusion of parallel and then associative play

Provide opportunity for sharing, turn taking, gesture reading during more enriched and teacher supervised peer activities such as story time, snack, art and music, table activities

Expand experiences to help child gain awareness of life routines more typical to peer group

VIII: Results and Outcomes

Wireless auditory trainer and added attention from aide is having positive impact on Peter's play development

Aide is active play partner, exploring theme development and initiating more appropriate peer contact

Aide is providing expanded experiences with opportunity for sharing with peer

Peter is demonstrating initial tolerance of short spans of parallel and associative play

Aide is using gross motor strengths to increase peer involvement

II: Observational Impressions

A = attained or mastered   E = emerging   * = working theme
P = practicing   N = not observed

LEVEL 1 (BIRTH–18 MONTHS)

WORKING THEME   Seeks pleasure from bodily sensation and movement to get and take in experience, leading to a balance of pleasure from nurturance (trust) with growing urge for self-sufficiency

WHAT YOU OBSERVE

A   *Expresses personal and shared pleasure (feeding, sucking, mouthing, cuddling, physical care), as well as oral and motor aggression (biting, scratching, throwing, poking)*

A   *Enjoys early imitative play as a way to maintain an emotional connection with the caregiver (attachment)*

A   *Seeks and derives pleasure, and comfort from activities involving own body (mouth, other body openings, skin) and caretaker's body, leading to the enjoyment of soft transitional objects*

A   *Derives pleasure and feelings of elation from mobility, robust–action schemes, and from movable toy*

LEVEL 2 (19–36 MONTHS)

*   **WORKING THEME**   *Integrates ambivalent feelings of love and hate, dependence and autonomy, holding on and letting go,* leading to cooperating with adult rules of social interaction, safety, and self-care

WHAT YOU OBSERVE

P   *Experiments in play with vacillation between intake/elimination, hoarding/sharing, filling/dumping, hurting/being hurt, messiness/cleanliness, construction/destruction, elation/soberness, nurturing/destroying, impulsivity/regulation to strike a balance between extremes*

A   *Expresses daily living and family caregiving themes through repetitive and ritualized actions with unchanging plot*

P   *Displays negativeness and combativeness as a way to defend autonomy and accept adult rules on their own terms*

N   Experiments with use of rules, rituals, routines, and fastidiousness to control unruly impulses

P   *Uses emerging locomotion and play themes to assert independence and act out ambivalence about fusion and separateness, devouring/being devoured, (shadowing and darting, chasing and catching, hide-and-seek)*

LEVEL 3 (37–60 MONTHS)

WORKING THEME   Seeks mastery of sexual and social roles and place in family, leading to internalization of sexual identity, social rules regarding eating and bodily hygiene, and social conventions of interaction

WHAT YOU OBSERVE

E   *Shows high-spirited, repeated sociodramatic plots that* recreate family drama and romance, feeling states and emotions, *hero and aggressor fantasies* with exhibitionism and voyeurism counterpointed against privacy and modesty

E   *Plays repetitive games that reflect fascination with expression of* affection, sexual intimacy vs. aggression; use, function and differences of genital organs; birth, death and vulnerability; *wish for affiliation with adults and jealousy of their skill, power, and relationships; wishes to be grown up; shows frustration at personal limitations;* preoccupied with love, rage, fear of retaliation, and the loss of the love of the love object

E   *Displays competitiveness (envy, jealousy, rivalry, possessiveness, bids for attention, winning exclusive relationship with preferred adult),* leading to an increase in protectiveness, generosity, curiosity, and nurturance

P   *Exhibits body mastery through challenging and vigorous activity*

E   *Uses symbolic, dramatic insignia, emblems, costumes and props (police badge, fire hat, nurse hat, etc.) to experiment with character roles and imaginary roles*

E   *Displays emerging passion for learning with pleasure in finished product*

III: Skills and Outstanding Characteristics Observed

Play themes may reflect issues about deafness.

Unable to incorporate peer or adult into sociodramatic play

Beginning to be able to use relationship with caregiver to relieve anxiety and modulate behavior

Pleasure in solitary play

Uses imagination to create multiple scene and varied theme play dramas

IV: Characteristic Patterns Limiting Play

Egocentricity or disturbed attachment (overdependent, insecure, ambivalent, unattached), *interfering with resolution of themes related to body competencies, needs, and controls; separation/individuation, dependency/independence;* sexual identification

Fixation on sensory and functional dimensions

Impoverishment of themes or content

Perseveration on themes

Excessive or insufficient inhibition around fear and aggression themes

Resistance to expansion of themes

Inability to adapt to adult or peer suggestions or involvement

Advancement of play skills elicits extremes of emotional experience, loss of control, and fear for safety

Emotionally charged play themes lead to overexcitement and overstimulation

Mismatch existing between play skill level and the level of themes being processed

Mismatch existing between cognitive level and the level of themes being processed

Play themes being inhibited by passivity, withdrawal, lack of motivation, overaggression, and overactivity

Play being inhibited by grief and sadness related to *issues of real or imagined loss* (death, hospitalization, divorce), confusion around finding a place in family and in adjusting to roles in the family, feelings of anger, entrapment, helplessness, and hopelessness *imposed by limitations related to disability*

Play themes inhibited by problems with oral intake, elimination, gross and fine motor skills, sensory functioning, state regulation, confused gender identity

Play themes inhibited by lack of appropriate role models, inability to organize and synthesize roles and play schemes (too loosened), inability to differentiate between reality and fantasy, limited or no motivation to play, *hoarding and inability to share*

Excessive passivity or *competitiveness interferes with play*

Other:

V: Discrepancy Analysis (GO TO LAST PAGE OF CHARTS)

VI: Intervention Goal/Facilitating Techniques

GOAL   Provide relationship, environment, and materials that support expression and resolution of developmental crises: body, love, relationship, and membership

WHAT YOU CAN DO

Consult with play therapist and, when appropriate, refer child and family for therapy

Accept the need for persistent themes; gradually challenge the repeated play scene by introducing minor variations in the sequence, content, and object use

Accept and woo the passive and withdrawn child

Assist child to identify and label feelings

Offer child words and explanations that foster understanding of worries or confused play themes

Provide toys and props that allow child to play out and experiment with bodily themes of feeding and being fed, elimination, and hygiene

Provide toys and props that allow child to play out and experiment with separation and reunion, hide-and-seek, run-and-catch

Provide toys and props that allow child to play out and experiment with themes of gender role and identity

Provide reassurance about fears of bodily injury and support bodily integrity with materials and activities such as mirrors, doctor kits, grooming materials, fantasy and realist heroic figures

Allow child to take control and show power in play; avoid battle of wills; tolerate child's normal ambivalence without overreaction

Accept expression of anxious feelings; developmental progress in play may induce regression and increased anxiety

Support exploration of unresolved themes that may be aided by return to presymbolic play; provide more adaptive outcomes in play scenarios; suggest/evoke alternative solutions to problems/conflicts that arise in play scenarios

Strive to strike a balance between opportunities for messiness and conformity to social rules of cleanliness and tidiness

Provide through play opportunities to practice rule attunement: slowing down, stopping, changing directions, cleaning up, eating, toileting, waiting, redirection of aggression, finishing, social order

Provide appropriate sensory and motor adaptive toys and props to facilitate the development of play themes

Other:

VII: Individualized Supportive Play Adaptations and Experiences

Direct teacher support to establish sociodramatic play skills appropriate to play themes; assist peers in play involvement at appropriate entry level

Through play participation and verbalization recognize and support resolution of play themes dealing with separation, dependency struggle, body integrity

Through play participation and verbalization recognize and support expression of emotions such as anger, excitement, anxiety, frustration, sadness, loneliness, and loss

Provide a variety of stimulating play materials to reinforce expanding range of life experiences and progressively maturing emotional play themes

VIII: Results and Outcomes

Aide's understanding and acceptance of Peter's emotional play needs has greatly reduced his tension and anxiety during play

Play interactions are now being used as a medium for clarification of emotional feelings

Whenever possible, aide is allowing Peter to design and lead in his own play

Expanding play opportunities are allowing Peter's play scenes to be more enriched and varied

II: Observational Guide

Type and frequency of contact between family and staff (attend parent's meetings; exchange daily log with staff; participate in regular conferences with parent coordinator or other staff member; participate in planning and placement team meetings; make regular classroom observations)

Family goals and motivation for child's placement in preschool (family's concerns about child's development and projection for future developmental outcome and programming)

Child's attachment patterns within the nuclear and extended family (preferred adult for varied activities and routines; separation and reunion issues at different setting)

Role and relationship of siblings with observed child and within family (nurturing, rejecting, baiting, etc.)

Extended family constellation, roles and functioning

Child's routine within the family's daily/weekly schedule

Details of child's home environment (sleeping arrangements, available toys, available play space indoors and outdoors, amount of television viewing, playmates in neighborhood, pets)

Availability of professional resources and family utilization of available resources

III: General Description

Parents are working to gain knowledge about impact of hearing impairment, but remain unrealistic with high expectations regarding Peter's social inclusion in a nursery group

Family lives in rural area offering Peter interesting experiences, but no peer contact

Parents are highly committed to Peter and willing to participate in the Supportive Play Model

Parents are finding Peter's behavior difficult to manage at home because of his high energy level and his resistance to adult controls

Parents are working with public schools for future planning and are active in state-wide parent support group for parents of the hearing impaired

IV: Characteristic Patterns Limiting Play

Expectations mismatched to child's development

Temperament or *style mismatch between child and parents*

Overinvestment in child's dependency

Overprotectiveness or defensiveness concerning peer reaction and lack of social interaction

Detachment and distancing

Lack of understanding of development and its implications

Provision of limited opportunities for child to experience outside the household

Overexposure of child to stimulation, activities, and experiences beyond his or her development and understanding

Driven search for innovative treatments

Inability to advocate for child

Use of education, health, and related service system in an adversarial and self-defeating way

Sibling relationships counterproductive for child or siblings

Limitations or lack of family resources and support systems

Home environment not supportive to child's individual developmental needs

Family environment not providing consistency and predictability of caregiving

Patterns of blaming and emotional unavailability between key family members, making coping difficult

Verbal commentary focusing on child's negative behavior and characteristics setting the stage for a self-fulfilling prophecy

Discussion of provocative and anxiety-ridden topics in child's presence

Other:

V: Discrepancy Analysis (GO TO LAST PAGE OF CHARTS)

VI: Intervention Goal/Facilitating Techniques

GOAL   Help family gain appreciation and understanding for child's unique qualities and developmental needs; help family maintain a system that supports mental health of all members; help family develop advocacy role in planning and management of child

THINGS YOU CAN DO

Accept parents' current level of functioning and understand that parenting is developmental process that needs nurturing

Assist family in establishing developmentally appropriate routine, environment, and expectations for child's temperament and style

Assist parents in the selection and organization of appropriate toys, materials, and *play-time experiences that match child's current development needs*

Encourage and guide parent–child play for its own sake and for pleasure

Support parental awareness of differences in temperament and *style in their child and help them to accommodate these differences*

Support family in understanding that sensorimotor exploration and play are precursors and subskills of preacademic and academic goals

Support parents as individuals in their own right

Support parents to reinforce self-identity and couple identity and total family focus so as not to become absorbed and overfocused on special child

Assist the family in helping to find a special place for the child in the family, rather than the child being at the center of the family

Assist parents in finding resources related to issues of disability and other issues

Reinforce parents' need to build support network (babysitters, respite care, therapy, support groups, etc.)

Support parents in maintaining a personal life, rather than being entrapped into "professional parent of the handicapped child" role

Work on reinforcing positive experiences shared between parent and child

Give positive feedback to parent about child's performance and positive characteristics

Understand that overprotection may be reflection of separation fears and issues of ambivalence

Allow parent appropriate access to program

Integrate parents of child with special needs into regular parent group

Assist parents in assessing strengths and limits of available services

Assist parents in selection of reasonable program of support therapies for themselves, siblings, and the child

Support family's effective advocacy for their child

Support parents in coping with what may be chronic nature of child's disability and its impact on the family

Heighten parents' awareness of the potential risk of the child's misunderstanding of anxiety-ridden and provocative commentary; worrisome material can be discussed, but at appropriate times and places, out of earshot of the child

Other:

VII: Individualized Supportive Play Adaptations and Experiences

Include parents as a resource in designing adaptation in curriculum and setting

Use parents as a resource to educate other parents and peers concerning needs of hearing impaired

Help parents understand scatter in Peter's overall development

Help parents to be more tolerant of Peter's needs for toddler like activities and emotional support

Encourage parents to locate appropriate play peers

VIII: Results and Outcomes

Fall parent's night included short presentation by speech and language pathologist concerning hearing and the preschool child; hearing impairment issues were discussed

Aide is exchanging weekly notebook with parents to improve adult consistency in expectations and responses

Classroom volunteer has made it possible for aide to spend more time with Peter to encourage peer friendships

Several classmates have been invited for play visits to Peter's home

II: Observational Guide

Number of adults available in group

Adult-to-child ratio

Adequate time available for training, staff meetings, team meeting with parents, consultation

Roles and responsibility of staff members

Affective tone of staff members with group and with observed child

Staff's ability and commitment to play

General description of adults' interactions with group and with observed child

Adults' style (directive/nondirective), tolerance of children's behavior and range of development

Adults' use of language, general relationship with child and children

Adults' teaming style and the overall school climate

III: General Description

1 teacher, 1 aide

Both early childhood trained (BA, AA)

Teacher is unsuccessfully attempting to modify Peter's play to include peers.

Teacher intervenes and removes Peter from playground when out of control.

Aide converses with Peter during snack, but unable to expand conversation to include peers.

Generally warm and accepting style and atmosphere in group

Peter raises staff anxiety level by not matching group expectations.

Teaching approach is predominantly verbal.

IV: Characteristic Patterns Limiting Play

Unresponsive or unempathetic to child's immediate needs, behaviors, or feelings

Inconsistent interest or acceptance toward child

Style and pace poorly matched to child's

Poorly defined roles and responsibilities

Communication and language poorly matched to affect and developmental level of child

Inadequate training to meet observed child's needs

Uninvolved with child's play

Too involved or *controlling*

Not reinforcing child's attempts for object mastery or peer affiliation

Confused about accepting the protective and guiding role (over permissive or authoritarian; inconsistent and ambivalent)

Anxious about child's disability

Poor team work

Inadequate adult-to-child ratio

Other:

V: Discrepancy Analysis (GO TO LAST PAGE OF CHARTS)

VI: Intervention Goal/Facilitating Techniques

GOAL   Provide individualized relationship to support all areas of child's development and to accommodate a family-focused approach; incrementally release child to relate with other adults and peers

WHAT YOU CAN DO

Provide adult-to-child ratio of one-to-one, progressing to one-to-five; consider special child to be equivalent to two or three normally developing children when establishing adult-to-child ratio

Seek and use network support system to increase skills for working with child (consult specialists, attend workshops, read about condition)

Prepare personally for working with child: empathy exercises, exploration of personal reaction to child (sadness, hopelessness, helplessness, fear, vulnerability, anger, and disappointment)

Accept and reach out to family for collaboration, to develop mutual support and respect

Adapt teaching style and interactive style to child's needs (activity level and passivity, loudness, *verbal intensity and rate of speech, use of physical contact*)

Know and believe that task is to assist in the child's growth and development, not to "cure" the child (progress, not *perfection); accept some misbehavior and regression*

Be alert to nonintrusive ways that child's developmental skills can be supported

Build team collaboration and consistency for communication and management

Be available as play partner by being actively involved in child's play; gradually disengage and allow child to play with other adults and peers

Prepare environment and give child emotional and physical space that allows him or her to experience, explore, experiment, and discover through trial and error; let child's product be his or her own—do not use art models

Reinforce discovery and learning by using techniques like "say, show, do, and review"

Accept that child sometimes needs to experience failures, bumps, and falls

Actively facilitate child-to-child interaction: verbally model, prompt, cue, and coach; physically and verbally support greetings, partings, negotiations, material and space sharing, and turn taking

Allow child to retreat, when necessary, from group activities or engage in solitary play; "tuning out" for interludes may allow child to reorganize and then reenter group activities

Support by sitting near child at group time, praising child's attempt at task, reinforcing child's approach to peers

Resist temptation to comment critically or sarcastically (to discuss any child while children present); all classroom conversation should be appropriate for children to hear and be centered on child's experiences and activities

Prepare family and staff for the reality that regression is a normal part of development; sometimes you have to go back to regroup in order to go forward

Other:

VII: Individualized Supportive Play Adaptations and Experiences

Increase number of adults in group

Maintain communication with public school special education personnel

Consult with speech and language pathologist to be trained with hearing aids and wireless auditory trainer

Learn about impact of hearing impairment on development of play

Design a plan for team consistency

Establish regular communication pattern with family (notebook exchange, telephone, meetings)

Regulate pace and amount of speech

Utilize wireless auditory trainer for direct verbal contact with child

Have adult be play partner; gradually include one peer

Accept that child not ready for peer play even though symbolic play is well established

VIII: Results and Outcomes

Significant progress is observable because of staff's increased understanding of special needs of child and family; community resource use and consultation; hearing impairment and its implications in a mainstreamed setting ; technological equipment

Staff to child ratio has improved

PEERS

II: Observational Guide

Total number of peers in group
Age range of peers
Male–female ratio of group
Ratio of normally developing children to children with disabilities
Interaction and style of peers with observed child during various activities
Pace of group
Child's awareness and involvement with peers
Peers' level of awareness, involvement, and interest in the observed child
Relative difference in developmental age of peers and observed child

III: General Description

17 children
Peter is 5 years old, remainder of children are 4-year-olds
8 males, 9 females
No peer skills observed between Peter and peers, no special friend
Peers are active, appropriate solitary, associate, and cooperate players

IV: Characteristic Patterns Limiting Play

Inappropriate group size or composition
Peer-driven climate and activity preferences incompatible with child
Group social behavior and play level unable to accommodate observed child
Peers intolerant of, uninterested in, or display *lack of understanding of child with special needs*
Pace too fast or too slow

Other:

SPACE

II: Observational Guide

Size of room and playground
Scale, division, and organization of play spaces
Defined areas for activities of daily living spaces: feeding, sleeping, toileting, hand washing, tooth brushing, group and personal storage
Defined play spaces: fine motor, constructive and dramatic play, expressive arts, gross motor
Traffic flow, circulation space
Variety of flooring and ground surfaces (hard and soft; varying textures)
Acoustics (separation of quiet and noisy areas, sound-absorbing surfaces, general noise level)
Attention to appropriate stimulation level: decor, use of color, lighting level, window treatment, visual clutter
Open and closed storage facilities
Areas for relaxation, retreat, and comfort
Display areas
Handicapped accessible

III: General Description

Room space and design fine
Organization and decor fine
No acoustic adaptations for sensory impairments
Inadequate indoor sensory and gross motor areas

IV: Characteristic Patterns Limiting Play

Disorganized, cluttered, or unsafe space
Sterile and uninviting or overplanned space
Too large, overstimulating, and unstructured space
Indoor and outdoor space not planned to respond to child's needs
Unclear division between activity areas
Inadequate opened and closed storage areas
Acoustics and lighting inadequate or *inappropriate*
Inconvenient or inappropriate toileting area
No space allocation for quiet, solitary, messy uses, clean-up
Inadequate large motor areas, indoors and outdoors
Traffic flow interferes with effective use of play spaces
Inadequate or inappropriate hard and soft play surfaces
No discrete display areas
Inadequate accessibility

Other:

V: Discrepancy Analysis (GO TO LAST PAGE OF CHARTS)

VI: Intervention Goal/Facilitating Techniques

GOAL Help normal peers to relate in a positive fashion to their peers with special needs, to gain understanding and tolerance of individual differences

WHAT YOU CAN DO

Form small, compatible, and complementary subgroups that contain children who show a balance in activity level, play and social level and in the range of verbal, cognitive, and motor skills

Educate normal peers for presence of child with special needs in group (peers may be unable to understand child's problem or intention, fear child's condition, and fantasize something similar is going to happen to them, and show disinterest, which may represent a form of avoidance or denial)

Emphasize strengths and interests of child with special needs; empower the child with interesting activities and materials to draw other peers to him

Support peers to include child with special needs, even if play is at lower level

Support peers to allow child with special needs not to participate in all group activities or to participate in a different way

Other:

VII: Individualized Supportive Play Adaptations and Experiences

Use consultants, including parents, to help peers understand handicap and special equipment

Help children tolerate Peter's need for solitary play at this time

Target key peers who can be gradually supported into parallel and then associative play with Peter

Allow Peter to carry out solitary, parallel activity while peer group is involved in sociodramatic theme, gradually move toward small role in drama

Begin play integration process in strong areas that do not raise Peter's anxiety level (gross motor, obstacle course, sharing story time)

Use vehicle play and gross motor equipment that allows Peter to interact with peer

VIII: Results and Outcomes

All children are benefiting from increased staff coverage

Children are more accepting and knowledgeable concerning Peter's equipment and disability

Key peers have been selected for gradual increase of peer interactions with Peter

Peter's strong skills are being better utilized to incorporate peer involvement

---

V: Discrepancy Analysis (GO TO LAST PAGE OF CHARTS)

VI: Intervention Goal/Facilitating Techniques

GOAL Design an environment that responds adaptively to the child's unique needs for flexible space

WHAT YOU CAN DO

Design flexible and accessible space: open and closed, movable and fixed elements and partitions, appropriately stimulating, clear divisions for activities and materials, logical and adequate storage, accessible sink and bathroom areas, messy activity area, *large motor area outdoors/indoors*, varied room textures

Give special consideration to acoustics (soft background music, white noise, *rugs as sound absorption*, ceiling height) and lighting (nonfluorescent lights, window shades, task spot lighting, mirror use)

Consult appropriate specialists concerning lighting and *acoustics when child's needs* are visual, *auditory*, motoric, or attention related

Other:

VII: Individualized Supportive Play Adaptations and Experiences

Consult audiologist about acoustics and a specialist to improve design of space and sound management

Design indoor gross motor areas for regular use

VIII: Results and Outcomes

Rug has been installed.

Indoor gross motor area is available daily.

Plans have been made to lower ceiling.

TIME

II: Observational Guide

Daily schedule and length of activities
Sequences of activities
Balance of active and quiet activities
Schedule responsive to children's needs, interests, moods, and
  daily tempo
Coordination and synchronization of arrival and departure with
  school schedule, transportation schedule and family needs

III: General Description

9:00–11:30 AM
Free play activity hour, group time, snack, outdoor play
Basic schedule suitable for majority of children

IV: Characteristic Patterns Limiting Play

Inflexible routine or no clear routine
Activities, all group-focused, long, and required
Imbalance of active or quiet activities
Routine pace too rushed, too slow, nonresponsive
Disruption in routine because of unscheduled arrival and depar-
  ture

Other:

MATERIALS AND EQUIPMENT

II: Observational Guide

Scale, size, weight, texture, color, and composition of furniture,
  materials, and equipment
Quantity, categories, and appropriateness of toys, materials and
  equipment available
Large and small motor material and equipment
Suspended equipment for vestibular and sensorimotor stimulation
Sensory materials (sand and water, paint, clay and play dough,
  etc.)
Constructive and dramatic materials and equipment
Adaptive and augmentative materials and equipment
Conceptual and creative materials
Availability of furniture and equipment for activities of daily liv-
  ing (feeding, hygiene, napping)
Maintenance of materials and equipment
General accessibility to materials and equipment

III: General Description

Need wireless auditory trainer
No computer available in the classroom
Gross motor equipment needs to be increased

IV: Characteristic Patterns Limiting Play

Choices and supplies inappropriately constrict child's selection of
  and experimentation with objects
Restrictive range of available materials
Poorly matched to child's needs (developmental level, size, etc.)
Not reflective of child's experiences
Not multisensory or creative in nature
Disorganized and poorly presented
Insufficient number of duplicate materials requiring premature sharing
Not adapted and accessible to child's specific limitations (chair and
  table height, grip handles on puzzles, etc.)
Broken, dirty, torn, and incomplete items
Inappropriate scale, size, weight, texture, color, and composition
Unavailable or insufficient toys that promote expanded play deal-
  ing with play themes

Other:

V: Discrepancy Analysis (GO TO LAST PAGE OF CHARTS)

VI: Intervention Goal/Facilitating Techniques

GOAL   Design an environment that responds adaptively to the child's unique needs for responsive routine.

WHAT YOU CAN DO
Provide predictable and responsive routine with adjustments for fatigue, *illness, overstimulation, or regression*
Experiment with schedule and activity variations relative to child's biological rhythms (slow starter, *highly active*, morning napper, etc.)
Allow ample time for solitary play, but encourage group participation
Allow sufficient periods in schedule to accommodate varying levels of play (solitary, interactive, onlooker, parallel, associative, cooperative)
Collaborate to identify and resolve scheduling problems

Other:

VII: Individualized Supportive Play Adaptations and Experiences

Allow opportunity for solitary play during group time.
Experiment with gross motor, sensory, or vestibular activities in first hour of day
Allow opportunity for short activities with one peer
Provide time out procedure and space for emotional reorganization

VIII: Results and Outcomes

Motor, sensory, and vestibular activities are available in first hour
Aide is providing short time away from groups with walks with one peer
Plan has been established by staff to maintain safety limits for Peter

---

V: Discrepancy Analysis (GO TO LAST PAGE OF CHARTS)

VI: Intervention Goal/Facilitating Techniques

GOAL   Design an environment that responds adaptively to the child's unique needs for adaptive materials and equipment.

WHAT YOU CAN DO
Consult, if necessary, with physical therapist, occupational therapist, speech and language specialist, audiologist, vision specialist, or other specialists *for appropriately adaptive materials and equipment*
Use toys, materials and equipment that promote a full range of learning, feeling, and playing experiences matched to children's developmental needs
Use materials that promote multisensory experiences (tactile: water, sand, clay, shaving cream; *vestibular: swings, hammock, bolsters; auditory: earphones, tape player, instruments,* background music, *language master;* visual: *computer,* light box, *pictures, books, language master cards*)
Choose materials with attention to tactile defensiveness, vestibular instability, and *sensory problems;* be attentive to material qualities that relate to size, weight, and volume
Repair or replace broken materials and equipment

Other:

VII: Individualized Supportive Play Adaptations and Experiences

Make gross motor options available in indoor space
Use wireless auditory trainer and other auditory support equipment throughout day
Increase options of sensory and vestibular materials and equipment
Provide some duplicate materials to encourage parallel play

VIII: Results and Outcomes

Record player with earphones and wireless auditory trainer are now in daily use.
Language master has been ordered.
Computer will be on loan to classroom.
Availability of sensory motor and vestibular materials and equipment has greatly increased.

Supportive Play Model

Section I. Discrepancy Analysis

Name: *Peter*

Date of birth: *July 24, 1989*

Date: *September*

Developmental Area	CA Level	Working Theme Level	Differences (below age level, age level, above age level)
Self/Social/Emotional	3	2	below age level
Motor/Self-Help	3	2	below age level*
Communicative/Language	3	2	below age level
Cognitive	3	2	below age level
Play Skills	3	2	below age level*
Play Themes	3	2	below age level

Highlight significant discrepancy issues:

CHILD: doesn't have group social skills; showing signs of anxiety, aggression, and frustration because can't express ideas as a result of limited verbal and nonverbal skills; good gross motor skills, but high activity level and lack of awareness for safety; many play skills are strong but because of social–emotional and interpersonal delays play is not yet interactive

FAMILY: very interested and involved in Peter's development; home is in remote location; Peter's high energy level has been over-whelming; have found it difficult to be consistent with Peter's behavior

PROGRAM: staff concerned about Peter's behavior in the group; he requires a great deal of attention; they question if other children are losing out; interrupts other children's activities

Application of the Supportive Play Model to a Child with a Physical Handicap and Related Chronic Health Conditions

More aggressive and effective care for medically at-risk infants and children, during and after life-threatening accidents and illness, has added to the population of children who are qualified for early intervention, special education services, and inclusion in regular educational settings. This "new morbidity" has increased survival rates in infants and children with handicaps, and means that more students with chronic health problems or physical handicaps attend schools and are participating in mainstreaming (Stabler, 1988).

Chronically ill children and children who have to go through repeated medical procedures for extended periods of time or throughout their lives have an added burden in their development that, if not appropriately supported, can lead to emotional and developmental consequences. The time of the origination of their condition and the extent of the condition's interference in normal daily living are significant in the developmental outcome Kessler & Milligan, 1979). Developing positive self-esteem may be difficult when the medical or health issues impede socialization and lead to social isolation (Cadman, Boyle, Szatmari, & Offord, 1987; Stabler, 1988). Breslau (1985) found increased risk for psychiatric impairment in children with chronic health conditions. In particular, conditions involving brain abnormalities were associated with more pervasive psychopathology, including social isolation. Pless's (1984) review studies the relationship of illness and psychological or social problems and finds that the order of magnitude of risk is 1.5 to 3 times that of healthy children.

One in 1,000 children needs medical technological assistance on an ongoing basis over an extended period or for all of his or her life (Palfrey et al., 1991). As a group, children who need medical technological assistance are those who need daily skilled nursing and are technologically dependent in order to avoid further disability and death (Office of Technical Assessment, 1987). Medically technologically assisted children are entering into integrated school situations in increasing numbers (Haynie, Porter, & Palfrey, 1989). Half of this population requires respiratory technology, such as suction, tracheotomy care, oxygen treatments, or ventilator support. Another 25% requires cardiorespiratory monitoring, and the remaining 25% relies on interventions, such as intravenous treatment for medication or nutrition, kidney dialysis, or tube feeding (Millner, 1991).

Children may require these medical measures because of spinal cord injury, neuromuscular disorders, cerebral palsy, kidney failure, illnesses such as cancer and AIDS, and diseases such as cystic fibrosis, asthma, and heart problems (Kirk, Gallagher, & Anastasiow, 1993; Trompeter, 1990). Premature birth or very low birth weight can lead to chronic lung disorder requiring respiratory technical assistance, including oxygen supplementa-

tion, tracheotomy, and mechanical ventilation; apnea, which may require electronic surveillance with cardiorespiratory monitoring; and poor sucking and swallowing, which may require tube feedings. Complications from prematurity may lead to kidney failure, muscle weakness, and brain damage (Aylward, Pfeiffer, Wright, & Verhulst, 1989; *Handbook for the Care*, 1991; Levy & Pilmer, 1992).

Children who are medically technologically dependent may need to be hospitalized for extended periods, or even indefinitely. This forced separation may lead to interference in parent–child attachment, emotional distress because of the necessity for repeated intrusive medical procedures, and feelings of abandonment (Levy & Pilmer, 1992). If these children can be cared for at home, there is the advantage of having them experience developmentally appropriate interactions with normally developing peers, because many of these children have the capacity for age-appropriate social and intellectual development. Children who are on ventilators may need support in developing social skills because of a lack of exposure to peers and a poor self-image (Levy, 1991). Children who have a tracheotomy tube during their first years of life are unable to speak during this period, unless they have a speaking valve or electrolarynx; consequently, most must depend on sign language or augmentative communication systems (Levy & Pilmer, 1992). If they are unable to speak throughout the language development years, they may develop problems in speech production, syntax, and articulation once the tube is removed (Simon, Fowler, & Handler, 1983; Singer et al., 1989). For all of these children, early intervention must be designed by parents and a team of appropriate professionals who understand the child's ongoing medical and developmental needs.

Families need a high level of support because of the emotional and financial stresses of raising a medically technologically dependent child. It takes emotionally strong parents who have good support systems to see their way through much of the uncertainty and stress that is part of the daily reality of living with many of these children (Burr, Guyer, Todres, Abrahams, & Chiodo, 1983; Lichtenstein, 1986; Quint, Chesterman, Crain, Winkleby, & Boyce, 1990).

There are numerous other chronic conditions that can affect the health of children and their early education. For instance, cystic fibrosis and asthma are two cardiopulmonary conditions that affect children who are participating in preschool programs. Cystic fibrosis, the most frequently occurring fatal genetic disease in the United States, affects 1 in every 1,600 children, and asthma has become one of the most common causes for chronic school absences and hospitalizations among children today (Neisworth & Bagnato, 1987; Roberts, 1990). Other conditions affecting children who are enrolled in preschool settings include diabetes, sickle cell anemia, and cancer. Children with these health issues can benefit emotionally, socially, and academically by participating in a normalized peer setting, but the adults in charge of the setting need to be sensitive to their ongoing health needs while planning for their participation. Fatigue, depression, and anger may be part of children's reaction to their illness. Full participation in all activities may not be advisable or even possible.

For many children with ongoing health problems, exposure to childhood illnesses, which is merely an inconvenience to most children, can be potentially life-threatening and must be monitored. For some, immunity problems may be the result of an illness or the outcome of some treatment programs. For instance, children who have had transplanted organs may have their immune systems depressed medically to reduce the chances of organ rejection. Decisions regarding group participation of immune-deficient children need to be carefully weighed by parents and physicians, but, if the risks can be minimized, participation with peers can be a wonderful support to the overall development of these children.

For children with chronic and serious health problems, fears about pain and dying may be foremost in their minds. It takes skilled adults to respond to their real need for empathy and understanding about these issues, and to draw them into the daily pleasures of interacting and learning with their peers. Fear of medical equipment, pain associated with medical treatment, and concerns about death and dying may also affect normal peers who need help in sorting through their fantasies regarding sickness and body constancy issues.

There is an additional group of children now being served in preschools. These are the 2 in 100 children who may have motor- or health-related problems and do not require medical technical assistance in their classroom, but who do require nonmedical technical assistance to successfully participate in daily living and preschool education (Millner, 1991; Levy & Pilmer, 1992). The equipment they need may include wheelchairs, hearing aids, computers, microswitches to control computers or other equipment, augmentative communication devices, adaptive equipment to improve positioning and seating, and adaptive toys (Church & Glennen,1992). This type of equipment is mandated by Public Law 100-47, the Technology Related Assistance for Individuals with Disabilities Act of 1988, and should be part of the intervention plan drawn up by the child's planning and placement team. This type of equipment may be a curiosity to preschool peers and may be utilized by a sensitive teacher as a modality to increase peer contact. If unexplained, though, it may add to peers' fears, to their need to reject the child, and to their sense of concern about the child with special needs or about their own sense of mastery and body-related competencies. Acquiring the appropriate materials and equipment to maximize the involvement of this group of children is crucial to success in the preschool setting. Since the equipment involved is not part of direct life support, it may appear to be less crucial to mainstream placements, but for the individual child who will be participating in the group, this type of non-medical equipment and adaptive materials can make a dramatic impact on the child's ultimate success in the program. Something seemingly as simple as a properly adapted chair and table can be the reason why a child can participate with peers in snack and fine motor activities. A voice output communication device or picture board can allow a child, who otherwise couldn't, to make friends and express needs. Negotiating with the child's public school system or other appropriate funding sources to provide the required materials and equipment is a high priority. Trying to

mainstream a child by "making do," without the appropriate nonmedical technical equipment, is a real disservice to children because they will experience unnecessary frustration and failure in attempting to interact with peers and participate in preschool play and other activities.

TWO HIGH-INCIDENT PHYSICAL HANDICAPS WITH LONG-TERM MEDICAL OR HEALTH IMPLICATIONS

Handicapping conditions that affect a child's motor skills and general mobility can be of major consequence to the child's self-esteem and general success in preschool and, ultimately, in life. Even if the child has normal intelligence and is highly motivated to socialize with peers, a physical disability sets up major barricades to success. In this section, we have chosen to describe two physically handicapping conditions, cerebral palsy and spina bifida, that lead to ongoing health and medical issues. These conditions were selected because they are the most frequent causes of locomotion problems in children and, thus, are the conditions that teachers are most likely to see in preschool. The developmental issues related to each condition will be described. Then, a case study will be presented to illustrate the use of the SPM process with a child who has **spina bifida**. Although there are numerous issues that are different in children with cerebral palsy and spina bifida, many of the play-related and overall developmental issues are similar.

Cerebral Palsy

Cerebral palsy, the most common mobility handicap affecting children, also affects global development and typically requires a wide range of therapies and frequent medical evaluation and intervention. Incidence statistics average 2 per 1,000 children with this condition, although some studies that include mild cases indicate as many as 6 per 1,000 children diagnosed with cerebral palsy (Mysak, 1982; Paneth & Kiely, 1984). Males have a slightly higher risk of being diagnosed with cerebral palsy (Perin, 1989). Because of advances in current neonatology, many hoped that the rates of cerebral palsy would decrease, but, in fact, the rate has stayed stable because the smaller premature and low-birth-weight babies who are currently surviving have a high risk of cerebral palsy (Hagberg, Hagberg, & Olow, 1975; Hagberg, Hagberg, & Zetterstrom, 1989; Paneth & Kiely, 1984; Russman & Gage, 1989).

Cerebral palsy is not a single disease, but rather a disability that is the result of nonprogressive damage to the motor control centers of the brain before they are fully developed; this damage compromises movement and posture (Bax, 1964; Perin, 1989). The severity of this disability can range from minimal to profound. The causes for this condition are numerous and can be either prenatal, perinatal, or postnatal, although for many children the specific cause can not always be determined (Russman & Gage, 1989). Most of the known causes are prenatal and include chromosomal abnormalities, rubella, Rh incompatibility, toxemia, and toxins (Scher, Belfar, Martin, & Painter, 1991). Far less common are perinatal causes, such as birth injury (Nelson & Ellenberg, 1986). Postnatal causes include head injury, anoxia, exposure to toxins, such as lead, and infections, such as encephalitis (Behrman & Vaughan, 1983). Between one third and two thirds of all children with cerebral palsy are premature or of low birth weight (Behrman & Vaughn, 1983; Bleck, 1982a; Hagberg et al., 1989; Russman & Gage, 1989). Premature babies, particularly, face a risk of intracranial hemorrhage that can be associated with paralysis and retardation (McCrae, 1986).

The most common types of cerebral palsy are **spastic**, **athetoid**, and **ataxia**. Spastic cerebral palsy leads to increased muscle tone, which limits movement and leads to abnormal movement patterns. Athetoid cerebral palsy leads to excessive movement and abnormal patterns of movement. Ataxia leads to problems in balance and posture, fluctuating muscle tone, and a lurching gait (Bleck, 1982a; Neisworth & Bagnato, 1987). **Hypotonia** is also seen in many children with cerebral palsy. Cerebral palsy is also categorized by the number of limbs that are affected, the most common being hemiplegia (one arm and one leg on the same side of the body), diplegia (the legs only), triplegia (usually both legs and one arm), and quadriplegia (all four limbs).

Depending on the category of cerebral palsy, between 25 and 90% of these children also have a seizure disorder (Aksu, 1990; Wallace, 1990). Other global developmental issues that are common to children with cerebral palsy include learning disabilities, mental retardation, speech impairments, eating problems, visual and hearing impairments, problems in **sensory integration**, tactile sensitivity, and joint and bone deformities (Black, 1980, Bleck, 1979, 1982a; Brett, 1983; Jones, 1989; Molnar, 1985; Mysak, 1982). This overlay of issues makes it imperative that children with cerebral palsy receive a cross-disciplinary early intervention program that deals with their developmental issues; otherwise, overall potential can be dramatically compromised, and lifelong needs will be increased.

Infants or children with cerebral palsy may have a difficult time conveying feeling states because their nonverbal communication skills, including reflexive and intentional motor behavior, gesture, and facial expression may be outside their control, or may not communicate what they intend. Hospitalizations and separations from parents are necessary to deal with problems related to prematurity, joint and bone deformities, **ocular motor imbalance**, and seizures. Parents may have to spend an inordinate amount of time carrying out physical care and therapy activities, so that pleasurable reciprocal interactions may be limited (Foley, 1986; Kogan, Tyler, & Turner, 1974; Peterson, 1987; Shere & Kastenbaum, 1966). Children with cerebral palsy may run the risk of emotional problems, hyperactivity, emotional immaturity, introversion, and depression (Batshaw, Perret, & Kurtz, 1992; Mysak, 1982; Peterson, 1987; Rutter, Tizard, & Whitmore, 1970).

All aspects of speech, language, and communication development can be problems for many children with cerebral palsy. About 20% of these children have hearing deficits (Robinson, 1973). But even without auditory problems, there are many other aspects of cerebral palsy that interfere with communication and speech. Because of poor development of head and trunk control, irregular and abnormal respiration patterns, primitive reflexes, high palate, and general motor control problems, up to 90% of children with cerebral palsy have articulation deficits and voice problems that may interfere with the production of oral language (Buch, Collins, & Gelber, 1978; Darley, Aronson, & Brown, 1975; Davis, 1978; Hagen, Porter, & Brink, 1973; Mecham, 1966; Morris, Escoll, & Wexler, 1956; Mysak, 1971; Peterson, 1987).

Because of their problems with expression, it is difficult to use standardized intelligence testing with children with cerebral palsy. It is estimated, though, that at least 40% of these children have normal intelligence, and of the children who are retarded, 15% are mildly retarded, 35% are moderately retarded, and the remaining 50% are severely to profoundly retarded (Robinson, 1973). Mental retardation is partially the result of the brain damage that causes the cerebral palsy, but it can also be the indirect consequence of the deprivation in physical and motor experiences (Rothman, 1987). Even the 40% of children with cerebral palsy who test as having average or better intelligence may have learning disabilities and perceptual impairments requiring adaptations in the learning environment (Crothers & Paine, 1959).

Mental and motor problems can also directly interfere with the development of exploratory and social play in children with cerebral palsy (Hewett, 1970). Parents are often so focused on the physical needs and the therapies that are part of their child's daily schedule that they may need support in enjoying simple interactive play activities with their child (Shere & Kastenbaum, 1966). Toys may need to be adapted to attract the child's attention, to reinforce simple movements, and to give the child control and some independence (Finnie, 1974). Most importantly the play activities should not be so programmed and motor-oriented as to inhibit the child's potential for initiative and spontaneity (Mogford, 1977; Sheridan, 1975; Musselwhite, 1986).

Sensory and motor problems related to cerebral palsy can also compromise many aspects of learning and living. Sensory disabilities in hearing and vision, sensory integration problems, and tactile defensiveness may all limit exposure to the materials and experiences necessary for learning (Ayres, 1972, 1978; Black, 1980; DuBose, 1979; Rosenbloom, 1975). Central nervous system damage also leads to delayed motor milestones and the related problems in movement that can, in turn, affect problem-solving, communication, and social skills. The result of central nervous system damage can also mean that normal daily activities and play are exhausting and unrewarding (Connolly & Russell, 1976; Neisworth & Bagnato, 1987). Even for children with mild cerebral palsy, learning to walk can be complicated because their disability leads to scissor walking and toe walking. Often required throughout the child's life, are the use of **orthotics** (such as braces and splints) to provide support and maintain range of motion and surgeries to avoid and correct joint and bone deformities.

Intervention plans for children with cerebral palsy should include a range of appropriate therapies, medical planning and intervention, and the design and use of adaptive materials and equipment. When planning for adaptive materials and equipment, the child's hearing, vision, and motor needs must be taken into account. Color, texture, size, weight, and design are all qualities that need to be considered when selecting toys that are market-ready. Many toys can also be adapted through the use of Velcro to hold a toy in place, knob enlargement to allow for a better grasp, and switches to allow a child with even minimal motor control to experience **cause and effect** during exploratory play. Diverse sensory and motor experiences are needed to improve sensorimotor and **spatial ability** (Finnie, 1990; Powell, 1985; Rothman, 1987, 1989). If a child is not speaking or experiences difficulties with spoken communication, **augmentative and alternative communication methods** must be explored. They may include simple picture books and language boards, as well as more sophisticated voice output or **electronic communication devices** and computers (Bruno, 1989; Fishman, 1987; McDonald, 1975; Neisworth & Bagnato, 1987; Silverman, 1980; Udwin & Yule, 1990, 1991a, 1991b). The impact of motor disabilities may be reduced with occupational therapy, which can also improve sensory integration and reduce defensiveness to textures, touch, and stimulation (Ayres, 1972, 1978). Physical therapy can design a plan for positioning and a treatment that may include **neurodevelopmental treatment**. This is planned to provide postural and sensorimotor opportunities which promote improved muscle tone and coordination to facilitate the experience of normal movement. A speech and language therapist will most likely be involved in the treatment to improve communication and to assist in oral motor therapy. Additional plans could include the use of **orthotics** and mobility equipment, such as walkers and wheelchairs. In some situations orthopedic surgery and neurosurgery may be warranted (Bobath, 1967, 1971; Finnie, 1990; Logan, Byers-Hinkley, & Ciccone, 1990; Manning, 1972; Palmer et al., 1990). Early intervention in the motor development of children with cerebral palsy can lead to significant improvement in mobility potential (Jenkins et al., 1982; Kanda, Yuge, Yamori, Suzuki, & Fukase, 1984).

Prognosis for children with cerebral palsy is more dependent on family support and the quality of education and training available than on the level of the disability (Russman & Gage, 1989). In the past, many individuals with cerebral palsy did not reach their social, educational, and vocational potential because of lack of adaptive equipment and inaccessible school and work environments. Until recently, only 10% of individuals with cerebral palsy have become self-supporting, but with current adaptive technologies, earlier intervention, and more inclusive school and community environments, the prognosis for a more fulfilling life experience will be available to children entering early intervention today (O'Grady, Nishimura, Kohn, & Bruvold, 1985).

Spina Bifida

Currently, approximately 1 in every 1,000 babies born in the United States has spina bifida, making the incidence of this birth defect second only to Down syndrome (Hobbins, 1991; Tappit-Emas, 1989). After cerebral palsy, spina bifida is the most common cause of locomotion dysfunction in children (Morrissey, 1978; Tappit-Emas, 1989). Current incidence figures show a major decrease from two decades ago when 2 in 1,000 were affected (Hobbins, 1991). Prenatal testing, therapeutic abortions, and vitamin therapy during early pregnancy account for a decrease in the of the incidence rate (Hobbins, 1991). Males and females are equally affected by this condition, which is the result of the **neural tube** failing to close properly in the first 4 weeks after gestation (Williamson, 1987). There are many suspected causes of spina bifida, including environmental pollution, genetic factors, iodine and vitamin deficiency, maternal alcohol use, antiepileptic drugs used by the mother, and genetic syndromes (Charney, 1992; McLone, 1982; Mills et al., 1989; Rosa, 1991; Scarff & Fronczak, 1981).

Approximately one third of babies with spina bifida are born with **anencephaly** (i.e., no central nervous system development above the brain stem). These children survive only for a few days. Until the mid 1970s, there was a practice of selective treatment for the remaining, nonanencephalic, children with spina bifida. Physicians made the determination concerning the overall chances for the child in question to live a healthy and productive life before performing surgery. Gradually, it became clear that many of these children, although physically handicapped, did have the potential for normal intellectual development and a meaningful existence. The current practice is immediate surgery to close any opening in the back to avoid life-threatening infection (Charney, Weller, Sutton, Bruce, & Schut, 1985; Rekate, 1991). Today, most children with spina bifida, except those with anencephaly, receive medical intervention to repair their spinal area. This surgery does not reverse any neurological damage that has already occurred, but it lowers the risk of infection from meningitis and **meningoencephalitis** (Swinyard, Chaube, & Nishimura, 1978; "Public Health Education," 1992). Because of more aggressive medical intervention, the survival rates for children with spina bifida have changed dramatically over the past decades. It used to be that only 10% of these children survived to adulthood; between 85 and 90% of the children with spina bifida survive to adulthood today (Dunne & Shurtleff, 1986; McLone, 1989; Tappit-Emas, 1989).

Children with the most mild form of spina bifida, **spina bifida occulata**, may go undetected because there is only a separation of the bones of the spinal column, but no protrusion of the **meninges** of the spinal cord and no sac or opening on the child's back. The only symptoms include some leg numbness and some mild loss of bladder control ("Public Health Education," 1992). Of the diagnosed children, 4% have **meningocele**, which means that, although their spinal cord developed normally, its covering, the meninges, protrudes into a fluid-filled sac on the child's back, leading to some muscle paralysis and incontinence (Swinyard et al., 1978). The remaining 96% of the children have **meningomyelocele**, which includes the malformed spinal cord protruding through the incomplete closure of the spinal column bones and an opening in the back skin. This malformation leads to failure of the nerves below the opening to develop, resulting in paralysis, loss of sensation, and incontinence of bladder and bowel (Charney, 1992).

Hydrocephalus and **Arnold-Chiari malformation** are problems common to children with spina bifida. In Arnold-Chiari malformation, the brain stem is herniated downward. This causes a blockage to the normal flow of **cerebrospinal fluid**, which results in spinal fluids collecting in the brain, referred to as hydrocephalus (Griebel, Oakes, & Worley, 1991; McLone, 1982; Moore, 1974; Tappit-Emas, 1989). **Shunting,** the placing of a tube with a pressure valve in the brain that drains into the stomach or heart, will reduce the chances of brain damage, seizures, and **spastic paralysis** (Peterson, 1987). Arnold-Chiari malformation can also lead to 6th cranial nerve palsy, which leads to **strabismus** (Charney, Rorke, Sutton, & Schut, 1987).

Lack of bowel and bladder control can be socially detrimental because of the extended need to wear diapers. Bladder voiding is managed through the Criaz method (deep pressure) or **catheterization**. Children are able to assist with these procedures and become independent by grade school. Some children suffer from repeated bladder and kidney infections because of incomplete voiding, so that taking antibiotics may be essential on an ongoing basis. It is necessary for some children to have a bladder bypass constructed. Many children are able to learn to void their bowels, if trained by a time-triggered method. This type of training is usually begun in the preschool years.

Once appropriate surgeries are complete and the children are medically stable, they are able to receive appropriate interventions for any physical handicaps that have resulted from neural damage. These children are regularly attending preschool and public schools today. Socially, these children, like most children with mobility disabilities and chronic medical issues, face many challenges. They are often more adult- than peer-oriented, dependent on adult care when other children have made strides in autonomy. The establishment of child–parent attachment may be compromised by repeated hospitalizations. Delayed mobility and incomplete separation may lead the child to display poor self-esteem and high levels of anger and frustration, or to become depressed in the preschool years (Foley, 1986). Many children with spina bifida use their imagination as a coping device and as an escape mechanism, imagining that they will some day be able to do all the things that they are currently unable to accomplish (Nielsen, 1980). By elementary school, poor self-image, perhaps caused by mobility problems and bladder control issues, school failure and problems in establishing peer relationships are reported in the literature (Charney, 1992).

It has been reported that many children with hydrocephalus have "Cocktail Party Syndrome," a propensity to use language in a chatty and apparently advanced fashion even while they have poor comprehension and confused and illogical thinking (Hadenius, Hagberg, Hyttnes-Bensch, & Sjogren, 1962; Ingram & Naughton, 1962). This style of language use is very misleading socially—people may believe that these children are more intelligent and in touch with the social interchange than, in fact, they are (Ingram & Naughton, 1962; Laurence & Coates, 1967; Reynell, 1970). An additional problem that may interfere with oral language development for some children with spina bifida and Arnold-Chiari malformation is **vocal-cord paralysis** with **inspiratory stridor** (Charney et al., 1987).

Two thirds of the children with spina bifida, including those with hydrocephalus who were shunted in a timely fashion, are likely to have normal cognitive development (Diller, Swinyard, & Epstein, 1978), although they may have some learning disabilities (Kirk et al., 1993; Williamson, 1987). The severity of a child's motor impairments does not have a direct relationship to cognitive functioning; more relevant is a child's history of brain infection and central nervous system damage (McLone, 1982; Tappit-Emas, 1989). Generally, the children with spina bifida who demonstrate "Cocktail Party Syndrome" have somewhat lower IQs; delays in reading, spelling, and mathematics; shorter attention spans; and more delayed social skills than children without this characteristic (Tew, 1979). Children with spina bifida, even if they have average or above average intellectual potential, often have visual—perceptual dysfunction, abnormal hand function, slow motor responses, and impaired concentration (Miller & Sethi, 1971; Spain, 1970; Tappit-Emas, 1989; Tew & Laurence, 1975; Wallace, 1973; Wills, Holmbeck, Dillon, & McLone, 1990).

Motor issues, such as range of motion of joints, muscle tone and strength, sensation, movement skills, postural control, and sensory integrative skills, should be assessed in the child's first year, and an appropriate intervention plan involving physical and occupational therapy should be initiated (Williamson, 1987). The motoric consequences of spina bifida are complex and can effect more than mobility alone. Loss of motor function affects performance in many daily activities (Williamson, 1987; "Public Health Education," 1992). Paralysis of the legs and lower trunk decreases overall stimulation received by the child, so that tactile, proprioceptive, and vestibular input is greatly reduced. This means that the child is not as free to explore the environment and does not gain as much information about the world as is typical in the sensorimotor learning phase. Paralysis in the lower body directly affects the stability of the children's upper body and head control, which in turn affects fine motor skills (Anderson & Plewis, 1977; Bobath, 1967, 1971; Manning, 1972; Schafer & Dias, 1983; Tappit-Emas, 1989). Depending on the extent of paralysis, some children with spina bifida are able to learn to crawl, some develop alternative methods of bottom-scooting or lying prone and pulling themselves with arm-and-elbow motion. Because of paralysis and the lack of sensation in the lower extremities, children with spina bifida need to be monitored carefully as they begin to move around more freely. It is not uncommon for them to develop pressure sores and to experience, but be unaware of, fractures and other injuries. Another risk is progressively increased skeletal deformities because of muscular imbalance in their feet, legs, and hips. Surgery and bracing may have to be employed to intervene in and curtail this progressive deformation (Blackman, 1983; Bleck, 1982b; Myers, 1975). Spinal deformities such as **scoliosis** are frequent, some of which require surgery for spinal fusion. Some children with scoliosis may have complications that affect posture, sitting, and the potential for walking. They may be fitted with body braces to reduce the impact of scoliosis (Ward, Wenger, & Roach, 1989).

The exact extent of a child's motor involvement from spina bifida is determined by the level of the sac or opening on the child's back. Children who have damage to the lower back can often walk with ankle bracing or no bracing by the age of 2 or 3. Mid-back paralysis usually requires bracing up to the hip and crutches for successful mobility. Children with an upper-back opening walk only with extensive bracing and crutches, and mobility may only be possible with a wheelchair (Charney, Melchionni, & Smith, 1991).

INCLUSION OF A CHILD WITH SPINA BIFIDA IN A NURSERY SCHOOL

In the following case study, you will see some of the issues raised when 4-year-old Felicia, who has spina bifida, is placed in a nursery school. Felicia's parents and teachers are concerned about their ability to handle the many complex social/emotional issues with which Felicia is dealing. A planning and placement team meeting has been called by the public school social worker, who is the service coordinator for Felicia. The team has requested additional information regarding Felicia's developmental functioning. This information will serve as a basis for identifying Felicia's strengths and weaknesses, and determining the appropriateness of her current placement. The program staff will work through the components of the SPM to help clarify the developmental issues interfering with Felicia's progress, and plan facilitating techniques to assist in the future program plan.

In the next section, background information on Felicia and her educational placement, as well as a descriptive initial observation of Felicia in the nursery school program is presented.

Background Information and Initial Observation

Felicia is a 4-year-old girl who is the middle child with an older brother and a younger sister, both of whom are developmentally normal. Felicia has spina bifida at the upper thoracic level, which was repaired at 2 days, and she was shunted for hydrocephalus at 7 days of age. She is considered severely motorically disabled with bilateral whole-leg paralysis. She has been using a wheelchair for the past year, and she wears a body brace several hours each day to help reduce the effects of scoliosis. While in the brace, she is suspended by two hooks on the sides of her wheelchair that fit into her brace. This provides traction on her spine and helps to stretch and straighten the scoliotic curvatures. When not in her wheelchair, Felicia likes to be on the floor and to scoot on her bottom using her hands to propel herself. While on the floor, if she is not in her body brace, she needs to use her hands to support herself in a sitting position, so she is not free to use her hands for any activities.

Felicia is a bright and articulate child who comes from a family very committed to her development. She has excellent linguistic skills, and a psychological evaluation has made it clear that she also has high average intellectual potential. Her strong language patterns are not typical of "Cocktail Party Syndrome," in which language is not backed by comprehension. Felicia has strabismus that was surgically corrected when she was 28 months. She wears glasses to strengthen her eye muscles. Until last year, when she was 3, Felicia was always seen as a delightful, cheerful, and friendly child, who seemed unfazed by some of the medical issues in her young life. But last year Felicia had a fracture in her right leg and had to be hospitalized for several weeks and was in a hip-high cast for 2 months. Felicia never suffered any pain from the fracture because of lack of sensation in her legs, so she was very confused about the necessity of the cast and hospitalization. She was very unhappy with the lack of mobility she experienced during her recuperation. She has vivid and negative colored memories of the cast and, particularly, of its removal. After this experience she had a period of nightmares and still remains very frightened of noises that remind her of the saw used to remove her cast. She still sobs hysterically if she hears a lawn mower, sewing machine, or chain saw. Felicia experienced additional stress last year when her favorite babysitter, who had cared for her daily while her parents worked, moved away. Now she is dealing with additional anxiety because she needs to have surgery this winter to correct secondary ankle and foot deformities that are typical to spina bifida. She is very distressed that she must go back to the hospital and will once again need to have a cast, albeit less extensive.

This is Felicia's second year in nursery school. This 3-year-old group consists of fifteen children, a teacher (Ted), and an aide (Sally). Last year she participated in a toddler group that met 2 days a week, for 2 hours each session. Felicia enjoys the group activities, such as story time and singing, but is most happy when she can spend time in the dramatic play corner, alone or with a teacher. Her initial adjustment to nursery school had been quite successful, although this year she is not particularly interested in the other children and has become very demanding of her teacher's attention. Since last month, when she went back to the children's hospital to be evaluated for her surgery, she has been agitated, crying easily both at home and at school. Her teacher and parents are worried that they are not able to handle the intensity of her accelerating distress. The staff and parents are unsure how much they should tell Felicia about her next medical procedure.

In the next section, a play observation is conducted by Felicia's teacher in late November as part of the SPM process.

Felicia is the first child to arrive in the classroom in the morning. Her mother pushes her in her wheelchair into the classroom and then helps her get into her body brace.

Felicia shows distress when her mother is ready to leave. She tries to delay her mother with a barrage of questions about her mother's plans for the day. After her mother gives her one last hug and leaves, Felicia tearfully wheels herself to the window to watch her mother walk back to the car. When she turns back to the group, she calls out to the Sally, the teacher's aide, in a whiny voice, " Hey, I need your help, I need your help now. I want to paint now." Sally comes over to help Felicia to put on a smock and make her way to the painting easel, which is set up to fit Felicia's wheelchair. Felicia paints with tentative strokes for several minutes, first using the brush in one hand and then switching to the other hand. She makes a swirling pattern using yellow and orange, and then proceeds to cover the design with a thick and dripping coat of dark brown. In the process of applying the brown paint, some drips down her smock and onto her overalls. At first she stares at the drip, but then burst into tears and rubs frantically at the brown spot. A classmate, Carol, notices her crying and walks over to see what is the matter. Carol puts her hand on Felicia's back and asks her why she is sad. Felicia draws back from her touch, ignores her question, and pushes her wheelchair away from the easel. The aide comes to her side and says that the paint will not hurt her and that it will wash out. Felicia will not calm down until the aide lifts her out of her wheelchair and holds her for several minutes. Once she calms down she says, "Let's play with Sweetie now." (Sweetie is a doll from home to which Felicia is very attached.) Sally places Felicia in her wheelchair and goes to her cubbie to retrieve Sweetie. They settle at a table away from the rest of the group. Felicia likes to play a game in which she directs Sally to make Sweetie do a variety of things. "Make Sweetie jump on the table." "Now make her hop on one foot." "Now make her crawl around the table." After giving each

direction, Felicia watches that Sally does exactly as she requests. She watches each action with great attention. "Make Sweetie fall down and bump her knee." When Sally follows the direction, Felicia adds, "Make her try to get up but she can't." Sally does this and says, for the doll, "I can't get up, I hurt myself." Then she makes the doll make crying noises. Felicia watches the scene with a distressed expression and when Sweetie cries, she calls out, "It's ok, it's ok, her legs work now." She takes Sweetie from Sally and says she is all done.

Circle time is about to begin, so Felicia leaves the table and heads toward the forming group. The children are seated on the floor, but she does want to get out of the wheelchair, so she stays slightly behind the circle of classmates. She enjoys the story time and answers several questions; during singing, she makes a request for a song and joins in all the singing. After the circle time, the children return to the tables for a craft activity. Felicia dislikes cutting and gluing activities, so she requests to play with Sweetie by herself. She takes Sweetie to the kitchen corner and spends time preparing for an elaborate pretend snack. Carol comes over to see what she is doing, but Felicia does not respond to her overtures for friendship. Sweetie is fed a pretend bottle, some plastic fried eggs, and several pieces of plastic toast. Once fed, Felicia changes Sweetie's diaper and wraps her in a blanket. She sits holding her against her shoulder for several minutes (appearing to be daydreaming). Felicia seems more relaxed when she joins her peers at snack. She sits near Sally and listens to the children discuss their plans for the first snow storm, which is forecast for this evening. Several children comment that the snow means it is almost winter. Felicia becomes quiet once the subject of snow and winter is discussed. She starts to whine that her cracker is no good because it is broken. Her distress about the cracker quickly gets out of control and the aide wheels her away from the table.

Utilizing the SPM

We suggest that you use a copy of the SPM, provided at the end of Chapter 2, and respond to points made in the vignette as if you were Felicia's teacher, reviewing and observing Felicia's development. As we have mentioned in the preceding case study, this process allows for clinical judgment in your interpretations of the child's behavior. Also, remember that, if you were completing this process after a period of time of working with the child, you would have more information than is available in our vignette.

Section I: Cover Sheet

In filling out the *Cover Sheet*, highlight that Felicia's parents and the nursery school staff are concerned about her adjustment to the program. Her experience in the toddler group last year was successful, so staff are confused as to why Felicia is having such a difficult year. They see her becoming more and more withdrawn, and retreating into her play with Sweetie.

Child: Sections II, III, and IV

To summarize your observation, underline and code *Section II: Observational Impressions* and put a star beside the most relevant working theme in each developmental area. Next, list key observations in *Section III: Skills and Outstanding Characteristics Observed*. Then, in Section IV, underline the relevant *Characteristic Patterns Limiting Play*.

The following section provides a developmental analysis from the initial observation in the areas of Self/Social/Emotional, Motor/Self-Help, Communicative/Language, Cognitive, Play Skills, and Play Themes. After reading this section, return to your chart and make any appropriate changes or adaptations.

SELF/SOCIAL/EMOTIONAL. At this time, Felicia's current working theme in the Self/Social/Emotional area is at Level 1, although she has emerging skills at Level 2. She has made good attachments to significant adults and, because of her physical needs, remains very dependent on these adult-focused relationships. Her sense of trust and affection are strained at this point because of the stress of the medical procedures that have been so prominent in her life. Felicia is showing distress during leave-taking with her mother. Children who have delays in locomotion may experience extended issues around separation because they are not as free to practice physical separation and reunion as easily as children who are mobile. Felicia is able to signal her emotions to adults, but is having difficulty with self-regulation. Her emotions are very near the surface, and it takes a great deal of energy for her to stay in control of her distress. Felicia's needs are predominant in interpersonal interactions, and her negotiation skills are minimal. She is self-assertive to the point of being controlling, and her interactions are predominately with adults. Felicia has little interest or energy to be involved with peers. She uses her doll, Sweetie, as a way to soothe herself and to attempt to explore some of her worries. There is a clear overflow of emerging skills into Level 2. It can be speculated that her current working theme is at Level 1 which may be a sign of regression because of the current acceleration of stress on Felicia. Her shaken self-identity and self-esteem, along with weakened feelings of self and other constancy, are conspicuous in her behavior. Additionally, the past separation from her family because of the hospitalization, the confusing experience of being restrained in a large cast, and fear of being injured while having it removed are all feelings that have been reawakened because of the upcoming surgery.

MOTOR/SELF-HELP Although Felicia has a serious physical disability, she has gained a broad array of motor and self-help skills that are within her physical capacity. We place her Motor/Self-Help working theme at Level 2 because she is working on adaptive mobility, is expanding her fine motor skills, and is attempting to increase self-help skills. She has achieved the basic fine motor skills in Level 1 and several at Level 2. She can use a marker to draw a circle and can make simple constructions with 1-inch cubes and small blocks. In general, though, she avoids messy and textured materials (shaving cream and sand), but she greatly enjoys any play activities involving water. Felicia has a weak grasp and her hands are often not free or situated in an ideal position for easy rotation or **prehension**, but, when encouraged and physically comfortable, she can carry out Level 2 fine motor tasks, such as completing simple puzzles, threading beads, and stacking items of various sizes and shapes. However, because of visual–motor delays, these items have to be large and colorful, and the puzzles can only consist of 3 or 4 interlocking pieces. In art activities, Felicia has many Level 2 skills, but she feels compelled to produce only a perfect product, so is easily frustrated when trying to paint a picture, or when the activity becomes messy. When given any options, she often finds ways to avoid many of these fine motor and visual motor tasks.

In spite of her paralysis, Felicia is working on becoming physically active and mobile by relying on bottom scooting or using her wheelchair for mobility. She is able to move from low chairs to the floor, or to move between two seats of the same height. Because of her low muscle tone, motor exertion activi-

ties easily fatigue Felicia, but, nevertheless, she particularly enjoys the freedom of being out of her body brace and wheelchair. Felicia has a few self-dressing skills (helps pull shirt on, unbuttons larger buttons), is quite independent in eating, and can brush her own teeth. Felicia does not indicate toileting needs because of lack of sensation, but is aware of the basic timing of these personal hygiene routines. She is on routine catheterization for bladder relief, which is carried out by her mother before and after school. Her bowel movements are timed and triggered during the time that Felicia is at home. Because of paralysis and mobility problems, Felicia is more dependent on her mother than typical of a child her age. This undermines separation, because she does not have the typical opportunities to "do it herself" and practice leaving and returning to mother and task.

Felicia has a good sense of personal safety and is aware of her need to stay away from fast-moving traffic in the classroom. The adults are encouraging Felicia to let the other children know that she is in the play area ("Scott, I am behind you.") to ensure her comfort and safety in the space. When she is in the wheelchair, Felicia is able to maneuver into a play area where other children are present, but she shows fear of children's quick movements by screaming or crying out.

COMMUNICATIVE/LANGUAGE Felicia's working theme in the Communicative/Language area is at Level 3, with expressive skills her strongest developmental area. She can use complex sentences to converse, question, request, and generally gather and organize information. She is equally competent at following directions and understanding questions, comments, descriptions, and story sequences from others. However, her level of competence in these skills is reduced in times of anxiety and stress. When anxious, she reverts to patterns of rote conversation and although the quantity of verbal output may be increased, the quality tends to be more rigid and repetitive. She becomes further agitated when an adult tries to break into these patterns.

Felicia uses her well developed linguistic skills almost exclusively with adults. She tends to withdraw from conversations with children, or will redirect her comments and questions through an adult ("Tell Susie that I want to use those play pans for cooking."). When Felicia is having a hard time waiting her turn and sharing materials she whines or cries and says, "Is she done yet? I want to play with the stove" to the adult in the area, rather than expressing her wishes or needs directly to her peer. In general, Felicia's communication is very focused on her own needs and time frame for fulfilling these needs.

COGNITIVE In the area of cognitive skills, Felicia 's working theme is at Level 2. Although there are a variety of skills emerging and a few skills attained at Level 3, her current working theme is determined at Level 2 because of her short attention span, limited repertoire of interests, reduced awareness of the viewpoint of others, and her **perseveration** on themes of fear and injury. She is starting to play simple interactive games with an adult that include songs, rhymes, and finger plays with different favorite props (musical instruments, books). She understands the concept of one, knows correct gender, and identifies at least 6 body parts. In Level 3, Felicia likes to dramatize a favorite story or song. The areas that are beginning to emerge include classification of objects (shape, size, color), and recognition of the alphabet. These are not areas of great interest for Felicia. She would prefer to be in the housekeeping area.

PLAY SKILLS Felicia's play skills' working theme is determined to be at Level 2. Many of her skills at this level are emerging, but her motor disabilities have directly interfered with her wish or motivation to practice certain activities. Her mobility-oriented play is limited, because, when out of the wheelchair and brace, she is unable to use her hands freely. Her poor eye–hand coordination also contributes to an avoidance of simple constructive play. She is interested and able to use certain types of objects, such as kitchen items, and enjoys autorepresentational play and allorepresentational play, particularly with her doll, Sweetie. Her preference is for solitary play, unless the interaction is with an adult who allows her to orchestrate the exact actions of the scenario. At this time, she is not at all tolerant of peers entering into her play and has only limited interest or tolerance for parallel play. At Level 2, some of her developing skills include functional–combinatory play, particularly as open-ended and exploratory activities at the water table. Her ability to use deferred imitation is supported by realistic props, but she is unwilling to be involved in any activity that involves a common stockpile. Her limited mobility and possible perceptual weaknesses have kept her play patterns restricted, and her delayed social interaction skills have inhibited more expansive play development.

PLAY THEMES In the area of Play Themes, Felicia's working theme is set at Level 1. Her pressing worries about her body, its sensations and its functioning, are particularly marked at this point because of her medical history and her upcoming surgery. She does relate willingly to adults, but her demanding style reflects her shaky trust in their power to protect and comfort her. She is forced to accept a high degree of bodily care from the adults in her life, which may leave her feeling vulnerable and overly dependent. Even while she has to rely on their care for some of her physical needs, her wheelchair and brace often keep her separated from both peers and adults in her nursery school so that contact comfort is minimized. She has established an effective transitional object in Sweetie, which is helpful in maintaining emotional equilibrium.

She does enjoy scooting on her bottom to explore the playroom when she is not in her brace and wheelchair, but her physical disability does not always allow her to experience a great deal of pleasure from independent mobility, which usually supports play by her age. Her physical mobility is helped by the wheelchair, but it also can be confining and restricting to her play. She sometimes demonstrates aggression with her wheelchair, intentionally using it to bump into her peers.

Felicia also demonstrates some emerging Level 2 behaviors, particularly ambivalence, anger, envy, and need to control. There is also some scatter into Level 3, because of her body issues and anxiety, that is more Oedipal in its content. Concerns about bodily loss and sexual identification may be particularly confusing for Felicia because of her lack of physical sensation and function below her waist.

In her play, she does act out daily routines with her doll and seems comforted by this type of play. Felicia is easily overwhelmed by her fears even in play situations in which she is in charge of the content. She is trying to approach some of her intense emotions through play, but her anxiety often forces her to either stop or to revert to repetitive play scenes. These scenes may be comforting, but do not help her explore or resolve any of her emotional issues.

Family: Sections II, III, and IV

Using *Section II: Observational Guide*, fill in *Section III: General Description* for Family. Next, underline appropriate items in *Section IV: Characteristic Patterns Limiting Play.*

Felicia's family is very involved in the nursery school. Her mother brings her to the school daily. The father is in the Navy, which means that during Felicia's infancy and toddlerhood he was gone for months at a time on sea duty. Because of Felicia's disability, the father has been assigned to land duty so he can assist with the many appointments and hospitalizations, and to support the other two children who are at home. Perhaps because of lengthy absences from the family, her father now tends to let Felicia have her own way. The siblings are an older sister, Judy (age 6 and in 1st grade), and a younger brother, Alex (age 2). The parents placed Felicia in the nursery school because of their concern about the impact of her repeated hospitalizations and her lack of interest in peers. They are proud that Felicia is bright, but they also want her to have the opportunity to play and have fun with her peers. They are aware of her emotional distress, but feel overwhelmed by her anxiety and phobias and tend to avoid talking about spina bifida and hospitalization issues if at all possible. Felicia is most attached to her mother, since she has been the primary caretaker and carries out most of her daily care routines. Felicia slept in a crib in her parents' room until a few months ago, when she was moved into a small room with her little brother.

Judy, Felicia's older sister, treats Felicia like a baby, anticipates her every need, and is generally very protective. Judy has few friends and does not want to invite other children to her house. She spends a great deal of time playing with Felicia and taking her places in her wheelchair.

Alex walked at 9 months, has always run from Felicia when she approached, and tends to have more temper tantrums when she is around. Since the family's favorite sitter has moved away, he is often left at the "short stop" nursery at the naval base and is very independent from both parents.

There are no extended family members nearby. The maternal grandmother came to stay with the other children when Felicia was hospitalized and is very supportive of her daughter, but otherwise her visits are no more than once a year. The paternal grandparents also live at a distance and are not able to visit frequently. They tend to blame their daughter-in-law for Felicia's disability and say that spina bifida must run in her side of the family. Felicia's parents have little opportunity to socialize and interact with friends except through their local church, which they attend regularly. The family tends not to go out for meals or for any other outings. The father stays with the children when the mother goes shopping, and this usually occurs late in the evening after the children are in bed.

Neither the parents nor Felicia have known another child with spina bifida or met many other parents who have children with special needs, except during Felicia's hospital stays. Felicia receives most of her specialized care at a large pediatrics hospital that is 1 hour away. She has numerous doctors (neurologist, orthopedic, etc.); her local pediatrician is only involved in basic health care needs and refers the parents back to the specialized hospital team for any nonroutine questions. This specialized care is totally paid for by insurance, which is provided through the father's military employment.

Program: Sections II, III, and IV

Use *Section II: Observational Guide* to fill in *Section III: General Description* under Staff, Peers, Space, Time, and Materials and Equipment. Next, underline *Section IV: Characteristic Patterns Limiting Play* where appropriate.

STAFF The staff consists of an early childhood teacher, Ted, who has a BS in child development and has been with the program for 3 years, and the teacher's aide, Sally, who has been with the program for 5 years. Ted and Sally function very much as co-teachers. They divide responsibilities during the day, though Ted usually leads the group times. The staff create a warm and accepting atmosphere in the classroom. They are very open to parent contact, though they have limited time to talk to the parents at the end of the day. Both Ted and Sally use a developmental philosophy in their teaching. They are nondirective, but facilitate the child's play when necessary. They are generally in agreement about methods to use when dealing with issues related to behavioral management, but Felicia has been a puzzle to them because they have never had a child quite like her in their group. Last year they had a little boy with Down syndrome in the 3-year-old group, but he was very compliant and easy to manage. Neither Ted nor Sally have had any special education courses. They have both attended some workshops and worked with the speech pathologist last year in their work with the little boy with Down syndrome. They are desperate for help with Felicia, and realize that they are not working with her effectively. Her needs are not being met in their classroom, and they are frustrated by the fact that she takes so much of their time. Most of the other children avoid Felicia because they are afraid of her or have given up in their attempts to include her.

The staff's approach to Felicia is inconsistent. Ted feels sorry for her and tends to let her get her way with behavior that he would not accept from other children in the group. Sally feels that Felicia should not run the show and tries to limit her demands, but is unsure how to accomplish this effectively. Neither staff member has any knowledge about spina bifida and both have assumed that a child with this disability is also retarded. They have both been amazed by Felicia's verbal and cognitive abilities, but are confused about why these skills vary from day to day. They both feel they do not have adequate staff coverage to spend much time with Felicia. They are concerned that the other children are suffering from lack of attention and this makes them feel guilty. They are comfortable talking with the mother, but hesitate to ask her too many questions, because they fear this would offend her. They try to divert the other children when they ask about Felicia's disability. The physical and the occupational therapists, who are contracted by Felicia's town school system, see Felicia at the local rehabilitation center. The nursery staff have little contact with these therapists.

PEERS There are fifteen other children in the group. All of the children are 3 years old. There are an equal number of boys and girls in the group. Felicia is the only child with an identified special need in the group. Although most of the peers seem to shy away from Felicia, Carol and a few of her friends attempt to approach Felicia and include her in their play or enter into her play. They are consistently met with rebuffs from Felicia.

During the observation, the group, in general, tends to be very active with several of the children involved in building a large and complex structure in the block corner. At this time, there are also several children at the art table making a collage out of scraps of paper. There are two children in the housekeeping area dressed up in play clothes. Felicia tends to play most associatively with her peers during group time (singing and story time). Her strong verbal skills allow her to respond appropriately, and she seems most as ease because the children are all stationary during these activities. She sometimes tolerates parallel play with her peers at the water table, as long as the play does not become noisy. Otherwise, she tends to retreat to a quiet corner to play with Sweetie.

SPACE The classroom is divided into five areas by low shelf dividers (tables for fine motor activities and snack time, a block area, a dramatic play area, an area with an easel, and a book area with a rug on the floor). Each area can accommodate 3 to 5 children comfortably. The classroom flooring is linoleum, except for the area rug in the book area. The classroom tends to get very noisy during the free play time. There are storage shelves within the classroom for all of the materials that are available. Pictures the children have created are hung on the wall in the hallway. The size of the classroom is appropriate for the number and age of the children. The storage in the classroom tends to be somewhat casual, giving the room a cluttered and overstimulating look. There are several posters and alphabet letters on the classroom walls, allowing for little room to hang the children's art. The ceiling in this room is very high, which makes the acoustics poor. There is no indoor area for gross motor activities. The traffic flow routes are narrow between interest areas, which makes it difficult for Felicia to maneuver her wheelchair. The bathroom that adjoins the classroom has three child-sized toilets and two low sinks. There is room for Felicia to pull up to the sink to wash her hands easily.

TIME A typical routine is followed each day, offering a good balance between active and quiet activities. Typically, children enter at 8:45 am and move to a play area for the first 45 minutes. The staff circulate to the different play areas to facilitate the activities. After the children have been given a timely warning to finish up their play activity, there is a cleanup time. The snack is taken at three round tables in the classroom. Felicia usually sits at the table nearest the door and always asks Ted or Sally to sit next to her. Snack consists of crackers and juice. Sometimes the children help set up for snack. After the snack, the teacher reads three or four simple books to the children. The children request songs at singing time. There are many finger plays incorporated into all of the songs. After singing, the children go outside. The play yard is large and flat, with a sand box, a climbing apparatus, a swing with three seats, and a tube slide. There is an asphalt area for riding tricycles and an adjoining grassy area. The children play freely in the different areas of the playground, until they are picked up by their caregivers around 11:15 am. There is very little for Felicia to do in this play yard as it is presently designed. She typically sits and holds Sweetie and talks with her. She is afraid of some of the large equipment, and the other equipment and materials are inaccessible to her.

The regular daily schedule is very comforting to Felicia. Felicia knows the routine, and can tell the teacher what comes next. Transitions between activities are hard for Felicia; she dawdles or refuses to help pick up materials. She becomes anxious when the group goes on a walk or on a field trip because she worries that her mother will come to the school to pick her up while she is away.

MATERIALS AND EQUIPMENT There are a variety of materials offered in the five activity areas of the classroom. Some of the materials are changed at the end of each week. In the block area, the large wooden building blocks are always available. This week, the teachers have added different vehicles and other related props. In the dramatic play space, the stove, refrigerator, and sink are always available. This week the teachers have included some dress-up clothes. The paint area has a two-sided easel and various materials are provided for painting or drawing (chalk, water paint, crayons, markers). The fine motor activity/snack tables are changed weekly with materials from the nearby shelves. These materials include items such as Lego, puzzles, lotto games, and magnetic boards. The book area has a book shelf with a variety of books that are changed every 2 weeks when the group goes to the public library to get new books for the classroom. There is neither indoor gross motor equipment available nor opportunities for sensory exploratory play (sand, rice, beans, shaving cream, finger paints). There are a few simple games available—*Candyland,* and *Chutes and Ladders.* There is no computer available in the classroom, although children can go to the 4-year-old room to use the computer when it is available. Although there are dress-up costumes, there are no puppets and only a few dolls available in the classroom. Occasionally, Ted brings in some of these materials, but he does not have a selection that is in good repair. The outdoor equipment is adequate, but not suited to Felicia and her wheelchair. She can be taken out of her wheelchair and placed in the sand box, but will only do this when an adult is available to play with her. She is terrified of the swing and the tube slide.

Section V: Discrepancy Analysis

After this review of skills and limiting factors, the working themes are transferred to *Section V: Discrepancy Analysis* (found at the end of the chart). Compare and contrast Felicia's chronological age (Level 3) and the working themes of the individual areas of development (Self/Social/Emotional: Level 1, Motor/Self-Help: Level 2, Communicative/Language: Level 3, Cognitive: Level 2, Play Skills: Level 2, and Play Themes: Level 1). Then, fill in the Chronological Age (CA) Level (Level 3); write in differences between chronological age and theme levels (all areas are below age range, except Communicative/Language); star developmental areas in which you perceive significant scatter (Self/Social/Emotional, Cognitive, Play Themes); finally, highlight significant discrepancy issues in Child, Family, and Program. This discrepancy analysis should begin to provide insights into Felicia's current placement. You are now prepared to consider some suggestions along with the questions and ideas already generated.

The overriding factors that emerge from exploration of Felicia's development through the SPM are the complex, pervasive issues related to her physical handicap and how these compromise all areas of her development. Felicia's age is at Level 3, but all but one of her working levels are at Level 1 or 2.

In her Self/Social/Emotional development, Felicia appears to be experiencing a regression and her working theme is currently at Level 1, which is probably the result of the immediate situational stress of having to face another surgery. Also, as she has matured, she may be more aware of her differences and may be in need of some direct help in organizing her thoughts and feelings about these differences. Her urgent need for adult contact and adult protection is juxtaposed with her shaken trust in adults' power and expressed in her desire to be in control of the adults and the setting. This may constitute an overcompensation for feelings of helplessness and powerlessness.

Her anxiety dominates and can only be controlled for short periods of time.

Although Felicia's major handicap is in the Motor/Self-Help area, her motivation to compensate has contributed to the formation of comparative strengths in this area reflected in a working theme at Level 2. Although she does not seek out many fine motor tasks, she is able to accomplish many tasks typically found in a nursery school setting (puzzles, markers, painting). She is intent, nevertheless, on avoiding most messy materials, perhaps because of her tactile defensiveness. Felicia has had limited gross motor experience as a result of her handicap, but is showing good adjustment to a wheelchair. She enjoys self-ambulation when able to **cruise** on her bottom, although she is fearful of many activities that involve rapid movement. Felicia is beginning to show an interest in self-care skills. She likes to look nice and is very interested in having stylish clothing.

Felicia's Communicative/Language skills are at a working Level 3 and are her strongest developmental skill at this time. However, her communication is not as well developed as her general command of language. Interpersonal communication is restricted to adults, and she is not truly reciprocal because she has such a need to direct both the content and the direction of verbal discourse. These skills are easily compromised by stressful situations, anxiety, and other emotions that require the other party to adapt to Felicia's level and complexity of message (simple, short phrases with rephrasing for repetition).

Felicia's Cognitive working theme is at Level 2, which may reflect her limited experiences, plus the additional issues related to visual functioning and perceptual functioning. These issues may significantly affect her perception of objects and activities and her motivation to deal with new materials or new concepts. She exhibits brief attention to a task or perseveres with only one aspect of the task. Felicia gives up quickly if she does not succeed in a task and moves on to another area. She has difficulty generalizing from one situation to the next and needs the adult support to see connections between tasks.

Felicia's Play Skills are also at Level 2, with autorepresentational and allorepresentational play developing, especially around domestic themes that can be acted out on her favorite doll. These play skills again reflect a rigidity of control over theme and direction that has been observed in Felicia's social, language, and cognitive skills. She does not want peers to participate, or sometimes even to observe her play. Her interest is more limited when it comes to constructive play, but she does enjoy open-ended water play.

Felicia's play themes are at a working Level 1, which is in concord with her current self/social/emotional behavior. She is focused on the issue of trust and struggles with ways to gain pleasure from mobility and sensation. This intense focus on such primary themes in self/social/emotional development are confounding all other growth that contains a social component. This is particularly true when the activity requires her to be interactive with peers, because her own initial sense of self is still quite underdeveloped and inhibited.

The overall impression gained from this *Discrepancy Analysis* gives us a picture of a potentially very bright little girl who is experiencing serious situational stress that puts her current development and performance at serious risk. She is not without strengths, but an observation of her behavior makes it clear that she is fraught with anxiety and seriously affected by inconsistencies in skill level and what appear to be islets of regression. The unevenness of her current functioning makes it difficult to plan for Felicia. Her strong language skills convince others that she is ready to participate more fully in a nursery setting. Once the uneven pattern is clear to the observer, particularly the marked delays in self/social/emotional and play themes, it will be easier to understand why she is experiencing so little contentment in the group situation.

Felicia's family wants her to enjoy her peers and to function in a typical nursery setting. They have not fully understood the impact of Felicia's disability on her overall development, or the serious consequence that repeated hospitalizations have on her sense of security and well being. The family has not started talking about spina bifida in any direct way among themselves and most specifically with Felicia. They all are affected by her disability, and the family needs are sometimes being overwhelmed by Felicia's needs.

The staff want to include her in their group, but they are made anxious by her behavior and feel helpless. They don't know how to change their setting, their expectations, and particularly their approach to help Felicia have a more successful time in school. At this time, the staff does not have adequate information related to Felicia and her disability to effectively integrate her into the classroom setting. They also do not have enough personnel resources to plan for her needs.

Felicia's peers have a mixed response to her presence in their group. Some are curious and even friendly toward her, but even these children are losing the motivation to make a continued effort to include her in their activities due to her many rebuffs of them. Many children are made anxious by some of her behavior, and some children are reporting at home that they do not like her because she has legs that don't work and that she hurts them with the wheelchair.

The basic schedule is well structured for Felicia's needs, but she needs more help dealing with transitions and in coping with changes in the schedule, such as field trips. Space, both inside the classroom and in the playground, presents many issues that need to be addressed. The internal design of the classroom and outdoor space could be more suitable to Felicia's needs. Many of the materials are appropriate for Felicia, but the variety of materials could be expanded to offer her choices that more directly meet her needs.

Section VI: Intervention Goals/Facilitating Techniques and Section VII: Individualized Supportive Play Adaptations and Experiences

With the issues highlighted so far by the SPM, you can now review and underline pertinent items in *Section VI: Intervention Goals/ Facilitating Techniques* and write your suggestions in *Section VII: Individualized Supportive Play Adaptations and Experiences*. Then read the following narrative that reflects a composite of Section VI and Section VII. Check your charts to this point and make additions as necessary.

SELF/SOCIAL/EMOTIONAL   Because of Felicia's current level of high anxiety and distress, it is crucial that the adults in her life supply an emotional safety net for her. The adults living and playing with her need to be calm and reassuring. They should be able to tolerate a degree of regression and provide empathetic support and reassurance. To bolster her fragile ego, it is important to recognize her intense emotions, but to also provide opportunities and experiences in which she can feel control and satisfaction. At this point in time it may be wise to minimize expectations concerning peer interactions. Felicia may feel too vulnerable to negotiate with peers. Nonthreatening activities

that could be useful with Felicia include routine-oriented dramatic play that allows Felicia to play the role of the "in charge'" adult. She also enjoys being the nurturer, so activities where she is the caregiver may be helpful. Caring for plants, fish, or gerbils all may increase her feelings of adequacy and competency, thus emphasizing what she can do, not what she can't do.

The adult needs to be empathetic to her strong emotions, but also provide some resolution and closure. Reflection of Felicia's emotions would be useful, but the staff should not probe or ask for extensive details because they may lead to further stress and disorganization. If her anger or distress precipitate excessive disorganization or anxiety, the adult could model more appropriate outcomes or resolutions.

MOTOR/SELF-HELP   It is essential that the occupational therapist and the physical therapist who are involved with Felicia's case at the local rehabilitation center work closely with the nursery staff to help make appropriate changes in the materials, equipment, activities, and expectations in the classroom. By working on the classroom setup, materials can be made more accessible for Felicia. More low shelving may need to be built to allow her independent access to materials. There is a need for some higher tables so Felicia can pull her wheelchair up to the table to use materials and participate in art activities. Chairs of appropriate height should also be available to peers, to be placed at this table to enable them to join Felicia.

The occupational therapist may be helpful in positioning materials for Felicia so she will have better access and strength for carrying out these activities. This may include placing a nonskid pad on the wheelchair tray so the items don't slide around. The tray on the wheelchair can be tipped toward Felicia to give her a better visual perception of the objects, and allow her to experiment with more materials. She may respond to a work surface illuminated from beneath which highlights various high contrast shapes, puzzles, and forms. The adult can also offer verbal feedback related to the task that Felicia is working on ("You put all of the red pieces together" or "Where is the shape that is just like that one?") The physical therapist should work on exercises and positioning that provide better trunk stability for Felicia in the wheelchair. This will help her to be more adaptive in the use her arms. During individual occupational therapy sessions, the therapist can help desensitize Felicia's tactile defensiveness by incrementally introducing more textured and messy materials. Incorporating these activities with Felicia's favorite songs may be additionally therapeutic.

The physical therapist may be helpful in assisting with Felicia's safe and functional mobility in the classroom, whether in the wheelchair or scooting about on her bottom. The therapist can continue to help Felicia practice maneuvering her wheelchair in different positions in the classroom. It may be determined that Felicia will be removed from her wheelchair less frequently in the classroom. This will provide for more stability, so she can access materials more easily. Floor times may be most appropriate during singing time, story time, or other group activities. During more active classroom activity times, Felicia will remain in her wheelchair, so she will be safer and able to be more readily available for interactions with her peers. The therapist can practice throwing and catching (balls, beanbags) activities with Felicia in her individual sessions. The goal is eventually to invite another child to the session to introduce him or her into the interactive games and eventually carry these activities over into the classroom. The peers will need assistance from the staff to understand what Felicia can do in relation to her motor skills.

Felicia also requires continuing reinforcement concerning her wheelchair and safety-related issues. She should both verbalize the rules of the classroom and playground and demonstrate her understanding by her performance in these areas.

Outdoors, there should be activities in which Felicia can be included and feel safe as she participates. The paved area in the play yard is an ideal location to play simple games and make obstacle courses that other children could use with bikes and Felicia can use in her wheelchair. Hopefully, Felicia may eventually want to try going down the small slide with an adult beside her. This activity and others involving height may need to be practiced first during individual sessions with the physical therapist.

Felicia can practice dressing skills on Sweetie. This can also be a motivator during the physical therapy sessions ("Let's take Sweetie's shirt off, and then we will take your shirt off.").

COMMUNICATIVE/LANGUAGE   Felicia requires adult assistance to accomplish the most basic precursors to communication skills. She needs to have the adult model to facilitate turn taking in both verbal activities and in situations where nonverbal skills are essential. Felicia is extremely ego-centered and does not use her communication skills beyond a few people. Singing is useful for expanding communication. Felicia is excited and involved in the singing activities, so working on songs that have parts and turn taking can be a way to practice verbal interchange. Felicia can also be encouraged to label her feelings rather than cry and scream. If the activity is structured and directly supported by an adult, Felicia could also be encouraged by an adult model to expand her interests in the dramatic play area to include another child. This may initially require the adult to warn Felicia about the entry of the other peer in the area, and then lead into a shared material or experience. This shared dramatic play may work best when it involves the dramatization of a simple story where two children take two parts from a story and the teacher actually narrates the action. Again, turn taking and reciprocal behavior can be practiced, and the script offers Felicia both structure and direction that may reduce her anxiety and need to control. Also, Felicia enjoys having the adults write down little stories she tells about Sweetie or to write out the words of a favorite song.

COGNITIVE   When carrying out a task that requires several steps, Felicia responds best when the adult asks her to repeat the sequence or when the teacher and Felicia first make a list of the steps involved. Very few fine motor materials, games, or activities interest Felicia. These activities may have to be interspersed with favorite activities ("First, complete this puzzle and then you can play in the housekeeping area"). Additionally, housekeeping materials can be used to explore issues of size, shape, and category. First, the adults need to support Felicia's pleasure in this process, and then gradually she will gain more interest in the finished product. Felicia may be interested in some computer activities and games that allow her to explore basic cause and effect and other simple concepts. Computers have the added advantage of giving immediate feedback to Felicia and allowing her absolute control. She can be encouraged to try these computer activities with a peer, to practice taking turns, and to be able to demonstrate her good verbal skills in these activities. Also, Felicia's interest in water and water activities can be used to introduce different concepts, such as size, shape, number, and quantity.

PLAY SKILLS   Although Felicia is not interested in peer-oriented play at this time, in other ways, particularly in her allorepresentational play with Sweetie, she offers the staff an excellent oppor-

tunity to help her reorganize her current stressful reality. A trusted adult can provide several opportunities each day for the development of simple play scenarios that offer Felicia a direct opportunity to strengthen her interpersonal skills. Introduction of additional props in the house playing corner, with the adult playing a related role can offer suggestions for more adaptive behavior. The adult may need to guide and suggest expansion of the play, watching for all opportunities to have actual reciprocal exchanges and turn taking. New props can be introduced to expand Felicia's play ideas and allow her to build more elaborate story lines. Puppet play can be explored as a method of brief interactional exchanges. Turn taking may also be supported through simple constructive play that allows Felicia to gain confidence in her motor skills. Water play offers excellent opportunities for her motor exploration in an open-ended framework. An adult could add some suggestive props so that the simple filling and dumping or pouring can take on a more social meaning, such as washing the baby or sailing the boats into the harbor. Since Carol has shown interest in Felicia, she may join in some parallel play situations that do not make Felicia overanxious. But, if this is clearly too stressful, the adult can be the play partner until Felicia is more sure of herself with peers.

PLAY THEMES   The most important intervention in this case is to provide Felicia with some emotional crisis intervention. The social worker, who has been working with Felicia's public school, recommends that Felicia start immediately with play therapy at a nearby clinic. Felicia's parents can also meet regularly with a therapist who has experience with chronic health issues. Felicia and her parents need help in sorting out the issues that are facing them this winter. Felicia is facing another separation from her family and additional surgery. She may not understand exactly what will be happening to her or why the surgery must be done. Her attachment to Sweetie as a transitional object is very adaptive at this time and should be used to help her explore her feelings in her play and to supply comfort to her in her distress. Adults need to begin to help label some of Felicia's emotions that are revealed in her play. This should be done as a gentle reflection, with the expectation that at first Felicia will deny any fear or sadness. Supplying some labels for her will help make the feelings less pervasive. Any adult who is playing with Felicia can also offer some reality framing ("It's ok to be sad, but I am here to help you." "We will miss you when you are in the hospital, but we will send you cards and visit you."). The toy supply should be expanded to include some hospital materials and also some dolls with disabilities to allow some dramatic play that is more specific to the hospital and disability themes. These toys will allow Felicia to explore some of her aggression and anger relative to her own hospitalization experiences. It is also natural for her to have curiosity about her body and other children's bodies, including gender and sex. The geography of the body is a theme that can be explored through doll play and animal care. Play needs to help her explore the charged issues of changeability and constancy, especially in regard to body constancy. Some things can change (clay can be molded and pounded, blocks can be built up and knocked down), but the body is constant and still remains truly hers even as she grows or as she under goes surgery.

FAMILY   The parents would like to be introduced to other parents of children with spina bifida and have Felicia meet other children who have spina bifida or mobility disabilities. Felicia's siblings could also benefit from meeting other siblings of children with special needs. Judy may need assistance in explaining Felicia's disability to her friends so that she feels more comfortable having friends over to the house. The parents have requested information on how to access resources that are available to them. They may be interested in joining a parent support group and contacting an advocacy center to receive ongoing information on current laws and other issues related to children with disabilities and their families. These groups could be helpful with issues related to Felicia's disability, her development, public response to her disability, and extended family issues. The parents have a good relationship with the staff, but may prefer a more regular contact and feedback pattern.

The parents could hire a babysitter for a night out for themselves on a regular basis. Also, Judy and Alex could benefit from the opportunity to experience their own special time with their parents. Occasionally, Judy and Alex could each have a special time with one parent while the babysitter stays home with Felicia.

STAFF   Consultation with the play therapist will help the staff understand Felicia's inner life. They can then assist Felicia in expressing these emotions and dealing with them appropriately within the classroom setting. The staff need information on spina bifida to gain a better understanding of this condition and Felicia's limitations, capabilities, and prognosis. The staff could ask the parents permission to talk with Felicia's doctor at the children's hospital to gather this information. The staff would greatly benefit from being part of a diagnostic team that takes a comprehensive look at the issues related to Felicia's development. The staff and parents should meet regularly to talk about Felicia's strengths and weaknesses, and discuss management and teaching approaches that will allow consistency in approach and limit setting. The staff need an additional helper to allow better coverage in the classroom to meet Felicia's needs and the needs of the other children. There should be at least monthly meetings with the physical therapist, occupational therapist, and play therapist to discuss goals and strategies with the staff and parents. All three therapists should come into the classroom at least monthly to observe and to model techniques for the staff that will increase consistency in adults' approach to Felicia. Better staff coverage should help the classroom teachers assist the other children in understanding and accepting Felicia's disability and being more willing to include her in their play.

PEERS   Felicia may be able to show more interest in her peers once the play therapist begins to help her deal with her fears and anxieties. The adults can be prime facilitators with both Felicia and her peers to help them express feelings and wishes, while clarifying misunderstandings. In time, a peer could be selected to go with Felicia to her therapies to see this as a special time and share with the other classmates activities from the sessions. Also, as the result of the therapists working with Felicia in the classroom monthly, there will be less of a mystery about what Felicia does during her therapy sessions. This will also provide opportunities for discussion about spina bifida, giving the disability a name and helping children understand that it is not a contagious condition. A peer who enjoys dramatic play may be included in some of Felicia's play, although she will need an adult's guidance to feel comfortable expanding and sharing these play experiences. If a special friend emerges in school, the parents could invite this child over to the house for a short play time.

SPACE   The areas in the classroom need to be opened up for better wheelchair access, while still allowing for protection and privacy in the play spaces. A gross motor area should be added to one corner of the room. The staff could ask some of the fathers to help with the installation of a cross ceiling beam in the classroom on which to hang equipment such as a hammock, a hanging platform, or a small swing. The storage area should have closed cupboards in a separate area to reduce the messy, distracting appearance that exists in the classroom. There should be a goal to add acoustic tiles to the ceiling or to consult with an audiologist or acoustician concerning the most economical way to reduce the sounds in the classroom. The physical therapist and the occupational therapist can be helpful in looking at the classroom in terms of accessibility. These modifications should be funded by Felicia's board of education, with some additional support from some civic organization (Lions Club, Rotary) to ensure that the setting is truly accessible.

TIME   Photographs that show the daily routine would be helpful for Felicia and the other children. The teachers could send home a monthly activity calendar to help in preparing Felicia for a change in the schedule or a special event. The parents can use the calendar at home to help Felicia understand the sequence of the week and to talk about the program for the next day. Felicia may be called upon to help announce the clean-up time—she loves to sing the clean-up song and it seems to help organize her. Felicia also responds to "if and then" suggestions to move her through less favorite activities, "If you finish your snack, then we will go outside and play at the water table."

MATERIALS AND EQUIPMENT   It may be necessary to have a fund-raising project by the parents to obtain a greater variety of toys and equipment for the nursery school. The nursery school could also apply to local civic groups for funding. All of the children would benefit from a greater supply of materials for sensorimotor activities. The addition of a table that will hold water, sand, and other textured materials in the classroom would be beneficial for all of the children, and a definite attraction for Felicia, who enjoys water play. Felicia can practice the use of these materials, first in her individual occupational and physical therapy sessions and then, when the therapists model their use, in the classroom.

Puppets could be used during story time, singing time, or in the housekeeping area to dramatize stories or incidents. The puppets could also be used by Felicia to express some of her themes of worry and anxiety about spina bifida, her hospitalizations, and her ability to cope in general. The play therapist needs to talk with the program staff about the use of the puppets and keeping the themes manageable in the classroom setting. They have learned to say to Felicia when she seems to be getting anxious about the play, "You may want to talk with Alice [her play therapist] about this when you see her." This shows Felicia that they accept her feelings, but are channeling the discussion into a more appropriate setting. There should also be different dolls and stuffed animals available for play. There may need to be some dolls with disabilities (with a cast on, in a wheelchair). This will allow Felicia and her peers to include these dolls in some play themes and encourage discussion about people with differences—how they can be included, as well as how they handle different situations. The other items that should be included in the classroom are puzzles of people that can be taken apart and reassembled, dolls with Velcro clothes that can be changed, and a Mister Potato Head whose body parts can be removed and replaced. These items, with removable body parts and clothing, are important for Felicia and her peers. They all can experiment with parts that work and don't work.

The small tables usually used for fine motor activities and snack could also be used for shaving cream or finger paints, rather than just relegating these activities to the easel area. Simple games should be available for the table area. An adaptive tricycle that is propelled with hand pedals would be helpful for Felicia to use on the asphalt area outdoors. The tricycle would allow Felicia more movement and interaction on the playground. The therapist has been working with Felicia on the use of the tricycle in her individual sessions.

Review of Initial Observation

With the benefit of the information that has been collected thus far by completing sections I through VII of the SPM, review a short segment of the first vignette to see how Sally might have dealt with Felicia's separation issues. This review will allow you to put yourself in the adult's place and imagine how you might have interacted with Felicia now that you are more aware of some of her developmental characteristics and needs. Reread the section of the vignette that follows and note adaptations you would have made as Felicia's teacher. See how your ideas compare with the suggestions that follow the vignette.

Felicia shows distress when her mother is ready to leave. She tries to delay her mother with a barrage of questions about her mother's plans for the day. When her mother gives her one last hug and kiss and leaves, Felicia tearfully wheels herself to the window to watch her mother walk back to the car. When she turns back to the group, she calls out to the Sally in a whiny voice, "Hey, I need your help, I need your help now. I want to paint now." Sally comes over to help Felicia to put on a smock and to help her make her way the paint easel, which is set up to fit Felicia's wheelchair. Felicia paints with tentative strokes for several minutes, first using the brush in one hand and then switching the brush to the other hand. She makes a swirling pattern using yellow and orange, and then proceeds to cover the design with a thick and dripping coat of dark brown. In the process of applying the brown paint some drips down her smock and onto her overalls. At first she stares at the drip, but then bursts into tears and rubs frantically at the brown spot. A classmate, Carol, notices her crying and walks over to see what is the matter. Carol puts her hand on Felicia's back and asks her why she is sad. Felicia draws back from her touch, ignoring her question and pushing her wheelchair away from the easel. Sally comes to her side and says that the paint will not hurt her and that it will wash out. Felicia will not calm down until the aide lifts her out of her wheelchair and holds her for several minutes.

Felicia is making a valiant effort to manage her own distress, first by using her verbal skills to hold on to her mother rather than acting out, and secondly by using her painting skill to help herself to tolerate the separation. Her strategies are not totally effective, though. It would have been helpful for an adult to step in to verbally support this separation process for Felicia, particularly by helping her to verbally identify and modulate her feelings. Upon seeing Felicia's distress, Sally might have said, "I can see you are unhappy about having to let Mommy go, but she will be back later this morning after we play outside. Let's wave good-bye to Mommy through the window, and then I will help you find something to do." When Felicia suggested painting, the adult might have said, "That sounds like a good idea. Maybe painting can help you feel more comfortable letting Mommy go home. I can stay and help you if you want with your painting." These types of comments might have helped make Felicia's anxiety more conscious, without requiring her to comment or elaborate on her immediate feelings. Painting had the possibility of being a good transition activity for Felicia, but because her feel-

ings were never brought to the surface by adult verbalizations, her anxiety stayed unresolved, which may have led to her overreaction to dripping paint on her clothing. It also would have been helpful for an adult to stay near Felicia through her first activity, even as a quiet observer, to offer her support. The peer, Carol, senses her distress and tries to be comforting. Because Felicia is so disorganized and vulnerable by this point, she is not able to accept any comfort or help from a peer. Sally does step in at this point and offer some physical comfort by holding Felicia. It could be speculated that if the adult help had been offered earlier and if a more direct verbal approach had been used to identify the cause for Felicia's anxiety, she might have been able to sustain herself through this separation anxiety and painting activity.

Supportive Play Model Adaptation

In this section you will have an opportunity to see how the SPM adaptations have been incorporated into Felicia's school experience.

Felicia had her surgery in late December and returned to school by mid-January, wearing a cast on one lower leg and foot. She has continued to be involved in the individual play therapy at the local child guidance clinic that began a few weeks before her surgery. In this scene, we begin to see some of the changes taking place in Felicia's development as a result of the implementation of the SPM process. A commentary has been added to the observation (in italics and brackets) to offer some possible explanation.

Felicia is playing at the water table with two other peers. The table height has been adapted so that Felicia can pull her wheelchair up to it. Felicia is resisting having a child stand on the side of the water table where she is playing, but she tolerates two children, who tend to be calm in their play, on the opposite side of the table. Duplicate materials are available in the water table and she is able to carry out simple associate play while having some conversation regarding their shared experience. The teacher stays nearby to help facilitate the conversation.

Felicia then wheels herself to the dramatic play area where there is another peer. She sets up three babies on the table and plans a group meal. A dispute arises when the peer takes a baby bottle Felicia is using. Sally comes over and talks through the issue with Felicia and the other child. Felicia compromises in that she will let her classmate have the bottle "in three minutes." But once the compromise is struck, she loses interest in the play and wheels herself over to an empty table set up with several puzzles. She works for several minutes on a shape puzzle, and comments as she works that it makes her angry when she can't have her baby play the way she wants it. Sally then says, "You are getting bigger now, and you share sometimes. It is hard sometimes, but sometimes it is fun." Sally then changes her focus to the puzzle, which is of a school bus. She begins to softly sing a favorite song of Felicia's about a bus. After listening for a minute, Felicia starts singing the lyrics also and soon puts all the pieces in place.

[This sharing of play space and activity has been facilitated by including a peer in some of her physical therapy sessions where they have played with the same materials and shared simple activities. Felicia still prefers the water activities, and the dramatic play materials, but will now occasionally select a puzzle when an adult is nearby to offer verbal support. The staff has tried to incorporate her interest in stories and singing in these activities. They encourage story development from even a simple puzzle or will sing a song while Felicia's arranging some pegs in a design.]

Felicia next moves over to the reading center, where a teacher joins her and Carol to read them one of the *Curious George* stories. Both girls have a monkey puppet and act out parts of the story they particularly enjoy. Felicia and Carol each know many of the story lines by heart, and they laugh when the teacher finishes reading the story and have their puppets hug each other.

Felicia next participates in group story time and song time. In story time she joins three other children in answering the parts for three little animals in the story. She knows all the songs and volunteers to pick a partner to sing a verse together for the group. Felicia was able to wait her turn, with a reminder. She did not give away answers or talk during the other child's turn. Next ,Felicia joins the group in helping the teachers write a story about their trip to a local shopping mall. Felicia contributes a sentence about riding in the elevator with Sally and her friend Carol.

[Felicia is more secure with a clear sense of the rules of the classroom, the schedule of the classroom, and general safety rules in the classroom and on the playground. In fact, Felicia can recite the rule related to a given situation, and has to be helped by the adult to refrain from telling the rules to the other children.]

After snack, it is raining and the children stay inside. Felicia chooses to play Mister Potato Head with Sally. This has become a very popular activity with her. She first walks the legs around on their own, then she fills in all of the facial parts and limbs in their correct locations and has Mister Potato Head walk around the table to meet Sally's Mrs. Potato Head. Then she starts to roughly grab parts from Mrs. Potato Head's face and body shouting, " I have your ear, I have your leg." Then she reconstructs a new Mister Potato Head with the parts at random, facial parts attached to the limb holes and limbs sticking out where the facial parts belong. Sally tells Felicia that this play is making her too noisy, so they had better put their potatoes away. After whining for a minute, Felicia complies.

*[This play demonstrates some of Felicia's anxiety about herself as a physical person. Perhaps this toy is so interesting to her because it is mostly a head and the limbs are added and removed and exchanged at whim. Her body and limbs may not be well integrated into her body image at this time. When she animates the body parts, she may be revealing some wish that her limbs could take on life of their own too (animistic thinking). When she grabs body parts from Sally's Potato Head, she may be expressing a wish to replace her body parts or to initiate a more infant type reciprocal activity with Sally. This may be similar to how a parent plays with an infant to have them point to their body parts or pretend that they are playfully taking away their nose or ear and then returning them. How does a child with paralyzed limbs gain a sense of body wholeness and bodily integrity? Since Felicia does not receive sensations from her lower body to know where it is or how it is moving, she must use vision and other more indirect methods to learn about her own limbs. She needs to lay claim to her limbs and include them in her overall picture of herself, even though they do not function like her peer's limbs. Felicia is showing good progress in this scene because she is directly dealing with an emotional area that is integral to her development of a sense of self. Perhaps because of her own **countertransference** and anxiety, Sally becomes uncomfortable with the intensity of the play and needs to bring it to a halt. This play situation would be an excellent one for Sally to discuss with the play therapist to gain further insight into Felicia's and her own behavior.]*

Next, the children must dress in their outdoor clothing because it is time to go home. Felicia becomes very helpless and giggly and wants Sally to do everything for her. She allows her arms to go limp and says her name is baby Sweetie. Sally says that Felicia is getting to be a big girl now, and big girls can dress themselves. Felicia scowls at Sally and says, "Baby Sweetie go home to Mommy. Baby Sweetie no love you." Sally says, "Well I love you, and now I need you to help me get you dressed. I know you can put your arms into your jacket and then I can do your zipper." Sally swings the jacket in front of Felicia in a playful way allowing her to poke her arms in and out of the sleeves several times before getting her into her jacket. Then Sally says, "If we are ready in time, I need you to help me check that the gerbils have enough food and water for the weekend." Felicia perks up and asks if she can hold one of the gerbils for a minute after they check the food supply. Felicia quickly puts on her own hat and scarf and then begins asking questions about the gerbils. Sally comments that Felicia can do many things well.

[Felicia is again expressing frustration about some of the limitations imposed by her spina bifida. Dressing is a complicated activity for her. It could be helpful to have the occupational therapist discuss with her mother the clothing that would afford her the most ease in self-dressing. The fact that she must be directly assisted by an adult at a time when her peers can independently prepare for going outside once again must underline for Felicia some of the effects of her

disability . For her to regress first into silliness, then into being her own infant doll, and finally speaking in baby talk, may indicate that she is trying to express that this activity makes her feel no more than a helpless baby. In this segment, Sally is generally helpful to Felicia. She shows some of her frustration when she pressures Felicia with her comments indicating that big girls can dress themselves, even though realistically she knows that Felicia can't be independent at this time. She catches herself, though, and does not rise to the bait of being told she is not loved. She does not get into a battle of wills. She helps Felicia stay on the task and experience success by reminding her that she does have many skills. She allows for a degree of regression by setting up the bargaining and reciprocity game of "I'll do this and then you do that" with the dressing and then has Felicia end her day by being involved in the caretaking of the gerbils.]

Section VIII: Results and Outcomes

Felicia's play therapy sessions give her a place where she can verbalize and play out her worries and anxieties. The parents confer with the play therapist weekly and receive suggestions on how to deal with Felicia at home, and how to help her siblings and other family members cope with and help Felicia. The play therapist has worked with the family and the nursery school staff concerning the appropriate language to use with Felicia about her disability. It is important to give a name to her condition and talk realistically about her legs and not being able to walk. No one had previously discussed this directly with Felicia, and she made it clear in her play sessions that she thought that more of her parts might "break."

The parents have been able to refocus some of their own energy on the other children, and have found a babysitter who will stay with Felicia, alone or with the other children. During her hospitalization, her teachers tried to visit weekly and brought pictures from the children and a video of a day at school. While Felicia was at home recuperating, the class went to the hospital for a pediatric tour and met with the child life specialist, who helped familiarize them with the hospital.

The school staff confer with the play therapist monthly and they now feel more comfortable with the details related to spina bifida and more prepared to help Felicia talk about her handicap. The discussion of feelings related to spina bifida is still an area that makes the staff very anxious. Recently, Felicia told Sally that she hates spina bifida and wants the doctor to fix her. She has also frequently been mentioning dying during her baby play in school. Clearly, Felicia still has many fears and anxieties that manifest themselves around issues related to her body integrity and her feelings of overall fragility. The staff continues to try to assist Felicia in identifying her feelings, so she can use words instead of screaming and withdrawing as she did last fall.

Felicia is more comfortable with her wheelchair since the physical therapist taught her how to maneuver it more skillfully in all settings. The classroom design has changed so there are larger spaces, and the play corners are more open to allow for easier wheelchair access. Felicia's adapted wheelchair tray has helped her succeed at different activities and try materials that she would have previously resisted. She has demonstrated better pressure with her use of markers, and enjoys experimenting with water colors on paper. There is now a small table available for three or four children that Felicia can wheel up to with her wheelchair. She especially likes to play simple games with an adult and another child at this space (*Concentration, Candyland*). Felicia can now tolerate being in the area of ball play and has learned how to use hands to defend herself when she thinks the ball is approaching. She can verbalize when the ball movement scares her and she needs to move to another area. A hammock seat swing has been hung in the reading corner. Felicia is beginning to enjoy some reading time in this swing It is important that she create her own motion by trunk and arm movement, but she does not like to be pushed. She has a picture book in the classroom with the photographs of her family and Sweetie, which she will periodically look at during the day.

Felicia is showing more tolerance for messy activities. She started using play dough, probing it with a stick and poking it with her fingers, and now makes little cookies and muffins with it. She still hates to have her hair combed or cut. The staff have found that sometimes they can comb her hair while singing or while also combing a doll's hair. Under the occupational therapist's guidance, Felicia is brushed therapeutically several times a day, along with joint compression activities. This seems to increase her tolerance for touch and closeness to others. She has tried the low sliding board that is in the physical therapy room, going down it while an adult sings.

Although Felicia is still ambivalent about self-dressing, she is more willing to actively help when the dressing leads toward an activity that she enjoys. She is very interested in looking stylish and is opinionated about her clothing. Now that she has the short leg cast she wants to wear pants and matching tops to school rather than dresses.

SUMMARY

Using the SPM has clarified many of the issues facing the adults who are living and working with Felicia. Her current medical needs and her ongoing physical disabilities require support, patience, and insight. Her regression is often difficult to respond to because of the unevenness in her development. Her intellectual strengths allow her to be at least partially aware of age-appropriate issues, but her emotional stress has reawakened old issues that must be dealt with prior to tackling the more age-appropriate tasks. Helping her intense emotions surface and giving her the language to begin to talk about some of her own feelings and experiences has freed Felicia to be a more playful and spontaneous child. She will need ongoing support in sorting through the many challenges that confront her, but with the help of the adults in her life she can be an active participant in the process of understanding her thoughts and feelings, rather than being overwhelmed by feelings of disorganization, helplessness, anger, or depression.

REFERENCES

Aksu, F. (1990). Nature and prognosis of seizures in patients with cerebral palsy. *Developmental Medicine and Child Neurology, 32,* 661–668.

Anderson, E. M., & Plewis, I. (1977). Impairment of a motor skill in children with spina bifida cystica and hydrocepalus: An exploratory study. *British Journal of Psychology, 68,* 61–70.

Aylward, G. P., Pfeiffer, S. I., Wright, A., & Verhulst, S. J. (1989). Outcome studies of low birth weight infants published in the last decade: A metaanalysis. *Journal of Pediatrics, 115,* 515–520.

Ayres, A. J. (1972). *Sensory integration and learning disorders.* Los Angeles: Western Psychological Services.

Ayres, A. J. (1978). Learning disabilities and the vestibular system. *Journal of Learning Disabilities, 11*(1), 18–29.

Batshaw, M. L., Perret, Y. M., with Kurtz, L. A. (1992). Cerebral Palsy. In M. L. Batshaw & Y. M. Perret (Eds.), *Children with disabilities: A medical primer* (3rd ed., pp. 441–469). Baltimore: Paul H. Brookes.

Bax, M. C. O. (1964). Terminology and classification of cerebral palsy. *Developmental Medicine and Child Neurology, 6,* 295–297.

Behrman, R. E., & Vaughan, V. C., III. (1983). *Nelson textbook of pediatrics (12th ed.), Sec. 21.13, Cerebral palsy,* (pp. 1570–1572). Philadelphia: Saunders.

Black, P. D. (1980). Ocular defects in children with cerebral palsy. *British Medical Journal, 281,* 487.

Blackman, J. A. (1983). Orthopedic Problems. In J. A. Blackman (Ed.)., *Medical aspects of developmental disabilities in children birth to three* (pp. 179–185). Iowa City: The University of Iowa.

Bleck, E. E. (1979). Orthopaedic management of cerebral palsy. *Saunders Monographs in Clinical Orthopaedics* (Vol. 2). Philadelphia: Saunders.

Bleck, E. E. (1982a). Cerebral palsy. In E. E. Bleck & D. A. Nagel (Eds.), *Physically handicapped children: A medical atlas for teachers* (2nd ed., pp. 59–132). New York: Grune & Stratton.

Bleck, E. E. (1982b). Myelomeningocele, meningocele, and spina bifida. In E. E. Bleck & D. A. Nagel (Eds.), *Physically handicapped children: A medical atlas for teachers* (2nd ed., pp. 345–362). New York: Grune & Stratton.

Bobath, B. (1967). The very early treatment of cerebral palsy. *Developmental Medicine and Child Neurology, 9,* 373–390.

Bobath, B. (1971). Motor development, its effect on general development, and application to the treatment of cerebral palsy. *Physiotherapy, 57,* 526–532.

Breslau, N. (1985). Psychiatric disorder in children with physical disabilities. *Journal of the American Academy of Child Psychiatry, 24*(1), 87–94.

Brett, E. M. (1983). Cerebral palsy, perinatal injury to the spinal cord and brachial plexus birth injury. In E. M. Brett (Ed.), *Paediatric Neurology* (pp. 245–274). London: Churchhill Livingstone.

Bruno, J. (1989). Customizing a minspeak system for a preliterate child: A case example. *Augmentative and Alternative Communication (AAC), 5*(2), 89–100.

Burr, B. H., Guyer, B., Todres, I. D., Abrahams, B., & Chiodo, T. (1983). Home care for children on respirators. *New England Journal of Medicine, 309,* 1319–1323.

Cadman, D., Boyle, M., Szatmari, P., & Offord, D. R. (1987). Chronic illness, disability, and mental and social well-being: Findings of the Ontario Child Health Study. *Pediatrics, 79* (5), 805–813.

Charney, E. B. (1992). Neural tube defects. In M. L. Batshaw & Y. M. Perret (Eds.), *Children with disabilities* (3rd ed., pp. 471–488). Baltimore: Paul H. Brookes.

Charney, E. B., Melchionni, J. B., & Smith, D. R. (1991). Community ambulation by children with myelomeningocele and high-level paralysis. *Journal of Pediatric Orthopaedics, 11*(5), 579–582.

Charney, E. B., Rorke, L. B., Sutton, L. N., & Schut, L. (1987). Management of Chiari II complications in infants with myelomeningocele. *Journal of Pediatrics, 111,* 364–371.

Charney, E. B., Weller, S. C., Sutton, L. N., Bruce, D. A., & Schut, L. B. (1985). Management of the newborn with mylomeningocele: Time for a decision-making process. *Pediatrics, 75*(1), 58–64.

Church, G., & Glennen, S. (1992). *Handbook of assistive technology.* San Diego, CA: Singular Publishing Group.

Connolly, B., & Russell, F. (1976). Interdisciplinary early intervention program. *Physical Therapy, 56,* 155–159.

Connor, F. P., Williamson, G. G., & Siepp, J. M. (1978). *Program guide for infants and toddlers with neuromotor and other developmental disabilities* (pp. 206–217). New York: Teachers College Press.

Crothers, B., & Paine, R. S. (1959). *The natural history of cerebral palsy.* Cambridge, MA: Harvard University Press.

Darley, F. L., Aronson, A. E., & Brown, J. R. (1975). *Motor disorders of speech.* Philadelphia: Saunders.

Davis, L. (1978). Prespeech. In F. P. Connor, G. G. Williamson, & J. M. Siepp (Eds.), *Program guide for infants and toddlers with neuromotor and other developmental disabilities* (pp. 183–205). New York: Teachers College Press.

Diller, L., Swinyard, C. A., & Epstein, F. J. (1978). Cognitive function in children with spina bifida. In C. A. Swinyard (Ed.), *Decision making and the defective newborn* (pp. 34–49). Springfield, IL: Thomas.

DuBose, R. F. (1979). Assessment of visually impaired infants. In B. L. Darby & M. J. May (Eds.), *Infant assessment: Issues and applications* (pp. 163–179). Seattle: WESTAR.

Dunne, K. B., & Shurtleff, D. B. (1986). The adult with meningomyelocele: A preliminary report. In R. L. McLaurin (Ed.), *Spina Bifida: A multidisciplinary approach* (pp. 38–51). New York: Praeger.

Finnie, N. R. (1974). *Handling the young cerebral palsied child at home* (2nd ed., pp. 228–267). New York: Dutton.

Finnie, N. R. (1990). *Handling the young cerebral palsy child at home* (3rd ed.). New York: Dutton.

Fishman, I. (1987). *Electronic communication aids.* Boston: College Hill Press.

Foley, G. M. (1986). Emotional development of children with handicaps. In N. E. Curry (Ed.), *The feeling child: Affective development reconsidered.* New York: Haworth.

Griebel, M. L., Oakes, W. J., & Worley, G. (1991). The Chiari malformation associated with myelomeningocele. In H. L. Rekate (Ed.), *Comprehensive management of spina bifida* (pp. 67–92). Boca Raton, FL: CRC Press.

Hadenius, A. M., Hagberg, B., Hyttnäs-Bensch, K., & Sjögren, I. (1962). The natural prognosis of infantile hydrocephalus. *Acta Paediatrica 51*, 116–118.

Hagberg, B., Hagberg, G., & Olow, I. (1984). The changing panorama of cerebral palsy in Sweden. IV. Epidemiological trends 1959–1978. *Acta Paediatricia Scandinavia, 73*, 433–440.

Hagberg, B., Hagberg, G., & Zetterstrom, R. (1989). Decreasing perinatal mortality—Increase in cerebral palsy morbidity? *Acta Paediatricia Scandinavica, 78*, 664–670.

Hagen, C., Porter, W., & Brink, J. (1973). Nonverbal communication: An alternate mode of communication for the child with severe cerebral palsy. *Journal of Speech and Hearing Disorders, 38*(4), 448–454.

Handbook for the care of infants and toddlers with disabilities and chronic conditions. (1991). Lawrence, KS: Learner Managed Designs.

Haynie, M., Porter, S. M., & Palfrey, J. S. (1989). *Children assisted by medical technology in educational settings: Guidelines for care.* Boston: Project School Care, The Children's Hospital.

Hewett, S. (1970). *The family and the handicapped child.* Chicago: Aldine.

Hobbins, J. C. (1991). Diagnosis and management of neural-tube defects today. *New England Journal of Medicine, 324*(10), 690–691.

Ingram, T. T. S., & Naughton, J. A. (1962). Paediatric and psychological aspects of cerebral palsy associated with hydrocephalus. *Developmental Medicine and Child Neurology, 4*, 287–292

Jenkins, J. R., Sells, C. J., Brady, D., Down, J., Moore, B., Carman, P., & Holm, R. (1982). Effects of developmental therapy on motor impaired children. *Physical and Occupational Therapy in Pediatrics, 2*(4), 19–28.

Jones, P. M. (1989). Feeding disorders in children with multiple handicaps. *Developmental Medicine and Child Neurology, 31*, 404–406.

Kanda, T., Yuge, M., Yamori, Y., Suzuki, J., & Fukase, H. (1984). Early physiotherapy in the treatment of spastic diplegia. *Developmental Medicine and Child Neurology, 26*, 438–444.

Kessler, M. S., & Milligan, W. L. (1979). Effect of age-of-disability-onset on self-esteem and anxiety in wheelchair-bound individuals. *Rehabilitation Psychology, 26*(3), 105–112.

Kirk, S. A., Gallagher, J. J., & Anastasiow, N. J. (1993). *Educating exceptional children* (7th ed.). Boston: Houghton Mifflin.

Kogan, K. L., Tyler, N., & Turner, P. (1974). The process of interpersonal adaptation between mothers and their cerebral palsied children. *Developmental Medicine and Child Neurology, 16*, 518–527.

Laurence, K. M., & Coates, S. (1967). Spontaneously arrested hydrocephalus. *Developmental Medicine and Child Neurology, 13* (Suppl. 13, 4), 4–13.

Levy, S. E. (1991). Nonpharmacologic management of disorders of behavior and attention. In A. J. Capute & P. J. Accardo (Eds.), *Developmental disabilities in infancy and childhood* (pp. 489–494). Baltimore: Paul H. Brookes.

Levy, S. E., & Pilmer, S. L. (1992). The technology-assisted child. In M. L. Batshaw & Y. M. Perret (Eds.), *Children with disabilities* (3rd ed., pp. 137–157). Baltimore: Paul H. Brookes.

Lichtenstein, M. A. (1986). Pediatric home tracheostomy care: A parent's guide. *Pediatric Nursing, 12*(1), 41–48, 69.

Logan, L., Byers-Hinkley, K., & Ciccone, C. D. (1990). Anterior versus posterior walkers: A gait analysis study. *Developmental Medicine and Child Neurology, 32*, 1044–1048.

Manning, J. (1972). Facilitation of movement—The Bobath approach. *Physiotherapy, 58*, 403–408.

McCrae, M. Q. (1982). *Medical perspectives on brain damage and development.* Reading, PA: Family Centered Resource Project.

McDonald, E. T. (1975). Design and application of communication boards. In G. C. Vanderheiden & K. Grilley (Eds.), *Non-vocal communication techniques and aids for the severely physically handicapped.* Baltimore: University Park Press.

McLone, D. (1982). *Neurosurgical management and operative closure for myelomeningocele.* Presented at the Annual Myelomeningocele Seminar, Chicago.

McLone, D. G. (1989). Spina bifida today: Problems adults face. *Seminars in Neurology, 9*(3), 169–175.

Mecham, M. J. (1966). Appraisal of speech and hearing problems. In M. J. Mecham, M. J. Berko, F. G. Berko, & M. F. Palmer (Eds.), *Communication training in childhood brain damage* (pp. 49–69). Springfield, IL: Thomas.

Miller, E., & Sethi, L. (1971). The effects of hydrocephalus on perception. *Developmental Medicine and Child Neurology,* (Suppl. 25), 77.

Millner, B. N. (1991). Technology-dependent children in New York State. *Bulletin of the New York Academy of Medicine, 67*(2), 131–142.

Mills, J. L., Rhoads, G. G., Simpson, J. L., Cunningham, G. C., Conley, M. R., Lassman, M. R., Walden, M. E., Depp, O. R., Hoffman, H. J., & The National Institute of Child Health and Human Development Neural Tube Defects Study Group. (1989). The absence of a relation between the periconceptional use of vitamins and neural-tube defects. *New England Journal of Medicine, 321*(7), 430–435.

Mogford, K. (1977). The play of handicapped children. In B. Tizard & D. Harvey (Eds.), *Biology of Play* (pp. 170–184). Philadelphia: Lippincott.

Molnar, G. E. (1985). Cerebral palsy. In G. E. Molnar (Ed.), *Pediatric Rehabilitation.* Baltimore: Williams & Wilkins.

Moore, K. L. (1974). *The developing human* (2nd ed.). Philadelphia: Saunders.

Morris, H. H., Escoll, P. J., & Wexler, R. (1956). Aggressive behavior disorders in childhood: A follow-up study. *American Journal of Psychiatry, 112*, 991–997.

Morrissey, R. T. (1978). Spina bifida: A new rehabilitation problem. *Orthopedic Clinics of North America, 9*, 379–389.

Musselwhite, C. R. (1986). *Adaptive play for special needs children.* San Diego: College Hill Press.

Myers, B. R. (1975). The child with a chronic illness. In R. H. A. Haslam & P. J. Valletutti (Eds.), *Medical problems in the classroom* (pp. 97–127). Baltimore: University Park Press.

Mysak, E. D. (1971). Cerebral palsy speech syndromes. In L. E. Travis (Ed.), *Handbook of speech pathology and audiology* (pp. 673–694). New York: Meredith.

Mysak, E. D. (1982). Cerebral palsy. In G. H. Shames & E. H. Wiig (Eds.), *Human communication disorders: An introduction.* Columbus, OH: Merrill.

Neisworth, J. T., & Bagnato, S. J. (1987). *The young exceptional child.* New York: Macmillan.

Nelson, K. B., & Ellenberg, J. H. (1986). Antecedents of cerebral palsy. *The New England Journal of Medicine, 315*(2), 81–86.

Nielsen, H. H. (1980). A longitudinal study of the psychological aspects of myelomeningocele. *Scandanavian Journal of Psychology, 21*, 45–54.

Office of Technical Assessment. (1987). Technology-dependent children: Hospital v. home care: A technical memorandum (DHHS Publication no. TM-H-38). Washington, DC: U.S. Government Printing Office.

O'Grady, R. S., Nishimura, D. M., Kohn, J. G., & Bruvold, W. H. (1985). Vocational predictions compared with present vocational status of 60 young adults with cerebral palsy. *Developmental Medicine and Child Neurology, 27*, 775–784.

Palfrey, J. S., Walker, D. K., Haynie, M., Singer, J. D., Porter, S., Bushey, B., & Cooperman, P. (1991). Technology's children: Report of a statewide census of children dependent on medical supports. *Pediatrics, 87*(5), 611–618.

Palmer, F. B., Shapiro, B. K., Allen, M. C., Mosher, B. S., Bilker, S. A., Harryman, S. E., Meinert, C. L., & Capute, A. J. (1990). Infant stimulation curriculum for infants with cerebral palsy: Effects on infant temperament, parent–infant interaction, and home environment. *Pediatrics, 85*, 411–415.

Paneth, N., & Kiely, J. (1984). The frequency of cerebral palsy: A review of population studies in industrialized nations since 1950. In F. Stanley & E. Alberman (Eds.), *The epidemiology of the cerebral palsies.* Philadelphia: Lippincott.

Perin, B. (1989). Physical therapy for the child with cerebral palsy. In J. S. Tecklin (Ed.), *Pediatric physical therapy.* Philadelphia: Lippincott.

Peterson, N. L. (1987). *Early intervention for handicapped and at-risk children.* Denver: Love.

Pless, B. (1984). Clinical assessment: Physical and psychological functioning. *Pediatric Clinics of North America, 31*(1), 33–45.

Powell, N. J. (1985). Children with cerebral palsy. In P. N. Clark & A. S. Allen (Eds.), *Occupational therapy for children* (pp. 312–337). St. Louis: Mosby.

Public Health Education Information Sheet: "Spina Bifida". (1992). *March of Dimes Birth Defects Foundation.* White Plains: NY.

Quint, R. D., Chesterman, E., Crain, L. S., Winkleby, M., & Boyce, W. T. (1990). Home care for ventilator-dependent children. *American Journal of Diseases of Children, 144*, 1238–1241.

Rekate, H. L. (1991). Neurosurgical management of the newborn with spina bifida. In H. L. Rekate (Ed.), *Comprehensive management of spina bifida* (pp. 1–28). Boca Raton, FL: CRC Press.

Reynell, J. (1970). Children with physical handicaps. In P. Mittler (Ed.), *The psychological assessment of mental and physical handicaps* (pp. 443–469). London: Methuen.

Roberts, L. (1990, January). To test or not to test. *Science, 247*(5), 17–18.

Robinson, R. O. (1973). The frequency of other handicaps in children with cerebral palsy. *Developmental Medicine and Child Neurology, 15*, 305–312.

Rosa, F. W. (1991). Spina bifida in infants of women treated with carbamazepine during pregnancy. *New England Journal of Medicine, 324*(10), 674–677.

Rosenbloom, L. (1975). The consequences of impaired movement—A hypothesis and review. In K. S. Holt (Ed.), *Movement and child development* (pp. 8–13). Philadelphia: Lippincott.

Rothman, J. G. (1987). Understanding order of movement in youngsters with cerebral palsy. *Perceptual and Motor Skills, 65*(2), 391–397.

Rothman, J. G. (1989). Understanding of conservation of substance in youngsters with cerebral palsy. *Physical and Occupational Therapy in Pediatrics, 9*(3), 119–125.

Russman, B. S., & Gage, J. R. (1989). Cerebral palsy. *Current Problems in Pediatrics, 19*(2), 65–111.

Rutter, M., Tizard, J., & Whitmore, K. (Eds.). (1970). *Education, health and behavior.* London: Longman.

Scarff, T. B., & Fronczak, S. (1981). Myelomeningocele: A review and update. *Rehabilitation Literature, 42*(5–6), 143–147.

Schafer, M. F., & Dias, L. S. (1983). *Myelomeningocele: Orthopaedic treatment.* Baltimore: Williams & Wilkins.

Scher, M. S., Belfar, H., Martin, J., & Painter, M. J. (1991). Destructive brain lesions of presumed fetal onset: Antepartum causes of cerebral palsy. *Pediatrics, 88*(5), 898–906.

Shere, E., & Kastenbaum, R. (1966). Mother–child interaction in cerebral palsy: Environmental and psychosocial obstacles to cognitive development. *Genetic Psychology Monographs, 73*(2), 255–335.

Sheridan, M. (1975). The importance of spontaneous play in the fundamental learning of handicapped children. *Child Care, Health, and Development, 1*, 3.

Silverman, F. H. (1980). *Communication for the speechless* (pp. 85–161). Englewood Cliffs, NJ: Prentice-Hall.

Simon, B. M., Fowler, S. M., & Handler, S. D. (1983). Communication development in young children with long-term tracheostomies: Preliminary report. *International Journal of Pediatric Otorhinolaryngology, 6*, 37–50.

Singer, L. T., Kercsmar, C., Legris, G., Orlowski, J. P., Hill, B. P., & Doershuk, C. (1989). Developmental sequelae of long-term infant tracheostomy. *Developmental Medicine and Child Neurology, 31*, 224–230.

Spain, B. (1970). Spina bifida survey. *GLC Research and Intelligence Quarterly Bulletin, 12*(5).

Stabler, B. (1988). Perspectives on chronic childhood illness. In B. G. Melamed, K. A. Matthews, D. K. Routh, B. Stabler, & N. Schneiderman (Eds.), *Child health psychology* (pp. 251–263). Hillsdale, NJ: Erlbaum.

Swinyard, C. A., Chaube, S., & Nishimura, H. (1978). Spina bifida as a prototype defect for decision making: Nature of the defect. In C. A. Swinyard (Ed.), *Decision making and the defective newborn* (pp. 17–33). Springfield, IL: Thomas.

Tappit-Emas, E. (1989). Spina bifida. In J. S. Tecklin (Ed.), *Pediatric physical therapy.* Philadelphia: Lippincott.

Technology Related Assistance for Individuals with Disabilities Act of 1988. 29 U.S.C. § 2201. (1988)

Tew, B. (1979). The "cocktail party syndrome" in children with hydrocephalus and spina bifida. *British Journal of Disorders of Communication, 14*(2), 89–101.

Tew, B. J., & Laurence, K. M. (1975). The effects of hydrocephalus on intelligence, visual perception and school attainment. *Developmental Medicine and Child Neurology, 17*(Suppl. 35), 129–134.

Trompeter, R. S. (1990). Renal transplantation. *Archives of Disease in Childhood, 65*, 143–146.

Udwin, O., & Yule, W. (1990). Augmentative communication systems taught to cerebral palsied children—A longitudinal study. I. The acquisition of signs and symbols, and syntactic aspects of their use over time. *British Journal of Disorders of Communication, 25*, 295–309.

Udwin, O., & Yule, W. (1991a). Augmentative communication systems taught to cerebral palsied children—A longitudinal study. II. Pragmatic features of sign and symbol use. *British Journal of Disorders of Communication, 26*, 137–148.

Udwin, O., & Yule, W. (1991b). Augmentative communication systems taught to cerebral palsied children—A longitudinal study. III. Teaching practices and exposure to sign and symbol use in schools and homes. *British Journal of Disorders of Communication, 26*, 149–162.

Wallace, S. J. (1973). The effect of upper-limb function on mobility of children with myelomeningocele. *Developmental Medicine and Child Neurology, 15*(Suppl. 29), 84–91.

Wallace, S. J. (1990). Risk of seizures (Annotation). *Developmental Medicine and Child Neurology, 32*, 645–649.

Ward, W. T., Wenger, D. R., & Roach, J. W. (1989). Surgical correction of myelomeningocele scoliosis: A critical appraisal of various spinal instrumentation systems. *Journal of Pediatric Orthopaedics, 9*, 262–268.

Williamson, G. G. (Ed.). (1987). *Children with spina bifida: Early intervention and preschool programming.* Baltimore: Paul H. Brookes.

Wills, K. E., Holmbeck, G. N., Dillon, K., & McLone, D. G. (1990). Intelligence and achievement in children with myelomeningocele. *Journal of Pediatric Psychology, 15*(2), 161–176.

CHAPTER 6

Application of the Supportive Play Model to a Child with Moderate Pervasive Developmental Disorder/Autism

There is confusion among parents and professionals regarding the type of educational program (self-contained to mainstreamed), and the approach (behavioral, play training, responsive/relationship-centered) that is appropriate for young children with pervasive developmental disorder (PDD)/autism. These children are typically attractive, free of physical handicaps, and may display extraordinary splinter skills (early reading, unusual memory for names and dates). These skills may make them appear to be more developmentally capable than they actually are, leading to an educational placement that may not be developmentally appropriate.

In this chapter we review the general background for the diagnosis, some of the theories concerning the potential cause of PDD/autism, and the impact of this condition on development. Different intervention approaches used with this population and the important role of parents in this intervention process are discussed. A case study is presented to demonstrate the use of the SPM with a child who has PDD.

GENERAL BACKGROUND ON PDD/AUTISM

A young child who is rocking in a corner, flicking his fingers in front of his eyes, repeating words in a sing-song fashion, and twirling the wheels on a truck can be described as having PDD/autism. The childhood disability of autism was first defined by Kanner in 1943 and has been consistently observed in males three to four times more often than in females. Current theories suggest that PDD/autism has physiological roots, including possible neurological, genetic, or biochemical dysfunction that causes widespread developmental problems. In the past, some theorists suspected autism had psychological roots, with at least part of the problem caused by poor parenting or a traumatic event that interfered with appropriate attachment and the development of **symbolic functioning** (Bettelheim, 1967; Kanner, 1943; Lanyado, 1987; Mahler, 1965). Fortunately, findings in current developmental and neurological research have moved away from blaming parents and now focus on the child's inborn vulnerabilities in receiving and processing stimulation. Freud's (1920/1955) idea of an inadequate stimulus barrier, an inability to sort and screen the stimuli that constantly bombard humans, is a helpful metaphor in understanding the experiential reality of the child with autism. Additionally, Mahler (1965) has suggested that children with autism are constitutionally vulnerable and, therefore, often psychologically unable to establish appropriate interpersonal relationships (object relations). Thus, an inadequate stimulus barrier and inappropriate interperson-

al relationships do not cause the child to withdraw, but rather these vulnerabilities do not allow the child to enter into the experiential world and into relationships with caregivers in a typical fashion. PDD/autism is not a condition of intentional retreat, but a condition in which the most basic building blocks of personal and interpersonal development that are needed for learning and living are inhibited from developing in the normal way. These deficits lead to qualitative differences in relationship, development, communication, sensory perception and integration, object exploration, and social responsiveness (Wenar, Ruttenberg, Kalish-Weiss, & Wolf, 1986).

With the publication of *Diagnostic and Statistical Manual of Mental Disorders, Third Edition, Revised (DSM III-R)* in 1987 (American Psychiatric Association), this perplexing developmental condition of autism was redefined under the broader term of pervasive developmental disorder (PDD). PDD includes problems with social interaction, communication, the development of imagination, and range and type of activities and interests. These problems are apparent in infancy or early childhood. The diagnosis of autistic disorder is reserved for children at the more severe end of this spectrum disorder (4 or 5 children out of 10,000). Pervasive developmental disorder not otherwise specified (PDDNOS) is diagnosed in 10 to 15 children out of 10,000 who demonstrate fewer characteristics. Since PDD/autism can be applied to a very heterogeneous group of children, these diagnoses do not immediately indicate the children's intellectual potential or their overall prognosis for development (Allen, 1988; Rescorla, 1988). Most children with PDD, including children with autism, have life-long social and communication disabilities, but some perform quite well academically and many learn to interact more effectively with people. Early intervention is crucial to help these children gain an awareness of themselves in order to progress to their fullest potential. Intervention is also crucial to provide families with support and empathy while helping them to understand and interact more successfully with their children.

THE IMPACT OF PDD/AUTISM ON EARLY DEVELOPMENT

This section reviews key areas of development and how autism/PDD may affect growth in these various zones. After careful consideration of this information, the parent and professional will be better prepared to plan and implement more appropriate intervention options for the child with PDD/autism through the use of the SPM.

Self/Social/Emotional Development

A variety of factors may be responsible for the deficits apparent in children with PDD/autism. Some theorists emphasize that emotional, social, adaptive, and interpersonal deficits are central in PDD/autism (Baron-Cohen, 1987; Hobson, 1989, 1990; Provence & Dahl, 1987; Rodrique, Morgan, & Geffken, 1991; Volkmar, Sparrow, Goudreau, Cicchetti, Paul, & Cohen, 1987). Socially, children with PDD/autism react in ways that may make them appear unmotivated, detached, and disinterested in people. They may not understand the relationship between parts and the whole, so that they may use people as objects; for instance, using an adult's hand as a tool to reach for a desired object. Although children with PDD/autism generally do attach to their parents, patterns of eye contact, response to physical touch, smiling, and other affective responses tend to be inconsistent or unusual (Dawson, Hill, Spencer, Galpert, & Watson, 1990; Klin, 1991; McGee, Feldman, & Chernin, 1991; Snow, Hertzig, & Shapiro, 1987). They may not look at the adult when spoken to; in fact, they may become anxious when looked at and avert their gaze, with the result that mutual eye contact in not shared between the parent and the child (Hutt & Ounsted, 1966; Richer & Coss, 1976). These children do visually check in with the adult, particularly during their own monologues, but not during two-way interactions (Mirenda, Donnellan, & Yoder, 1983).

Although children with PDD/autism develop feelings and experience a range of emotions, to the observer they may appear flat emotionally, showing little variation in their facial expression or body language and giving few visual cues to their inner emotional state. They learn to smile, but not necessarily in synchrony with situational or social interaction; instead, they are more likely to smile while carrying out a repetitive activity by themselves (Dawson et al., 1990). Some may show dramatic mood variations that are difficult to connect to events in their environment.

Motor/Self-Help Development

Children with PDD/autism display unusual patterns in their **sensorimotor development**, sensory integration, and self-regulation. These may include difficulties with eating and sleeping, hypo- or hyper-responses to sensory input, and reduced reaction to pain. Many of these children may be **hypersensitive** to light, physical contact (for instance, they may be irritated by clothing), while they may simultaneously enjoy deep touch sensations, such as being swaddled tightly or firmly tucked into bed (Bergman & Escalona, 1949). Furthermore, they may be totally unaware of the pain usually associated with injuries or illnesses (Ayres, 1989). Their arousal threshold and self-regulation may also be affected so that they become easily overstimulated, developing patterns of repetitive and ritualized behavior that may serve to filter stimulation, reduce anxiety, and help them organize (Mundy & Sigman, 1989b). Although these types of behavior (arm flapping, rocking, head and body hitting, eye blinking, and finger wiggling) may calm the child, they look odd and frequently interfere with the children's ability to interact effectively with people and objects.

Although sensory and motor functioning are areas of relative proficiency, they, too, are delayed and may be quantitatively and qualitatively different (Lösche, 1990; Sigman & Ungerer, 1984). For instance, most children with PDD/autism, regardless of their mental ability, prefer visual–motor performance tasks, such as puzzles. However, they may not focus on the image on the puzzle and can just as successfully put the picture together upside-down. Although parents frequently wonder about the child's visual and auditory acuity, these are usually within normal limits when tested by traditional methods. However, children with PDD/autism may have subtle auditory and visual perceptual problems. They may be unable to screen out irrelevant background noise in order to focus on the words they are speaking or that are being directed to them. They may cry uncontrollably when soft music is played in another room, yet be oblivious to someone calling their name. They may not seem to notice people right beside them, but may observe and become agitated if a small trinket is missing from a shelf.

Communicative/Language Development

NONVERBAL COMMUNICATION/GESTURE USE   The inability of children with PDD/autism to develop nonverbal communication and gestural skills is a feature repeatedly noted in the literature. For children to ultimately function symbolically, it is necessary for them to develop communicative intent and presymbolic communication skills, including eye gaze, **joint attention**, **intentionality**, use of gestures, and shared meanings (Greenspan, 1992a, 1992b; Landry & Loveland, 1989; McCaleb & Prizant, 1985; Prizant, 1988). Children with PDD/autism are less skilled in gesture use, especially for establishing joint attention (Landry & Loveland, 1989; Mundy, Sigman, & Kasari, 1990). This deficit is highly significant because gesture use is related to cognitive skill and highly correlated to language use potential (McCaleb & Prizant, 1985; Mundy, Sigman, & Kasari, 1990; Mundy, Sigman, Ungerer, & Sherman, 1987).

Patterns of social interchange are highly dependent on gesture and eye contact as well. These patterns are typically compromised in children with PDD/autism, as evidenced by their difficulty in participating in games such as peek-a-boo, watching a jack-in-the-box with an adult, or pointing to a desired toy (Landry & Loveland, 1989). Without the normal development of joint attention and the sharing of an object or an activity, the foundations of social interchange, play, communication, and learning are in jeopardy (McCaleb & Prizant, 1985; Mundy & Sigman, 1989a; Mundy, Sigman, Ungerer, & Sherman, 1987).

VERBAL COMMUNICATION   A most striking feature in children with PDD/autism is their unusual use of words, which reflects a serious underlying communication disorder involving deficits in language form, content, and use (Bloom & Lahey, 1978; Lahey, 1988). Between 25 and 60% of children with PDD/autism never develop meaningful oral communication (Rutter, 1979; Rutter & Lockyer, 1967), but, after intensive intervention, may be able to communicate to some degree with sign language or other augmentative communication systems.

In the children who do use speech, their language may be characterized by extensive use of **echolalia**, which may consist of immediate or delayed repetition of words and/or phrases heard. It is currently believed that echolalia may serve a sociocommunicative function for the child—a turn filler, a processing aid, a behavioral self-regulator, or a form of rehearsal, affirmation, or request (Prizant, 1982). Other issues for children who do become verbal include problems with poor vocal intonation (monotone) and a tendency to reverse pronouns. Children with PDD/autism have difficulty with abstract concepts and use language in a very literal sense. They are confused by words that have multiple meanings. Their literal thinking also makes it difficult for them to understand humor.

Another debilitating aspect of the disorder is evident in the difficulty with functional and adaptive use of language as a means of social communication through conversation, and as a way to direct the child's own and other's behavior. For example, many of these children are not able to make adaptations in their dialogues to reflect the social situation; their conversational patterns tend to be rote, and they become stuck when the pattern of exchange is changed to include a new concept or direction. They are less likely to use gestures to support their language, and often do not respond to conversational overtures. They initiate, affirm, and expand conversations less (Loveland, Landry, Hughes, Hall, & McEvoy, 1988; Loveland & Tunali, 1991). In two-way interactions and conversations, the child with PDD/autism is likely to use compulsive questioning, demonstrates poor understanding of turn taking, and is unable to take another's point of view. (Baron-Cohen, 1988; Wetherby & Prutting, 1984). Because overall symbolic functioning is interrelated, children who use language most effectively are also those who will be able to gesture, draw, and play most effectively (Abrahamsen & Mitchell, 1990; Atlas & Lapidus, 1988; Baron-Cohen, 1987).

Cognitive Development

Baron-Cohen (1988) underlines the cognitive dimension as central to understanding the development of children with PDD/autism. The mental ability of children with PDD/autism can range from intellectually superior to profoundly retarded. It must be kept in mind that many children with PDD/autism are considered untestable or prove to be very inconsistent in their test results. Standardized testing that fails to include affective development may also result in inflated and inaccurate scores. With these limitations in mind, note that 25% of these children test as having IQs between 70 and 100 as measured by standard intelligence tests; 5% test as having IQs above 100; and the remaining 70% test as mildly, moderately, or severely retarded (Minshew & Payton, 1988). The subtest scatter on the Stanford Binet is similar across children with PDD/autism, regardless of their full-scale IQs. The absurdities subscale, which does not focus on factual knowledge but requires understanding of what is different or illogical, typically has the lowest score. On the other hand, pattern analysis, which reflects **visual–spatial**, and perceptual discrimination, is typically the highest scoring area in this population (Harris, Handleman, & Burton, 1990). Additionally, regardless of intellectual functioning level, object permanence is a concept that most of these children are capable of developing (Rogers, 1988).

Most children with PDD/autism have difficulties developing **metacognition** (the ability to think about and monitor one's own thinking), thus rendering their thought processes less efficient, effective, or intentional (Rogers, 1988). Some cognitive theorists hold that children's autistic problems rest in their lack of a "theory of mind." This concept refers to affective cognition, an ability to conceptualize one's own emotional state and the emotional state of others. Assuming a "theory of mind," children with PDD/autism are unable to differentiate and conceptualize their own emotional status, which makes it very difficult for them to understand emotions, attitudes, beliefs, and points of view (Baron-Cohen, Leslie, & Frith, 1985). If you can not differentiate and conceptualize your own affect, it may mean that you can't conceptualize another person's thinking as a separate experience. This cognitive deficit is reminiscent of the psychological theories that focus on issues of "me" and "not me" and ego boundaries (Tustin, 1988).

Yet other theorists focus on other cognitive difficulties that include some of the following: the inability to imitate (Rogers & Pennington, 1991), problems with **metarepresentation** (i.e., knowing how to pretend) (Baron-Cohen, 1987; Leslie & Happé, 1989; Mundy & Sigman, 1989b), difficulty in mastering means-end and causality (Rogers, 1988), and delays in the development of symbolic functioning (Baron-Cohen, 1987, 1988; Harris, 1989; Hobson, 1989). These cognitive deficits, all, in turn, affect language, communication, social interaction and play development (Leslie & Happé, 1989; McCaleb & Prizant, 1985; Mundy & Sigman, 1989a; Mundy, Sigman, Ungerer, & Sherman, 1987).

Play Skills and Themes Development

Predominant characteristics of PDD/autism are an uneven developmental profile and scatter in skill acquisition. This pattern is evident yet again in their play, which is delayed and distorted, with functional and constructive play far surpassing imitative and symbolic play. Functional and constructive play come closer to norm because these children are able to respond to the clear use of an object, as well as imitate at a very basic level (Baron-Cohen, 1987). However, even their functional and constructive play, which is a relative strength, is less frequent, less diverse, and less mature than might be expected in relation to their more general cognitive ability (McCune, 1986; Sigman & Ungerer, 1984). This may be exhibited when they choose to manipulate small objects (small toy people or vehicles) or complete a number of puzzles. At first glance, these may appear to be adaptive and developmentally appropriate activities, but with closer examination the unusual quality and nature of the use of the materials becomes more apparent (i.e., perseverative handling of the toy people, repetitive actions, compulsively completing the pile of puzzles to avoid other activities or to avoid peer or adult interactions). Typical in the play of many children with PDD/autism is a preoccupation with one part of the play object, rather than the whole. Wheels, switches, or moveable parts may mesmerize the child. This may suggest a fixation at the level of part-object relations, implying an inability to delay gratification to assimilate and comprehend the whole object. The interaction is based on the children's need for immediate feedback, limiting their interactions to what they can do here and now with the object. This focus on the part rather than the whole frequently extends to human objects as well; for example, when we see the children use the adult hand as a tool, disassociated from the whole person (Freud, 1966; Kline, 1937).

Children with PDD/autism display delays and differences in imaginative play, peer play, and imitative skills when compared to their normal counterparts (Stone & Lemanek, 1990). For instance, even though spontaneous symbolic play is positively correlated with expressive and receptive language skills, the play of children with PDD/autism never reaches the same level of spontaneous expression as their language (Mundy, Sigman, Ungerer, & Sherman, 1987). Additionally, play ability remains below the level of their general cognitive skills (Power & Radcliffe, 1989).

Numerous hypotheses exist to explain the generally depressed play ability of children with PDD/autism. Contributing to their difficulties in play development are deficits in metarepresentation, delays in social interaction, attachment, joint attention (Kasari, Sigman, Mundy, & Yirmiya, 1990; McHale, Simeonsson, Marcus, & Olley, 1980; Quinn & Rubin, 1984; Sigman & Mundy, 1989), and deficits in nonverbal indicating behavior like pointing (Mundy, Sigman, Ungerer, & Sherman, 1986; Sigman, Mundy, Sherman, & Ungerer, 1986). Additional factors that compromise play include an inability to **substitute objects** or to use imagination and fantasy. These children may be able to function at the level of direct representation (e.g., pretending to sip from an empty cup), but they are less able to move from the concrete into the abstract or from the sign to the symbol (e.g., being able to substitute a block for a car) (Hammes & Langdell, 1981; Langer, 1962; Rogers, 1988). Additionally, they have problems in forming social representation of themselves and others as seen, for instance, in doll play (Rogers & Pennington, 1991; Wulff, 1985). Even when these individuals do develop simple symbolic play, they seldom initiate it unless guided by an adult (Gould, 1986; Rogers, 1988a).

TRENDS IN INTERVENTION

Various intervention approaches have been used with the young child with PDD/autism. These have included behavioral approaches that include peer trainers, play training, responsive/relationship-centered approaches, and others. As we explore how to work most effectively with these children, it is imperative that we understand the implications for the use of each of these approaches and to examine how they involve the child, the staff, and the parents. Some philosophical underpinnings, as well as examples of implementation of these approaches, are described in this section.

Behavioral Approaches

Since the 1970s, a body of research focusing on behavior modification as an intervention technique has been amassed, claiming high levels of success with children with PDD/autism. This research has focused on training word production and extinguishing undesirable behavior (Lovaas, 1987). Although specific skills can be acquired through behavior modification, current practice questions the long-term benefits of this training because it is often situation-and trainer-specific, with little known about transfer and generalization.

Currently, there is emphasis in the literature on the role of modeling and the benefits of integration. Inclusion of children with PDD/autism in regular settings is recommended because of the potential benefit of peers modeling socially appropriate behavior and learning. Peer models have proven to be useful in increasing correct responses in discrimination tasks and in modeling socially appropriate behavior (Bandura, 1973). Some research indicates that the learning is maintained after the model is removed (Egel, Richman, & Koegel, 1981). Normally developing peers have been trained to initiate, interact, and respond to their PDD/autistic peers through individual and group-oriented contingency reinforcement. It is important to note that, without such training, normal peers do not spontaneously prompt children with PDD/autism to play (Kohler, Strain, Maretsky, & DeCesare, 1990). Likewise, children with PDD/autism do not benefit simply from the presence of normal peers, but must be helped with a carefully prepared individualized plan over an extended period of time to benefit from the integrated setting.

Even those committed to a more behavioral approach in intervention are finding that there are factors beyond skill training that must be carefully considered. For instance, it has also been shown that establishing a predictable but adaptive schedule can be helpful to children with PDD/autism to increase their responsiveness and to assist in mood maintenance (Ferrara &

Hill, 1980). There are a variety of daily living, social, and communication skills that must be incorporated into any integrated school experience to be successful (Chastain & Merzer, 1982; Guralnick, 1990; Quill, Gurry, & Larkin, 1989; Strain, 1985).

In order for regular educational placement to be successful for most children with PDD/autism, it is crucial that they become more aware and more skilled in social interaction with their classmates (Gresham, 1981). Initiating and sustaining social interaction with peers has been shaped through direct training and the use of various reinforcement systems (Lefebvre & Strain, 1989; McEvoy et al., 1988; Oke & Schreibman, 1990; Shafer, Egel, & Neef, 1984). However, once again, serious questions have been raised as to the generalization and maintenance of these skills when they are taught through behavioral techniques (McEvoy & Odom, 1987).

Play Training

Play training has also received attention in the behavioral literature. Without play skills, children with PDD/autism are limited in their ability to make to meaningful connections with adults and peers. In an effort to remediate these deficits, play training has focused on initiation skills, specific toy training through the use of peer confederates and peer models, and direct adult coaching of play behavior (Haring & Lovinger, 1989; McCune, 1986; Rogers, 1988; Santarcangelo, Dyer, & Luce, 1987; Sigman, Mundy, Sherman, & Ungerer, 1986; Tryon & Keane, 1986). Some success has been reported in activities that are highly structured by the teacher so that the child's role is prescribed by an adult and the materials are used in specific, predetermined ways. Although children with PDD/autism can be trained to increase their play in these highly staged scenarios, questions arise once again concerning the generalization of these skills and their meaningfulness to the child (Coe, Matson, Fee, Manikam, & Linarello, 1990).

Responsive/Relationship-Centered Approaches

In contrast to skill training is a responsive and relationship-centered approach, which focuses on maximizing the child's spontaneous play behavior, affect, and communication, even if particular behaviors of the children are atypical. Because these children develop in patterns qualitatively different from normally developing children, intervention strategies should neither adhere rigidly to traditional ideas about stage-specific development nor be focused on extinguishing symptomatic behavior (Powell & Jordan, 1991). There are a number of theorists and practitioners who emphasize relationship-centered intervention. For example, Margaret Wood's developmental therapy (Wood, Combs, Gunn, & Weller, 1986) presents play as the medium for encouraging the children into a social setting with peers. The teacher first focuses on helping the children gain trust of adults and of themselves. This allows the children to respond to their environment first with pleasure and then, ultimately, with success.

Greenspan (1992a, 1992b) and others stress the centrality of engagement and the development of two-way communication as a means to move the children from the gestural to the symbolic level and to affective elaboration and differentiation. Within Greenspan's methodology there are several strategies of particular importance. These include the goals of establishing attention and engagement, establishing intentionality and two-way communication (opening and closing circles of communication) through following the child's lead, and engaging with emotional empathy. He stresses that interventionists should avoid rigidity, fragmentation, hollow parallel commentary, or relating to the child either too far above or too far below the child's developmental level.

Along similar lines, Uline (1982), Mahoney and Powell (1986, 1988), and others (Chastain & Merzer, 1982; Dawson & Galpert, 1990; Gartner & Schultz, 1990) have documented the importance of parents and interventionists developing an interactive style that is responsive and promotes the child's participation in the most basic reciprocal interactions that will be the foundation for further social, communicative, and play development (Kalmanson & Pekarsky, 1987). Koegel, Dyer, and Bell (1987) also found that allowing the child to choose activities increases socially appropriate behavior and diminishes social avoidance. Responsiveness, including imitating the child's actions, thereby building a pattern of interchanges, helps the child across developmental areas, especially in play skills (McCune, 1986; McCune-Nicolich & Carroll, 1981). Imitation of a child's object use can also help the child maintain the interaction and improve eye gaze (Tiegerman & Primavera, 1981, 1984). Some suggest that an interactive style characterized as "low intrusive" can be helpful (Meyer et al., 1987), while Prizant & Wetherby (1990) and others encourage the interventionist to lure children into interaction by the strategic use of a mildly challenging style.

It is often pointed out by practitioners that the interventionist should avoid the trap of over-focusing on splinter skills that may give an artificial reading of a child's competencies (Greenspan, 1992b; McHale, Simeonsson, Marcus, & Olley, 1980). For instance, the child's vocabulary may be strong and overshadow the lack of skill in social language use, which really should be the focus of intervention. Splinter skills can sometimes be used, though, as a vehicle to engage the child and facilitate development in areas of weakness. For example, a child's reading ability can be used to increase the child's interpersonal skills by asking the child to carry a written message to another adult and read the message to him or her.

Additional Approaches

Somewhat parallel, but we believe associated to the relational approach, are a number of strategies that seem to make children more available for interaction, play, and learning. Some children with PDD/autism have been helped by the use of auditory trainers (the wireless microphone and receiver used with hearing impaired) to help them focus on their own utterances and to increase attentiveness (Smith, McConnell, Walter, & Miller, 1985; Smith, Olson, Barger, & McConnell, 1981). **Auditory integration training** (a technique used to reduce hypersensitivity to sound) has also been used with children who have PDD/autism (Bérard, 1993). **Sensory integration therapy**, (brushing, joint compression), techniques described by Ayres (1989) and Wilbarger (1993), are also used with some children with PDD/autism. Visual training (Getman, 1965), and **facilitated communication** (Biklen, 1993) are techniques that have also been described in the literature and appear effective for certain children. Another intervention technique for ameliorating some language and communication issues is the simultaneous use of sign language with speech (Barrera, Lobato-Barrera, & Sulzer-Azaroff, 1980; Barrera & Sulzer-Azaroff, 1983; Benaroya, Wesley, Ogilvie, Klein, & Clarke, 1979; Konstantareas, 1984; Konstantareas, Webster, & Oxman, 1979; Kouri, 1988). Others report that a multisensory–intrusive approach including tickling and rough-housing may increase focus and comprehension (Benaroya, Wesley, Ogilvie, Klein, & Meaney, 1977).

New intervention approaches are continually being described in the literature and becoming available in practice. There is always the need to balance the desire to find a good match between an intervention to the child's development issues and the risk of getting caught in an endless search for a cure for PDD/autism. There is seldom an easy answer or a pat solution to designing an intervention plan for children with this complex condition. The intervention process is usually arduous and life-long.

INVOLVING AND SUPPORTING PARENTS AND FAMILIES

The involvement of families in early intervention is integral because building an emotional relationship is the primary task of childhood. In families with a child who has PDD/autism, as with all families who have a child with special needs, family-collaborative involvement in the intervention is essential to increase the likelihood of long-term effectiveness. Agencies and professionals working with families need to be very alert to the necessity of finding a balance in asking for the family's active collaboration, while also providing the family members with appropriate supports, such as respite care, parent support organizations, and individual and family therapy (Bristol, 1984a; DeMyer, 1979; Kalmanson & Pekarsky, 1987; Schopler & Reichler, 1971; Wing, 1974). It is crucial to remember that the parents are not the patients but rather the co-designers of intervention, and should be very active in the intervention process (Bristol, 1984b). But it is also important to remember that the parents have a life beyond parenting the child with special needs.

A child with PDD/autism can cause great distress in a family, leaving parents feeling inadequate, responsible, and isolated; these stressors can be particularly severe before a diagnosis is established. Because these children are usually physically quite attractive and well-formed, the general public may show little patience with their unusual behavior. Extended family members may exacerbate the situation by blaming the parents' lack of childrearing skills. On diagnosis, parents are likely to experience the guilt and grief that is a natural reaction to this family crisis. Parents may sense that the old belief that they are somehow responsible for their child's condition still lingers in the minds of some relatives or professionals (Bristol, 1984a).

During the preschool period, parents need support around a variety of important issues. Their child may have a poor feedback system, so despite a parent working very hard at being loving and responsive, there may be little sign of the child being comforted and the child's communication back to the parent may not reflect any awareness of the parent's efforts. Parents need the opportunity to express their anger and frustration. Parents may need extra support during the periods when their child is in a disorganized or distressed phase and they are feeling particularly exhausted, defeated, or criticized. They also need affirmation of their understanding of their child's issues when relatives and friends dismiss the developmental problems as transient and short term.

The parents of children with PDD/autism are consistently faced with a unique set of circumstances when they consider educational placement and planning for their child with autism/PDD. As was mentioned earlier, these children are typically attractive and may appear to be quite normal. Parents of these children have said to the authors "If there is anything consistent about a child with PDD/autism, it is their inconsistency."

One moment, they are very cooperative and communicative and the next, they are having a temper tantrum and are intractable. For instance, parents describe the routines and rituals that they have to incorporate into the day to get their children ready for school in the morning. One parent described the exact sequence that had to be followed each day; if there was a change in that sequence the whole process had to begin again. Another parent described that they had once stopped at a sandwich store on their way out of the mall and from then on, each time they went to that mall, they had to stop at the same store before the child with PDD/autism would leave. These parents say they never know what will be added into the list of daily rituals or when they will begin or end. They are often exhausted trying to maintain order, without centering their life around the child with PDD/autism.

Although it is very stressful to have a child with significant developmental disabilities, it is also clear that many families possess the resilience to be responsive both to their child's and their own personal needs. Research reinforces the idea that, given a responsive, family-oriented intervention and support system, effective parental coping strategies can be developed and sustained (Bristol, 1984a, b). This does not trivialize the seriousness of the crisis of raising a child with PDD/autism, but speaks to the adaptive capacity of most people when provided with the refueling and affirmation that comes with adequate support systems.

CHILDREN WITH PDD/AUTISM IN A GROUP SETTING

Children who are at the milder end of the PDD/autism spectrum have been served in nursery school settings for decades. Often, the developmentally sensitive nursery school teacher was the person who first identified and referred this type of child for developmental evaluation. Blatant or even subtle interpersonal, communicative, behavioral, and cognitive differences made this child stand apart from peers in the nursery school. But the highly motivated teacher could include this child in a nursery class and support his or her development, even if the child remained aloof from peers throughout daily activities. With the current inclusive movement, more children with moderate and severe PDD/autism are being placed in preschool settings with normally developing peers. Although this may be done with the best of intentions, the potential for failure is high. An inappropriate placement can be disastrous to the child, the family, the peers, and the teachers involved.

As is clear from both research and clinical experience, the nature of PDD/autism is such that these children are, in many ways, dissimilar from normally developing children and from many other disabled children as well. For that reason, simplifying the curriculum and working as with a developmentally younger or retarded child will typically prove inadequate. Although children with PDD/autism are likely to be delayed in their development, an equal, if not more important defining, aspect of this condition is that their course of development is qualitatively different from normative development. These children may have splinter skills and islets of ability far ahead of their general development, contradicting what is generally thought to be the normal course of stage- and phase-specific progression. For instance, a child may read before he speaks or remember complicated directions to a grandparent's house, but at the same time not be able to go and retrieve a familiar object in the next room. Planning for such a child within the context of a group is indeed a challenge, as is illustrated in the following case.

THE INCLUSION OF A CHILD WITH PDD IN A HEAD START PROGRAM

In the following case study, you will see some of the challenges that arise when 5-year-old Scott, who is diagnosed PDD, is placed a Head Start group composed of 3 year olds and housed in a public elementary school. Scott's parents and teachers are not happy with his progress thus far in this placement, so the parents have requested that the planning and placement team (PPT) meet. The PPT resulted in the team requesting that additional information be gathered through the use of the SPM including both Scott's developmental strengths and weaknesses and the appropriateness of his current placement. The program staff will work through the components of the SPM process to help clarify the developmental issues that are interfering with Scott's progress in this group and plan facilitating techniques. In the next section, background information on Scott, a history of his educational placements, and a descriptive initial observation of Scott in the Head Start Program, are presented.

Background Information and Initial Observation

Since September, Scott, a 5-year-old with PDD, has been enrolled in a Head Start group of twenty 3-year-olds. When Scott's parents enrolled him in their church nursery school at age 3, the teacher realized that Scott's needs were not compatible with her setting. She referred the parents to a Department of Health Clinic where neurological and psychological testing was conducted. No hearing, visual, or neurological problems were identified. Scott was diagnosed as having moderate PDD with some near age-appropriate preacademic skills and with his most severe delays in expressive language and social development. Through their local public school, Scott was provided with speech and language intervention for 1 hour per week and placed in a small special education class with six other children three mornings each week throughout his 3rd and 4th years.

Even though Scott had been a moody and hard-to-reach child, his parents had not been overly worried about his delayed development because his father had also been a very difficult baby with delayed language acquisition. Scott has two younger sisters who are developing normally and who are usually very tolerant of his unusual behavior, even though he seems unaware of them as individuals and is interested in them only when they are a source of desired objects. Scott's parents had believed that with patience and ample stimulation he would learn to talk and relate more effectively with other children. Scott's parents have spent many hours reading to Scott and his little sisters. Looking through books and finding alphabet letters has turned into one of his favorite activities. His parents are very proud of the fact that Scott can identify numerous words in print and has recently shown interest in counting and simple addition.

Scott had made good strides in his special education class over the previous year, so that at his annual review and placement meeting everyone concerned was very enthusiastic about his joining this Head Start group. Since the Head Start children are 2 full years younger than Scott and not nearly as advanced as he is in many preacademic skills, his parents felt very strongly that he could experience success in this placement, while still benefiting from the 3-year-olds' social and play skills. The special education teacher reported increased verbal communication, although he still tended to be very echolalic, repeating whatever the teacher said and sometimes carrying out lengthy monologues from favorite books and television programs. He resisted answering direct questions, but could communicate more successfully when the adult provided the structure of a thought and let Scott fill in the missing word. "Now it is time for us to have _____," the teacher might say while pointing to the juice and popcorn at the table. He usually refers to himself as "you," "good boy," or "bad boy," depending on the circumstances. His special education teacher also indicated that he enjoyed Lego, puzzles, and pegs, but that he was disinterested in any interpersonal games like peek-a-boo or chasing games or activities that include imaginative play with human figures or vehicles. He knew the words to several songs and could be overheard "singing" to himself in a monotone; but Scott hated any group singing or music activities and often became agitated at the sight of the musical instruments or another child singing.

The 3-year-old group is in the last room off a long hallway that also contains a 4-year-old group, two kindergarten classrooms, and two self-contained special education classes, one of which was Scott's classroom the previous year. The classroom is large, bright, and cheery with a good supply of equipment and materials. The classroom is staffed by a teacher, Liz, and an aide, Sue. As part of the Head Start family-involvement program, a parent outreach worker is sometimes in the classroom, and often several parents are present for part of the day. The classroom is divided into several interest areas, which are defined by low storage cupboards. There is a piano at one end of the room and a children's bathroom and sink behind a partition at the opposite end of the room. The group is together four mornings a week from 8:30 am to 12:30 pm. Breakfast and lunch are served each day to the group. On Friday, the parent outreach worker and the teacher make home visits on a rotating schedule. Each morning after breakfast children are free to select any activity that is set up in the choice areas. Usually there are manipulatives, art materials, dress-up and housekeeping, and a block corner. After 45 minutes of self-directed play, the children are called together for a calendar activity, some group discussion about events of current interest (holidays, weather changes), and the reading of a story. After story time there is often some singing and then a small snack before going out to the playground with the two kindergarten classes. If the weather is inappropriate for outdoor play, the children sometimes go to the indoor gym and once a month they have begun to walk to a local Y for a swimming class. The day ends with lunch and a short rest time when children can rest on their cot or read a book to themselves on the reading cushions. The observation that follows was made in early October beginning at 8:30 in the morning.

Scott arrives at the door after coming to school in the special education van. He is carrying several pencils and a small notebook. He stands by his cubbie, flipping though the notebook and reading words aloud to himself. Liz gently suggests that it is time to take off his coat and come to one of the breakfast tables. Scott looks over at Liz and then turns his back to the group and begins to gently rock on this heels while he continues to repeat words to himself. Once everyone is seated except Scott, Sue goes to his side with some apple slices to show him what fruit they are having for breakfast. He looks at the fruit and gives a sideways glance at Sue. She says, "Apples, Scott, one, two, three," as she hands him the apple slices. He puts down his notebook, lets her remove and hang up his jacket, and allows her to lead him to a table. He sits down, lines up several apple slices on the table and then begins to eat his breakfast with a good appetite, but he does not look at or speak to the children seated around him. They, in turn, glance over at him occasionally but make no effort to talk with him. Sue watches Scott's food supply, and when he is running low on juice or toast, she places the serving dish or pitcher near him, and he helps himself.

During the 45 minutes the children are self-selecting and moving from one area of the room to another, Scott drifts back to his cubbie and retrieves his notebook and pencils. He lies on the floor and takes great care in writing the letters to his name. He then looks around the room and walks over to the bookshelf where he picks up books and points out and names alphabet letters randomly. All of the adults in the room are busy supporting the play of the children in the various choice centers and Scott goes basically unnoticed for 20 minutes. When Sue is able to leave the five children who are involved in playing house, she goes over to Scott and asks to see his notebook. He turns away from her but repeats, "Can I look at your notebook?" Sue reaches for a book that has pictures of farm animals and begins to point to various pictures, saying, "I see a cow and a horse, and a pig." Scott looks over her shoulder and says, "Cow? Horse? Pig?" Sue pats the floor beside her and asks Scott to sit with her and read the book. He says, "Time to read the book, read the book. Good boy." and sits down with one shoulder leaning against Sue. They look through several pages when a major disruption takes place in the block corner that requires Sue to get up quickly and leave Scott alone again. For the next 15 minutes Scott stays in the book corner, passively flipping through pages of the farm book. When Sue is able to return to Scott, she brings with her a basket of farm animals and a small barn, hoping to help Scott move from the farm animal book to some play with the animals. Scott watches her as she places several of the animals into the barn while saying their names. He repeats the animal names but does not show any interest in handling the animals. He becomes focused on the mechanism of the barn door, which makes a mooing sound when opened and closed. Scott takes the barn off the floor, shakes out the animals and proceeds to play with the doors while holding the barn upright on his lap. Sue comments to Scott that he does not want the animals, but that he likes the barn door noise.

Liz goes to the piano and plays a short tune that announces group time. Scott grimaces and covers his ears while Liz plays the piano. The children put away their toys and noisily come to sit around a large painted circle on the floor up near the piano. Scott does not join the group until Sue leads him over and has him sit on her lap. He has his pencils with him and occupies himself by twisting them in his fingers so that they make a fan shape in the air. He suddenly comes to attention when Liz brings forward a large calendar and asks the children what the day and the date are. Scott starts to excitedly call out various numbers, Liz tries to include him in this activity, but becomes frustrated because he keeps jumping up and running to the calendar to touch various numbers. His interest is just in the naming of the numbers and he seems unaware of the task. Sue takes him away from the group so the exercise can continue uninterrupted. She lets him write numbers on a large sheet of paper until story time. Today's story is about the monkey with the hats. Scott returns to the group and relaxes in Sue's lap and smiles to himself as the story progresses. Several times he calls out the appropriate line as the Liz turns to a new page. The children sitting near Scott are impressed that he knows the story and they, too, try to anticipate what will happen on the next page. Liz adjusts her storytelling to allow the children to give their suggestions. Scott is correct several times and he smiles shyly when the other children spontaneously clap when he calls out the correct story line.

When story time is over, a mother, who is helping in the classroom, starts to walk around the circle, handing out triangles and rhythm sticks. Scott becomes very tense and within seconds starts to talk unintelligibly in a rapid fashion. Sue tries to calm him, but her efforts only seem to frustrate him more, until he jumps from her lap and runs to the bathroom area saying, "All done? Pull up your pants, that's a good boy." This causes a lot of laughter among the children in the circle. Liz asks the children to settle down so that the music activity can begin.

When Scott comes out of the bathroom, after urinating independently and washing and drying his hands, he walks along the edge of the wall, jabbering to himself and ultimately positioning himself behind a shelf of puzzles. Liz and Sue are involved in the music activities and let him occupy himself with the puzzles while the group sings and plays their instruments. While jabbering loudly, he dumps out a puzzle and quickly completes it outside its frame on the table top. He then searches for a particular puzzle that has numbers and works diligently at completing this puzzle by himself. One of the number pieces causes him repeated problems, which he reacts to by whining, hitting himself on the side of the head, and finally throwing the piece under the table. When it is time for everyone to go outside, the speech and language pathologist arrives to take Scott for his individual speech session. He leaves calmly with her because she has brought a collection of flash cards that he enjoys.

He comes back and joins the group for lunch, but he is very agitated because the soup does not contain the letter noodles that were in the last soup they had. He shouts , "A B C , A B C" at Liz and flaps his arms with distress; Liz eventually removes him from the room until he can calm down. He rejoins the group for a peanut butter sandwich Liz makes for him and then joins the rest of the group for rest time. He lies contentedly on his cot with several favorite books. He is upset once again when it is time to get into his jacket and return home. He wants to take the classroom farm book home with him. Sue explains several times that he can read the book again tomorrow. He does not look at her when she talks to him, but he calms down enough to be helped into his jacket. He goes to the van and keeps repeating to himself, "Stop it, stop it. No more gum. Bad boy, bad boy."

Utilizing the Supportive Play Model

We suggest that you use a copy of the SPM, provided at the end of Chapter 2, to respond to this vignette, as if you were a member of the team that is observing and reviewing Scott's development. As we have mentioned in preceding chapters, this process allows for interpretation and the use of clinical judgment. If you had been working with this child for a while you would also have additional information to use, consequently our descriptions may be more detailed than you are able to construct.

Section I: Cover Sheet

In filling out the *Cover Sheet*, highlight that the staff and Scott's parents are very concerned about Scott's adjustment to the group. His parents and former special education teacher were confident that the setting would work. It is now clear to Scott's mother, after participating in the group as a helping parent, that some adjustments are necessary. The teacher and aide are finding his presence very disruptive to the group and his behavior confusing and frustrating. Although he has gained academic skills in the setting, he has not shown any signs of wanting to associate with other children or to function as a group member.

Child: Sections II, III, and IV

To summarize your observations, underline and code *Section II: Observational Impressions* and put a star at the most relevant working theme in each developmental area. Next, list key observations in *Section III: Skills and Outstanding Characteristics Observed*. Then, in Section IV, underline the relevant *Characteristic Patterns Limiting Play*.

The following section provides a developmental analysis from the initial observation in the areas of self/social/emotional, motor/self-help, communicative/language, cognitive, play skills, and play themes. After reading this section, return to your chart and make any appropriate changes or adaptations.

SELF/SOCIAL/EMOTIONAL   Scott's self/social/emotional skills are very delayed with his working theme at Level 1. Even in this infant–toddler level, his skills are only emerging or are still underdeveloped. Scott's range of emotion is either muted or extreme. He does not demonstrate aggression toward others, but is likely to hurt himself when angry. Scott's facial expressions are generally flat, so that there is little hint of what emotion he is experiencing until rage or laughter erupts. He is highly impul-

sive and reactive to whatever is in his immediate environment with little self-regulation, so that, when frustrated, his temper is very infantile with little modulation between his periods of passivity and withdrawal and his display of a full tantrum. Because of this emotional volatility, he is still highly dependent on external controls, particularly routine and environmental stability. Changes in routine and even transitions between activities can elicit emotional disorganization in him.

Scott is still exploring at a sensorimotor level and is showing only fleeting awareness and interest in others. He is only minimally aware of the kind of reciprocal behavior that infants use interpersonally and in play. Scott does not show any clear preference for particular adults nor does he seek comfort from adults when he is distressed. He finds people useful, but does not seem aware that they are discrete individuals. Scott's predominately passive style makes it easy for him to drift in the group and not come to the staff's attention when he is quietly self-involved. Scott is basically unaware of his peers and most of the social cues offered by the children and the staff. He shows some beginning signs of attachment to his parents but shows little sign of differentiation or self-identity. Scott does not typically respond to physical pain and can be quite ill before his parents know he is sick. He is using transitional objects, particularly his pencil and pad, to soothe himself. Although this behavior has some qualities of a transitional object, it is likely to represent a fragment (part-object) of his experience rather than evoking a more whole memory of the parent as we see in more typical children.

MOTOR/SELF-HELP   Although not fully age-appropriate, Scott's relative strengths lie in the motor and self-help areas, placing his working theme at Level 2. Although. he has some delays in motor skills, this is the developmental area in which he displays the most competence. He has attained or mastered everything in Level 1; he has attained all fine motor skills in Level 2 except the use of scissors. Level 2 gross motor skills, such as walking, jumping, stair climbing, and ball use are also mastered. To an observer, Scott often appears to be unaware of environmental dangers, but he is almost never hurt and seems able to keep out of harm's way. His impulse control is still poor and it takes an indirect tactic on the teacher's behalf to have him comply with behavioral guidelines.

At Level 3 Scott shows some attained skills and several that are emerging or that he is practicing. He can, when he chooses to, build a tower of nine blocks, balance on one foot, catch a large ball, walk downstairs, hop, button and unbutton, pour, spread with a knife, undress, brush his teeth, bathe with supervision, and toilet independently. Although he is not very physically and motorically active, he has mastered many motor planning and complex gross, fine motor and self-help skills, but, except for his stereotypic activity choices, he does not show much pleasure or pride in his motor skills, perhaps, because he does not possess a significantly differentiated sense of self to invest with pleasure.

Scott's general gross motor patterns are natural and smooth, although he has not shown interest in many of the gross motor activities popular in preschool, such as skipping and bike riding, and displays no general interest in exploration of his physical surroundings. His fine motor skills are more developed compared to other areas. Scott demonstrates age-appropriate skills using pencil and paper and puzzles, but does not show any interest in exploring new materials and has established ritualized use of the limited constructive and manipulative materials with which he is willing to play. He displays many oversensitivities. For instance, he finds most music very aversive and is irritated by light touch as shown by his discomfort with shirt labels, hats, wool, collars, cuffs, and elastic waistbands. He is passive about self-dressing; although he has the skills, he is not usually motivated to dress. Scott prefers his pajamas and has very specific clothing preferences, so that trying to get him ready for school or into outdoor clothing can be difficult.

COMMUNICATIVE/LANGUAGE Scott's communication and language skills are misleading because his ability to speak in an articulate fashion is much more advanced that his actual ability to communicate. This major inconsistency between his apparently strong ability to use words and his actual ability to communicate is compounded by his serious delays in all the interpersonal skills that are integral to communication: eye contact, shared attention, and turn taking. His Communicative/Language working theme is at Level 1, but even at Level 1 some of the skills are just beginning to emerge, and many skills have not been observed. Scott does not use a social smile in a typical fashion and he is only beginning to participate in joint attention and joint action rituals (patty-cake, peek-a-boo); he does not look for family members when they are named but will search for his dog, who both excites and frightens him. He can follow simple commands, although he often ignores them. Scott does not point to indicate his wants, but is likely to drag an adult by the hand to the area of a desired object. He does not use much intentional communication, but his echolalia sometimes can be understood to contain a message. Scott does use words to attract attention and to protest. Splinter skills at Level 2 include his willingness to use simple sentences and to listen to a story, but his word use is deceptive because his expressive vocabulary exceeds his comprehension and his vocalizations often do not appear to be communicative. He can combine words much like a 3-year-old, although his pronoun use is atypical. Most frequently, Scott uses language in a nonsequential and fragmented fashion. He has difficulty understanding much language as it is spoken to him unless it is simplified and supported by concrete objects and physical gestures.

COGNITIVE In the area of cognitive development, Scott has very divergent and scattered skills. His working theme falls at Level 1 with a scattering of skills into Levels 2 and 3. Even at Level 1, intentionality and cause and effect are weakly established. He does not identify himself in a mirror and will not point to named body parts. Some pleasure in seek-and-discover games is emerging. At Level 2, he enjoys favorite stories, picture books, and interlocking puzzles, but does not use creative materials and does not enjoy interactive exchanges. He understands the concept of one, but seems unaware of his own and others' sex. At Level 3, he has an emerging awareness of the significance of letters and words, pretends to read a story, and knows words to songs.

At the broadest level, his cognitive development is most curtailed by issues related to differentiation and synthesis in the self/social/emotional and communicative/language areas. His passivity and resistance to new experiences have limited his exposure to many of the learning opportunities available to him both at home and at school. At this time, Scott will have difficulty reaching his cognitive potential without access to concrete materials and a very direct approach to teaching. His general lack of motivation, lack of curiosity, and inconsistent attention inhibit the kind of spontaneous learning that would typically be found in a preschooler. Although object permanence has been established, he does not yet demonstrate much ability to problem solve because of a lack of understanding of cause and effect, and his inability to generalize and expand, sequence, imitate, or categorize.

PLAY SKILLS Scott's play skills are predominately at working theme Level 1 with sensorimotor and functional–combinatory play dominating. He prefers solitary play with little interest or skill in onlooker, parallel, or interactive play, even at an infant level. Scott rarely engages in autorepresentational play. He does a lot of walking around a room, picking up and then discarding objects, much like a young toddler.

Scott's play skills include a lack of interest in exploration, perseveraion on objects and routines, and a fixation at the functional–combinatory level of object use. His rigid style of using materials and his limited activity choices make it difficult to describe much of his behavior under the title of play. Even when engaged in an activity there is little feeling of spontaneity or pleasure. At this time Scott's response to materials is directly linked to the physical qualities of the object. Concrete materials would be necessary, then, if any representational activity is to be encouraged. His lack of cognitive concepts and skills, lack of life experience, and lack of social skills all greatly inhibit his play; his preference for adult interaction over peer interaction inhibit any benefit that might come from being in a peer group.

PLAY THEMES Scott's play working theme is at Level 1, but even at this level his skills are depressed or poorly developed. He does use sensory and motor activity to explore, but his interests are predominately in objects, rather than in himself or others. Scott does not convey a well-established sense of trust regarding the adults at school, initiates little or no imitating or mirror play, but does tolerate an adult briefly imitating him. He prefers solitary play and does express some aggression through motor behavior, for example, by throwing objects and hitting himself. He tends to be noninteractive and at present does not show many clear signs of pleasure from bodily experience or nurturance except possibly in his stereotypic behaviors. Scott's play themes exist only in a very rudimentary form because he is still sensoricentered, has poorly formulated attachment patterns, and little differentiated sense of self.

Family: Sections II, III, and IV

Using *Section II: Observational Guide*, fill in *Section III: General Descriptions for Family*. Next, underline appropriate items in *Section IV: Characteristic Patterns Limiting Play*.

Family concerns center on establishing realistic expectations for Scott, his readiness to participate in a 3-year-old group, and his parents understanding of PDD and its impact on his long-term development. His parents are encouraged by his academic skills, but they are not fully aware of how his self/social/emotional delays affect his overall success in this group setting. They believe that his interest in letters and numbers is a sign of his intellectual potential, but worry about his lack of interest in his sisters.

Scott's parents have little opportunity to go out together and, except for attendance at a local church, where they find the minister to be very supportive, they seldom take their three young children out in public places. Otherwise, the parents have no friends. They have met some of the parents of children in the nursery school, but because Scott's needs are so different, no friendships have formed.

Program: Sections II, III, and IV

Continuing with the SPM, use *Section II: Observational Guide* to fill in *Section III: General Descriptions* for Program (Staff, Peers, Space, Time, and Materials, and Equipment). Next, underline appropriate items in *Section IV: Characteristics Patterns Limiting Play*.

STAFF   There are adequate adults available in Scott's Head Start group, but at the time of our observation, they are not working effectively on behalf of Scott's needs. They are insufficiently coordinated to provide consistency for Scott and they do not know how to join with him to make use of objects and materials in his environment. They are not fully skilled at assisting him in object mastery or in reinforcing his initial attempts to affiliate with adults and peers. The adults seem unsure and hesitant in taking a guiding role with this child. They may be anxious about including this child in their setting because of a lack of knowledge about PDD and the feelings he may evoke in them.

PEERS   Aspects of the peer setting are also inhibiting Scott's progress. The large group size, the activity format, and the group expectations all are developmentally inappropriate for Scott's current needs. The children in his group do not understand his aloof behavior and are made anxious by his tantrums and atypical behaviors. All of the children are involved with playing at an associative and cooperative level, using symbolic play, which is far too advanced for Scott.

SPACE, TIME, AND MATERIALS AND EQUIPMENT   Several environmental issues also contribute to limiting Scott's success in this placement. The present arrangement of the classroom does not contain any large motor space that would allow Scott nonstructured exploration or opportunites for the vestibular and postural (climbing, swinging, creeping up an inclined plane) stimulation he currently needs. The classroom routine and activity focus is all group-oriented, which is unrealistic considering Scott's current developmental levels. Many of the materials and equipment are too advanced for Scott and there are no materials available to encourage multisensory and exploratory behavior.

Section V: Discrepancy Analysis

After this review of skills and limiting factors, the working themes are transferred to the *Discrepancy Analysis* (found at the end of the chart). You can then compare and contrast Scott's development against his Chronological Age Level (Level 3) and also his relative discrepancies among working themes across the individual areas of development (Self/Social/Emotional: Level 1, Motor/Self-Help: Level 2, Communicative/Language: Level 1, Cognitive: Level 1, Play Skills: Level 1, Play Themes: Level 1). Fill in the differences between Chronological Age and Working Theme levels (all below age range expectation); star developmental areas where you perceive significant scatter (Motor/Self-Help, Communicative/Language, Cognitive); finally, highlight significant discrepancy issues under Child, Family, and Program. This Discrepancy Analysis should facilitate insights to improve Scott's current placement. You should consider the implications of this analysis before moving to the next section.

Scott's behavior is delayed in most areas, although some of his motor, linguistic, and cognitive skills are comparable to the 3-year-olds in his class. The most serious deficits in self/social/emotional, communicative/language, cognitive,

play skills, and play themes, have made his successful integration much more difficult. His self-help and motor skills give the illusion of strength and a certain air of independence, but his inability to control his impulses and problems with accepting appropriate adult restraints, guidance, and direction means that he often uses his motor skills and self-help skills as a method to separate himself from adults and peers. This seemingly antisocial quality reflects the difficulty Scott has in interpersonal interactions and relationships—the crux of his PDD. Many of his scatter skills in language contribute to his quality of separateness and isolation. Some of his language is self-stimulating, some is self-soothing, and some is communicative. Reading his verbal and nonverbal messages and helping him to be more socially interactive will be a challenge and a key focus of the facilitating techniques.

Scott's play skills and play themes are most seriously undermined at this time by his weakness in self/social/emotional development. He handles and explores materials in an infantile way, but conspicuously lacking are the self-awareness, self-observing, and interpersonal skills that are the foundation of the representational, symbolic, and social play that would be expected at his age.

Scott's family only wants to emphasize his intellectual abilities and are struggling with the idea that his delays also need to be formally addressed in his intervention plan. The Head Start staff anticipated a much easier job in integrating Scott into their setting. They are frustrated and discouraged and wonder if the placement is right for Scott at this time. The peers are basically leery of Scott and circle and avoid him in their play. The setting can be made more appropriate by expanding motor areas, creating enclosed areas, including activities that do not require group participation, and providing a wider array of materials that are more appropriate for Scott's sensorimotor level exploration.

Sections VI and VII

At this point of the SPM process, keep Scott's developmental discrepancies and the limiting factors that are inhibiting his play in mind and underline in *Section VI: Intervention Goals/Facilitating Techniques* the items that will be most useful in his intervention plan. Then write some of your ideas that will be helpful to Scott in *Section VII: Individualized Supportive Play Adaptations and Experiences*. Next, read the following narrative that reflects a composite of these two sections and check your worksheets to this point and make additions as necessary.

SELF/SOCIAL/EMOTIONAL   It is crucial to help Scott formulate basic attachments and organize a core sense of self. A primary relationship with an adult will help Scott differentiate among adults at school and establish some attachment behavior. This relationship can provide Scott with the structure to help him regulate and contain his mood and to promote more typical emotional expression. The team agrees that he is most uniformly responsive to Sue. Likewise, Sue is clearly drawn to Scott and is not put off by his aloof style. The new plan calls for several times each day during which Sue and Scott can play together, separate from the group. Each morning will begin with a one-to-one play session in an enclosed carpeted area in the classroom. Most of the SPM facilitating techniques are relevant to this child.

Because Scott's social and emotional behavior is so infantile, Sue will need to use a different interaction style than typically seen in a nursery school setting. Scott needs emphasis on becoming progressively more aware of himself and then aware of the presence of others. Sue must be reassured that it will take some time for Scott to recognize his style of interaction; she will need support from the other staff because progress may be slow and regressions will probably be frequent. Helping Scott discover some pleasure in being with an adult and exploring his world is a key goal. Sue and Scott need extended times to carry out infant games and routines as well as open-ended gross motor and sensorimotor play. These activities will afford Scott the opportunity to practice the establishment and maintenance of eye-contact, shared attention, disengagement and reorganization, turn taking, time on task, and expansion and elaboration. She will need to be creative and open-minded in her experimentation to see what attracts Scott's attention, often gaining entry into Scott's world by following his lead. All this will require a major shift in perspective, but with acceptance of Scott's actual functional level and building on what he can do, Scott can begin to experience more success and gratification in interpersonal and shared activities.

To engage his attention, Sue could begin by **mirroring** his spontaneous behaviors and interjecting interactive opportunities. She will need to identify and verbalize Scott's actions, feelings, and needs using simple words and phrases. Exaggerating her facial expression and her vocal intonation, much as we naturally do with a baby, will assist Scott in sustaining shared attention and comprehending her message. Sue should stress routine, provide physical containment, and visual reminders of schedule and transitions. She will stay with Scott in selected group situations (story time, meal time), supporting his presence, but also watching to see when he needs to retreat. Initially, meal time may prove to be the most successful group time. Scott should be encouraged to signal his needs, not just be served. As Scott acquires social skills, aggressive and negative behavior are also likely to emerge. Sue should anticipate this, stay calm, and set and maintain clear behavioral expectations for Scott, similar to those an adult would set for an older infant. In order to gain control over himself and his environment, Scott can be expected and encouraged to make some choices regarding daily living activities, much as you might ask an older infant (e.g., does he want apple juice or water, does he want to wear a striped or plaid shirt?). Body scheme and image are important building blocks of the core self. Intervention strategies will need to include mirror play, body-part games, nurturing, and comforting experiences which all contribute to the early birth of the self.

MOTOR/SELF-HELP   The motor/self-help area, which is a relative strength for Scott, can also be used as an avenue to help Scott expand body awareness, self-image, and conscious self-regulation. Scott's motor development is complicated by the fact that at one level he appears to be very competent, but at another level he is showing many issues related to sensory-integration concerns not atypical in children with PDD/autism. He appears to crave vestibular sensation, and although he is sensitive to light touch on his skin, he seeks and is organized by experiences that involve deep pressure. The planning and placement team decides that it is important to have input from an occupational therapist in introducing a variety of activities tailored to Scott's needs. The occupational therapist evaluated Scott's development, met with the staff to explain some of the techniques used to improve sensory integration, and will provide consultation every other week in the classroom. Her recommended interventions include wearing a weighted vest 15 minutes each day, brushing his skin with a small surgical scrub brush, and activi-

ties that include weight bearing and joint compression. The occupational therapist will teach Sue how to do these activities so that they can be incorporated at natural times in the day. To decrease tactile sensitivity, activities that provide deep pressure, such as rolling Scott tightly in a blanket, and sensory activities such as playing in sand and water may be helpful. There should be a large motor area added to the classroom to allow for more vestibular activity (swings, hammocks, large bolsters and balls, tunnels and slides). Scott will first need to work in this area alone with the aide. Initially she can mirror his motions and actions, gradually expanding his repertoire and awareness.

Daily outside activity is also important and can include walks with Sue and a gradual introduction of biking, swinging, climbing, and sliding. Sue will work with him individually to increase competence skills in activities that can ultimately be shared with peers. A movement consultant could be hired to conduct several workshops to introduce movement activities for the entire group (without music until Scott is less auditorially sensitive) and to help the staff with a more responsive motor approach. Scott enjoys swimming and this will be built into his weekly schedule with his parents participating as often as possible. Scott can be encouraged to practice dressing skills as part of an activity that motivates him. Although he may exhibit extended dependence in dressing, this can be used by the adult as a method to encourage Scott to make requests and participate in turn taking. The noise in the pool can be overwhelming for Scott so Sue could take him a half hour before the whole group arrives to acclimate him to the setting. Eventually, simple, interactive ball games could be introduced in the pool to include a peer into the play.

Since Scott's strength in certain self-help skills actually has the capacity for pulling him away from social interaction, these skills need to be blended within a small group context. Snack and meal times are positive times for Scott so they need to be linked with a shared activity (setting the snack table with Sue, and eventually with a peer, asking an adult or a peer for desired food, sharing food preparation with an adult or peer).

COMMUNICATIVE/LANGUAGE   Since Scott's language skills are more advanced than his communication skills, the emphasis should be on both nonverbal and verbal communication. The goal is to develop a key interpersonal relationship that elicits and sustains the social, nonverbal, and verbal aspects of communication, including eye contact, shared attention, turn taking, pleasure with making sound, and gesturing, all of which will be the basis for interpersonal communication and the foundation for future verbal exchanges. Sue and the speech and language pathologist will need to work together on games that encourage interactive patterns, such as peek-a-boo, "chase me," and "find the toy."

The staff and the parents need to coordinate with the speech and language pathologist to closely coordinate communication expectations for therapy sessions, classroom, and home. Throughout all interactions, simplification of adult verbal messages and reinforcing communication with gesture and exaggerated expression may be helpful. In communication development it is important to explore the value of specific augmented communication supports such as pictures, signing, computer use, augmentative communication devices, and, cautiously, facilitated communication (Biklen, 1993). Since Scott appears to respond best to a **multisensory approach**, speech should be combined with objects, pictures and photographs, manual signs, and gestures. A list of about 50 signs should be drawn up that can be used both at home and at school. Signs will be used along with one or two word utterances by the adult to stress key ideas, such as commands (come, stop, no); emotions and feeling sensations (happy, sad, tired, hungry, sleepy, thirsty); and objects, activities, and routines (eating, sleeping, toileting, bathing, playing, swimming, riding, coat, hat, shoes, ball, pencil, paper). Pictures of activities, people, and places should be introduced into Scott's daily experience. The adult can point to the appropriate picture, saying the name and using the appropriate sign. A sequence board using pictures or photographs with a key word may be useful in the classroom showing the daily schedule. Sue needs to explore simple picture activities, lotto games, interactive computer games, to see if any of these attract Scott's attention; they could be excellent ways to increase interaction behaviors that are necessary for interpersonal and cause and effect relations as well as communication.

During a speech and language session, the speech and language pathologist may experiment with using earphones or a wireless auditory trainer to help Scott focus on key words that relate to his communication. A **language master** card reader with cards designed to match his immediate interests may also be useful both in therapy and as an activity choice in the classroom. Pictures taken during activities and field trips, in school, and at home should be put into photo albums that allow Scott to review real life experiences with Sue and to improve receptive, expressive, and interactive communication skills. Scott needs to understand that words are a way of connecting with people and that they are also a way of getting his wishes fulfilled. Activities that allow for large motor, vestibular, and multisensory stimulation may be helpful in eliciting sound production and language from Scott. During such activities Sue needs to reflect Scott's actions and vocalizations with simple verbal statements ("Scott is swinging, swinging, swinging, up, up, up."). Sue needs help from the speech and language therapist to learn how to interpret echolalia and to be alert to when it has a communicative intent. Scott's jargoning and echolalia should be judiciously imitated and accepted as he attempts to communicate. Even though his gestures and words may not initially always be communicative, responding to them as if they were facilitates interaction and teaches cause and effect relationships and interpersonal reciprocity.

COGNITIVE Scott's apparent intellectual strengths are deceptive—many crucial foundation skills are deficient or missing. Consultation with the psychologist will help staff better understand evaluation materials and better differentiate between splinter skills and Scott's base line cognitive functioning. His interest in numbers and letters is not built on a solid cognitive foundation, but it is, nonetheless, possible to use these number and letter based activities to motivate Scott to practice important underlying skills such as imitation and cause and effect (e.g., write simple directions for him to follow or have him write directions for the teacher). Also, these preferred number and letter activities can be used as reward for broader involvement with materials and activities. Adults need to strongly encourage new exploration, starting with looking and touching. Working one-on-one, the adult can introduce a wider range of materials and model their use. There needs to be a focus on concrete, daily-living, and experiential activities, which may help Scott become more attuned to his world (cooking, cleaning, preparing the table for snack, and cleaning up). At first Sue and Scott, and then eventually Scott and his parents and siblings can plan field trips to expose him to new people, places, and routines. Picture books

can be made to summarize field trips, and reinforce memory and recall of both familiar and new places. Additionally, the staff can use pictures of real life events and lotto cards with real pictures to work on categorization (weather, clothing, feelings, people, and places), the reinforcement of the daily schedule, and people identification. The cognitive component is focused on completing his developmental sequences which will give him a more meaningful foundation for moving forward.

PLAY SKILLS To help Scott gain play skills is essential before he will be able to attain his overall developmental potential. As previously discussed, Scott will benefit from a key relationship, more infant and toddler materials, and direct support for him to experience pleasurable learning from progressively more complex object use and, ultimately, social interactions through play. A playful infant–adult type style and imitation and gentle expansions will be a mainstay of the process of encouraging play skills in Scott. A relaxed acceptance of Scott's behaviors, along with direct mirroring of his actual sounds and actions, will raise Scott's awareness of himself as well as of the adults in his life. Once he is slightly more focused by this type of mirrored interaction, Sue should experiment with small modifications in the play interactions. Shared attention and turn taking will be the most immediate goals in play. Scott will need time for solitary, functional–combinatory play, but the adult involved will need to gain skill at breaking into these play sequences and leading Scott to more exploration and interaction. As described under self/social/emotional, play skills that need to be emphasized include body image formation, turn taking, self-recognition, interactive sequences, "**act on agent**" play, and social inclusion. Scott will also need support to combine objects and to use objects functionally.

Two characteristics that greatly inhibit his play are perseveration and attention to a part of an object, instead of to a whole object. Rather than attempting to completely extinguish perseveration, our aim is to try to incorporate it into some functional play. Rocking can be incorporated into hammock swinging or peek-a-boo, finger flicking can be transformed into bubble popping. If Scott insists on **perseverative play patterns**, Sue can challenge him gently, being careful not to precipitate a break in control.

Part object play should be directed toward a more meaningful context, for example, Scott's preoccupation with opening and closing the barn door was redirected to more purposeful opening and closing: in and out concepts by placing cows in the barn which have letters of the alphabet affixed to them.

Although it is too early to expect peer play, toys and technology can ultimately be used as mediators to help Scott interact with his peers. Some possibilities include two-person computer activities that encourage taking turns in naming pictures on the screen. Scott's ability to play will be liberated as he expands his repertoire of actions on objects and his understanding of their relationship to himself and others.

PLAY THEMES To develop the ability to ultimately use play as a form of expression, Scott must gain a sense of his own body and being.

The types of materials and activities described in play skills are ideal to begin the process of helping Scott to begin to be aware of his own body, its boundaries, its pleasures and discomforts, and its potential to be a link to others. His play themes at this time appear devoid of much emotional content as the child may look flat and mechanical. The inclusion of an adult in this play who is capable of finding pleasure with the child's primitive rituals and play is a first step to making an emotional connection. The art of intervention is also knowing when to challenge these body-centered sensory rituals by introducing novelty and optimal stress with the aim of moving the child into more reality based play. Taking what he does, even if it looks vacant to an adult, and using it as the building blocks of contact and interaction will begin the process of enriching Scott's play themes.

FAMILY It is crucial that Scott's family be part of this plan for reorganizing his preschool experience. Basic to this process will be for his parents, along with program staff, to gain a more complete understanding of the complexity of PDD and the unique patterns of Scott's strengths and weaknesses. Scott's parents' goals for Scott need to be a priority in program planning. At this time Scott's parents are interested in his being more cooperative for hair cuts. (Now his mother has to resort to cutting his hair while he sleeps.). They would also like to be able to take Scott into church without his causing a disturbance.

Since Scott's parents are very pleased with his cognitive splinter skills and want to focus on them, it may take some time for the parents to accept that Scott needs to focus more on early level skills. Stressing infant behaviors may feel like supporting regression to the parents, rather than actually building a necessary foundation.

Staff and parents should maintain a regular communication pattern with each other through notebooks and phone calls. When appropriate, Scott's parents can be encouraged to observe the classroom and speech and language sessions to see what techniques work. Additionally, staff can encourage the parents to participate in the regular parents groups to gain support from as well as provide information for other parents. School personnel also need to support and assist the parents in their process of being advocates for their child.

Family members may be interested in seeking out extended support systems because of the stress of living with a child who has such complex developmental needs. They may need encouragement to take some of their attention away from Scott and reinvest in themselves and in their daughters. Family therapy or sessions with a psychologist may assist them in fulfilling some of their own needs and express some of their frustrations, anger, sadness, and regret concerning Scott's developmental issues. The family may be interested in locating babysitters and resource groups for families with autistic children.

STAFF The adults in the setting are focal to improving Scott's adaptation to this classroom. The individual relationship between a primary adult and Scott will be essential to his progress. Since Sue is doing well with him, the Planning and Placement team recommend that she becomes the key classroom contact person (with Scott's town covering her salary so that another aide can be hired to assist the teacher with the group). Once this relationship is established, Scott can be helped to relate more successfully with a range of adults and, ultimately, to include peers into his experience. All the staff involved with Scott need support in dealing with him and in developing an understanding of the complexities of PDD/autism. Learning more about PDD/autism and having a consultant (a psychologist from the public school) to help them in observing and interpreting his behavior will help them understand Scott better and not take his negative behavior personally. Adults working with children who are diagnosed with PDD/autism may experience extreme emotional reactions to the child. If the adult does not understand the thought process and interpersonal problems intrinsic to this condition, it is easy to take the child's impersonal behavior personally. If the adult interprets the behavior as a personal rejection, it is easy to become angry at the child and to reject the child in return.

Because of Scott's unusual behavior, it is easy to be attracted by splinter skills, hoping to make the child look normal. All staff need to understand the disadvantages of over focusing on these skills for the sake of Scott's overall development. Since all growth requires some failure, staff must accept some failure with each success, and some regression after progress. Accepting Scott as a unique individual of value, even with all of his unusual behavior, can turn some of the emphasis from fixing his behavior, to supporting his unique developmental pattern.

As methods are developed that are helpful to increasing Scott's responsiveness, spontaneity, and involvement, Sue needs to demonstrate these techniques to the speech and language pathologist, other staff, and parents, helping staff and parents work as a team to coordinate goals and approaches. The need for an interdisciplinary approach with this child should be very apparent. This type of intense intervention plan is costly, both financially and from a personnel perspective, but if the full team is able to communicate and collaborate effectively with each other, the chances for a dramatic improvement in this child will be greatly increased.

PEERS It is necessary that the peers in this setting gain some tolerance and sensitivity to individual differences including how people look, learn, and relate to others so they can gain an appreciation of their own uniqueness and those of their classmates. They will need direct support from the staff to include Scott in any activities where he can be successful. Children who seem interested in and are tolerant of Scott could join him for snack, on gross motor equipment, walks, swimming trips, and field trips. The classroom library could also include several books that raise children's awareness and sensitivity to individual differences. Sue will need to speak for Scott when he is frustrated in a peer situation, but she can also comment on and encourage peer interactions when they are successful ("Scott enjoys it when you swing together."). Although we typically think of the child with the handicap benefiting from normal peers, we often fail to recognize what the normal peer can gain from the child with special needs. Such experiences foster in the typical child an appreciation for human variation, a capacity for compassion and empathy, a greater acceptance of their own idiosyncrasies, and new, and sometimes creative making sense out of experience.

SPACE The immediate need is for an appropriate indoor motor space. This must be large enough to accomodate a swing, climbing and floor activities. Contained space is also desirable. This can include boxes with pillows and places for retreat. Within these enclosed spaces, Scott and Sue can experiment with materials, and carry out routine interpersonal games and interchanges.

TIME Routine is essential for Scott, but his routine will have to be individualized and may not initially conform to the group schedule. Each day, Sue can review the schedule for the day so Scott will be prepared for the day's events. Each day should include one-to-one time with Sue in an enclosed area to work on interaction skills, play and communication behaviors, and an outside time on gross motor equipment.

Other changes include changing the time of his individual speech sessions so that they are held during group music time, because Scott finds this activity intolerable. On Friday mornings there is no group program, but plans are made so that Sue will take Scott on field trips into the community (barber shop, fast food stores, grocery shopping, local mall). These trips will be based on places the parents would like to be able to take Scott, either alone or with the family. One of his parents will participate in this activity, as his or her schedule allows.

Each afternoon, Scott's program will be expanded to include participation in a resource room with Sue as his aide. This class consists of seven other children, ages 5 to 8, who are working on individualized skills and activities in this smaller setting. One afternoon a week, Scott will go swimming with Sue, another child, and his or her aide.

MATERIALS AND EQUIPMENT   Because of the relative breadth of Scott's skill repertoire he will require a range of materials from the infant toddler level to those found in the traditional nursery school. The speech and language pathologist and the physical and occupational therapists can prove helpful in the selection of these materials. Attention should be paid to choosing these materials with both solo and interactive goals in mind. Infant–toddler materials can include jack-in-the-box, speak and say, pop-up toys, and cause and effect toys with knobs and levers. Action toys, such as balls and cars, can encourage "act on agent" play such as running the car down the slide and throwing a ball through a hoop. To support body mastery Scott will also benefit from motor equipment such as swings, hammocks, bolsters, large foam shapes for climbing, a carpet lined barrel, and a tunnel. For fine motor and sensory development, water and sand, beans and foam chips, playdough, finger paint, and shaving cream are all useful. As representational play skills unfold, it will be important to have concrete props available for Scott. These include hats, tea sets, workbenches, shopping carts, and fireman gear. Once interactive and social skills develop, Scott should be exposed to lotto games, picture activities and games, language master activities, and simple interactive computer games.

Review of Initial Observation

With the benefit of the information that has been compiled by completing Sections I through VII of the SPM, we now review a short segment of the first vignette to see how Sue might have dealt with Scott differently. This review will allow you to put yourself in the adult's place and imagine how you might have interacted with Scott. Reread the section of the vignette that follows and then make notes describing your own strategies. See how your ideas compare with the suggestions that follow the vignette.

When Sue is able to return to Scott, she brings with her a basket of farm animals and a small barn, hoping to help Scott move from the farm animal book to some play with the animals. Scott watches her as she places several of the animals into the barn, while saying their names. He repeats the animal names, but does not show any interest in handling the animals. He becomes focused on the mechanism of the barn door, which makes a mooing sound when opened and closed. Scott takes the barn off the floor, shakes out the animals, and proceeds to play with the doors while holding the barn upright on his lap. Sue comments to Scott that he does not want the animals, but that he likes the barn door noise.

Sue is already demonstrating a significant level of empathy and understanding in her work with Scott. She is respectful of his messages and it is clear that they are beginning to build a relationship. With the benefit of your more thorough under-

standing of Scott, what do you suggest she change in this short interaction? How could Sue have used Scott's play behavior of repeatedly opening and closing the barn door to expand their interaction. Some suggestions could include the following: She might have responded to each "moo" sound with mock surprise and delight, seeing if Scott made a connection between the door and her surprised response. Does he continue to open and close the door, checking back for her surprised expression, thus attempting to make an interesting response last? She could have conveyed her knowledge and appreciation of their interaction by a smile and a look of anticipation. She might also have verbally echoed the sound along with the sign for cow. She could also take a second barn and repeat the same action on her door to see if they could develop a pattern of parallel behavior. Sue might have physically realigned herself so that she and Scott were sitting side by side, with her supporting him briefly with an arm around his shoulder while she introduced a change in the play pattern. If Scott seemed receptive to her joining in his play in this way, she could then have tried to "walk" one of the discarded animals in the direction of his barn to see if he would allow her to put it into his barn while the door was open. All of this should be attempted with minimal vocalization, focusing on the shared actions. This could be the beginning of an exchange of delivering animals to each others' barns. As suggested previously she could also affix letters to the cows, highlighting their interest to Scott and increasing his motivation to participate. Not all attempts at this type of play expansion will be calmly received by Scott, but if Sue is sensitive to his cues and is not intrusive, most children like Scott can respond to this type of social overture.

Supportive Play Model Adaptation

Now we can move ahead 2 months in time for a return observation. There are some significant changes in Scott's behavior following the implementation of the SPM process. All days have not been easy, but everyone involved is pleased to see some progress. In this scene, a commentary (in brackets) has been added to the observation to offer some possible explanations for what is observed.

The morning starts with Scott arriving in the classroom with his notebook and pencils in hand. He is met by Sue who is waiting outside the classroom. They go together to the back of the classroom where a large refrigerator box is turned on its side and filled with pillows. After eagerly putting on the weighted vest, Scott climbs inside, chanting the alphabet in a high sing-song voice. Sue sits outside the box and gives him a minute to arrange the pillows, then she peeks in the side window echoing some of the alphabet. Scott looks briefly at her and then waits with an expectant expression. Sue takes this as a cue to begin the day. She initiates a peek-a-boo game through the window in the box. Scott watches for her to appear in the window and smiles each time she appears. She waits for him to make a chattering sound as a signal that he wants her to pop into the window. They repeat this interaction pattern several times. Sue places a puppet on her hand, and when Scott makes his chatter request, she pops her hand through the window, which causes Scott to yell out in a tense laugh. They repeat this twice, but then his voice becomes more anxious, so Sue takes off the puppet, ending the sequence by smiling at Scott through the window. *[The box, filled with pillows, is a perfect place for Scott to start his day because it allows him to feel safe, helps him organize and prepare for the stimulation of joining a group, and assists him in establishing boundaries between himself and others. Sue starts her interaction by imitating some of the alphabet letters that Scott is chanting. Even though his alphabet use is stereotypic, she accepts it as a first vehicle for interaction. Once she sees that she and Scott are attuned, she moves to another interactive sequence in which he vocalizes to invite her to surprise him in a peek-a-boo sequence. She tries to move this play to a more complex level by introducing a hand puppet. Scott is made anxious by this change away from reality and she hears the tension in his voice, so she knows that this may be testing his limits. It was important for her to experiment with new items, like the puppet, but it was equally important to stay attuned to Scott's reaction and not get stuck in insisting that the puppet become part of their interaction.]*

Sue then knocks at the door of the box, saying, "Hello, hello, who wants to read a book?" as she pushes a picture book through the doorway. Scott takes hold of the book, which causes her to hold on and pull back a bit. He whines and says "Read a book?" Sue answers "Scott and Sue can read a book," and she accepts this as an invitation to join him in the pillow-filled box. Scott sits beside her, surrounded by pillows and rests lightly on Sue's arm. They look through the first pages of the book, which contain the pictures for today's schedule. Then they look at Scott's favorite series of photos, which show him going to the swimming pool. There is a simple statement with each picture. The sequence of photos includes the van, the locker room, Scott undressing, the shower, the pool area, the life guard, swimming with Sue, and a few photos of Scott getting ready to go back to school. He taps at different pictures when he wants Sue to read the words and tell him about the details. Sue tries to reverse this process by asking, "where is the ___?" This makes Scott fuss and he tries to pull the book away from Sue. Sue says, "Scott wants to ask the questions today. OK." After completing the swimming story, Sue puts the book down and starts to chant a rhyme about a mouse who is hunting for a house. This game involves her touching Scott's hands, nose, mouth, and hair. Scott anticipates each contact and pretends to hide behind a pillow, but clearly indicates that Sue can continue. At one point Scott tentatively reaches out and touches Sue's hair and nose, but then pulls back his hand and ends the sequence. Sue changes pace a bit by helping Scott cover himself completely with pillows, pretending she can not find him. He lies quietly and then actually chuckles when Sue picks off the pillows and shows great surprise in finding him.

[Sue helps Scott relax by returning to his favorite activity, reading. Reading is a useful transitional activity for Scott, allowing a regression away from the more interactive games to a passive–receptive role, but still allowing some turn taking and requesting. Reading may also function as a type of refueling for Scott; it is a popular activity between him and his parents. Also, it allows for some physical contact and comfort between Scott and Sue. After reading with Scott, Sue introduces another physical contact game that allows for more playfulness and shared pleasure. Scott is involved enough in this exchange to even take the risk of reaching out and tentatively beginning to explore Sue's face, much like small infants will do when they are beginning to "hatch" and differentiate themselves from their mothers' bodies as Mahler, Pine, and Bergman (1975) describe it.]

They leave the box and sit at a small table with three other children for breakfast. Scott walks around the table with Sue, handing a cup to each child and repeating their name. He then sits down and, after showing Sue that he wants the juice pitcher, pours himself juice. He fusses and twists to leave the table when Sue does not automatically hand him a cereal box. She says, "Tell me what you want and you can have breakfast." Scott's expression is tense and he pushes back his chair from the table. Sue turns to the other children and quietly asks them a question about their plans for the day. Scott makes angry noises and starts to chatter the alphabet. In the midst of the letters he says "More, more, more, good boy". Sue turns to Scott and says "Scott wants cereal, you want cereal." His face is still tense, but he pulls his chair up to the table and accepts the cereal box.

[Sue waits for Scott to find a way to communicate his wishes to her. Sue might have facilitated this interaction by letting Scott point to a picture or use the sign "to eat," but they managed to come to a successful conclusion because she was able to be flexible enough to respond to his inferred intent, rather than to insist on an exact request. Even though asking is difficult for Scott, Sue conveys the expectation and trusts that he can comply. She offers language to clarify his request. This helps him organize himself and relieves some of his anxiety.]

Later in the morning, Scott pulls Sue toward the hammock. Another boy is swinging and looking at a picture book. After check-ing if it is all right with this child, Sue helps Scott climb onto the hammock. She steps back a little to see what will happen. Scott lies on his stomach and pushes with his hands. The second child does not like the faster swinging so he closes his book and climbs off, leaving Scott on his own. Sue touches one of Scott's hands and he looks up at her briefly. She then begins a pattern of touching his right hand and then his left. This causes him to move his hand a little to the side, causing the hammock to move. This becomes an interaction, with Sue tapping the area all around Scott's hands and then suddenly tapping his hand. He reacts each time and begins to smile. When Sue stops and turns away a bit, Scott calls out "One, two, three," which is a way that Sue often introduces a game. Sue accepts this as a request for her to continue, so she says "Scott wants more tap, tap, tap" and she restarts the game. She reaches over for the puppet they had used earlier and tries to continue the game using the puppet on her hand and talking in a puppet voice. Scott tolerates this for two turns, but then turns himself away so that Sue can not reach his hands. When she persists with the puppet, he becomes upset and begins to kick his legs and grimace. Sue says and signs "All done" and removes the puppet from her hand.

Scott is scheduled for speech during group time. The speech pathologist comes to the door with several of Scott's favorite language master cards in her hand. He goes willingly. Sue joins these sessions to observe and gain techniques for working with Scott.

Outdoor play includes several wagons and tricycles. Scott is upset when he sees that all the wagons are busy. He loves to lie in a wagon making guttural noises while Sue pulls him over the blacktop. He is not able to wait calmly and refuses to be distracted by other activities. Even a swing, which a child offers to him, does not help him to stop screaming. The teacher talks to the children about how angry Scott is because he is having trouble waiting his turn. Sue moves him away from the children and tries to calm him by reminding him that he can have a turn in a few minutes. Her words only lead to further screaming, and Scott lunges at her, crashing his head into her stomach. She is surprised and angry. She holds him by the shoulders and says very firmly, "No, you can not hurt Sue. No hurting." She takes his hand and leads him inside where he climbs into the box and hides under the pillows. She repeats, "No hurting." She gives him several minutes alone and then asks if Scott wants to return outside and see if the wagon is free. She shows him the wagon picture and he climbs out of the box and joins her to go outdoors. Most of the children are now on the climbing equipment, and several wagons are free. They spend several minutes with Sue pulling Scott around the playground.

[In this segment of the vignette we see how difficult waiting is for Scott. His tolerance for frustration is still very low, and it takes an adult to help him reorganize himself so that he can end the day with a feeling of success. Crashing his head into Sue's stomach is the type of behavior some children with PDD/autism revert to when upset. Head banging, face smacking, and pinching are all self-stimulation actions that may be a way to block one unpleasant sensation with another. It may also resonate with themes related to merger and separateness, and the anxiety related to "me" and "not me". Sue holds Scott's shoulders, providing the type of compression that is comforting and organizing. Sue lets Scott retreat into the box to calm himself. Once he is more in control she shows him the picture of the wagon and suggests they try again. Instead of being punitive, she allows him the opportunity to master his anger and to then enjoy a choice activity. Sue was appropriately firm and angry when Scott hurt her, but she did not stay angry longer than was necessary. Excessive anger would have been threatening to Scott, because their relationship is only in its formative stages. She does not take his aggression personally, but she does provide a clear response to his aggressive behavior and sets clear guidelines for the behavior she will allow. This type of clarity reduces anxiety in children. It is very frightening for children to believe they are so powerful that an adult does not know how to control them.]

Section VIII: Results and Outcomes

Scott is displaying more clearly differentiated emotions, including pleasure, anxiety, and anger. He is showing more involvement with materials, often following Sue's lead and responding to her cues. Sue is pleased with some of the progress, but also discouraged and frightened by sudden displays of anger and anxiety. She finds that she goes home exhausted some days and is surprised at how angry she has felt with Scott. At the same time, she expresses real pride in Scott's willingness to interact with her. She is gaining a great deal of confidence in her ability to read his cues.

As Scott is demonstrating developmental changes at school, the parents report that they are experiencing more difficult behavior at home. These behaviors include more extreme emotional outbursts and an intolerance for change of family routines. However, they also report that Scott is using more words to tell them why he is upset, "I want bath now." and "I don't want to go in car."

Scott is more aware of his peers and the classroom environment in general. His new awareness can actually cause him to become anxious and upsets him when the group gathers. Scott is still unable to sort out all of the simultaneous stimuli. All adults involved in Scott's program need ongoing assurances that these changes will ultimately result in developmental progress. Scott is more attuned to his world and is struggling with integrating all of the information and his responses. At times his parents and the staff may wish for a return to his more removed, self-involved behavior, but they need to realize that some of his new anxiety is actually integral to his mastering the world outside of himself, the "not-me". The increase in his emotional display causes adults to react to him with stronger feelings; this shows that Scott is more developed as person now and he has the capacity to evoke and respond to strong feelings. But his atypical patterns of behavior still confound the cues he gives to adults, leaving them feeling angry and confused.

There are still signs of Scott pushing away and resisting activities and interactions. At the same time, there are more indications of involvement with materials, some peers, and the teacher aide. These new expressions of ambivalence suggest evolving autonomy, growth of personal boundaries, self-awareness and organization, and a beginning delineation of a core self.

SUMMARY

Using the SPM has not cured Scott of his PDD, but he is showing improvements and progress that are both qualitative and quantitative. The qualitative aspects of his development are our primary goals, an integration of feelings, states, and emotions. These are the changes that will make him more successful in interpersonal relations and in the emotional business of living. Through the efforts initiated as part of the SPM process, Scott is beginning to build a relationship with the aide. They are clearly involved in a reciprocal relationship, even though Scott will continue to test Sue. Her consistent reactions and expectations will need to be implemented and shared by other staff members working with Scott and with his parents. It is fortunate that Scott's mother volunteers in the class because she can observe, practice, and help develop new strategies that can be used with Scott. She can also see that what works one day for Scott may not work the next day. The staff have just as hard a time working with Scott as she, and they do not have all the answers. However, together they are developing a repertoire of techniques that are effective with Scott. It is through the interaction of Scott and his aide that play skills begin to develop. These skills are not trained in a mechanical or rote sense; they are nurtured so that the motivation to play with objects and to interact with people is internally driven.

Placing children like Scott in typical settings requires a very intensive intervention plan, a wide range of highly trained personnel, and a high level of communication and collaboration between home and school. This type of plan may seem very costly, but a less multidisciplinary approach would not meet Scott's needs.

Regular reassessment of this placement plan is crucial because his needs are subtle and in many areas more basic than in most children attending Head Start programs. In some cases, a team may have to come to the decision that, after a careful and organized attempt, a placement is not appropriate for a particular child and group. Although this is always a very difficult decision to face, it is far better than perpetuating a situation that is counterproductive to a child's developmental needs. Scott's placement looks positive at this time, which is very encouraging, but his new skills and evolving personality development will require a great deal of support to maintain him within this typical setting.

REFERENCES

Abrahamsen, E. P., & Mitchell J. R. (1990). Communication and sensorimotor functioning in children with autism. *Journal of Autism and Developmental Disorders, 20*(1), 75–85.

Allen, D. A. (1988). Autistic spectrum disorders: Clinical presentation in preschool children. *Journal of Child Neurology, 3*, (Suppl. 1988), S48–S56.

Atlas, J. A., & Lapidus, L. B. (1988). Symbolization levels in communicative behaviors of children showing pervasive developmental disorders. *Journal of Communication Disorders, 21,* 75–84.

Ayres, A. J. (1989). *Sensory integration and the child.* Los Angeles: Western Psychological Services.

Bandura, A. (1973). *Aggression: A social learning analysis.* Englewood Cliffs, NJ: Prentice-Hall.

Baron-Cohen, S. (1987). Autism and symbolic play. *British Journal of Developmental Psychology, 5*(2),139–148.

Baron-Cohen, S. (1988). Social and pragmatic deficits in autism: Cognitive or affective? *Journal of Autism and Developmental Disorders, 18*(3), 379–402.

Baron-Cohen, S., Leslie, A. M., & Frith, U. (1985). Does the autistic child have a "theory of mind"? *Cognition, 21,* 37–46.

Barrera, R. D., Lobato-Barrera, D., & Sulzer-Azaroff, B. (1980). A simultaneous treatment comparison of three expressive language training programs with a mute autistic child. *Journal of Autism and Developmental Disorders, 10*(1), 21–37.

Barrera, R. D., & Sulzer-Azaroff, B. (1983). An alternating treatment comparison of oral and total communication training programs with echolalic autistic children. *Journal of Applied Behavior Analysis, 16,* 379–394.

Benaroya, S., Wesley, S., Ogilvie, H., Klien, L. S., & Clarke, E. (1979). Sign language and multisensory input training of children with communication and related developmental disorders: Phase II. *Journal of Autism and Developmental Disorders, 9*(2), 219–220.

Benaroya, S., Wesley, S., Ogilvie, H., Klein, L. S., & Meaney, M. (1977). Sign language and multisensory input training of children with communication and related developmental disorders. *Journal of Autism and Childhood Schizophrenia, 7*(1), 23–31.

Bérard, G. (1993). *Hearing equals behavior.* New Canaan, CT: Keats.

Bergman, P., & Escalona, S. K. (1949). Unusual sensitivities in very young children. In A. Freud, H. Hartmann, & E. Kris (Eds.), *The psychoanalytic study of the child* (Vols. 3–4, pp. 333–352). New York: International Universities Press.

Bettelheim, B. (1967). *The empty fortress.* New York: Free Press.

Biklen, D. (1993). *Communication unbound.* New York: Teachers College Press.

Bloom, L., & Lahey, M. (1978). *Language development and language disorders*. New York: Wiley

Bristol, M. M. (1984a). Family resources and successful adaptation to autistic children. In E. Schopler & G. B. Mesibov (Eds.), *The effects of autism on the family* (pp. 289–310). New York: Plenum.

Bristol, M. M. (1984b). *Needs of parents of young autistic children: Some covert assumptions*. Unpublished manuscript. University of North Carolina, Carolina Institute for Research on Early Education for the Handicapped, Chapel Hill, NC.

Chastain, L., & Merzer, S. (1982). *Social skills: Assessment and interventions*. (available from Lyle Chastain, Suite 113, 1375 Willow St., Minneapolis, MN.)

Coe, D., Matson, J., Fee, V., Manikam, R., & Linarello, C. (1990). Training nonverbal and verbal play skills to mentally retarded and autistic children. *Journal of Autism and Developmental Disorders, 20*(2), 177–187.

Dawson, G., & Galpert, L. (1990). Mothers' use of imitative play for facilitating social responsiveness and toy play in young autistic children. *Development and Psychopathology, 2*(2), 151–162.

Dawson, G., Hill, D., Spencer, A., Galpert, L., & Watson, L. (1990). Affective exchanges between young autistic children and their mothers. *Journal of Abnormal Child Psychology, 18*(3), 335–345.

DeMyer, M. K. (1979). *Parents and children in autism*. New York: Wiley.

Diagnostic and statistical manual of mental disorders (DSM-III-R). (1987). Washington, DC: American Psychiatric Association.

Egel, A. L., Richman, G. S., & Koegel, R. L. (1981). Normal peer models and autistic children's learning. *Journal of Applied Behavior Analysis, 14*(1), 3–12.

Ferrara, C., & Hill, S. D. (1980). The responsiveness of autistic children to the predictability of social and nonsocial toys. *Journal of Autism and Developmental Disorders, 10*(1), 51–57.

Freud, S. (1920/1955). *Beyond the pleasure principle*. In J. Strachey (Ed.), *The standard edition of the complete psychological works of Sigmund Freud* (Vol. 18, pp. 7–64). London: The Hogarth Press.

Freud, A. (1966). The concept of developmental lines. In A. Freud, *Normality and pathology in childhood: Assessment of development* (pp. 11–30). New York: International Universities Press.

Gartner, D., & Schultz, N. M. (1990). Establishing the first stages of early reciprocal interactions between mothers and their autistic children. Special Issue: Motherhood: A feminist perspective. *Women and Therapy, 10*(1–2), 159–167.

Getman, G. (1965). The visuomotor complex in the acquisition of learning skills. In J. Hellmuth (Ed.), *Learning disorders* (Vol. 1; pp. 49–76). Seattle: Special Child Publications.

Gould, J. (1986). The Lowe and Costello symbolic play test in socially impaired children. *Journal of Autism and Developmental Disorders, 16* (2), 199–213.

Greenspan, S. I. (1992a). *Infancy and early childhood: The practice of clinical assessment and intervention with emotional and developmental challenges*. Madison, CT: International Universities Press.

Greenspan, S. I. (1992b). Reconsidering the diagnosis and treatment of very young children with autistic spectrum or pervasive developmental disorder. *Zero to Three, 13*(2), 1–9.

Gresham, Frank M. (1981). Social skills training with handicapped children: A review. *Review of Educational Research, 51*(1), 139–176.

Guralnick, M. J. (1990). Peer interactions and the development of handicapped children's social and communicative competence. In H. C. Foot, M. J. Morgan, & R. H. Shute (Eds.), *Children helping children* (pp. 275–305). New York: Wiley.

Hammes, J. G. W., & Langdell, T. (1981). Precursors of symbol formation and childhood autism. *Journal of Autism and Developmental Disorders, 11*(3), 331–346.

Haring, T. G., & Lovinger, L. (1989). Promoting social interaction through teaching generalized play initiation responses to preschool children with autism. *Journal of the Association for Persons with Severe Handicaps, 14*(1), 58–67.

Harris, P. L. (1989). The autistic child's impaired conception of mental states. *Development and Psychopathology, 1*, 191–195.

Harris, S. L., Handleman, J. S., & Burton, J. L. (1990). The Stanford Binet profiles of young children with autism. *Special Services in the Schools, 6*(1/2), 135–143.

Hobson, R. P. (1989). On sharing experiences. *Development and Psychopathology, 1*, 197–203.

Hobson, R. P. (1990). On psychoanalytic approaches to autism. *American Journal of Orthopsychiatry, 60*(3), 324–336.

Hutt, C., & Ounsted, C. (1966). The biological significance of gaze aversion with particular reference to the syndrome of infantile autism. *Behavioral Science, 11*, 346–356.

Kalmanson, B., & Pekarsky, J. H. (1987). Infant–parent psychotherapy with an autistic toddler. *Zero to Three, 7*(3), 1–6.

Kanner, L. (1943). Autistic disturbances of affective contact. *The Nervous Child, 2*, 217–250.

Kasari, C., Sigman, M., Mundy, P., & Yirmiya, N. (1990). Affective sharing in the context of joint attention interactions of normal, autistic, and mentally retarded children. *Journal of Autism and Developmental Disorders, 20*(1), 87–100.

Klin, A. (1991). Young autistic children's listening preferences in regard to speech: A possible characterization of the symptom of social withdrawal. *Journal of Autism and Developmental Disorders, 21*(1), 29–42.

Klein, M. (1937). *The psycho-analysis of children* (2nd ed.). (A. Strachey, Trans.). London: Hogarth Press.

Koegel, R. L., Dyer, K., & Bell, L. K. (1987). The influence of child-preferred activities on autistic children's social behavior. *Journal of Applied Behavior Analysis, 20*(3), 243–252.

Kohler, F. W., Strain, P. S., Maretsky, S., & DeCesare, L. (1990). Promoting positve and supportive interactions between preschoolers: An analysis of group-oriented contingencies. *Journal of Early Intervention, 14*(4), 327–341.

Konstantareas, M. M. (1984). Sign language as a communication prosthesis with language-impaired children. *Journal of Autism and Developmental Disorders, 14*(1), 9–25.

Konstantareas, M. M., Webster, C. D., & Oxman, J. (1979). Manual language acquisition and its influence on other areas of functioning in four autistic and autistic-like children. *Journal of Child Psychology and Psychiatry, 20*, 337–350.

Kouri, T. (1988). Effects of simultaneous communication in a child-directed treatment approach with preschoolers with severe disabilities. *Augmentative and Alternative Communication, 4*, 222–232.

Lahey, M. (1988). *Language disorders and language development*. New York: Macmillan.

Landry, S. H., & Loveland, K. A. (1989). The effect of social context on functional communication skills of autistic children. *Journal of Autism and Developmental Disorders, 19*(2), 283–299.

Langer, S. K. (1962). *Philosphy in a new key*. New York: Mentor Books.

Lanyado, M. (1987). Asymbolic and symbolic play: Developmental perspectives in the treatment of disturbed children. *Journal of Child Psychotherapy, 13*(2), 33–44.

Lefebvre, D., & Strain, P. S. (1989). Effects of a group contingency on the frequency of social interactions among autistic and nonhandicapped preschool children: Making LRE efficacious. *Journal of Early Intervention, 13*(4), 329–341.

Leslie, A. M., & Happé, F. (1989). Autism and ostensive communication: The relevance of metarepresentation. *Development and Psychopathology, 1*, 205–212.

Lösche, G. (1990). Sensorimotor and action development in autistic children from infancy to early childhood. *Journal of Child Psychology and Psychiatry and Allied Disciplines, 31*(5), 749–761.

Lovaas, O. I. (1987). Behavioral treatment and normal educational and intellectual functioning in young autistic children. *Journal of Consulting and Clinical Psychology, 55*(1), 3–9.

Loveland, K. A., Landry, S. H., Hughes, S. O., Hall, S. K., & McEvoy, R. E. (1988). Speech acts and the pragmatic deficits of autism. *Journal of Speech and Hearing Research, 31*, 593–604.

Loveland, K. A., & Tunali, B. (1991). Social scripts for conversational interactions in autism and Down syndrome. *Journal of Autism and Developmental Disorders, 21*(2), 177–186.

Mahler, M. S. (1965). On early infantile psychosis: The symbiotic and autistic syndromes. *Journal of the American Academy of Child Psychiatry, 4,* 554–568.

Mahler, M. S., Pine, F., & Bergman, A. (1975). *The psychological birth of the human infant.* New York: Basic Books.

Mahoney, G., & Powell, A. (1986). *Transactional intervention program.* Farmington, CT: Pediatric Research and Training Center.

Mahoney, G., & Powell. A. (1988). Modifying parent–child interaction: Enhancing the development of handicapped children. *The Journal of Special Education, 22*(1), 82–96.

McCaleb, P., & Prizant, B. M. (1985). Encoding of new versus old information by autistic children. *Journal of Speech and Hearing Disorders, 50,* 230–240.

McCune, L. (1986). Symbolic development in normal and atypical infants. In G. Fein & M. Rivkin (Eds.), *Reviews of research: Vol. 4. The young child at play* (pp. 45–61). Washington, DC: National Association for the Education of Young Children.

McCune-Nicolich, L., & Carroll, S. (1981). Development of symbolic play: Implications for the language specialist. *Topics in Language Disorders,* 1–14.

McEvoy, M. A., & Odom, S. L. (1987) Social interaction training for preschool children with behavioral disorders. Special Issue: Social interactions of behaviorally disordered children and youth. *Behavioral Disorders, 12*(4), 242–251.

McEvoy, M. A., Nordquist, V. M., Twardosz, S., Heckaman, K. A., Wehby, J. H., & Denny, R. K. (1988). Promoting autistic children's peer interaction in an integrated early childhood setting using affection activities. *Journal of Applied Behavior Analysis, 21*(2), 193–200.

McGee, G. G., Feldman, R. S., & Chernin, L. (1991). A comparison of emotional facial display by children with autism and typical preschoolers. *Journal of Early Intervention, 15*(3), 237–245.

McHale, S. M., Simeonsson, R. J., Marcus, L. M., & Olley, J. G. (1980). The social and symbolic quality of autistic children's communication. *Journal of Autism and Developmental Disorders, 10*(3), 299–310.

Meyer, L. H., Fox, A., Schermer, A., Ketelsen, D., Montan, N., Maley, K., & Cole, D. (1987). The effects of teacher intrusion on social play interactions between children with autism and their nonhandicapped peers. *Journal of Autism and Developmental Disorders, 17*(3), 315–332.

Minshew, N. J., & Payton, J. B. (1988). New perspectives in autism. Part I: The clinical spectrum of autism. Part II: The differential diagnosis and neurobiology of autism. *Current Problems in Pediatrics, 18,* 561–694.

Mirenda, P. L, Donnellan, A. M., & Yoder, D. E. (1983). Gaze behavior: A new look at an old problem. *Journal of Autism and Developmental Disorders, 13*(4), 397–409.

Mundy, P., & Sigman, M. (1989a). The theoretical implications of joint-attention deficits in autism. *Development and Psychopathology, 1,* 173–183.

Mundy, P., & Sigman, M. (1989b). Second thoughts on the nature of autism. *Development and Psychopathology, 1,* 213–217.

Mundy, P., Sigman, M., & Kasari, C. (1990). A longitudinal study of joint attention and language development in autistic children. *Journal of Autism and Developmental Disorders, 20*(1), 115–128.

Mundy, P., Sigman, M., Ungerer, J., & Sherman, T. (1986). Defining the social deficits of autism: The contribution of non-verbal communication measures. *Journal of Child Psychology and Psychiatry and Allied Disciplines, 27*(5), 657–669.

Mundy, P., Sigman, M., Ungerer, J., & Sherman, T. (1987). Nonverbal communication and play correlates of language development in autistic children. *Journal of Autism and Developmental Disorders, 17*(3), 349–364.

Oke, N. J., & Schreibman, L. (1990) Training social initiations to a high-functioning autistic child: Assessment of collateral behavior change and generalization in a case study. *Journal of Autism and Developmental Disorders, 20*(4), 479–497.

Powell, S., & Jordan, R. (1991). A psychological perspective on identifying and meeting the needs of exceptional pupils. *School Psychology International, 12*(4), 315–327.

Power, T. J., & Radcliffe, J. (1989). The relationship of play behavior to cognitive ability in developmentally disabled preschoolers. *Journal of Autism and Developmental Disorders, 19*(1), 97–107.

Prizant, B. M. (1982). Gestalt language and gestalt processing in autism. *Topics in Language Disorders, 3,* 16–23.

Prizant, B. M. (1988). Communication problems in the autistic client. In N. J. Lass, L. V. McReynolds, J. L. Northern, & D. E. Yoder (Eds.), *Handbook of speech-language pathology and audiology.* Toronto: Decker.

Prizant, B. M., & Wetherby, A. M. (1990). Assessing the communication of infants and toddlers: Integrating a socioemotional perspective. *Zero to Three, 11*(1), 1–13.

Provence, S., & Dahl, E. K. (1987). Disorders of atypical development: Diagnostic issues raised by a spectrum disorder. In D. J. Cohen, A. M. Donnellan, & R. Paul (Eds.), *Handbook of autism and pervasive developmental disorders* (pp. 667–689). New York: Wiley.

Quill, K., Gurry, S., & Larkin, A. (1989). *Daily life therapy: A Japanese model for educating children with autism.* New York: Plenum.

Quinn, J. M., & Rubin, K. H. (1984). The play of handicapped children. In T. D. Yawkey & T. D. Pellegrini (Eds.), *Child's play: Developmental and applied.* Hillsdale, NJ: Erlbaum.

Rescorla, L. (1988). Cluster analytic identification of autistic preschoolers. *Journal of Autism and Developmental Disorders, 18*(4), 475–492.

Richer, J. M., & Coss, R. G. (1976). Gaze aversion in autistic and normal children. *Acta Psychiatrica Scandinavica, 53,* 193–210.

Rodrique, J. R., Morgan, S. B., & Geffken, G. R. (1991). A comparative evaluation of adaptive behavior in children and adolescents with autism, Down syndrome, and normal development. *Journal of Autism and Developmental Disorders, 21*(2), 187–196.

Rogers, S. J. (1988). Cognitive characteristics of handicapped children's play: A review. *Journal of the Division for Early Childhood, 12*(2), 161–168.

Rogers, S. J., & Pennington, B. F. (1991). A theoretical approach to the deficits in infantile autism. *Development and Psychopathology, 3,* 137–162.

Rutter, M. (1979). Diagnosis and definition. In M. Rutter & E. Schopler (Eds.), *Autism* (pp. 1–25). New York: Plenum.

Rutter, M., & Lockyer, L. (1967) A five to fifteen year follow-up study of infantile psychosis. I. Description of sample. *British Journal of Psychiatry, 113,* 1169–1182.

Santarcangelo, S., Dyer, K., & Luce, S. C. (1987). Generalized reduction of disruptive behavior in unsupervised settings through specific toy training. *Journal of the Association for Persons with Severe Handicaps, 12*(1), 38–44.

Schopler, E., & Reichler, R. J. (1971). Parents as cotherapists in the treatment of psychotic children. *Journal of Autism and Childhood Schizophrenia, 1*(1), 87–102.

Shafer, M. S., Egel, A. L., & Neef, N. A. (1984). Training mildly handicapped peers to facilitate changes in the social interaction skills of autistic children. *Journal of Applied Behavior Analysis, 17*(4), 461–476.

Sigman, M., & Mundy, P. (1989). Social attachments in autistic children. *Journal of the American Academy of Child and Adolescent Psychiatry, 28*(1), 74–81.

Sigman, M., Mundy, P., Sherman, T., & Ungerer, J. (1986). Social interactions of autistic, mentally retarded and normal children and their caregivers. *Journal of Child Psychology and Psychiatry and Allied Disciplines, 27*(5), 647–656.

Sigman, M., & Ungerer, J. A. (1984). Cognitive and language skills in autistic, mentally retarded, and normal children. *Developmental Psychology, 20*(2), 293–302.

Smith, D. E. P., Olson, M., Barger, F., & McConnell, J. V. (1981). The effects of improved auditory feedback on the verbalizations of an autistic child. *Journal of Autism and Developmental Disorders, 11*(4), 449–454.

Smith, D. E. P., McConnell, J. V., Walter, T. L., & Miller, S. D. (1985). Effect of using an auditory trainer on the attentional, language, and social behaviors of autistic children. *Journal of Autism and Developmental Disorders, 15*(3), 285–302.

Snow, M. E., Hertzig, M. E., & Shapiro, T. (1987) Expression of emotion in young autistic children. *Journal of the American Academy of Child and Adolescent Psychiatry, 26*(6), 836–838.

Stone, W. L., & Lemanek, K. L. (1990) Parental report of social behaviors in autistic preschoolers. *Journal of Autism and Developmental Disorders, 20*(4), 513–522.

Strain, P. S. (1985). Social and nonsocial determinants of acceptability in handicapped preschool children. *Topics in Early Childhood Special Education, 4*(4), 47–58.

Tiegerman, E., & Primavera, L. (1981). Object manipulation: An interactional strategy with autistic children. *Journal of Autism and Developmental Disorders, 11*(4), 427–438.

Tiegerman, E., & Primavera, L. H. (1984). Imitating the autistic child: Facilitating communicative gaze behavior. *Journal of Autism and Developmental Disorders, 14*(1), 27–38.

Tustin, F. (1988). The black hole: A significant element in autism, *Free Associations, 11*, 35–50.

Tryon, A. S., & Keane, S. P. (1986). Promoting imitative play through generalized observational learning in autisticlike children. *Journal of Abnormal Child Psychology, 14*(4), 537–549.

Uline, C. (1982). Teaching autistic children to play: A major teacher intervention. In P. Knoblock (Ed.), *Teaching and mainstreaming autistic children* (pp. 94–119). Denver: Love.

Volkmar, F. R., Sparrow, S. S., Goudreau, D., Cicchetti, D. V., Paul, R., & Cohen, D. J. (1987). Social deficits in autism: An operational approach using the Vineland Adaptive Behavior Scales. *Journal of the American Academy of Child and Adolescent Psychiatry, 26*(2), 156–161.

Wenar, C., Ruttenberg, B. A., Kalish-Weiss, B., & Wolf, E. G. (1986). The development of normal and autistic children: A comparative study. *Journal of Autism and Developmental Disorders, 16* (3), 317–333.

Wetherby, A. M., & Prutting, C. A. (1984). Profiles of communicative and cognitive–social abilities in autistic children. *Journal of Speech and Hearing Research, 27*, 364–377.

Wilbarger, P. (1993, April). *Sensory intervention for infants and young children.* Paper presented at the meeting of the New York Chapter of Zero to Three Study Group on Sensory Functions in Infancy, New York.

Wing, L. (1974). *Autistic children: A guide for parents and professionals.* Secaucus, NJ.: The Citadel Press.

Wood, M , Combs, C., Gunn, A., & Weller, D. (1986). *Developmental therapy in the classroom.* Austin, TX.: PRO-ED.

Wulff, S. B. (1985). The symbolic and object play of children with autism: A review. *Journal of Autism and Developmental Disorders, 15*(2), 139–148.

CHAPTER 7

Application of the Supportive Play Model to a Child with Multiple Risk Factors

This chapter takes a somewhat different turn in organization. The previous chapters were constructed around defined and differential diagnostic categories. Increasingly, however, we are seeing a group of young children who present a complex composite of symptoms that cut across developmental zones and diagnoses. Language delay is frequently the presenting problem and cardinal feature. In children who are talking, the organization of connected discourse may be labored and the pragmatic aspects of language thin. Yet one is inclined to suspect a greater store of inner language than can be expressed. These children frequently have subtle motor difficulties not always apparent through their flurry of activity. Only when they are settled down to more discrete and refined tasks do we note hesitancy, postural fixing, and awkwardness in their executions. They may be overreactive to touch and poorly regulated to incoming stimuli. Their attention span is limited. They are distractible and sometimes impulsive. This configuration of traits makes them highly susceptible to peer and caregiver conflicts alike. This is particularly underlined when circumstances demand some adherence to a dawning social order, as in the nursery school classroom or even in the routines of an average home environment.

These children are puzzling in that they present with an array of symptoms suggesting a range of developmental trajectories and possible outcomes. Because they are young and not yet fully formed developmentally, any definitive differential diagnosis is both premature and a disservice, at the risk of creating a self-fulfilling prophecy.

Vagueness, however, may undermine intervention as much as premature specificity. An enriched environment alone is insufficient, just as a regimen of individual therapies may be excessive and inefficient. We suggest a balance between discipline-specific therapies and a therapeutic environment or classroom when planning for these children. In the early years, development is more malleable, which allows for the corrective potential of early intervention. It is hoped that such support can alter a suspected atypical course or ameliorate the severity or complexity of the outcome. To do this effectively requires describing the symptoms carefully, defining the symptoms that most compromise function across developmental zones, identifying the configuration of contributing causal factors, and constructing a hypothetical map of the child and family's strengths, challenges, supports, and adversities. Such a developmental approach is predicated on the clinical concept that most perceptible handicaps are the result of multiple factors operating over time, rather than the outcome of some single unitary event. Intervention, then, aims to at least interrupt, if not correct, this cycle of cumulative adversity.

In this chapter, we identify the configuration of factors that seem to be most significant in contributing to the developmental problems you observe in the multirisk child. These include poverty, teratogens (lead, alcohol, drugs), acquired immunodeficiency syndrome (AIDS), language delay, behavior problems, and attention deficit hyperactivity disorder (ADHD). The second half of the chapter consists of a case study that exemplifies the supportive play approach to intervention with a child whose symptoms fit into this multirisk pattern.

RISK FACTORS

Poverty

Over 20% of all American children under age 18 and nearly 25% of children under age 6 are living in poverty (Patterson, Kupersmidt, & Vaden, 1990; Children's Defense Fund, 1992). Even more dramatic, 40% of children in young families live in poverty, a rate that has doubled since 1973 (Children's Defense Fund, 1992), and 50% of African-American children are born to single mothers and live in poverty (Laosa, 1988; Patterson et al., 1990). The effects of poverty include lower birth weights from preterm births and a higher risk of infant mortality, with the current African-American infant mortality rate nearly twice as high as that of white infants. This is similar to the mortality rates in third world countries (Escalona, 1982; Sabol, 1991; Children's Defense Fund, 1992). In general, children of color are more likely to be born into poverty, be born to a single parent, and suffer many of the social, health, and educational consequences of poverty (Glick, 1981; Laosa, 1988; Miranda & Santos de Barona, 1990; Patterson et al., 1990; Santos de Barona & Barona, 1991; Slaughter, 1988; Walker, 1989).

It is estimated that 10,000 children die from poverty annually in the United States, but many more live with hunger, family stress, poor health care, homelessness, and inadequate education and social services (Children's Defense Fund, 1992). The interaction of these physical and emotional stresses affect the child's general vulnerability and cognitive and psychosocial development (Escalona, 1982). Problems associated with poverty, such as substance abuse, parenting stress, health issues including AIDS, and increased rates of abuse and neglect all add to the vulnerability of children (McLoyd, 1990).

The literature suggests a strong correlation between poverty and developmental problems. Realizing that correlation does not prove causation, we suggest that it is the adverse impact of poverty that exacerbates underlying developmental vulnerability, setting in motion a cumulative tide of adversity sufficient to tip the imperceptible handicap into the diagnosable category (McCrae, 1986). Thus the ameliorate of social factors is no small part of the role of early intervention.

Foster Care

The stresses of poverty often make it difficult for parents to care adequately for their children, perhaps because of patterns of abuse, parental addiction, illness, or homelessness. Over 250,000 children are in foster care in the United States because of these familial problems, with abuse and neglect being the most dominant causes (Sabol, 1991). Some studies indicate that these children in foster care are functioning adequately (Fein, 1991; Fanshel & Shinn, 1978; Fein, Maluccio, Hamilton, & Ward, 1983; Festinger, 1983). But there are numerous issues raised in the literature that speak to the psychological risks of being placed in temporary foster care. Although two thirds of foster children are fortunate enough to have stability in their foster placement, one third of all foster children experience multiple placements (Fein, Maluccio, & Kluger, 1990; Fein, 1991). In addition, up to 30% of foster children experience multiple entries into the foster care system (Ooms, 1990).

In evaluating the effectiveness of foster care, it must be emphasized that many of the children enter the system with serious emotional and developmental issues that are the result of their past family experience. It is, therefore, difficult to differentiate whether adjustment issues and placement success relate to less-than-ideal placements or developmental problems that preexisted the placement (Polit, 1989).

There are reports of abusive foster parents (Fein & Staff, 1991), but some of this mistreatment may be a result of foster children's acting-out behavior ,which may be related to their crisis in readjustment. Hawkins, Meadowcroft, Trout, and Luster (1985) report that it is possible to place children who have difficult behavior into foster care with a high success rate, if the foster parents are carefully selected and receive more extensive and ongoing support. Foster parents and welfare workers need to be more aware of the psychological crisis that can be precipitated by placement. Although the welfare worker and foster parents may see removal from an abusive home as an act of kindness, the children involved may not feel the same way. Their loyalty to their biological parent or parents and their experience of severe loss can lead to generalized hostility and disruption of their identity, with a resulting unwillingness to form new attachments or solid relationships (Horner, 1982, 1986; Mullan, 1987). Minuchin and Elizur (1990) believe that foster parents need to be trained and then supported to envision themselves as helpers to the child's family, not just to the child, much like an extended family member would step in to help in a crisis. This would break some of the patterns of competitiveness between the biological and foster parents. Of course, in some situations, caused by parental addiction, failing health, imprisonment, or death, the child will not be able to be permanently united with the biological parents. These complex cases increase the need for support to both the children and the foster parents (White, 1992).

Lead

Lead poisoning is a preventable childhood disease, but it remains the major environmental problem affecting our babies and children (Alliance to End Childhood Lead Poisoning, 1993). It is true that we have made an effective reduction of airborne lead, and currently, as a society, we have one third less lead in our blood as a direct result of lowering our dependence on leaded gasoline (Mahaffey, Annest, Roberts, & Murphy, 1982). But it is also true that prenatal exposure to lead affects 400,000 babies a year. These babies are born with toxic levels of lead that have crossed the placenta into their systems (Alliance to End Childhood Lead Poisoning, 1993). For children under age 6, whose neurological systems are still developing, the risks of lead poisoning are high. Most particularly, poorly nourished children are at risk for lead poisoning because their bodies absorb more lead when they have low levels of calcium and iron in their diet (Blumenthal, 1992). Nationally one sixth of our children, both rich and poor alike, are affected. Seventeen percent of urban children, with rates as high as 50% in some city areas, have dangerous levels of lead in their blood (Alliance to End Childhood Lead Poisoning, 1993).

Lead contaminates children from many environmental sources. Lead comes into baby formula and food directly from the water through lead pipes or lead solder in the pipes of the water system (Alliance to End Lead Poisoning, 1993; Waldman, 1991). Lead in paint that is chipping or the dust of this paint that is being removed during renovations is a major cause of contamination to children (Blumenthal, 1992; Alliance to End Lead Poisoning, 1993; Waldman, 1991). Bridge repainting projects can be another major source of airborne contamination (Blumenthal, 1992). Additional lead can be brought into the home on workplace clothing or may be lying in the soil where the child plays (Blumenthal, 1992; Alliance to End Lead Poisoning, 1993). For young children who are likely to pick up and put contaminated paint chips or soil into their mouths, even minute amounts of lead can result in lead poisoning. Children who have poor nutrition are more likely to have a condition known as pica, a craving for nonnutritive substances, which increases their likelihood of picking at peeling paint or eating soil (Batshaw & Perret, 1992).

Dangerous lead levels can be diagnosed through blood testing even before children show any of the behavioral or developmental symptoms of lead poisoning. Blood testing can be started at 12 months, but 9 out of 10 children are not screened (Alliance to End Lead Poisoning, 1993). Because it is possible to reverse early toxicity, more wide scale screening would save many children from the permanent cognitive, learning, growth, and behavioral disabilities that can be the result of undetected poisoning (Blumenthal, 1992).

Possible physical signs of prenatal poisoning include low birth weight and premature delivery (Alliance to End Lead Poisoning, 1993). In young children, some signs suggesting possible exposure to lead include pica, fatigue, stomach aches, and headaches (Blumenthal, 1992). Children may show a loss in motor skills, slower reaction time, clumsiness, and problems in sensory perception (Waldman, 1991). As levels increase, lead is stored in the brain, nerves, bones, blood, and digestive system. Advanced symptoms can include anemia, kidney damage, muscle weakness, neurological damage, hearing loss, vomiting, and, ultimately, blindness, coma, convulsions, and, in extreme cases, death (Blumenthal, 1992; Peterson, 1987).

Because lead poisoning affects neurological development and functioning, children suffer a loss of their intellectual capacity, reduced attention span, and lowered IQ. They may also experience a delay in language development and, ultimately, experience learning disabilities, reading problems, and mental retardation (Alliance to End Lead Poisoning, 1993; Shapiro, 1992; Waldman, 1991). Children who have been exposed to dangerous levels of lead have a greatly increased chance of reading disabilities and learning disabilities and are four times less likely to graduate from high school (Alliance to End Lead Poisoning, 1993; Morris, 1991; Waldman, 1991).

Along with intellectual problems, lead poisoning leads to a cluster of potential emotional and behavioral problems. Parents may notice their child becoming less interested in play, lethargic, and distractible, or they may be irritable, impulsive, aggressive, and antisocial in their behavior (Blumenthal, 1992; Alliance to End Lead Poisoning, 1993; Waldman, 1991).

The timeliness of intervention is crucial. If the toxicity is discovered early and the source of the lead can be eradicated, a good level of recovery is possible. Treatment involves removing the lead from the child's system with medication (edetate calcium disodium [EDTA] and penicillamine), providing good nutrition, and removing the source of lead from the child's environment (Batshaw & Perret, 1992; Davis, 1988). Additionally, it has been shown that when the exposure to lead is low, once the source is removed, some of the children's learning problems can be ameliorated by good nutrition and developmental stimulation (Waldman, 1991).

Alcohol

Prenatal exposure to alcohol was identified two decades ago as the source of Fetal Alcohol Syndrome (FAS), a condition that negatively affects the physical, intellectual, and social development of 2 out of every 1,000 babies worldwide (Abel, 1984; Jones & Smith, 1973; Jones, Smith, Ulleland, & Streissguth, 1973). FAS is the leading known cause of mental retardation; 7,000 babies with this syndrome are born annually in the United States (Abel & Sokol, 1987; Freilberg, 1991; Hoyseth & Jones, 1989; Streissguth et al., 1991). Up to an additional 6 children out of every 1,000 are born with Fetal Alcohol Effect (FAE). These children do not have the physical anomalies found in FAS, but have similar, although more subtle, intellectual and behavioral consequences (Abel, 1990; Day et al., 1990; Streissguth et al., 1991). It is estimated that 5% of all congenital anomalies and up to 20% of mild mental retardation is the result of FAS and FAE (Olegård et al., 1979).

FAS is found among children of all ethnic groups and social classes. There is suspicion of some genetic vulnerability, and surveys have shown a higher proportion of identified children from the lowest socioeconomic groups (Abel, 1990; Abel & Sokol, 1987; Rosett & Weiner, 1985). It is estimated that approximately 3% of women who are of childbearing age are alcoholics or problem drinkers (Abel & Sokol, 1987). Since the alcohol molecule is small, it rapidly passes through the placental membrane and directly affects the fetus by impairing cellular growth, decreasing protein synthesis and the production of neurotransmitters, and interfering with the myelination of nerves (Pietrantoni & Knuppel, 1991; Streissguth, Barr, Sampson, Darby, & Martin, 1989). A mother's chronic or binge drinking during pregnancy can have a dramatic effect on the fetus' physical development, intellectual potential, and behavior (Driscoll, Streissguth, & Riley, 1990; Jones, Chernoff, & Kelley, 1984; Streissguth, Barr, & Sampson, 1990; Streissguth et al., 1989). It is suspected that excessive drinking by the father may also affect the sperm and lead to negative developmental consequences in the fetus (Russell, 1990; Wallace, 1987). It is interesting that few babies with FAS are diagnosed at time of delivery. This is unfortunate because intervention for the baby and the parents is crucial to modify the negative consequences of this condition (Abel, 1990; Little, Snell, Rosenfeld, Gilstrap, & Gant, 1990). The specific guidelines for establishing this diagnosis include a prenatal and infant growth rate and head circumference below the 10th percentile, damage to the central nervous system (CNS), and facial characteristics including small eyes, thin upper lip, and underdeveloped midfacial jawbone (Rosett & Weiner, 1985; Sokol & Clarren, 1989).

Excessive drinking of alcohol in the first trimester is implicated with causing the physical and intellectual characteristics of FAS; drinking starting in the second trimester is implicated with decreased growth and intellect, and excessive drinking in the third trimester has its major impact on intellect (Conlon, 1992). General physical anomalies have been found in cardiovascular, renal, orthopedic, dermatological, and connective tissue development. Respiratory dysfunction, seizures, vision problems, and hearing loss are all possible physiological problems found in children with FAS (Burd & Martsolf, 1989; Church, 1987; Graham, Hanson, Darby, Barr, & Streissguth, 1988; Streissguth & Giunta, 1988).

The impact of FAS on the CNS includes tremors, a weak suck response, fitful sleeping, hyperexcitability, and irritability (Clarren & Smith, 1978; Murray, 1989; Sokol, Miller, & Reed, 1980; Streissguth, Barr, Martin & Herman, 1980; Streissguth & Giunta, 1988; Wallace, 1987). The weak suck response can be particularly concerning because it leads to feeding difficulties and makes these children vulnerable for failure to thrive (Streissguth & Giunta, 1988).

Many children with FAS and FAE have been found to have emotional and behavioral problems, similar to those found in ADHD, that continue into their adulthood. Other specific developmental issues mentioned in the literature that may have an emotional component include enuresis, encopresis, and schizophrenia (Abel, 1984; Burd & Martsolf, 1989; Driscoll et al., 1990; Hoyseth & Jones, 1989; Nanson & Hiscock, 1990; Phelps & Grabowski, 1992; Streissguth et al., 1991; Streissguth & LaDue, 1987).

In language development, delays in articulation, vocabulary, grammar, and comprehension are reported (Becker, Warr-Leeper, & Leeper, 1990). Once language does start to develop, the children may mask their comprehension problems by asking excessive questions (Streissguth & Giunta, 1988). For children who are identified as FAE, language delay appears to be more related to the quality of parenting than to the level of maternal drinking (Greene, Ernhart, Martier, Sokol, & Ager, 1990).

Cognitive development is most affected by FAS, with children being mildly retarded or in the dull–normal range. In general, the children who have the most conspicuous physical signs of the syndrome suffer the most intellectual compromise (Streissguth et al., 1986; Streissguth, Clarren, & Jones, 1985; Streissguth & Giunta, 1988). Specific cognitive problems reported in the research include attentional and distractibility problems, learning disabilities, sequential memory problems, and problems in mathematics-related skills (Becker, Warr-Leeper, & Leeper, 1990; Bingol, et al., 1987; Coles et al., 1991; Marino, Scholl, Karp, Yanoff, & Hetherington, 1987).

Early diagnosis and early intervention are important in order to reduce the impact of emotional and learning problems. Approaches similar to those used with children with ADHD have been suggested. These include small classes, clear expectations, and a focus on communication skills and behavioral management. Fine motor skills and perceptual organization should be addressed as well because of sensory problems associated with FAS and FAE. (Becker et al, 1990; Myers, Olson, & Kaltenbach, 1992; Nanson & Hiscock, 1990; Streissguth & Giunta, 1988; Streissguth et al, 1991).

Intervention must focus not only on the child but also on the family members who are nurturing the child. Of great significance is the fact that fewer than 10% of children with FAS grow up with natural parents; two thirds of mothers die in the child's early years because of cirrhosis, car accident, suicide, and overdose (Abel & Sokol, 1987). Many children with FAS are removed from their natural parents because of neglect or abuse. When children do stay at home, 86% of mothers are accused of neglect and 52% of abuse (Streissguth et al., 1991). Obviously, the risks from FAS are multidimensional and require an intervention plan that takes all these variables into consideration.

Illegal Drugs

It is estimated that 100,000 babies are born each year in the United States who have been exposed to drugs prenatally. Use of illegal drugs, especially cocaine and crack, is a current reality among women of child-bearing age, with a large increase in use over the last 10 years (Chasnoff, 1988; Schutzman, Frankenfield-Chernicoff, Clatterbaugh, & Singer, 1991; Singer, Garber, & Kliegman, 1991). For instance, in hospitals with many low-income patients, between 10 and 20% of newborns have been exposed to cocaine in utero (Chasnoff, Landress, & Barrett, 1990; Frank et al., 1988; Sabol, 1991). Drug abuse is evident across all racial groups; research has indicated that white women experiment more with drugs over their lifetime, but that African-American or Hispanic women are more likely to use drugs regularly (Adams, Gfroerer, & Rouse, 1989). Because individuals who use cocaine during pregnancy are also more likely to use other drugs and alcohol, lack prenatal care, have poorer nutrition, have more sexually transmitted diseases, and give birth to more low-birth-weight babies, it must be questioned whether the developmental compromises observed in these children are caused by the drug exposure or by the multirisk factors that are intrinsic to their social environment (Allen, Palomares, DeForest, Sprinkle, & Reynolds, 1991; Chasnoff, 1988; Frank et al., 1988; Schutter & Brinker, 1992). It is suspected that paternal cocaine use can also affect development since the sperm may carry cocaine into the egg (Yazigi, Odem, & Polakoski, 1991).

Physiological effects seen in babies who were repeatedly prenatally exposed to cocaine include risk of early delivery; decreased weight, length, and head circumference; and malformations of the heart, gastrointestinal tract, genitourinary tract, skeleton, and brain (Bingol, Fuchs, Diaz, Stone, & Gromisch, 1987; Chasnoff & Griffith, 1989; Chasnoff, Griffith, MacGregor, Dirkes, & Burns, 1989; Doberczak, Shanzer, Senie, & Kandall, 1988; Dominguez, Vila-Coro, Slopis, & Bohan, 1991; Finnegan, 1985; Hadeed & Siegel, 1989; Hoyme et al., 1990; MacGregor et al., 1987; Oro & Dixon, 1987; Zuckerman et al., 1989). For children who were repeatedly exposed to cocaine in utero during the first trimester, 10% have malformations (Yazigi et al., 1991).

Damage to the central nervous system (CNS) can result in an abnormal electroencephalogram (EEG), tremors, increased muscle tone, vomiting, seizures, bleeding in the basal ganglia and frontal lobes, and problems in regulating mood and in experiencing pleasure. These, in turn, can lead to irritability, lethargy, restlessness, abnormal sleep patterns, poor feeding, and a high-pitched cry (Dixon & Bejar, 1989; Doberczak et al., 1988; Finnegan, 1985; Hadeed & Siegel, 1989; Howard, 1989; Lester et al., 1991).

These neurological issues potentially have a direct effect on the social and emotional experience of the infant and on the relationship between the infant and the caregivers. When overstim-ulated, this baby is likely to shut out the environment either through excessive crying or sleeping. When organized enough to attend to stimuli, the baby easily becomes overstimulated and disorganized. These patterns are difficult to anticipate and manage, so that it is unlikely for a caregiver to feel successful in comforting and caring for this baby. Even when the child attempts to communicate, the message may be unusual, indirect, and disorganized (Davidson, 1991; Main & Solomon, 1986). The combination of a difficult baby and a parent who may be compromised by continued drug abuse all too often leads to child abuse (Davidson, 1991; Dixon, Bresnahan, & Zuckerman, 1990). These children have been described as having flat affect with little display of either positive or negative emotions. Their play behavior is immature, with little manifest fantasy or curiosity (Howard, Beckwith, Rodning, Kropenske, 1989). At this time it is difficult to differentiate if the social problems seen in this population are a result of prenatal drug exposure or of the multirisk home environment many of these children experience (Allen, Palomares, DeForest, Sprinkle, & Reynolds, 1991; Elliott & Coker, 1991). Schutter and Brinker (1992) describe the overgeneralizations that are currently in the literature about prenatal cocaine exposure. They point out that, at this time, research has not filtered the multiple factors that are involved in the development of these children, so they suggest great caution before these generalizations become part of the common belief system.

Although most of these children have IQs in the normal range, their learning is compromised, most often in the area of language and communication (Conlon, 1992). Additionally, their increased muscle tone, tremors, and primitive reflexes may interfere with their fine and gross motor exploration and development. The increased tone may limit the motor control of the hips and knees and lead to delays in sitting and walking (Chasnoff, 1988; Dominguez et al., 1991; Schneider & Chasnoff, 1987).

Intervention for the children who are cocaine exposed must be highly family-focused. The question of environment versus biology is a very important one in working with these children and their families. How much of the neurological insult can be rectified with good parenting and family support? There is no such thing as a "crack or cocaine baby"; the interventionist must be aware that the neurological, physical, and behavioral ramifications of prenatal cocaine exposure are as individual as the babies and their family and social systems. Some programs of intervention are behavioral in their orientation employing reduced environmental stimulation and little experiential learning (Dixon et al., 1990). But no matter what philosophical approach is used, it is crucial to focus on the child within the context of his or her dynamic ecological system and to design intervention that is neither punitive nor focused exclusively on the child's remediation (Myers et al., 1992; Schutter & Brinker, 1992).

Treatment for addicted mothers and their children must first deal with the addiction. It has been suggested that for some addicted parents their primary relationship is not with their child, rather it is with the drug; they can not read their own behavior, and can not self-regulate and, therefore, they are not able to read their own child. Mothers may be emotionally depressed, and this depression may be linked to use of both legal and illegal drugs, cigarettes, and alcohol. The baby may be at risk, but environmental intervention can improve the situation in some cases. Interventionists need to think in a dynamic, transactional model (Werner & Smith, 1982). Intervention must focus on the family unit, gradually building a therapeutic relationship, and continually ensuring family safety. At some points in the treatment, separation of the child from the parent may be necessary to ensure safety (Kaplan-Sanoff & Rice, 1992). Weston and colleagues (1989) point to the strain on the foster care system because of the number of drug-exposed babies in need of placements; many of these children are also HIV positive. In all cases, intervention must focus on a multidimensional, social–ecological perspective that includes family and community (Davidson, 1991).

Acquired Immunodeficiency Syndrome (AIDS) and Human Immunodeficiency Virus (HIV)

AIDS is becoming a major cause of developmental disability and early death in children. By 1995, AIDS is predicted to be the fifth leading cause of death in infants and young children (Pizzo et al., 1988). Currently, children and women are the two populations showing the greatest growth rate in incidence of AIDS. Approximately 2,000 infected children were born in 1989 in the United States (Chu, Buehler, Oxtoby, & Kilbourne, 1991). It is estimated that for every child diagnosed with AIDS, there are at least 10 more children who are HIV positive; that is, the antibodies to the virus are detectable, but the child is not ill (Gwinn et al., 1991, Hopp & Rogers, 1989). Eighty-five percent of infected children are African-American or Hispanic (Chu et al., 1991). Mortality statistics are even more dramatic along the east coast and in Puerto Rico, where 75% of the AIDS infected children live (Conlon, 1992). For African-American and Hispanic children under age 4 who are living in New York state, AIDS is the first and second leading cause of death (Chu et al., 1991).

Eighty percent of children with AIDS are infected perinatally from their mothers, with the remaining children becoming infected through blood products or through sexual contact and drug abuse as adolescents (Hutto et al., 1991). Jason (1991) advises that sexually abused children need to be screened for HIV because this is another potential source of childhood infection. In 1989, a nationwide screening of pregnant mothers found that 1.5 out of 1,000 mothers were HIV positive; 30% of these infected women gave birth to babies who were HIV positive (Gwinn et al., 1991). The incubation period for perinatal infection can be anywhere from 2 months to 5 years (Epstein et al., 1986). Eighty percent of HIV-positive babies developed AIDS in the first 2 years of their lives (Hutto et al., 1991), with a median age of 8 months (Scott et al., 1989).

The remaining infants who are HIV positive at birth do not develop AIDS; thus, HIV antibodies are not a sufficient grounds for diagnosis of AIDS in an infant because maternal antibodies may persist for as long as 18 months (Conlon, 1992). Diagnosis is generally made when a wide range of physical symptoms become apparent: the child may become chronically ill with enlarged lymph nodes, liver, and spleen; fevers; diarrhea; failure to thrive; acute weight loss; bacterial and viral infections; joint infections; and problems with heart, lung, kidney, and CNS (Hauger & Powell, 1990). Some children develop paralysis, have seizures, and show sudden changes in their mood and mental state (Belman, 1992; Belman et al., 1988; Brouwers, Belman, & Epstein, 1991; Butler, Hittelman, & Hauger, 1991; Ultmann et al., 1985). In general, young children who develop perinatal AIDS have a poor prognosis. After diagnosis, their median survival rate is 38 months, although antiviral medical treatment is very important in improving quality of life and longevity (Scott et al., 1989; Belman et al., 1988; Pizzo et al., 1988). A second group of children with perinatal infection develop AIDS-related complex (ARC) instead of AIDS. These children are not as negatively affected, showing more variability in their development (Scott et

al, 1989). From a medical treatment perspective, Meyers and Weitzman (1991) describe AIDS as childhood's newest chronic illness. A chronic illness is one that "interferes with an individual's activities on a daily basis for at least three months per year and leads to a hospital stay involving at least one month per year" (Williams, 1989, p. 259).

Along with physical illness, developmental abnormalities are seen in 75 to 90% of HIV-positive children (Pizzo, 1990). As a result of damage to the CNS, many children experience a delay in developmental milestones or a loss of developmental abilities previously in place (Belman et al., 1985; Ultmann et al., 1985). Some children with AIDS show a rapid loss of skills, others follow a pattern of reaching a plateau of skills and then demonstrating a progressive loss followed by a leveling off and then another loss (Dokecki, Baumeister, & Kupstas, 1989; Butler et al., 1991). Butler and colleagues (1991) points out that research is not yet conclusive as to whether these learning patterns are caused exclusively by AIDS or compounded by the effects of prenatal drug exposure, chaotic family life, and the need for frequent hospitalizations.

The loss of developmental skills may affect motor and sensory skills, communication, as well as cognitive areas. The delays may be progressive; however, in some cases, they may be forestalled and even temporarily reversed with medical treatment. Motor and sensory problems include spasticity, visual motor functioning problems, visual-spatial deficits, poor fine motor coordination and abnormal tone and gait (Belman, 1992; Butler et al., 1991; Conlon, 1992; Diamond et al., 1987; Dokecki et al., 1989; Mintz, Epstein, & Koenigsberger, 1989; Ultmann et al., 1985).

Communication profiles include sparse production and delays or regressions in speech and language development (Belman, 1992; Condini et al., 1991; Conlon, 1992; Pressman, 1992). Specific cognitive problems associated with brain infection that is identified in the literature include problems in short-term memory, attentional difficulties, and generalized cognitive deficits (Belman et al, 1988; Butler et al., 1991; Conlon, 1992; Mintz et al., 1989). Although Belman (1992) mentions that these children demonstrate impairments in their play, details are lacking in the literature.

Intervention, both medical and educational, should begin with diagnosis. If appropriate, treatment with AZT (zidovudine, an antiretroviral medication) and other medical treatments may forestall many of the developmental complications experienced by children with AIDS (Pizzo et al., 1988). An immunization program to prevent routine childhood illness is also crucial in the child's plan because common diseases, such as measles and chicken pox, can be life threatening (Burroughs & Edelson, 1991). Older children who are dealing more directly with their diagnosis may become depressed and need psychotherapy to validate their experiences; they may also possibly benefit from antidepressant medication (Spiegel & Mayers 1991; Vas Dias, 1990).

Establishing appropriate educational intervention for a child with AIDS requires preparing educational and allied health professionals to care for children with this infection (Hopp & Rogers, 1989). Meyers & Weitzman (1991) recommend that the child with AIDS be looked upon like any other child with a chronic illness. As with all children with chronic illness, quality-of-life issues need to be a focus of intervention (Khan & Battle, 1987). Because of the developmental disabilities that are the result of AIDS, these children need and can benefit from special education, occupational, physical, and speech/language therapy (Epstein et al., 1986; Conlon, 1992). But frequently, the attempt to place a child who is known to have AIDS or to be HIV positive in a nursery school or daycare setting raises a high level of public concern because of fear of contagion (Jason, 1991).

Social isolation and ostracism are serious consequences of this diagnosis and necessitate a high degree of confidentiality from professionals working with children who have AIDS or are HIV positive (Lockhart & Wodarski, 1989). Current legislation makes it clear that all children should be served in as natural a setting as possible, so that access questions and public education need to be dealt with for this population (Dokecki et al., 1989). If the child is developmentally able, in stable health, has had appropriate inoculations, and has his or her physician's approval, medical experts believe that social contact with peers is of major benefit (Berry, 1988; Task Force on Pediatric AIDS, 1988; Klug, 1986). There is no indication that the fears of contagion to peers or staff through contact in a day care center or school are based on any reality (Rogers et al., 1990; Schwarcz & Rutherford, 1989). As general practice, the Task Force on Pediatric AIDS (1988) suggests that universal precautions be used to limit contagion of all communicable diseases. The risk is really to the children unable to fight infections that they are exposed to in a group setting (Spiegel & Mayers, 1991). Once the child's health has declined, an alternative setting with medical supervision may be more appropriate ("Task Force," 1988).

Intervention must be child-centered and family-focused. Many of these children come from families who have a variety of risk factors that need to be addressed in a culturally sensitive and non-judgmental fashion (Conlon, 1992; Khan & Battle, 1987). If the AIDS was transmitted prenatally or perinatally, the mother will need help dealing with her guilt and, like all parents of any chronically ill child, she will need support to grieve about her child's illness (Conlon, 1992). If the child is the only infected person in the household, family members need to be assured that home transmission is not a real risk, even with the exposure that is normal in daily life (Rogers et al., 1990). The most crucial emotional support for the family will center around the social isolation that they may encounter because of public reaction to AIDS. If the mother is also infected, interventionists will need to facilitate decisions concerning the mother's ability to meet the child's needs and arrange alternative care, if necessary, while retaining the mother–child attachment, if possible. Many mothers of HIV-positive infants and toddlers die while the child is quite young. This has led to the necessity of establishing an expanded foster-care program in many urban areas. The homes that specialize in the care of these children need specialized recruitment, training, and support services because of all of the social, emotional, and medical issues that are part of their commitment to the care of children with AIDS (Gurdin & Anderson, 1987; Hart, 1987; Jason, 1991; Skinner, 1989; Taylor-Brown, 1991). Education is crucial as the primary intervention in the spread of HIV and AIDS to children. This is a health tragedy that is avoidable for the vast majority of children.

COMMUNICATION AND BEHAVIORAL ISSUES IN DEVELOPMENT

We know that language and communication, general intellectual development, attention, and social and emotional behavior are intertwined in early development, so that difficulties in one area will have a negative impact on other developmental areas. In preschool settings, many teachers are seeing children who display such a cluster of behaviors that they are troublesome in a group situation and frustrating to both the children's and the teachers' sense of success. These children may have a known diagnosis or a known cause for some of their behavior, but it is just as likely that no specific cause has been identified. Whether or not the etiology is known, these children are challenged when placed in a setting where it is assumed that children can initiate their own learning, interact with peers in a prosocial fashion, and work toward shared goals. In fact, some of these children have difficulty listening and following directions; others confuse us because they may seem to understand most of what is said to them but are slow in establishing effective patterns of expressive communication. They are not necessarily retarded, but tend to be mildly delayed to average in their cognitive development. Yet they have difficulty attending to materials and activities so that their learning is negatively affected. They may exhibit very erratic behavior, moving around a room quickly, upsetting both objects and people, seemingly unable to restrain their own emotions and actions. They may seem emotionally stressed or distressed, timid or overly familiar, depressed or aggressive, and prone to temper tantrums. When they reach elementary school, they are often identified as being learning disabled, emotionally disturbed, or as having ADHD. In preschool settings, many children can be described as having these characteristics.

Often these children are not diagnosed as having a specific problem but rather are judged to be problem children. The reasons for these types of behaviors are often unknown, but may be multiple, including neurological damage caused by various viruses, chronic ear infections (otitis media), and prenatal exposure to toxins, such as lead, drugs, and alcohol. There may be a genetic predisposition that may compromise children's learning and behavioral development (Biederman, Faraone, Keenan, Knee, & Tsuang, 1990). Children may come from backgrounds of financial poverty, homes where poor nutrition and familial stress may lead to their experiencing additional developmental risks, or they may come from financially secure and stable homes. Whether we know the exact cause or not, the need for early intervention is not deminished.

Language Delay

Children who demonstrate delays in the acquisition of communication skills that cannot be attributed to hearing impairment, mental retardation, pervasive developmental disorder, or neurologic disorder can be diagnosed as having developmental articulation disorder, developmental receptive language disorder, and/or developmental expressive language disorder ("Diagnostic and statistical manual," 1987). Other terms used include speech and/or language delay, speech and/or language disorder, communication disorder, and aphasia/dysphasia. These terms do not describe a single condition, but a variety of symptoms related to different aspects of speech, language, and communication development; for example, a significant expressive language delay could be related to developmental **apraxia** or to a **phonological disorder**. Estimates of the incidence of language delays in children range from 1 to over 12% (Lahey, 1988), with males predominating. Language delay has been associated with low IQ, reading and academic problems, and behavioral problems (Aram & Nation, 1980; King, Jones, & Lasky, 1982; Cantwell & Baker, 1987b; Silva, Williams, & McGee, 1987). This is not surprising given the interrelatedness of developmental domains in early development.

Children with poor verbal expressive skills may become frustrated and resort to inappropriate acting-out behaviors to express themselves or may withdraw from social situations. Children who are impulsive and display a short attention span may have difficulty following directions. This may be perceived as a language difficulty, which may or may not be the case. Such children may also exhibit difficulties "reading" social cues; this may be reflected in inappropriate behaviors and language use (e.g., laughing when another child falls and is hurt). Unfortunately, these children may have progressively fewer opportunities to interact, because other children will tend not to seek them out (Siegel, Cunningham, & van der Spuy, 1985).

A strong link has been established between language delay and behavioral difficulties by a number of researchers (Cantwell & Baker, 1987a, 1987b; Richman, Stevenson, & Graham, 1982). This relationship has been found independent of sex differences, family stressors, and poor reading ability (Silva et al., 1987). Other studies have shown a high rate of psychiatric disorders in children referred for communication delays (Cantwell & Baker, 1987a). This combination of language and behavioral difficulties may be related to an underlying neurodevelopmental immaturity or subtle CNS deficits (Beitchman & Peterson, 1986; Cantwell & Baker, 1987b; Tallal, Dukette, & Curtiss, 1989).

Speech and language therapy alone has not been found to be effective in reducing the negative impact on social–emotional development (Cantwell & Baker, 1987a). Intervention must address the needs of the developing child in an integrated manner. Collaboration among speech and language pathologists, educators, and mental health professionals is essential when planning appropriate programs for these children.

Preschool children who have language delays frequently also have cognitive delays that become evident in the elementary grades. Global or general language delay (i.e., receptive and expressive delays) strongly suggests underlying developmental delay in cognition, and children with this disability have an increased likelihood of being diagnosed as mentally retarded (Cantwell & Baker, 1987c; Coplan, Gleason, Ryan, Burke, & Williams, 1982). Expressive language delay at the preschool age is highly related to low verbal and full-scale IQ scores (verbal and performance) in elementary school and low reading scores (Silva, 1980; Silva, McGee, & Williams, 1983; Silva et al., 1987). Additionally, preschool language problems continue for many of these children into the elementary school years, when the majority may demonstrate specific academic and learning problems (Aram & Hall, 1989; Aram & Nation, 1980). Children with language delay also have been found to have problems in auditory memory, thinking skills, and the ability to sequence gestures related to a familiar event (Morgan, Dawson, & Kerby, 1992; Thal, 1991). In follow-up studies, preschoolers with general language delay also have an increased likelihood of having been diagnosed as having learning disabilities or ADHD in elementary school (Beitchman, Hood, Rochon, & Peterson, 1989; Cantwell & Baker, 1991).

Examination of the play of children with language impairments has yielded mixed results. In some studies, a strong relationship between play development and language development has been reported for children with language impairments when matched to normally developing children for age (Snyder, 1978). Terrell and colleagues (1984) found that children with language impairments performed better, although below age expectations, on symbolic play tasks than younger children who were matched for language age. In contrast, Roth and Clark (1987) found that children with language impairments performed more poorly on symbolic play tasks than on linguistic tasks. In addition, significant individual variability in play–language corre-

spondences has been documented for children with developmental delays (Kennedy, Sheridan, Radlinski, & Beeghly, 1991). Rescorla (1987) found that, despite normal cognitive development, 2-year-olds with expressive language delay demonstrated relatively poor pretend-play skills. They showed fewer and less varied play behaviors and demonstrated a lack of socially directed play. Rescorla suggested that this may result from a lack of understanding of the social communicative value of both words and objects.

Bates and her colleagues have shown that the relationship between linguistic development (comprehension, production) and nonlinguistic cognitive skills (gestures, symbolic play) varies at different points in development (Bates, Bretherton, & Snyder, 1988). Two areas (comprehension and gesture) may be highly correlated at one point in time and show little or no correlation at another point in time (Thal, Tobias, & Morrison, 1991). This may account for some of the contradictory findings in the literature. The variability may also result from differences in maturation, cognition, and parental stimulation of language and play (Tamis-LeMonda & Bornstein, 1989).

Children with play and language delays need carefully planned developmental programming that focuses on both the underlying areas of deficit and the ongoing integration of all developmental areas. The teacher and speech-language pathologist should work together in developing a program that incorporates the expansion of various play skills and play themes while facilitating the child's growing linguistic skills. Structured play situations with play props that are interesting and motivating to the child (puppets, dress-up clothes) serve as a catalyst for the development of these skills. Parents may also need assistance understanding the significance of supporting both their child's language and play development.

Attention Deficit Hyperactivity Disorder

In 1980, Diagnostic and Statistical Manual of Mental Disorders, Third Edition (DSM III) defined attention deficit disorder (ADD) as inappropriate levels of inattention, impulsivity, and hyperactivity. The different behaviors were listed separately according to the presence (ADHD) or absence (ADD) of hyperactivity. Since that time, further delineations have indicated that ADD without hyperactivity is a distinct subtype that may co-occur more frequently with learning disabilities, while ADHD may be more prevalent in children with behavior disorders (Barkley, DuPaul, & McMurray, 1990; Hynd et al., 1991; Lahey & Carlson, 1991). Therefore, the diagnosis of ADHD can be and is used with preschool children.

Between 2 to 10% of children in the United States are diagnosed as having ADHD (Shaywitz & Shaywitz, 1988). As toddlers, these children are in constant motion, to a degree that goes far beyond the typical activity pattern of the busy toddler (Hechtman, Weiss, Perlman, 1984). As they grow older, they continue to be unusually active, have difficulty attending to prominent features in the environment, have poor responses to questions, may make verbal comments that are disconnected to immediate events, and may show a pattern of inappropriate and/or excessive questioning. They are also prone to impulsive behavior, which may put them into danger, and to demonstrating behavior that shows a lack of awareness of appropriate interpersonal cues in social situations. They may also have motor–perception problems.

This diagnosis is given when physical causes for the behavioral symptom are not present and no other cause can be established. ADHD is usually diagnosed in the absence of discernible brain damage and is seen more frequently in boys than in girls; therefore, it is suspected to have some genetic components (Biederman et al., 1990; "Diagnostic and statistical manual," 1987; Goodman, 1989). Other factors that may be causative include prenatal lead exposure (Bellinger & Needleman, 1983), prenatal exposure to alcohol (Abel, 1984), prenatal exposure to cocaine (Giacoia, 1990), prematurity and low weight at full term (Hawdon, Hey, Kolvin, & Fundudis, 1990), brain infections, errors of metabolism (Shaywitz & Shaywitz, 1988), chromosome abnormalities (Borghgraef, Fryns, & van den Berghe, 1990; Eldridge et al., 1989; Reiss & Freund, 1990), or other genetic syndromes (Comings & Comings, 1990; Shaywitz & Shaywitz, 1988). Other explanations include neurotransmitter abnormalities (Shaywitz & Shaywitz, 1988) and less activity in the brain section that controls attention (Lou, Henriksen & Bruhn, 1990; Zametkin et al., 1990).

Treatment for ADHD may be multifaceted, including stimulant drugs, which can improve focus and the general ability to learn and relate (Barkley, 1988; Forness & Kavale, 1988; Gadow, 1986; Hallahan, Kauffman, & Lloyd, 1985; Mercer, 1992). Educational interventions may include the use of structured and low-stimulating learning environments; the use of simplified instructions; the use of visual and auditory materials and equipment to supplement usual classroom instruction; and the use of behavioral management techniques (Kirk, Gallagher, & Anastasiow, 1993). Counseling for both the child and the family may also be helpful (Mercugliano, 1992).

THE INCLUSION OF A CHILD WITH MULTIPLE RISKS IN A HEAD START PROGRAM

The following case study will illustrate some issues raised when Patty, a child with multiple risks, is placed in a Head Start program. The foster mother and program staff are concerned about Patty's adjustment to the placement and have requested a planning and placement meeting. At the Planning and Placement Team (PPT) meeting, information gained from working through the SPM will assist in determining Patty's strengths and weaknesses, relevant family information, and the appropriateness of this current placement. The characteristics limiting play, a discrepancy analysis, and goals for intervention and facilitating techniques are proposed. In the following section, background information on Patty and her educational placement, as well as a descriptive observation of Patty in the Head Start Program, is presented.

Background Information and Initial Observation

Patty is a 3-year-old girl who has been enrolled in a 5-day-per-week Head Start program for 2 months. Patty is currently in a foster home, one of the three in which she has been placed since birth. Her biological mother, who was 17 years old at Patty's birth, has used cocaine since she was 12 years old. Patty has two younger brothers: 2-year-old John resides in the foster home with Patty and 1-year-old Tom is in a different foster home.

Patty was born at term weighing $4\frac{1}{2}$ lbs. and demonstrating signs of prenatal cocaine exposure. She moved through the stages of withdrawal at a large medical center. When she was stabilized, she was sent to the first foster home where she stayed for 6 months. The biological mother agreed to participate in a drug treatment program soon after Patty was born and wanted her daughter returned to her. Reunion was not approved,

though, because Patty's mother did not have a consistent domicile. The mother soon became pregnant with the second child. John was born when Patty was 1 year old and in her second foster home. The mother began using cocaine again soon after John came home from the hospital at which time he joined Patty in her foster home. The mother was soon pregnant again, and the third child, Tom, was born exposed to cocaine. Tom was placed in another foster home. In the meantime, Patty was in her third foster home, with Mr. and Mrs. Jones, and had started in a Head Start program. The biological mother was still hopeful of a reunion with all three of her children as she had been drug free for 6 months. Consequently, Patty and John make supervised visits with their mother every other Saturday.

Patty has been aggressive and acting out in all of her foster home placements. The families have all seen her as a moody, unstable child. She is always seeking out her brother John to hit or push and she grabs his toys, frequently assigning the blame to John when the adult appears. All of these behaviors are amplified after the visitations with her mother. The current foster family, the Jones, hope to adopt Patty and John and are exploring those possibilities.

Patty is an attractive child, tall and slender for her age. She is always well dressed in pretty dresses and patent leather shoes; her long dark hair is usually curled in ringlets, with a matching ribbon. A psychological evaluation indicated her overall cognitive level in the low average range. Patty was sick a lot during her first 18 months with repeated upper-respiratory and ear infections. Independent walking did not emerge until she was 16 months old.

The Head Start program, housed in the gymnasium/auditorium area of an old elementary school, is composed of seventeen 3-year-olds in a group with a head teacher, two teacher aides, and a volunteer grandmother. Patty enjoys the housekeeping area, fine motor materials, and arts and crafts activities. She is competent and curious about the gross motor equipment, but seldom chooses these activities, because she has been cautioned to keep her clothes clean.

The following observation is recorded by a public school speech and language pathologist who has been working with Patty. The observation takes place in October after Patty has been enrolled in the program for 1 month.

Patty is usually one of the last children to arrive at school. Mrs. Jones reports terrible battles in the morning getting both children ready. Patty typically provokes her brother every chance she can, so the foster mother seems relieved when she is able to leave Patty at the program. Mrs. Jones waves good-bye, Patty returns the waves and goes directly to the housekeeping corner. She scans the area to see what is available and touches many of the items. She looks at the items the other children are using, then moves on to another area, and repeats the same behaviors. She eventually returns to the housekeeping area because several of the children have left to do an art project. Patty picks the doll up and slams it back in the crib saying, "Bad baby, no more crying." The teacher is standing nearby and asks her why the baby has been bad. Patty says "Baby wet her pants, all dirty." Patty picks up the baby bottle and jams it in the baby's mouth. She lifts the doll up again and jerks the leg, so it drops off. Patty has a panicked look on her face and the teacher comes over to pop the doll's leg back on. Patty then goes to the art project area. The children are pasting scraps of different materials on paper to form a collage. Patty reaches for the materials and gets some glue on her arm. She tries to rub the glue off, but it is too sticky. Patty looks at the teacher aide and says "Glue off, now!" The aide tells her to go to the bathroom to wash it off. Patty goes in the bathroom and applies a large quantity of liquid soap on the drying glue. She rubs and rubs with a paper towel; the sink is overflowing with bubbly water. The aide comes in and finds her, tells her she has used too much soap and is to dry her hands and return to the classroom. Patty's skin is red where she rubbed the glue spot. She goes out and shows the other teacher that the glue finally came off. The teacher nods her head and asks Patty to finish her picture. Patty shakes her head and says, "All done with the glue."

Patty moves to the puzzle area and quickly completes about six puzzles, each with eight to ten interlocking pieces. She leaves the puzzles scattered on the table. It is time to clean up for singing and story time. Patty again moves from one area to the next, checking and touching the materials in each area. She takes the sponge and cleans all of the tables. The teacher aide asks her to come and put the puzzles away. Patty looks up from her cleaning and screams, "No." The teacher looks at Patty, who has resumed sponging the tables, and puts the puzzles away herself. Patty continues to clean the tables and the teacher asks her to join the group. She yells "No." The teacher aide goes over to help her finish the cleaning and Patty throws the sponge at her and runs around the table yelling "I not done." The aide goes back to the group and Patty comes to sit beside her after a few minutes. Patty enjoys singing the songs and knows all of the finger and hand movements. When asked to choose a song, Patty can now say "Spider song" and is enthusiastic as they sing her selection. She talks to the aide next to her about "The spider eating her up." The aide tries to redirect her attention to the group. Patty leans over on the aide and lays down on her lap. Her attention and interest in the activity have ended after three short songs. The children now have a book time, where they can look at books in small clusters. Patty grabs a book and throws it against the wall. The other children look at Patty. She runs over to the housekeeping area, grabs the doll, and throws it down.

Utilizing the Supportive Play Model

In this section we highlight the components of the SPM that were used to identify the developmental issues that interfere with Patty's progress in this group. We suggest that you use the SPM chart provided at the end of Chapter 2 as if you were a member of the team that is observing and reviewing Patty's development. Record the data you gather from the background information and the observation section. Then read the following sections, which summarize the steps of the process of the staff and foster parents completing the chart. Remember, you would have more information had you actually been working with the child and you would also feel more prepared to make interpretations and use your clinical judgment. Nevertheless, the exercise will help you to feel more prepared to use the SPM with a real child in the future.

Section I: Cover Sheet

When filling out the *Cover Sheet* highlight the foster mother's concern about Patty's development, especially her aggression towards her brother and her disorganized use of materials. The school staff, however, have not observed any aggression toward other children at the program. Staff concerns that could be noted on the *Cover Sheet* include Patty's inability to settle with materials or complete a task and her rough handling of the materials, particularly doll figures. Additionally, transition times are difficult for Patty, often resulting in resistance or tantrums. The teachers feel that sometimes Patty "gets lost in her play" with dolls and they are unsure how to redirect her.

Child: Sections II, III, IV

To summarize your input from several observations and discussions, underline and code *Section II: Observational Impressions* and put a star at the most relevant working theme in each devel-

opmental area. Next, list key observations in *Section III: Skills and Outstanding Characteristics Observed*. Underline the relevant items in *Section IV: Characteristic Patterns Limiting Play*. The following section provides a developmental analysis from the observations and team discussions in the areas of self/social/emotional, motor/self-help, communicative/language, cognition, play skills, and play themes. After reading this section, return to your chart and make any appropriate changes or additions.

SELF/SOCIAL/EMOTIONAL Patty continues to work on themes related to constancy, attachment, and autonomy. She is ambivalent about trusting adults and her own self-sufficiency, which renders her rather insecure and unstable. She is still very toddler-like in her interactions. Her working theme in the self/social/emotional area is deemed to be at Level 2.

Patty appears to have a glimmer of an awareness of herself, her peers, and their impact on her in the classroom. However, she is listening more to their exchanges as she moves from one activity to the next and often watches how the other children use the materials. She can then be seen trying to imitate what she has observed. Her difficulty with self-regulation often results in extremes of emotional response. She shows abrupt changes of mood that are reported to be even more marked at home. In the classroom, this is usually exhibited at transition time or when the schedule and routine of the day are different. Patty can still be described as impulsive, but when the adults can explain to her the reason to wait or stop, she can usually modulate her behavior appropriately. She displays a range of affect, and can be happy, angry, sad, and so forth.

MOTOR/SELF-HELP Patty currently exhibits mild delays in motor/self-help skills that are compounded by her impulsivity and lack of regard for safety. Her current working theme is Level 2, with scatters of skill into Level 3. Patty's activity level is poorly regulated, toddler-like, and an area of continued concern. This pattern is seen as situational rather than pervasive.

She is capable of using any of the gross motor equipment at school, but will stand and watch because she says that she does not want to "get my clothes dirty." She can dress and undress herself, shows definite clothes preferences, can button small buttons, and push snaps closed. Patty is competent with fine motor skills. She can complete 8–10-piece interlocking puzzles with ease and uses different writing implements adaptively. Patty enjoys using magic markers and tries to draw pictures of her family or her pets. Patty can use scissors and cut around objects with good control.

Patty has a hearty appetite. She will eat any food and often is unable to stop eating or drinking until she sees that the food or drink is gone.

Patty toilets independently and does not have accidents. She is fascinated with tooth brushing, and would use all of the toothpaste in the tube, if not monitored. Mrs. Jones has reported that Patty loves a bath and will empty a whole bottle of the bubble bath in the tub, if left to her own devices.

COMMUNICATIVE/LANGUAGE Patty has age-appropriate receptive language and delayed expressive language as indicated by testing. Her overall communicative/language working theme is at Level 2. She has been receiving speech and language therapy for the past 6 months, which is paid for by her public school. Her language is egocentric and still bears a private quality. The lack of investment in social interactions for their own sake is demonstrated by Patty using language mainly for the fulfillment of her own needs, particularly around objects and materials. She uses simple sentences to express herself, frequently omitting or using immature grammatical forms. Patty still is unable to express herself when she gets upset or angry, and yells, has temper tantrums, and/or retreats. Her problems attending and staying- on-task affect her ability to communicate. Patty is often moving from one area to the next, showing little interest in communicating unless it is around her use of an object or problem with the activity. She can follow a 2–3 step direction, even when she seems not to be listening. Patty will respond to an adult's question, sometimes even as she is moving on to another area, by shaking or nodding her head. Her peers get frustrated when she does not answer their questions or respond to their overtures. Patty will not talk about events at home, but will listen to the teacher's questions.

COGNITION The area of cognition, at working theme 2, is significantly affected by Patty's inability to stay with a task and see it to completion. Patty appears to be primarily a visual–spatial, and incidental learner. She is weak in concept formation, which means she cannot make the leap from her action-oriented learning to more symbolic or abstract learning. Process is still her focus when involved in an activity, while product and outcome are often irrelevant to her actions. This may suggest difficulty with constancy or an inability to hold an image in mind to serve as a referent. Her chaotic life experiences most likely have contributed to her difficulty finding organized outcomes.

Patty enjoys all of the puzzles in the classroom and may complete from six to eight a day. She can follow rules that are part of the daily routine. However, new situations are often challenging for her, and she may have a tantrum. Patty enjoys simple songs and rhymes. She can be heard singing some of the songs when she is in the housekeeping area. Patty knows at least 10 body parts and the names and genders of all her classmates. It is hard for Patty to listen when another child talks directly to her. She will typically look away or walk away. Patty likes short simple books that are read to her at home or in a one-on-one situation at school. She loses interest in books with a larger group of children.

PLAY SKILLS Patty's play reflects a preoccupation with sensory exploration and some growing interest in functional combinations and allorepresentational play. Her working theme in play skills is at Level 2. Sensory play often leads to overstimulation and disorganization, rather than pleasure in the manipulation of the materials for tension reduction.

Patty especially likes to play chasing games with her teacher. She enjoys running and being caught, as well as hiding and being found. She giggles with glee when other peers join in the game. Patty likes all sensory materials and enjoys playing in the sand box, moving, piling, and pouring the sand; this type of activity is successful when an adult is nearby to help support her, otherwise she may become disorganized and hyperactive. She sometimes intrudes on the other children's space, but can be redirected by the adult to stay in her own area or to "make room for John's truck." It is easiest for Patty to share from a common stock pile in sand play or water play activities, but she still needs adult assistance. She is extremely aware of equal portions for each child, making sure that she gets her share. She is focused on any differences that occur and has a temper tantrum when she does not think she is getting the same as another child. Sometimes Patty starts to prepare meals in the housekeeping area and feeds the teacher and the doll. Patty wears the dress-up clothes

and talks to the teacher while she feeds her, saying "Time to eat. Don't get dirty."

PLAY THEMES Patty's play themes are focused on messiness/cleanliness, hoarding/sharing, filling/dumping, impulsivity/regulation, and nurturing/destroying. This places her working theme at Level 2 for play themes. These themes may have their origin in her mother's great concern about cleanliness which outstrips Patty's readiness and ability. In efforts to conform to her mother she has relied on behaviors such as ritualizing, washing, and demanding. Because her external behaviors are inconsistent with her internal impulses, she experiences ambivalence and breaks in control. Her deep-seated feelings of deprivation, which may be related to her interrupted attachments, pervade her play themes.

Patty is using materials to explore all of the themes in different ways. She always helps clean up and wipe the tables, but has difficulty stopping this activity. Patty can play endlessly in water and likes to pour or spread the water on different surfaces. She also likes play dough and often starts with one shape and make duplicates until the quantity is gone. Patty has trouble putting materials away and ends up having a temper tantrum or escaping to another area when requested to do so.

Patty is beginning to participate in some housekeeping themes, including cooking, washing the baby, sweeping, and ironing. She has watched the other children do some of these activities and has imitated them at a later time. Patty can become aggressive when washing the doll, getting excited as she dunks it, and then holding it under the water. The teachers try to keep her calm while she participates in this activity and say to her "Patty, calm down" or "Washing baby is all done." At this time, Patty will become angry, throw the doll on the floor, and go to another area as she scowls at the teacher.

Patty does have nurturing times with the doll, changing its diapers and telling the doll "You are dry" as she holds it close to her. Patty is always testing her relationship and status with the adults in school. She seeks their attention and help mainly around issues that are important to her. When an adult makes a request, Patty often becomes oppositional and can easily get lost in this resistive behavior.

Family: Sections II, III, and IV

Using the *Observational Guide*, fill in *Section III: General Description for the Family*. Then underline the appropriate items in *Section IV: Characteristic Patterns Limiting Play* that relate to family. Use general background information and any additional information offered below to complete Section III and Section IV. Patty's foster mother transports her to school daily. Mrs. Jones is invested in the children's appearance. They are always immaculately groomed and dressed in good clothes. The foster mother is distressed by the children's visits to the biological mother. She complains that the children are always dirty when they return from the visits, and she worries that they have been exposed to drugs. Patty has gone through periods of fecal smearing, which were of great distress to Mrs. Jones.

Patty has always been a poor sleeper, which is also upsetting to Mrs. Jones. She wakes up crying several times a night, and the foster mother goes to her room to try and comfort her.

Mrs. Jones is well organized and articulate around the planning meetings for Patty with the school. She wants Patty to get what she needs and has worked with the family case worker to see that she receives these services.

Program: Sections II, III, and IV

Using the *Observational Guide*, fill in *Section III: General Descriptions for Program*. Next, underline appropriate items in *Section IV: Characteristic Patterns Limiting Play* that relate to the Program.

STAFF A head teacher, two teacher aides, and a volunteer grandmother are in the class every day. The staff are all committed to working with Patty, but are puzzled by her behaviors. They have met with the family case worker, who has explained Patty's background. The staff has no experience or information on children whose parents have been substance abusers. One of the aides, Mrs. Scott, has expressed a particular interest in Patty, so she tends to deal with her most of the time in the classroom.

The atmosphere created by the program staff is an accepting, developmental approach. The staff find the foster mother hard to talk to because sometimes she seems disinterested in Patty's problems or blames everything on her "addiction" problem. She has told the staff not to give Patty too many hugs, because she needs to grow up. This has puzzled the staff and caused some disagreement among the team. Repeated requests by the staff for Patty to wear play clothes, instead of good clothes, have met with lack of cooperation. This annoys the staff because they think that Patty is missing out on some activities and that this makes her feel the need to be compulsively clean. The staff can always tell the weekends that Patty has visited her biological mother. She is angry and more aggressive the following day.

PEERS There are sixteen other 3-year-olds in the group, equally split between boys and girls. Patty is one of the older children in the group. She is the only child with special needs in the group. This group tends to be a very active and verbal. The boys play a lot in the block building area and the girls prefer the housekeeping and art areas.

Her peers tend to give Patty a wide berth. They find her behavior erratic and unpredictable and are afraid of her. In the past, when children have made overtures to play with her, she has either grabbed their toys or tried to start a battle over something. The children have said that Patty does not share. They notice that she always stuffs her mouth full of food at snack time and tries to take their food. Several of the children refuse to sit at her table at snack time. During the other group times, the children accept Patty's distractability and wandering.

SPACE The group is housed in an old stone school building and uses a room that was formerly the gym with a stage. The large open area is divided into housekeeping, block building, art, and a table area. There is no area inside for large motor activities. The floors are hardwood, with an area rug in the block area. The ceilings are high, so the acoustics are poor. There is no quiet area or indoor gross motor area. There is no place to display the children's work. The storage area is in one corner of the room; the open shelves visible and cluttered looking. There is a bathroom off the main room. The outdoor playground is a large fenced-in, asphalt area.

TIME A set routine is followed each day. There is an opening group time, free play time, group art, music, and story time, and an outdoors play time. The group times tend to last from 15 to 20 minutes. The children all arrive and leave at the same time. Some of the children are brought to school by the Head Start van.

MATERIALS AND EQUIPMENT The materials and equipment are all in good condition, in spite of their heavy use. There is an especially large puzzle supply, but there are not many other fine motor games and activities (Lego, lotto, small figures, and so forth). There is only one small set of large building blocks, so the children often have to wait for a turn to use the materials. The housekeeping area is adequate and there is a nice supply of dress up clothes. The materials and equipment in the outdoor play area are sparse. There is a large open area with only one swing set. There are five tricycles, and these are always in use. The children tend to start their own chase games outside, and the staff try to expand upon these ideas. There are not adequate multisensory materials and activities available, either indoors or outside.

Section V: Discrepancy Analysis

After this review of skills, establishment of working themes, and specification of limiting factors, transfer the working themes to the *Discrepancy Analysis* (found at the end of the chart) so you can compare and contrast Patty's development against her Chronological Age Level (Level 3) and identify relative discrepancies among working themes (Self/Social/Emotional: Level 2, Motor/Self-Help: Level 2, Communicative/Language: Level 2, Cognitive: Level 2, Play Skills: Level 2, Play Themes: Level 2). Star the developmental areas in which staff members perceive significant scatter (all areas of development) and, finally, highlight significant discrepancy issues under Child, Family, and Program. This *Discrepancy Analysis* should provide insights into issues regarding Patty's current placement. You should consider the implications of this before moving to the next section. Now you are prepared to consider some suggestions we have generated along with the ideas that you have already formulated.

Patty's overall developmental profile shows a delay in the areas of social emotional, communicative/language, cognition, play skills, play themes, and motor/self-help, which are all at the working Level 2. Her pervasive feelings of deprivation, insatiability, and cleanliness/control issues are evident across her developmental profile. The emotional issues are at the crux of Patty's development, and her delays in this area interfere with all other developmental areas. She has attempted to make forays into more mature behavior, but tends to regress, suggesting a more toddler-like quality.

The limited use of language appears secondary to her emotional neediness. Her lack of vocabulary for experiences and objects outside of her immediate experience leaves her confounded in handling new concepts and dialogues. Linguistically, she has not crossed the threshold from the egocentricity of toddlerhood to a more independent world. Patty can understand more than she can express, but she has trouble linking action and words. Her activity level and tendency to become overexcited interfere with all that she tries to undertake. Patty's relatively strong receptive language skills are impeded by the delay in expressive language skills.

In spite of significant early delays in the motor/self-help area, Patty has made some good gains over the past year. The main concern at this time is that she lacks the opportunity to experiment and experience a variety of large motor activities due to the inappropriateness of the clothes that she wears to school and the overemphasis on cleanliness. Patty is also very competent in fine motor skills. She is willing to try all types of food but needs assistance in limiting the quantity and needs reassurance that there will be plenty.

Patty's overall cognitive functioning is affected by her short attention span, impulsivity, and poor investment in social interactions. Play skills are compromised by her delayed language skills, her lack of confidence, her poor attention span, and her lack of interest in socializing with her peers. Patty is dealing with play themes related to relationships, fears, anxieties about love/loss, and issues related to her own body competency. She easily loses control as she tries to explore areas that challenge her.

Patty's family situation is a complex one. The biological mother and the foster parents are both placing a claim on Patty. The foster mother's lack of information about the addiction and its impact on Patty has made it difficult for her to assess the real impact this has on her development.

The staff are eager to receive help concerning the issues related to Patty. There is disagreement among the staff about how to handle Patty. The staff all feel that Patty requires a great deal of staff attention and that this detracts from the needs of the other children. They resent what they perceive as the foster mother's lack of cooperation and feel that she is hindering Patty's progress.

The space is large and open, with a stage, high ceilings and a wood floor. There is no alternative location for storage. The acoustics are poor, and when a child is upset or the children are active, it is noisy. The outdoor space is unappealing. On hot days, it is too warm to play on the asphalt, so they often stay indoors. The group activity segments are too long for the 3-year-olds. There is no opportunity for the children to have active times interspersed with group times.

The materials are limited in number and variety, both indoor and outside. The children get bored with the small selection. The teachers use many creative materials in the art area, but there is only one set of blocks, so the teachers have to plan a rotating schedule to allow all of the children the opportunity to use this area. There is little to do outdoors, and the children tend to get overexcited and vie for the few materials that are available.

Section VI and Section VII

At this point of the SPM process, you should keep Patty's developmental discrepancies and the limiting factors that are inhibiting her play in mind and proceed to underline the items in *Section VI: Intervention Goals/Facilitating Techniques* that will be most useful in the intervention plan. Then, write some of your ideas to help Patty in *Section VII: Individualized Supportive Play Adaptations and Experiences*. Then read the following narrative that reflects a composite of these two sections. Check your worksheet at this point and make adaptations as necessary.

SELF/SOCIAL/EMOTIONAL Central to promoting Patty's development in the self/social/emotional areas is a pattern of consistent caregiving by the adults in her group. Adults who respond in similar fashion in their interactions with Patty, who themselves are secure enough to be able to ride through Patty's storminess without taking her explosions personally, as well as a program design that uses predictable routines, are all crucial to the plan. Patty needs many repeated experiences of adult constancy for her to begin to build some real trust. This will be a challenge to the adults working with her because, even as she improves, her sense of self will be fragile and regression may be frequent at first. She will need the adults to stand by her in these times of regression and refuel her in direct and physical ways (holding, rocking) much as one might do with a young toddler.

This is an important area for Patty because her fears and anxieties affect and compromise her willingness to try to use a variety of materials, participate in activities, and engage in social opportunities with both adults and peers. As an outcome of the analysis of Patty's needs, the team has recommended that a play therapist work individually with Patty and consult with parents and staff. In a play therapy setting, Patty can work on the many compromising issues, feelings, and concerns that intrude on her ability to experience, experiment, and enjoy her environment. She can benefit from many one-to-one practice experiences that can serve as a dress rehearsal for the larger setting in which she must function. An individual aide, Mrs. Scott, will be assigned to work with Patty. A great deal of individual attention in the classroom for a while will assist Patty with her play, interactions, appropriate use of materials, and with the expressions of her feelings. The adults must serve as a bridge to assist Patty in associating her feelings and actions with words. An available adult can reflect and help Patty articulate her feelings when she throws down the doll—"Oh, the baby went down so hard!" Building on the relationship with the teacher aide, Mrs. Scott, will serve, as a source of motivation to pull Patty to new activities. Simple picture books that relate to feelings, family, and basic experiences should be available for Mrs. Scott to read with Patty.

The staff must understand that Patty will have periods when she is scared, ambivalent, and regresses, but the adult must remain calm and provide a secure, accepting environment. If Patty lunges for materials that another child has, Mrs. Scott should be nearby to verbalize—"Paul is using that now. You can use it after Paul." If Patty destroys another child's structure, Mrs. Scott can help Patty pick it up and rebuild it and verbalize how this destruction upsets the other child. These behaviors may be repeated frequently and will need consistency from all of the staff to make a lasting impact. The other staff should continue their activities during these episodes and explain to the other children, for example, "Patty is having a hard time right now. We are going to clean up, and sing," rather than allowing the class to come to a complete halt.

MOTOR/SELF-HELP The facilitating techniques in this area should focus on activity level, adherence to safety, and concern about impulse control. Patty should try a variety of fine motor materials and be allowed to experiment with their properties, connections, relationships, first in a one-to-one situation with Mrs. Scott and then within the group. This will allow her to have an adult assist her to stay with a task, finish it, and realize the value of completion. This may require the establishment and clear definition of the physical boundaries that are safe through verbally interpreting what is happening or is about to occur, and what should happen.

Patty needs to have many more opportunities and experiences with all types of gross motor materials. A large ceiling beam in the corner of the room would provide the opportunity for hanging equipment (swing, hammock) to allow all of the children, and particularly Patty, the opportunity to engage in some vestibular stimulation that may facilitate her overall organization in selecting and using materials and enhance her ability to attend long enough to complete a task. It will be important to monitor these activities so that Patty does not become either overstimulated or isolate herself.

Patty may benefit from a small trampoline with a stabilizing handle or other weight-bearing activities that could serve as a calming influence. More appropriate clothes would allow Patty the freedom to climb, swing, slide, and jump, use and expand her good gross motor skills, and practice using her body appropriately in space. Patty's impulsivity and lack of regard for safety are significant impediments in her exploration of her environment. The adults must clearly verbalize class rules and safety considerations and ask Patty to repeat some of these important rules to ensure her understanding and internalization of these important concepts. This will help govern her access to open spaces and the use of a variety of large motor equipment and activities.

COMMUNICATIVE/LANGUAGE Adults' communication to Patty should be clearly stated. It is important to engage Patty before speaking to her and to wait for and expect a response from her. The modeling of the sequence "stop, attend, listen, and respond" is important to enable Patty to understand the intent, reciprocity, overall value, and power of communication. The staff and parents should be able to schedule a regular consultation time with the public school speech–language pathologist to receive tips and strategies on how to assist Patty in more successful communication. These strategies can be practiced in the individual language sessions first and must be eventually transferred to the larger group. The speech–language pathologist may introduce a peer to Patty's therapy session to allow her to practice her skills, which will help in the transfer back to the classroom.

Patty's participation in activities and games in which she can practice concepts, following directions, simple interactions, and turn taking is important. This could first be implemented with an adult as the play partner (perhaps with the teacher aide during speech and language sessions), and then in the classroom with a teacher, eventually adding other children. Perhaps the teacher could say, "Show me the game you played with Marianne (speech pathologist)." Patty's interest in songs and rhymes should be carried over to other activities. For example, her teachers could sing during transition, "This is the way we clean up our toys," and use the music as the message, the organizer, and a way to sustain Patty's attention through a transition. Adults can model connected speech for Patty that is slightly more complex than her utterance. For example, when she says "Ball falling," the teacher could say "Yes, the ball is falling."

COGNITIVE The adults should assume that Patty has the potential for average or better cognitive development. As they establish their expectations, they should not talk down to her or assume she cannot understand. Since Patty appears to be a visual–spatial and incidental learner, Patty's interest in fine motor materials also presents an opportunity to expand upon a variety of skills. This will increase her repertoire of interests, successes, and provide opportunities for completion of the task. A block-building activity that has different props, such as vehicles and road signs, could utilize some of Patty strong skills and interests while exploring rules and social expectations within the context of her play scenes (cows sleep in the barn, cars stop at red lights). She can build a structure and leave it up for the next day to add to or break down when she is ready. In a sand table, Patty could use other props to build a farm or construction site and develop a story about the sand structure. These activities will allow Patty control over materials to build and break down as she wishes, but also to develop plans that are meaningful to her.

PLAY SKILLS Patty can benefit from different opportunities and materials to both expand and solidify her play skills. The play equipment in the housekeeping area can be rotated in order to expand on the children's play topics. These could include stores, post office, doctor play, pet store, and a play bus for trips. Mrs.

Scott must be an active participant in the play to serve both as a model and a supporter of the play. In these different settings Patty can be helped to use the concrete props to play and also to observe the play of the other children for ideas and elaboration of her basic story lines. This may require a great deal of repetition, and the expansion may be slow and tedious. The other children can be encouraged through verbal support to include or tolerate the slower pace of Patty's play. During play with sensory materials, Mrs. Scott can offer Patty different props in order to give the play a conceptual framework and focus, so that it becomes more productive and satisfying. For example, during water play, she could introduce a water wheel, cups, funnels, or boat. Patty currently participates in a lot of onlooker play and, hopefully, she can be moved on to first tolerating playing next to peers and then entering into some simple play exchanges with them.

PLAY THEMES The stressors caused by multiple caregivers and multiple placements has led to the aggressive themes that pervade Patty's play. The play therapist can do more interpreting of the play in the individual sessions with Patty than the teacher or parent may feel comfortable doing. Acceptance of the play, as well as some gentle expansion and elaboration, will assist Patty with her confusions and fears. As a result of regular meetings with the play therapist, the staff have come to understand the reason for and need for Patty's perseverative activities (wiping the table) which help her to bind and contain some of her anxiety and feel more competent and in control. With this understanding they will feel more comfortable to step in, accepting but redirecting these activities. For example, they may say, "Nice job, Patty. Now it is time for books and you can pick which of these two books you want to read. Table wiping is all done." Different play props that would encourage more productive exploration of her world could include various sizes and types of building blocks, clay, a variety of dramatic play items (beauty parlor, doctor play), different types of doll play (washing, feeding), figure puzzles (boy and girl), action figures or small doll house figures, and various free-form art activities (gluing, cutting). This will allow Patty to build and knock down; roll, punch, and smash; nurture and punish; play out different roles; and create her own designs. Puppets could serve as safe messengers of feelings, questions, and a way to practice beginning interaction skills with adults and peers. Simple hide-and-seek games, as well as games of tag will allow Patty to experience some of the earlier stages in personality development and relationship building that she has missed. Such games will assure her of the permanence and constancy of people and allow her to explore themes of closeness and distance, losing and finding, and oneness and separateness.

FAMILY The foster parents need assistance in obtaining accurate information on prenatal drug exposure and its impact on later development. They should also be helped to understand that all undesirable behavior cannot be attributed to "the addiction." The family service case worker can provide direct information to the parents on the status of the biological mother, help determine if adoption is realistic and, if so, determine the time line. The foster parents need immediate assistance with Patty's sleep regulation because it is directly affecting all members of the household. Both the therapist and the teachers can share ideas with the parents that could alleviate the bedtime problems. Mrs. Jones needs support in becoming more relaxed about the children's cleanliness.

STAFF Children with volatile behavior like Patty's are quite provocative. Staff need help in accepting the intensity of their responses to Patty and then knowing what to do with their own feelings. Once their feelings are recognized, it will be easier to move ahead and plan the intervention techniques. The staff must collaborate in order to reach agreement on philosophy, approach, and techniques, and to gain an overall understanding of Patty's early history and how it relates to her current functioning. Any myths or misconceptions need to be allayed at this time. Patty's behavior can be very intense and irritating. The staff must learn how to refrain from overreacting to Patty's behavior, but provide a response that is firm, consistent, and supportive of her burgeoning self. The play therapist can be helpful in assisting the staff with understanding the issues that are pervading and limiting Patty's play. This will help the staff feel comfortable about the themes that arise in the classroom, talk about what they feel they can handle, and what should be dealt with in the individual play session with the therapist.

Mrs. Scott, who has been assigned as Patty's primary adult, can serve as the bridge in Patty's play, first as the recipient, then the play partner, then as a means to introduce other peers into the play. Because Mrs. Scott's time will be filled with Patty's needs, the public school agreed at the Planning and Placement Team (PPT) meeting to provide an additional aide for the classroom so that Mrs. Scott could focus on Patty. Mrs. Scott should be available to talk Patty through the activities and give feedback to her about what she is doing—"You are playing with the play dough"; " The doll is lying in the bed"; "The puzzle is all finished." Mrs. Scott can continue to sit by Patty during the group time to help her sustain an interest and expand on these activities. The play therapist can endorse the important role of the head teacher in overseeing the total plan and supervision of the aide. The staff could use inservice training about the impact of cocaine on development. This information will help make the staff less fearful of Patty. The therapist may also be able to serve as a liaison between the staff and the foster mother around the issues of cleanliness, not giving Patty hugs, and so forth.

PEERS The staff should brainstorm to find a compatible peer or peers that can play effectively with Patty. This may be an older, confident, sturdy child. These compatible peers can join Patty one at a time, first in an individual session, perhaps with the speech pathologist or teacher aide, in simple games or sensory activities both indoors and outside. These are the times that Patty is most receptive to having other children in her space. Patty is frequently watching her peers so the staff can articulate (carefully) "You are watching Michael build that Lego building" or "Susie is making some pies with her play dough," with the goal of moving toward an interaction "Do you want to build a car like Alex?"

SPACE The space needs some alteration. The parents group or a fund raising project may provide finances to improve this aspect. Perhaps a professional group such as the Professional Acoustical Engineers would be willing to look at the space and make some simple inexpensive recommendations for making the space more appropriate for a group of busy 3-year-olds. More rugs on the floor and acoustical tiles placed on the walls would help to dampen the sound. Separate activity areas can be more clearly defined by shelves or rugs. An indoor gross motor space would be an important addition (putting a ceiling beam across one corner for hanging equipment). Slides, tunnels, and other climbing equipment would add an enriching dimension to the activity choices. The storage areas should be covered or closed to cut down on visual stimulation.

TIME AND MATERIALS AND EQUIPMENT The group times are too long and not interspersed with more active choices. The activity areas that are available are nicely presented, but there are not enough materials or adequate choices, so the children spend too much time waiting. More fine motor games, more building materials, and additional gross motor options should be available both indoors and outside. There should also be sensory materials available in the classroom and outside on a daily basis. The dramatic play area has some nice choices, but rotating cooking, workbench, doctor play, housekeeping, and beauty parlor, would provide richer opportunities for all the children, and help to give Patty the opportunity to expand her play scenes. The use of puppets and other stuffed animals would offer Patty additional options for her play and introduce topics of comfort and nurturance. Patty enjoys music, so musical instruments, hand gestures, and playing with rhymes would all be helpful variations on a favorite activity. More activity options with the increased availability of materials both indoors and outside would provide more opportunities for positive interactions. Patty may still need to get up and move around, and the adults can say to the children "It is hard for Patty to sit for very long right now."

Review of Initial Observation

With these facilitating techniques in mind and a more indepth understanding of Patty's needs from working through the steps of the SPM, let's take a brief look at an incident from the first vignette and see how the situation might have been handled differently. Write out your thoughts about this segment and then compare your ideas to the interpretation that follows the vignette segment.

Mrs. Jones waves good-bye, and Patty returns the waves and goes directly to the housekeeping corner. She scans the area to see what is available and touches many of the items. She looks at what items the other children are using, then moves on to another area and repeats these same behaviors. She eventually returns to the housekeeping area because several of the children have left to do an art project. Patty picks up the doll and slams it back in the crib saying "Bad baby, no more crying." The teacher is standing nearby and asks her why the baby has been bad. Patty says "Baby wet her pants, all dirty." She picks up the baby bottle and jams it in the baby's mouth. She lifts the doll up again and jerks the leg, so it drops off. Patty has a panicked look on her face, and the teacher comes over to pop the doll's leg back on.

Patty appears quite agitated in this scene, which may reflect her separation anxiety and uneasiness acclimating to school. Her rather frantic activity suggests both discharge of and distraction from this uncomfortable feeling. Transitions are typically difficult for children, and adult guidance and little rituals help contain anxiety for children in constructive ways. A greeting and structured opening exercise may have helped Patty feel more safe, secure, and focused.

Left to her own devices, as we observe, Patty's play seemed to reflect her own concerns about managing bodily functions and impulses (toileting, getting dirty). Given the seeming proximity of the play scene to having separated from Mrs. Jones, it could be speculated that her play projects concerns about behavior that could keep Mrs. Jones at emotional distance and bears a coloring of projected anger and self-blame. The rather rough handling of the doll may give us a clue as to how Patty remembers her own early care. Dislodging the doll's leg would probably frighten, if not panic, all of the children. Not only is this the obvious worry of having done harm with possible fear of punishment for breaking the doll, but also the concern most children of this age have about the integrity and solidness of their own bodies.

Although there is no one right way to have more helpfully managed their interaction, more structure and guidance at least may have helped Patty stay better organized. The teacher might have suggested to Patty that together they find out why the baby is crying and reintervene with more appropriate ministrations. The teacher may have assured Patty that the baby can be rediapered and her clothes washed, and that Patty, being a big girl, can go to the bathroom herself and put on a smock to help keep clean. Should there be other problems, she can use her words to get help. As for the dismembered doll, assurance that there was no catastrophe and that the doll is fixable might have put the matter in perspective. Assurance that Patty had a complete and well functioning body may have addressed the hypothetical unspoken concern as well.

Supportive Play Model Adaptation

At the time of the return observation in 4 months, there are some significant changes in Patty's behavior following the implementation of the SPM process. The staff and foster parents have altered their approaches and expectations of Patty. Her progress is slow, but small inroads are being made into the many factors that are impeding her development.

Patty has been in individual play therapy for 2 months. The staff and the foster mother still see aggressive play with the dolls and other materials, but they feel that this has diminished. Patty is still very vigilant about who gets what, making certain that she gets her share, but the staff are now verbalizing more to help her monitor this worry and reassure her that, for example, "There will be plenty of juice for everyone." The staff are realizing that a great deal of repetition, consistency, and cues to anticipate transitions are important in dealing with Patty. The primary aide, Mrs. Scott, has helped to stabilize Patty in the setting and is now beginning to read her moods, so that she is able to help verbalize and anticipate some of the issues before they develop. In this scene, a commentary has been added in brackets to the observation to offer possible explanations related to the observation.

In this visit we find Patty in the new indoor gross motor area. She is seated in the swing and Mrs. Scott is pushing her while she sings a song about Patty swinging. Patty has a big smile on her face. She continues to be dressed in "party clothes" but Mrs. Jones has yielded and allows her to wear tennis shoes to school. Another child is waiting for the swing. Mrs. Scott alerts Patty that after five more swings it will be Matt's turn. She asks Patty to join her in calling out the numbers of each push and swing. *[At this point Mrs. Scott recognizes Patty's tendency to have trouble with transitions and provides her with a specific preparatory cue to help her manage the transition.]* After the five pushes, Mrs. Scott stops the swing and Patty is helped off the swing and shown the shaving cream activity at a nearby table. Patty goes over to a table where four other children are spreading their shaving cream on the table. She watches what her peers are doing. Mrs. Scott helps Patty into a smock, saying that she needs to cover her dress. Patty suddenly tries to put her hand in a design that another child has made on the table. Mrs. Scott reaches for Patty's hand, redirects it to her own shaving cream, and says "Patty, here is your shaving cream." Patty places both hands in her shaving cream and wildly moves her hands in circles, immersed in the activity. The other children stop to watch Patty's frenzied move-

ments. Mrs. Scott sits beside Patty and slowly moves her hands in her own shaving cream, while singing a simple song softly to the motions. This causes Patty to stop and look at Mrs. Scott. She starts alternating patterns with Patty that corresponds to stopping and starting the singing. A huge smile breaks out on Patty's face and the other children all relax and return to their activity. Another child joins Patty and Mrs. Scott in their game. Patty waits her turn and looks to Mrs. Scott and the peer to take their turns when the song stops. *[Patty's impulsive tendencies persist, but now the aide is more attuned and vigilant to intervene. Physical cuing, including firm touch, physical proximity, modeling, and the use of singing as an organizing and relaxing support all help to reduce Patty's impulsivity. On another level, Mrs. Scott uses social engagement and turn taking to create a rhythm that supports Patty's organization and control, but also prevents her from disrupting the group. This saves her from, once again, frightening her peers through her out-of-control behavior.]* .

Patty stays with the shaving cream for 10 minutes, spreading the cream up to her elbows. *[This extended play suggests an increased tolerance for sensory materials, less anxiety, and a more balanced position around the issue of cleanliness and messiness. Engaging in messy play has afforded Patty opportunities to internalize a code of cleanliness at her own pace and without excessive demands from the environment. Thus she relies less on defenses such as ritualizing, washing, and demanding to bind her anxiety.]* It is time for cleanup and snack, so Mrs. Scott says to Patty "It is time to clean up for snack. We are going to have apple juice and blueberry muffins today." Patty starts to cry, which quickly accelerates to a short period of screaming. The remainder of the class proceeds to sing the cleanup song while Mrs. Scott tells Patty that she will be able to play with the shaving cream tomorrow. She takes Patty aside and reminds her that she needs to be calm to join the group for snack. Patty darts from Mrs. Scott and smears shaving cream on the classroom wall. Mrs. Scott firmly stops her, saying "Patty, we need to clean the wall together and you need to wash up for snack." She leads her screaming to the bathroom to get paper towels. The crying gradually reduces to a whimper as Patty wipes the wall with paper towels with Mrs. Scott. Then they return to the bathroom where Mrs. Scott is nearby to verbalize the cleanup steps for Patty. "Let's wash off the shaving cream, dry our hands, and go to the snack table." Patty moves through this sequence and goes to the snack table. Mrs. Scott sits next to Patty and verbalizes the progress of the snack activity: "The apple juice is coming, Alan is pouring his now. Your turn is after Alan." Patty pours herself some juice and reaches for the muffin basket while listening to a child talk about a popular TV program. She nods enthusiastically and offers several brief comments that are related to a different TV show she has watched. *[Mrs. Scott's firm physical contact without harshness and direct verbal statements are helping Patty experience much more success within the classroom routine. She is clear, does not evoke feelings of failure in Patty, and intervenes before there is a total loss of control. Recognizing that part of Patty's distress in stopping the shaving cream activity may relate to her sensitivity about losses, Mrs. Scott verbalizes that the shaving cream will be available tomorrow for her. Mrs. Scott does not get caught up in Patty's screaming, but instead focuses on the problem; she helps Patty resolve the issue. The other staff help the remainder of the children keep within their routine so that they do not become overfocused on Patty's crying and so that the tension does not spread. With highly directed help, Patty is able to reorganize herself and rejoin her peers. She participates in snack time and is able to attune to the general topic of discussion with her peers.]*

Section VII: Results and Outcomes

There is an overall feeling of relief in the classroom (adults and peers) and with the foster parents in their management of Patty at home. Patty is less impulsive and unpredictable. She uses adults more appropriately and the adults have become more responsive and able to anticipate situations that previously would have resulted in a crisis. It can be speculated that Patty has become more confident in anticipating what is expected of her and that she views the environment as more satisfying, more predictable, and generally more supportive and accepting.

There is a larger and more challenging range of activities and materials available in the classroom. The addition of the indoor gross motor area has provided the opportunity for a variety of equipment (rope ladders, hammocks, swings) to provide new experiences and opportunities for all of the children. The staff have also included sensory materials both indoors and outdoors as daily activity choices. There are more building materials and other play props to assist with Patty's growing interest in different play skills and themes.

Important support personnel have assisted in the individualization of Patty's program. Mrs. Scott, as the individual teacher aide, plays an important role with Patty in the classroom. She serves as the primary liaison in the use of materials, in activities, and in interaction with other adults and children. The play therapist sees Patty individually and also meets with the foster mother, Mrs. Jones, and the school staff on a regular basis to offer support and clarification of issues that relate to all aspects of Patty's emerging development. The therapist has also assisted the foster parents to understand issues related to Patty's emotional state, ambivalence about cleanliness, sleep disturbance, the relationship of the mother's drug abuse, and the reality of Patty being available for adoption. The speech-language pathologist has assisted both the parents and the staff in understanding the complexity of Patty's language issues in the framework of her initial total developmental profile.

SUMMARY

The SPM has provided a process for the staff and the foster parents to both understand and then support Patty's development. She is showing some slow but steady changes that, at this point, are more qualitative than quantitative. She is refining existing skills and acquiring missing skills which contribute to stabilizing her developmental base. Particularly she missed many important building blocks in the social emotional domain. She started life in a state of physiological withdrawal and emotional turmoil. She has battled to make sense out of an ever-changing environment and relationships, as she has been moved to three foster homes. This has affected all other areas of development as she has sought to organize her world and understand the role that adults should play in that world. Patty is gaining trust in the adults so that she can reach out to the environment with more confidence and decreased anxiety. This emerging trust is allowing Patty to relinquish her need for excessive control and vigilance, thus allieviating her anxiety and allowing her to participate more fully and freely in the world around her. The aide has served as a play partner to provide a commentary to assist Patty to return to or maintain a play theme rather than abandoning the scene. Patty is more organized and is able to move to more elaborate play themes. Before the facilitating strategies were implemented, her play was laced with shadowing and darting and questions of loss and reunion.

Placing Patty in a large group when she has not had the experience of attaching to any significant adult figure was the crowning blow for this vulnerable 3-year-old. She was thrown into yet another setting where she had to deal with an environment with demands that exceeded her capacity and readiness. Mrs. Scott has been an important nurturing and guiding presence for this child. She has helped Patty beyond basic physical care, but she has also experienced ambivalence toward this difficult child. Children who have such serious attachment and loss issues are often self-defeating when an adult makes an earnest effort to build a meaningful attachment. Children may break the relationship themselves, just to avoid the disappointment of the adult disappearing from their life at some future point.

When working with children who are this easily regressive, another issue is that their breaks in control may create anxiety in the other children in the group. Since they have only recently begun to control their anger, aggression, and wish to mess and smear, the out-of-control child is a reminder of their own easily out-of-control behavior. The adults in the setting need to help the out-of-control child to regain control, and also reassure the remainder of the children that the problem is temporary and that the child is trying, but needs an adult's help.

In this case and in similar cases the SPM serves as a powerful change agent, one that does not just offer opportunities for child-oriented change, but assists in reframing the total environment that surrounds the child, including the peers, adults, and the caregivers. What results is a robust, developmentally appropriate setting for children with such confusing and complex profiles and, more important, a setting where any child can grow and prosper.

REFERENCES

Abel, E. L. (1984). Prenatal effects of alcohol. *Drug and Alcohol Dependence, 14,* 1–10.

Abel, E. L. (1984). *Fetal alcohol syndrome and fetal alcohol effects.* New York: Plenum.

Abel, E. L. (1990). *Fetal alcohol syndrome.* Oradell, NJ: Medical Economics Books.

Abel, E. L., & Sokol, R. J. (1987). Incidence of fetal alcohol syndrome and economic impact of FAS-related anomalies. *Drug and Alcohol Dependence, 19,* 51–70.

Adams, E. H., Gfroerer, J .C., & Rouse, B. A. (1989). Epidemiology of substance abuse including alcohol and cigarette smoking. *Annals of the New York Academy of Sciences, 562,* 14–20.

Allen, L. F., Palomares, R. S., DeForest, P., Sprinkle, B., & Reynolds, C. R. (1991). The effects of intrauterine cocaine exposure: Transient or teratogenic? *Archives of Clinical Neuropsychology, 6*(3), 133–146.

Alliance to end childhood lead poisoning. (1993). *Questions and answers about lead poisoning.* Washington, DC: Author.

Aram, D. M., & Hall, N. E. (1989). Longitudinal follow-up of children with preschool communication disorders: Treatment implications. *School Psychology Review, 18*(4), 487–501.

Aram, D. M., & Nation, J. E. (1980). Preschool language disorders and subsequent language and academic difficulties. *Journal of Communication Disorders, 13,* 159–170.

Barkley, R. A. (1988). The effects of methylphenidate on the interactions of preschool ADHD children with their mothers. *Journal of the American Academy of Child and Adolescent Psychiatry, 27*(3), 336–341.

Barkley, R. A., DuPaul, G. J., & McMurray, M. B. (1990). Comprehensive evaluation of attention deficit disorder with and without hyperactivity as defined by research criteria. *Journal of Consulting and Clinical Psychology, 58,* 775–789.

Bates, E., Bretherton, I., & Snyder, L. (1988). *From first words to grammar: Individual differences and dissociable mechanisms.* Cambridge: Cambridge University Press.

Batshaw, M. L., & Perret , Y. M. (1992). Good nutrition, poor nutrition. In M. L. Batshaw & Y. M. Perret (Eds.), *Children with disabilities* (pp. 171–196). Baltimore: Paul H. Brookes.

Becker, M., Warr-Leeper, G. A., & Leeper, H. A., Jr. (1990). Fetal alcohol syndrome: A description of oral motor, articulatory, short-term memory, grammatical, and semantic abilities. *Journal of Communication Disorders, 23,* 97–124.

Beitchman, J. H., Hood, J., Rochon, J., & Peterson, M. (1989). Empirical classification of speech/language impairment in children: II.

Behavioral characteristics. *Journal of the American Academy of Child and Adolescent Psychiatry, 28*(1), 118–123.

Beitchman, J. H., & Peterson, M. (1986). Disorders of language, communication, and behavior in mentally retarded children. *Psychiatric Clinics of North America, 9*, 689–698.

Bellinger, D. C., & Needleman, H. L. (1983). Lead and the relationship between maternal and child intelligence. *Journal of Pediatrics, 102*(4), 523–527.

Belman, A. L. (1992). Acquired immunodeficiency syndrome and the child's central nervous system. *Pediatric Clinics of North America, 39*, 691–714.

Belman, A. L., Diamond, G., Dickson, D., Horoupian, D., Llena, J., Lantos, G., & Rubinstein, A. (1988). Pediatric acquired immunodeficiency syndrome. *American Journal of Diseases of Children, 142*, 29–35.

Belman, A. L., Ultmann, M. H., Horoupian, D., Novick, B., Spiro, A. J., Rubinstein, A., Kurtzberg, D., & Cone-Wesson, B. (1985). Neurological complications in infants and children with acquired immune deficiency syndrome. *Annals of Neurology, 18,* 560–566.

Berry, R. K. (1988). Home care of the child with AIDS. *Pediatric Nursing, 14,* 341–344.

Biederman, J., Faraone, S. V., Keenan, K., Knee, D., & Tsuang, M. T. (1990). Family–genetic and psychosocial risk factors in DSM-III attention deficit disorder. *Journal of the American Academy of Child and Adolescent Psychiatry, 29*, 526–533.

Bingol, N., Fuchs, M., Diaz, V., Stone, R. K., & Gromisch, D. S. (1987). Teratogenicity of cocaine in humans. *The Journal of Pediatrics, 110*, 93–96.

Bingol, N., Schuster, C., Fuchs, M., Iosub, S., Turner, G., Stone, R. K., & Gromisch, D. S. (1987). The influence of socioeconomic factors on the occurrence of fetal alcohol syndrome. *Advances in Alcohol and Substance Abuse, 6*, 105–118.

Blumenthal, R. (May, 1992). Statement of Richard Blumenthal, Attorney General of Connecticut, before the Senate Committee on Governmental Affairs. Hartford, CT.

Borghgraef, M., Fryns, J. P., & van den Berghe, H. (1990). The female and the fragile X syndrome: Data on clinical and psychological findings in 7 fra (X) carriers. *Clinical Genetics, 37*, 341–346.

Brouwers, P., Belman, A. L., & Epstein, L. G. (1991). Central nervous system involvement: Manifestations and evaluation. In P. A. Pizzo & C. M. Wilfert (Eds.), *Pediatric AIDS: The challenge of HIV infection in infants, children and adolescents.* Baltimore: Williams & Wilkins.

Burd, L., & Martsolf, J. T. (1989). Fetal alcohol syndrome: Diagnosis and syndromal variability. *Physiology and Behavior, 46,* 39–43.

Burroughs, M. H., & Edelson, P. J. (1991). Medical care of the HIV-infected child. *Pediatric Clinics of North America, 38*(1), 45–67.

Butler, C., Hittelman, J., & Hauger, S. B. (1991). Approach to neurodevelopmental and neurologic complications in pediatric HIV infection. *Journal of Pediatrics, 119* (Suppl. 1, Part 2), S41–S46.

Cantwell, D. P., & Baker, L. (1987a). Clinical significance of childhood communication disorders: Perspectives from a longitudinal study. *Journal of Child Neurology, 2,* 257–264.

Cantwell, D. P., & Baker, L., (1987b). Prevalence and type of psychiatric disorder and developmental disorders in three speech and language groups. *Journal of Communication Disorders, 20*(2), 151–160.

Cantwell, D. P., & Baker, L. (1987c). Psychiatric symptomatology in language-impaired children: A comparison. *Journal of Child Neurology, 2*, 128–133.

Cantwell, D. P., & Baker, L. (1991). Association between attention deficit-hyperactivity disorder and learning disorders. *Journal of Learning Disabilities, 24*(2), 88–95.

Chasnoff, I. J. (1988). Drug use in pregnancy: Parameters of risk. *The Pediatric Clinics of North America, 35*(6), 1403–1412.

Chasnoff, I. J., & Griffith, D. R. (1989). Cocaine: Clinical studies of pregnancy and the newborn. *Annals of the New York Academy of Sciences, 562,* 260–266.

Chasnoff, I. J., Griffith, D. R., MacGregor, S., Dirkes, K., & Burns, K. A. (1989). Temporal patterns of cocaine use in pregnancy. *Journal of the American Medical Association, 261*(12), 1741–1744.

Chasnoff, I. J., Landress, H. J., & Barrett, M. E. (1990). The prevalence of illicit-drug or alcohol use during pregnancy and discrepancies in mandatory reporting in Pinellas County, Florida. *The New England Journal of Medicine, 322*, 1202–1206.

Children's Defense Fund. (1992). *The State of American's Children.* Washington, DC: Author.

Chu, S. Y., Buehler, J. W., Oxtoby, M. J., & Kilbourne, B. W. (1991). Impact of the human immunodeficiency virus epidemic on mortality in children, United States. *Pediatrics, 87*(6), 806–810.

Church, M. W. (1987). Chronic in utero alcohol exposure affects auditory function in rats and in humans. *Alcohol, 4*, 231–239.

Clarren, S. K., & Smith, D. W. (1978). The fetal alcohol syndrome. *The New England Journal of Medicine, 298*(19), 1063–1067.

Coles, C. D., Brown, R. T., Smith, I. E., Platzman, K. A., Erickson, S., & Falek, A. (1991). Effects of prenatal alcohol exposure at school age. I. Physical and cognitive development. *Neurotoxicology and Teratology, 13*(4), 357–367.

Comings, D. E., & Comings, B. G. (1990). A controlled family history study of Tourette's syndrome. I: Attention-deficit hyperactivity disorder and learning disorders. *Journal of Clinical Psychiatry, 51*(7), 275–280.

Condini, A., Axia, G., Cattelan, C., D'Urso, M. R., Laverda, A. M., Viero, F., & Zacchello, F. (1991). Development of language in 18–30-month-old HIV-1-infected but not ill children. *AIDS, 5*(6), 735–739.

Conlon, C. J. (1992). New threats to development. Alcohol, cocaine, and AIDS. In M. L. Batshaw & Y. M. Peret (Eds.), *Children with Disabilities: A medical primer* (3rd ed., pp. 111–136). Baltimore: Paul H. Brookes.

Coplan, J., Gleason, J. R., Ryan, R., Burke, M. G., & Williams, M. L. (1982). Validation of an early language milestone scale in a high-risk population. *Pediatrics, 70*(5), 677–683.

Davidson, C. E. (1991). Attachment issues and the cocaine exposed dyad. *Child and Adolescent Social Work Journal, 8*(4), 269–284.

Davis, D. R. (1988). Nutrition in the prevention and reversal of mental retardation. In F. J. Menolascino & J. A. Stark (Eds.), *Preventive and curative intervention in mental retardation* (pp. 177–222). Baltimore: Paul H. Brookes.

Day, N. L., Richardson, G., Robles, N., Sambamoorthi, U., Taylor, P., Scher, M., Stoffer, D., Jasperse, D., & Cornelius, M. (1990). Effect of prenatal alcohol exposure on growth and morphology of offspring at 8 months of age. *Pediatrics, 85*(5), 748–752.

Diagnostic and statistical manual of mental disorders (DSM-III). (1980). Washington, DC: American Psychiatric Association.

Diamond, G. W., Kaufman, J., Belman, A. L., Cohen, L., Cohen, H. J., & Rubenstein, A. (1987). Characterization of cognitive functioning in a subgroup of children with congenital HIV infection. *Archives of Clinical Neuropsychology, 2*, 245–256.

Dixon, S. D., & Bejar, R. (1989). Echoencephalographic findings in neonates associated with maternal cocaine and methamphetamine use: Incidence and clinical correlates. *The Journal of Pediatrics, 115*(5, Pt. 1), 770–778.

Dixon, S. D., Bresnahan, K., & Zuckerman, B. (1990). Cocaine babies: Meeting the challenge of management. *Contemporary Pediatrics, 7*(6), 70–92.

Doberczak, T. M., Shanzer, S., Senie, R. T., & Kandall, S. R. (1988). Neonatal neurologic and electroencephalographic effects of intrauterine cocaine exposure. *The Journal of Pediatrics, 113*(2), 354–358.

Dokecki, P. R., Baumeister, A. A., & Kupstas, F. D. (1989). Biomedical and social aspects of pediatric AIDS. *Journal for Early Intervention, 13*, 99–113.

Dominguez, R., Vila-Coro, A. A., Slopis, J. M., & Bohan, T. P. (1991). Brain and ocular abnormalities in infants with in utero exposure to cocaine and other street drugs. *American Journal of Diseases of Children, 145*, 688–695.

Driscoll, C. D., Streissguth, A. P., & Riley, E. P. (1990). Prenatal alcohol exposure: Comparability of effects in humans and animal models. *Neurotoxicology and Teratology, 12*, 231–237.

Eldridge, R., Denckla, M. B., Bien, E., Myers, S., Kaiser-Kupfer, M. I., Pikus, A., Schlesinger, S. L., Parry, D. M., Dambrosia, J. M., Zasloff,

M. A., & Mulvihill, J. J. (1989). Neurofibromatosis Type 1 (Recklinghausen's disease). *American Journal of Diseases of Children, 143,* 833–837.

Elliott, K. T., & Coker, D. R. (1991). Crack babies: Here they come, ready or not. *Journal of Instructional Psychology, 18*(1), 60–64.

Epstein, L. G., Sharer, L. R., Oleske, J. M., Connor, E. M., Goudsmit, J., Bagdon, L., Robert-Guroff, M., & Koenigsberger, M. R. (1986). Neurologic manifestations of human immunodeficiency virus infection in children. *Pediatrics, 78*(4), 678–687.

Escalona, S. K. (1982). Babies at double hazard: Early development of infants at biologic and social risk. *Pediatrics, 70*(5), 670–676.

Fanshel D., & Shinn, E. B. (1978). *Children in foster care.* New York: Columbia University Press.

Fein, E. (1991). Issues in foster family care: Where do we stand? *American Journal of Orthopsychiatry, 61*(4), 578–583.

Fein, E., Maluccio, A. N., Hamilton, V. J., & Ward, D. E. (1983). After foster care: Outcomes of permanency planning for children. *Child Welfare, 62,* 485–562.

Fein, E., Maluccio, A. N., & Kluger, M. P. (1990). *No more partings: An examination of long-term foster family care.* Washington, DC: Child Welfare League of America.

Fein, E., & Staff, I. (1991). Implementing reunification services. *Families in Society, 72,* 335–343.

Festinger, T. (1983). *No one ever asked us. A postscript to foster care.* New York: Columbia University Press.

Finnegan, L. P. (1985). Neonatal abstinence. In N. M. Nelson (Ed.), *Current therapy in neonatal-perinatal medicine, 1985–1986* (pp. 262–270). Toronto: Decker.

Forness, S. R., & Kavale, K. A. (1988). Psychopharmacologic treatment: A note on classroom effects. *Journal of Learning Disabilities, 21*(3), 144–147.

Frank, D. A., Zuckerman, B. S., Amaro, H., Aboagye, K., Bauchner, H., Cabral, H., Fried, L., Hingson, R., Kayne, H., Levenson, S. M., Parker, S., Reece, H., & Vinci, R. (1988). Cocaine use during pregnancy: Prevalence and correlates. *Pediatrics, 82*(6), 888–895.

Freilberg, P. (1991, April). Panel hears of families victimized by alcoholism. *American Psychological Association Monitor, 3,* 11.

Gadow, K. D. (1986). *Children on medication: Vol. 1* (pp. 31–95). San Diego: College Hill Press.

Giacoia, G. P. (1990). Cocaine in the cradle: A hidden epidemic. *Southern Medical Journal, 83*(8), 947–951.

Glick P. C. (1981). A demographic picture of black families. In H. P. McAdoo (Ed.), *Black families* (pp. 106–126). Beverly Hills, CA: SAGE.

Goodman, R. (1989). Genetic factors in hyperactivity. *British Medical Journal, 298,* 1407–1408.

Graham, J. M., Hanson, J. W., Darby, B. L., Barr, H. M., & Streissguth, A. P. (1988). Independent dysmorphology evaluations at birth and 4 years of age for children exposed to varying amounts of alcohol in utero. *Pediatrics, 81*(6), 772–778.

Greene, T., Ernhart, C. B., Martier, S., Sokol, R., & Ager, J. (1990). Prenatal alcohol exposure and language development. *Alcoholism: Clinical and Experimental Research, 14*(6), 937–945.

Gurdin, P., & Anderson, G. R. (1987). Quality care for ill children: AIDS-specialized foster family homes. *Child Welfare, 66*(4), 291–302.

Gwinn, M., Pappaioanou, M., George, J. R., Hannon, W. H., Wasser, S. C., Redus, M. A., Hoff, R., Grady, G. F., Willoughby, A., Novello, A. C., Petersen, L. R., Dondero, T. J., & Curran, J. W. (1991). Prevalence of HIV infection in childbearing women in the United States. *Journal of the American Medical Association, 265*(13), 1704–1708.

Hadeed, A. J., & Siegel, S. R. (1989). Maternal cocaine use during pregnancy: Effect on the newborn infant. *Pediatrics, 84*(2), 205–209.

Hallahan, D. P., Kauffman, J. M., & Lloyd, J. W. (1985). *Introduction to learning disabilities* (2nd ed., pp. 81–105). Englewood Cliffs, NJ: Prentice-Hall.

Hart, G. (1987). Placing children with AIDS. *Adoption and Fostering, 11*(1), 41–43.

Hauger, S. B., & Powell, K. R. (1990). Infectious complication in children with HIV infection. *Pediatric Annals, 19,* 421–436.

Hawdon, J. M., Hey, E., Kolvin, I., & Fundudis, T. (1990). Born too small: Is outcome still affected? *Developmental Medicine and Child Neurology, 32,* 943–953.

Hawkins, R. P., Meadowcroft, P., Trout, B. A., & Luster, W. C. (1985). Foster family-based treatment. Special Issue: Mental health services to children. *Journal of Clinical Child Psychology, 14*(3), 220–228.

Hechtman, L., Weiss, G., & Perlman, T. (1984). Young adult outcome of hyperactive children who received long-term stimulant treatment. *Journal of the American Academy of Child Psychiatry, 23*(3), 261–269.

Hopp, J. W., & Rogers, E. A. (1989). *AIDS and the allied health professions.* Philadelphia: Davis.

Horner, A. J. (1982). *Object relations and the developing ego in therapy.* New York: Jason Aronson.

Horner, A. J. (1986). *Being and loving.* New York: Jason Aronson.

Howard, J. (1989). Cocaine and its effects on the newborn. *Developmental Medicine and Child Neurology, 31*(2), 255–257.

Howard, J., Beckwith, L., Rodning, C., & Kropenske, V. (1989). The development of young children of substance-abusing parents: Insights from seven years of intervention and research. *Zero to Three, 3*(5), 8–12.

Hoyme, H. E., Jones, K. L., Dixon, S. D., Jewett, T., Hanson, J. W., Robinson, L. K., Msall, M. E., & Allanson, J. E. (1990). Prenatal cocaine exposure and fetal vascular disruption. *Pediatrics, 85*(5), 743–747.

Hoyseth, K. S., & Jones, P. J. H. (1989). Minireview: Ethanol induced teratogenesis: Characterization, mechanisms and diagnostic approaches. *Life Sciences, 44,* 643–649.

Hutto, C., Parks, W. P., Lai, S., Mastrucci, M. T., Mitchell, C., Munoz, J., Trapido, E., Master, I. M., & Scott, G. B. (1991). A hospital-based prospective study of perinatal infection with human immunodeficiency virus type 1. *Journal of Pediatrics, 118,* 347–353.

Hynd, G. W., Lorys, A. R., Semrud-Clikeman, M., Nieves, N., Huettner, M. I. S., & Lahey, B. B. (1991). Attention deficit disorder without hyperactivity: A distinct behavioral and neurocognitive syndrome. *Journal of Child Neurology, 6*(Suppl.), 37–43.

Jason, J. M. (1991). Abuse, neglect, and the HIV-infected child. *Child Abuse and Neglect, 15*(Suppl. 1), 79–88.

Jones, K. L., Chernoff, G. F., & Kelley, C. D. (1984). Outcome of pregnancy in women who "binge" drink during the first trimester of pregnancy. *Clinical Research, 32,* 114.

Jones, K. L., & Smith, D. W. (1973). Recognition of the fetal alcohol syndrome in early infancy. *Lancet, 2,* 999–1001.

Jones, K. L., Smith, D. W., Ulleland, C. N., & Streissguth, A. P. (1973). Pattern of malformation in offspring of chronic alcoholic mothers. *Lancet, 1,* 1267–1271.

Kaplan-Sanoff, M., & Rice, K. F. (1992). Working with addicted women in recovery and their children: Lessons learned in Boston City Hospital's Women and Infants Clinic. *Zero to Three, 13*(1), 17–22.

Kennedy, M. D., Sheridan, M. K., Radlinski, S. H., & Beeghly, M. (1991). Play–language relationships in young children with developmental delays: Implications for assessment. *Journal of Speech and Hearing Research, 34,* 112–122.

Khan, N. A., & Battle, C. U. (1987). Chronic illness: Implications for development and education. *Topics in Early Childhood Special Education, 6*(4), 25–32.

King, R. R., Jones, C., & Lasky, E. (1982). In retrospect: A fifteen-year follow-up report of speech–language-disordered children. *Language, Speech, and Hearing Services in the Schools, 13,* 24–32.

Kirk, S. A., Gallagher, J. J., & Anastasiow, N. J. (1993). *Educating exceptional children* (7th ed.). Boston: Houghton Mifflin.

Klug, R. M. (1986). Children with AIDS, Part 2. *American Journal of Nursing, 86,* 1126–1132.

Lahey, M. (1988). *Language disorders and language development.* New York: Macmillan.

Lahey, B., & Carlson, C. (1991). Validity of the diagnostic category of attention deficit disorder without hyperactivity: A review of the literature. *Journal of Learning Disabilities, 24* (2), 110–120.

Laosa, L. M. (1988). Ethnicity and single parenting in the United States. In E. M. Hetherington & J. D. Arasteh (Eds.), *Impact of divorce, single parenting, and stepparenting on children* (pp. 23–49). Hillsdale, NJ: Erlbaum.

Lester, B. M., Corwin, M. J., Sepkoski, C., Seifer, R., Peucker, M., McLaughlin, S., & Golub, H. L. (1991). Neurobehavioral syndromes in cocaine-exposed newborn infants. *Child Development, 62,* 694–705.

Little, B. B., Snell, L. M., Rosenfeld, C. R., Gilstrap, L. C., & Gant, N. F. (1990). Failure to recognize fetal alcohol syndrome in newborn infants. *American Journal of Diseases of Children, 144,* 1142–1146.

Lockhart, L. L., & Wodarski, J. S. (1989). Facing the unknown: Children and adolescents with AIDS. *Social Work, 34 ,* 215–221.

Lou, H. C., Henriksen, L., & Bruhn, P. (1990). Focal cerebral dysfunction in developmental learning disabilities. *Lancet, 335,* 8–11.

MacGregor, S. N., Keith, L. G., Chasnoff, I. J., Rosner, M. A., Chisum, G. M., Shaw, P., & Minogue, J. P. (1987). Cocaine use during pregnancy: Adverse perinatal outcome. *American Journal of Obstetrics and Gynecology, 157*(3), 686–690.

Mahaffey, K. R., Annest, J. L., Roberts, J., & Murphy, R. S. (1982). National estimate of blood levels: United States, 1976–1980. *New England Journal of Medicine, 307*(10), 573–579.

Main, M., & Solomon, J. (1986). Discovery of an insecure-disorganized/disoriented attachment pattern. In T. B. Brazelton & M. W. Yogman (Eds.), *Affective development in infancy* (pp. 95–124). Norwood, NJ: ABlex.

Marino, R. V., Scholl, T. O., Karp, R. J., Yanoff, J. M., & Hetherington, J. (1987). Minor physical anomalies and learning disability: What is the prenatal component? *Journal of the National Medical Association, 79*(1), 37–39.

McCrae, M. Q. (1986). *Medical perspectives on brain damage and development.* Reading, PA: Family Centered Resource Project.

McLoyd, V. C. (1990). The impact of economic hardship on black families and children: Psychological distress, parenting, and socioemotional development. *Child Development, 61,* 311–346.

Mercer, C. D. (1992). *Students with learning disabilities* (4th ed.). New York: Merrill.

Mercugliano, M. (1992). Attention deficit hyperactivity disorder. In M. L. Batshaw & Y. M. Perret (Eds.), *Children with disabilities: A medical primer* (3rd ed., pp. 387–406). Baltimore: Paul H. Brookes.

Meyers, A., & Weitzman, M. (1991). Pediatric HIV disease: The newest chronic illness of childhood. *Pediatric Clinics of North America, 38*(1), 169–194.

Mintz, M., Epstein, L. G., & Koenigsberger, M. R. (1989). Neurological manifestations of acquired immunodeficiency syndrome in children. *International Pediatrics, 4*(2), 161–171.

Minuchin, S., & Elizur, J. (1990, January–February). The foster care crisis. *Family Therapy Networker,* 44–51.

Miranda, A. H., & Santos de Barona, M. (1990). A model for interventions with low achieving minority students. I A. Barona & E. E. Garcia (Eds.), *Children at risk: Poverty, minority status, and other issues in educational equity* (pp. 119–134). Washington, DC: National Association for School Psychologists.

Morgan, R. L., Dawson, B., & Kerby, D. (1992). The performance of preschoolers with speech/language disorders on the McCarthy Scales of Children's Abilities. *Psychology in the Schools, 29*(1), 11–17.

Morris, V. (1991, Fall). Lead: The poison that never went away. *Yale-New Haven Magazine,* 7–11.

Mullan, B. (1987). *Are mothers really necessary?* New York: Weidenfeld & Nicolson.

Murray, J. B. (1989). Psychologists and children of alcoholic parents. *Psychological Reports, 64,* 859–879.

Myers, B. J., Olson, H. C., & Kaltenbach, K. (1992). Cocaine-exposed infants: Myths and misunderstandings. *Zero to Three, 13*(1), 1–5.

Nanson, J. L., & Hiscock, M. (1990). Attention deficits in children exposed to alcohol prenatally. *Alcoholism: Clinical and Experimental Research, 14*(5), 656–661.

Olegård, R., Sabel, K. G., Aronsson, M., Sandin, B., Johansson, P. R., Carlsson, C., Kyllerman, M., Iversen, K., & Hrbek, A. (1979). Effects on the child of alcohol abuse during pregnancy. *Acta Paediatrica Scandinavica*(Suppl. 275), 112–121.

Ooms, T. (1990). *The crisis in foster Care: New directions for the 1990s.* Washington, DC: Family Impact Seminar, American Association for Marriage and Family Therapy, Research and Educational Foundation.

Oro, A. S., & Dixon, S. D. (1987). Perinatal cocaine and methamphetamine exposure: Maternal and neonatal correlates. *Journal of Pediatrics, 111*(4), 571–578.

Patterson, C. J., Kupersmidt, J. B., & Vaden, N. A. (1990). Income level, gender, ethnicity, and household composition as predictors of children's school-based competence. *Child Development, 61,* 485–494.

Peterson, N. L. (1987). *Early intervention for handicapped and at-risk children.* Denver: Love.

Phelps, L., & Grabowski, J. (1992). Fetal alcohol syndrome: Diagnostic features and psychoeducational risk factors. *School Psychology Quarterly, 7*(2), 112–128.

Pietrantoni, M., & Knuppel, R. A. (1991). Alcohol use in pregnancy. *Clinics in Perinatology, 18*(1), 93–111.

Pizzo, P. A. (1990). Pediatric AIDS: Problems within problems. *Journal of Infectious Diseases, 161,* 316–325.

Pizzo, P. A., Eddy, J., Falloon, J., Balis, F. M., Murphy, R. F., Moss, H., Wolters, P., Brouwers, P., Jarosinski, P., Rubin, M., Broder, S., Yarchoan, R., Brunetti, A., Maha, M., Nusinoff-Lehrman, S., & Poplack, D. G. (1988). Effect of continuous intravenous infusion of Zidovudine (AZT) in children with symptomatic HIV infection. *The New England Journal of Medicine, 319*(14), 889–896.

Polit, D. (1989). National longitudinal study of child welfare: Planning phase. Washington, DC: U. S. Department of Health & Human Services, Office of Human Development Services.

Pressman, H. (1992). Communication disorders and dysphagia in pediatric AIDS. *American Speech-Language-Hearing Association, 34,* 45–47.

Reiss, A. L., & Freund, L. (1990). Fragile X syndrome. *Biological Psychiatry, 27,* 223–240.

Rescorla, L. (1987, April). Pretend play in 2-year-olds with SELD. Paper presented at the Biennial Meeting of the *Society for Research in Child Development,* Baltimore, MD.

Richman, N., Stevenson, J., & Graham, P. J. (1982). *Pre-school to school: A behavioral study.* London: Academic Press.

Rogers, M. F., White, C. R., Sanders, R., Schable, C., Ksell, T. E., Wasserman, R. L., Bellanti, J. A., Peters, S. M., & Wray, B. B. (1990). Lack of transmission of human immunodeficiency virus from infected children to their household contacts. *Pediatrics, 85*(2), 210–214.

Rosett, H. L., & Weiner, L. (1985). Alcohol and pregnancy: A clinical perspective. *Annual Review of Medicine, 36,* 73–80.

Roth, F. P., & Clark, D. M. (1987). Symbolic play and social participation abilities of language-impaired and normally developing children. *Journal of Speech and Hearing Disorders, 52*(1), 17–29.

Russell, M. (1990). Prevalence of alcoholism among children of alcoholics. In M. Windle & J. S. Searles (Eds.), *Children of alcoholics* (pp. 9–38). New York: Guilford Press.

Sabol, B. J. (1991). The urban child. *Journal of Health Care for the Poor and Underserved, 12*(1), 59–73.

Santos de Barona, M., & Barona, A. (1991). The assessment of culturally and linguistically different preschoolers. *Early Childhood Research Quarterly, 6,* 363–376.

Schneider, J. W., & Chasnoff, I. J. (1987). Cocaine abuse during pregnancy: Its effects on infant motor development—A clinical perspective. *Topics in Acute Care Trauma Rehabilitation, 2*(1), 50–69.

Schutter, L. S., & Brinker, R. P. (1992). Conjuring a new category of disability from prenatal cocaine exposure: Are the infants unique biological or caretaking casualties? *Topics in Early Childhood Special Education, 11*(4), 84–111.

Schutzman, D. L., Frankenfield-Chernicoff, M., Clatterbaugh, H. E., & Singer, J. (1991). Incidence of intrauterine cocaine exposure in a suburban setting. *Pediatrics, 88*(4), 825–827.

Schwarcz, S. K., & Rutherford, G. W. (1989). Acquired immunodeficiency syndrome in infants, children, and adolescents. *Journal of Drug Issues, 19*(1), 75–92.

Scott, G. B., Hutto, C., Makuch, R. W., Mastrucci, M. T., O'Connor, T., Mitchell, C. D., Trapido, E. J., & Parks, W. P. (1989). Survival in children with perinatally acquired human immunodeficiency virus type 1 infection. *New England Journal of Medicine, 321*(26),1791–1796.

Shapiro, B. K. (1992). Normal and abnormal development. In M. L. Batshaw & Y. M. Perrett (Eds.), *Children with disabilities: A medical primer* (3rd. ed., pp. 259–289). Baltimore: Paul H. Brookes.

Shaywitz, S. E., & Shaywitz, B. A. (1988). Attention deficit disorder: Current perspective. In J. F. Kavanaugh & T. J. Truss, Jr. (Eds.), *Learning disability: Proceedings of the national conference* (pp. 369–523). Parkton, MD: York Press.

Siegel, L. S., Cunningham, C. E., & van der Spuy, H. I. J. (1985). Interactions of language-delayed and normal preschool boys with their peers. *Journal of Child Psychology and Psychiatry, 26,* 77–83.

Silva, P. A. (1980). The prevalence, stability and significance of developmental language delay in preschool children. *Developmental Medicine and Child Neurology, 22,* 768–777.

Silva, P. A., McGee, R., & Williams, S. M. (1983). Developmental language delay from three to seven years and its significance for low intelligence and reading difficulties at age seven. *Developmental Medicine and Child Neurology, 25,* 783–793.

Silva, P. A., Williams, S., & McGee, R. (1987). A longitudinal study of children with developmental language delay at age three: Later intelligence, reading, and behavior problems. *Developmental Medicine and Child Neurology, 29,* 630–640.

Singer, L. T., Garber, R., & Kliegman, R. (1991). Neurobehavioral sequelae of fetal cocaine exposure. *Journal of Pediatrics, 119*(4), 667–672.

Skinner, K. (1989). Counselling issues in the fostering and adoption of children at risk of HIV infection. Special Issue: AIDS counselling: Theory, research and practice. *Counselling Psychology Quarterly, 2*(1), 89–92.

Slaughter, D. T. (1988). Black children, schooling, and educational interventions. In D. T. Slaughter (Ed.), *Black children and poverty: A developmental perspective.* New Directions for Child Development, No. 42. San Francisco: Jossey-Bass.

Snyder, L. S. (1978). Communicative and cognitive abilities and disabilities in the sensorimotor period. *Merrill-Palmer Quarterly, 24,* 161–180.

Sokol, R. J., & Clarren, S. K. (1989). Guidelines for use of terminology describing the impact of prenatal alcohol on the offspring. *Alcoholism: Clinical and Experimental Research, 13*(4), 597–598.

Sokol, R. J., Miller, S. I., & Reed, G. (1980). Alcohol abuse during pregnancy: An epidemiologic study. *Alcoholism: Clinical and Experimental Research, 4*(2), 135–145.

Spiegel, L., & Mayers, A. (1991). Psychosocial aspects of AIDS in children and adolescents. *Pediatric Clinics of North America, 38*(1), 153–167.

Streissguth, A. P., Aase, J. M., Clarren, S. K., Randels, S. P., LaDue, R. A., & Smith, D. F. (1991). Fetal alcohol syndrome in adolescents and adults. *Journal of the American Medical Association, 265*(15), 1961–1967.

Streissguth, A. P., Barr, H. M., Martin, D. C., & Herman, C. S. (1980). Effects of maternal alcohol, nicotine, and caffeine use during pregnancy on infant mental and motor development at eight months. *Alcoholism: Clinical and Experimental Research, 4*(2), 152–164.

Streissguth, A. P., Barr, H. M., & Sampson, P. D. (1990). Moderate prenatal alcohol exposure: Effects on child IQ and learning problems at age 7 1/2 years. *Alcoholism: Clinical and Experimental Research, 14*(5), 662–669.

Streissguth, A. P., Barr, H. M., Sampson, P. D., Darby, B. L., & Martin, D. C. (1989). IQ at age 4 in relation to maternal alcohol use and smoking during pregnancy. *Developmental Psychology, 25*(1), 3–11.

Streissguth, A. P., Barr, H. M., Sampson, P. D., Parrish-Johnson, J. C., Kirchner, G. L., & Martin, D. C. (1986). Attention, distraction and reaction time at age 7 years and prenatal alcohol exposure. *Neurobehavioral Toxicology and Teratology, 8,* 717–725.

Streissguth, A. P., Clarren, S. K., & Jones, K. L. (1985). Natural history of the fetal alcohol syndrome: A 10-year follow-up of eleven patients. *Lancet, 2,* 85–91.

Streissguth, A. P., & Giunta, C. T. (1988). Mental health and health needs of infants and preschool children with fetal alcohol syndrome. *International Journal of Family Psychiatry, 9,* 29–47.

Streissguth, A. P., & LaDue, R. A. (1987). Fetal alcohol: Teratogenic causes of developmental disabilities. In S. R. Schroeder (Ed.), *Toxic substances and mental retardation: Neurobehavioral toxicology and teratology* (pp. 1–32). Washington, DC: American Association on Mental Deficiency.

Tallal, P., Dukette, D., & Curtiss, S. (1989). Behavioral, emotional profiles of preschool language-impaired children. *Development and Psychopathology, 1,* 51–67.

Tamis-LeMonda, C. S., & Bornstein, M. H. (1989). Habituation and maternal encouragement of attention in infancy as predictors of toddler language, play, and representational competence. *Child Development, 60,* 738–751.

Task Force on Pediatric AIDS. (1988). Pediatric guidelines for infection control of human immunodeficiency virus (acquired immunodeficiency virus) in hospitals, medical offices, schools, and other settings. *Pediatrics, 82*(5), 801–807.

Taylor-Brown, S. (1991). The impact of AIDS on foster care: A family-centered approach to services in the United States. Special Issue: Child welfare around the world. *Child-Welfare, 70*(2), 193–209.

Terrell, B. Y., Schwartz, R. G., Prelock, P. A., & Messick, C. K. (1984). Symbolic play in normal and language-impaired children. *Journal of Speech and Hearing Research, 27,* 424–429.

Thal, D. J. (1991). Language and cognition in normal and late-talking toddlers. *Topics in Language Disorders, 11*(4), 33–42.

Thal, D., Tobias, S., & Morrison, D. (1991). Language and gesture in late talkers: A 1-year follow-up. *Journal of Speech and Hearing Research, 34,* 604–612.

Ultmann, M. H., Belman, A. L., Ruff, H. A., Novick, B. E., Cone-Wesson, B., Cohen, H. J., & Rubenstein, A. (1985). Developmental abnormalities in infants and children with acquired immunodeficiency syndrome (AIDS) and AIDS-related complex. *Developmental Medicine & Child Neurology, 27,* 563–571.

Vas Dias, S. (1990). Paediatric psychotherapy: The development of a technique for a service in a general paediatric outpatient clinic. Special Edition: Work with children with an illness or disability. *Journal of Child Psychotherapy, 16*(2), 7–20.

Waldman, S. (1991, July 15). Lead and your kids. *Newsweek,* 42–48.

Walker, B., Jr. (1989). Protecting our children. *Journal of the National Medical Association, 81*(7), 815–818.

Wallace, J. (1987). Children of alcoholics: A population at risk. *Alcoholism Treatment Quarterly, 4*(3), 13–30.

Werner, E., & Smith, R. (1982). *Vulnerable but invincible.* New York: McGraw-Hill.

Weston, D. R., Ivins, B., Zuckerman, B., Jones, C., & Lopez, R. (1989). Drug exposed babies: Research and clinical issues. *Zero to Three, 9*(5), 1–7.

White, E. (1992). Foster parenting the drug-affected baby. *Zero to Three, 13*(1), 13–17.

Williams, A. D. (1989). Nursing management of the child with AIDS. *Pediatric Nursing, 15*(3), 259–261.

Yazigi, R. A., Odem, R. R., & Polakoski, K. L. (1991). Demonstration of specific binding of cocaine to human spermatazoa. *Journal of American Medical Association, 266*(14), 1956–1959.

Zametkin, A. J., Nordahl, T. E., Gross, M., King, C., Semple, W. E., Rumsey, J., Hamburger, S., & Cohen, R. M. (1990). Cerebral glucose metabolism in adults with hyperactivity of childhood onset. *New England Journal of Medicine, 323*(20), 1361–1366.

Zuckerman, B., Frank, D. A., Hingson, R., Amaro, H., Levenson, S. M., Kayne, H., Parker, S., Vinci, R., Aboagye, K., Fried, L. E., Cabral, H., Timperi, R., & Bauchner, H. (1989). Effects of maternal marijuana and cocaine use on fetal growth. *New England Journal of Medicine, 320*(12), 762–768.

Conclusion

All children are complex and unique. It is this quality of individualism that makes working with them both exciting and challenging. Children who are developmentally at risk or born with a disability offer us special challenges in preparing a path for them that most completely enhances their chances for optimal development. Underlying principles and beliefs that have guided this book include a respect for the inner life of children, a belief in the centrality of play as a means through which development is enhanced, and a belief in the possibility that all children can weave some understanding of their unique development into their personal inner world. As our case studies have illustrated, being born with a special need casts an influence beyond the specific area of the disability. There is often a pattern of impact that means we must address areas therapeutically that may seem less than obvious. Sometimes it is more important to bolster a seemingly tangential area in order to remediate a specific problem. The SPM offers the student or professional a way to systematically review a child's development, process information, and then generate a highly individualized intervention plan. Using the SPM can help you gain a greater grasp of the complexity of development and the ability to look behind the obvious to development intervention strategies that are truly supportive.

As the case studies in this book have illustrated, a well designed inclusion plan is complex and multifaceted, often requiring increased staffing and coordination with support personnel. Preparation and support of the staff and peers in the setting is crucial. Inclusion should be selected only when it is the best developmental choice for the child, not because it seems to be the most economical plan, corroborates denial of the child's developmental issues, or meets the current educational fashion.

Carefully designed and developmentally appropriate early intervention promotes the development of children along their unique lines of feeling, learning, and knowing. It always encourages families to be full participant partners in planning for their children and helps families to cope effectively and function maximally in spite of the challenges they face in parenting. It is our hope that by reading this book you are now better able to design more appropriate early intervention strategies that will not only increase the potential for children to experience success in their early years, but also bolster the continued unfolding of their development toward successful and productive lives.

Glossary

"ACT ON AGENT" PLAY: Play in which the child is responsive to, interactive with, and/or instrumental on a human or inanimate object.

ACTION SCHEMES: Simple patterns of movement used to explore and/or manipulate objects, or to interact with people (patting, shaking, and poking).

ANENCEPHALY: A birth defect in which either the whole brain or all but the most primitive regions of the brain are missing.

APRAXIA: Difficulty in coordinating voluntary movements for speech.

ARNOLD-CHIARI MALFORMATION: A congenital disorder in which there is distortion of the base of the skull with protrusion of the lower brain stem and parts of the cerebellum through the opening of the spinal cord at the base of the skull.

ASSOCIATIVE PLAY: Play in which a number of children are engaged in the same activity, but with little, if any, social interchange (e.g., telephoning).

ATAXIA: Incoordination of voluntary muscular action, particularly of the muscle groups used in activities such as walking or reaching for objects; usually resulting from abnormalities in the cerebellum.

ATHETOID: Involuntary and constant movements characterized by recurrent, slow, wormlike, and more or less continual change of position of the fingers, toes, hands, feet, and other parts of the body.

AUDIOLOGIST: A person trained and certified in the identification, measurement, and study of hearing and hearing impairments; also recommends rehabilitative procedures when necessary.

AUDITORY INTEGRATION TRAINING (AIT): A process believed to reduce distortions and hypersensitivities of the auditory system. Filtered music is presented through headphones over a brief period of training.

AUGMENTATIVE AND ALTERNATIVE COMMUNICATION METHODS (AAC): Any method of communication that enhances or supplements speech. These may include gestures, facial expressions, writing, various sign languages, picture and/or symbol boards, and various electronic or computerized devices, such as switches or pointers, which may be necessary to operate the communication device.

AUXILIARY EGO: The role parents and other adults assume when assisting children to cope, adapt, or master some aspect of the real world. Thus, they amplify the child's immature ego with the benefits of one more well formed.

CATHETERIZATION: The insertion of a catheter—a long, thin, hollow surgical instrument, usually flexible, that is inserted into a body cavity, such as the bladder, for the purpose of drainage.

CAUSE AND EFFECT: The operative relationship between an agent or action and an outcome. Pushing the ball causes it to roll, pressing a switch activates a mechanical toy.

CEREBROSPINAL FLUID: A clear, watery liquid that bathes the spinal cord and flows through the ventricles, or cavities, within the brain; serves as a buffer for the central nervous system against sudden pressure changes and also helps to provide the system with nutrition.

COCHLEAR IMPLANT: An implant surgically attached to the cochlea that provides electrical current to stimulate the auditory nerve fibers, thereby allowing sound to be transmitted to the brain.

COOPERATIVE PLAY: Play in which children discuss, plan, and assign roles necessary to form a shared idea and embark on a joint venture.

COUNTERTRANSFERENCE: A therapist's unconscious emotional reaction toward his or her client.

CRUISE: A stage in the course of learning to walk, during which babies side-step while supporting themselves on items of furniture and shifting their grip from support to support.

DEFERRED IMITATION: The ability to replicate the behaviors of models in their absence.

DISASSOCIATION: The ability to isolate the movement of one part or segment of the body from the movement of others, such as poking with the index finger without generalized movement of the hand or other fingers.

ECHOLALIA: The immediate or delayed echoing or repetition of words and/or sentences that have been heard without necessarily understanding their meaning or function.

ELECTRONIC COMMUNICATION DEVICES: See **AUGMENTATIVE AND ALTERNATIVE COMMUNICATION METHODS.**

EQUILIBRIUM: A state of balance between or among opposing forces. A Piagetian concept referring to continuous movement between stages of equilibrium and disequilibrium. Describes how the assimilation of new information and the accommodation of this new information with previous understanding work together to produce cognitive change.

FACILITATED COMMUNICATION: A technique in which physical support on the hand or arm is provided to an individual in order to facilitate the spelling of messages on an alphabet board, keyboard, or typewriter.

FANTASY PLAY: Play in which the intent and/or content arise more from the imagination or inner life than from current situational factors or physical/descriptive reality.

FIGURE–GROUND DISCRIMINATION: The ability to differentiate foreground visual or auditory information that is the subject of attention from background data.

FORMAL SYMBOLIC COMMUNICATION: The expression of descriptions, categories, ideas, and feelings through a standard, culturally validated symbol system, such as a language and written alphabet.

HYDROCEPHALUS: A condition characterized by the abnormal accumulation of cerebrospinal fluid within the ventricles of the brain.

HYPERSENSITIVE: Prone to increased responsiveness to a particular stimulus.

HYPOSENSITIVITY: A state of decreased responsiveness to a variety of sensory stimuli.

HYPOTONIA: A state of reduced tension in muscles; often referred to as "low" or "floppy" muscle tone.

IMITATION: The ability to observe and duplicate the gestures and/or language of others.

INSPIRATORY STRIDOR: Crowing sound during the inhalation phase of respiration due to pathology involving the epiglottis or larynx.

INTENTIONALITY: Behavior that displays some degree of planning and foresight.

INTERACTIVE: Relating to reciprocity, as in a social exchange.

INTERACTIVE PLAY: Pleasurable exchanges that are reciprocal and may involve vocalizations, facial expressions, gestures, or exchange of objects.

JOINT ATTENTION: Ability to focus on an object, event, or conversational topic with another person.

KINESTHETIC: Relating to the ability to perceive movement and sense the position of the body and the relationship of its parts in space.

LANGUAGE MASTER: Small battery-operated device that can record and play speech using cards with a strip of magnetic tape at the bottom. Pictures and/or words can be drawn or pasted onto the cards.

MENINGES: The three membranes covering the brain and spinal cord.

MENINGITIS: An inflammation of the meninges caused by a viral or bacterial infection. Severe cases can lead to death. Bacterial meningitis can be treated with antibiotics. Viral meningitis does not respond to drugs, as a result, prolonged bed rest, darkness and quiet are the only treatments.

MENINGOCELE: A protrusion of the cerebral or spinal meninges through a defect in the skull or vertebral column, forming a cyst filled with cerebrospinal fluid.

MENINGOENCEPHALITIS: Inflammation of the brain and its membranes.

MENINGOMYELOCELE: A protrusion of a portion of the spinal cord and membranes through a defect in the vertebral column.

METACOGNITION: Awareness and understanding of one's own cognitive processes; thinking about thought.

METAREPRESENTATION: Conscious awareness and understanding of one's own content and process of mental imagery and imaging.

MIRRORING: Imitating the actions of another.

MULTIMODAL: A form of instruction or stimulation that draws upon and uses a variety of techniques such as positive reinforcement, modeling, task analysis, and verbal prompting, cuing, and interpretation.

MULTISENSORY APPROACH: A method of stimulation, instruction, or therapy that involves the activation of more than one sensory system.

NEURAL TUBE: The embryonic tube formed from the ectodermal neural plate that differentiates into brain and spinal cord.

NEURODEVELOPMENTAL TREATMENT (NDT): A specialized therapy approach that concentrates on encouraging normal movement patterns and discouraging abnormal reflexes, postures, and movements. Used by specially trained physical and occupational therapists and speech and language pathologists.

OBJECT PERMANENCE: Knowledge that an object exists even though that object can not be seen, heard, or validated by other sensory information.

OCULAR–MOTOR IMBALANCE: Concerned with uncoordinated eye movement.

ORTHOTICS: Lightweight devices made of plastic, leather, or metal that provide stability at the joints or passively stretch muscles.

PARALLEL PLAY: Two or more children playing side by side, obviously taking pleasure in each other's companionship, but without any real exchange.

PATHOLOGIST: A person trained and experienced in the study and practice of the branch of biological science that deals with the nature of disease through the study of its causes, process, and effects, together with the associated alterations of structure and function.

PERSEVERATION: Involuntary, pathological repetition of words or some activity.

PERSEVERATIVE PLAY PATTERNS: Play themes or actions that are repeated as though "stuck in a groove" and that seem to block developmental movement forward.

PHONOLOGICAL DISORDER: A disorder in the acquisition of rules governing the speech sound system.

PLAY SCENARIOS: Short "dramas" enacted in play.

PREHENSION: The act of grasping or seizing.

PRESYMBOLIC PLAY: Pleasurable interaction with object and others that is wedded to the physical/sensory or functional attributes of the object.

PROXIMAL JOINTS: Situated close to the origin, point of attachment, or median line of the body.

REPRESENTATIONAL THOUGHT: Ability to form and hold a mental image of an object or event, thus allowing it to be thought about even when not present.

ROLLS SEGMENTALLY: Rolling in which a portion of the body turns discretely, such as head, shoulder, trunk etc., as opposed to "log rolling," in which the whole body flips over as a unit.

ROTATION: Diagonal movement through the trunk; keeping the child's hips stable and turning the shoulders in one direction or vice-versa.

RULE ATTUNEMENT: Demonstration of a regard for an established order of conduct.

SCHEMES: A Piagetian term for a cognitive structure that changes with development.

SCOLIOSIS: Curvature of the spine.

SELF-REGULATION: Continuous, conscious monitoring and evaluation of one's progress toward a goal, including checking outcomes and redirecting unsuccessful efforts.

SENSORIMOTOR ACTIVITIES: Related to activities concerned with or functioning in both sensory and motor aspects of bodily activity.

SENSORIMOTOR DEVELOPMENT: Learning that takes place in the early years predominately through the use of the senses.

SENSORIMOTOR PLAY: Pleasurable sensory learning that dominates early development.

SENSORY INTEGRATION The ability of the central nervous system to process and learn from sensations such as touch, sound, light, smell, and movement.

SENSORY INTEGRATION THERAPY: A therapeutic technique designed to help children who have trouble with fine motor coordination or perceptual skills, such as reading, due to problems with sorting and organizing sensations.

SHUNTING: Insertion of a tube with a pressure valve that is implanted in the brain to allow proper circulation and drainage of fluid.

SOCIAL AFFILIATION: A bond or connection between people based on pleasurable exchanges and relationships.

SOCIODRAMATIC PLAY: Play that consists of the creation of themes related to human relations.

SOLITARY PLAY: Isolated play.

SPASTIC: Pertaining to or characterized by recurrent and continuous spasms.

SPASTIC PARALYSIS: A condition in which a group of muscles manifest increased tone, exaggerated tendon reflexes, depressed or absent superficial reflexes, and sometimes clonus, due to an upper motor neuron lesion.

SPATIAL ABILITY: Understanding of the relationships of objects to one another or in an arrangement or configuration.

SPINA BIFIDA: A developmental defect in which the newborn has part of the spinal cord and its coverings exposed through a gap in the backbone.

SPINA BIFIDA OCCULATA: The most mild form of spina bifida in which there is a separation of the bones of the spinal column, but no protrusion of the meninges of the spinal cord and no sac or opening on the back.

SPLINTER SKILLS: A proficiency or ability that seems unrelated to an individual's general level of development; may appear to exist out of context and be fragmentary in form.

STABILITY: Feeling of bodily security in space and movement.

STRABISMUS: A condition in which a person's eyes deviate inward or outward and/or wander as a result of a weakness of one or more of the six muscles that move the eyeball; this prevents the eyes from focusing on the same object simultaneously. Cannot be controlled voluntarily by the person.

SUBSTITUTE OBJECTS: Objects used to stand in the place of others that may imply the transfer of feeling, drive, or action from one to another; for example, a soft blanket may serve as a substitute for the contact comfort of mother's body.

SYMBOLIC FUNCTIONING: The ability to understand, create, and use words, ideas, or codes to represent something that is not present.

TACTILE: Relating to or affecting the sense of touch.

VESTIBULAR: Pertaining particularly to the vestibular part of the 8th cranial nerve; concerned with equilibrium and the perception of movement.

VISUAL–SPATIAL LEARNER: One who acquires information primarily through the analysis of the physical world and an understanding of the relationships of parts to wholes, as opposed to primarily relying on words.

VOCAL CORD PARALYSIS: Muscle weakness of the two folds of tissue that produce speech, song, and all other vocal noises.

Index

Author Index

Subject Index

About the Authors

Margaret K. Sheridan, Ph.D., is the Chair and a Professor of Child Development at Connecticut College where she has been Director of the Program for Children with Special Needs since it began in 1973. She has been active in numerous State task forces and has been a member on regional boards and agencies that assist children and their families. Dr. Sheridan has been a popular presenter to regional parent and professional groups and has served as an inservice provider for daycare, Head Start, and public schools. She has co-authored several articles and made numerous national and international conference presentations.

Gilbert M. Foley, Ed.D., is Associate Professor of School and Developmental Psychology at Ferkauf Graduate School of Psychology, Yeshiva University, New York City. He also serves as clinical supervisor of child life services in the Pediatric Resource Center, Bellevue Hospital Center and maintains a private practice. For 11 years, Dr. Foley directed the Family Centered Resource Project, a Federally funded Model/Demonstration and outreach project program that provided consultation and technical assistance to early intervention programs across the nation. Dr. Foley has lectured widely and is co-author of the *Cognitive Observation Guide* and the *Attachment-Separation-Individuation Scale*. He has written and produced media or video resources on the transdisciplinary approach.

Sara H. Radlinski, Ph.D., has been the Associate Director of the Connecticut College Program for Children with Special Needs for the last 20 years and is an Adjunct Assistant Professor of Child Development. Dr. Radlinski is also a clinical faculty member for the Connecticut Infant and Toddler Developmental Assessment Project (IDA). She has been a member of numerous State task forces and on boards and agencies that work with children and their families. She consults regularly in Head Start, day care, and public schools. Dr. Radlinski has made numerous presentations at national and international conferences and has co-authored several articles dealing with children with special needs.